# The Artist in the Counterculture

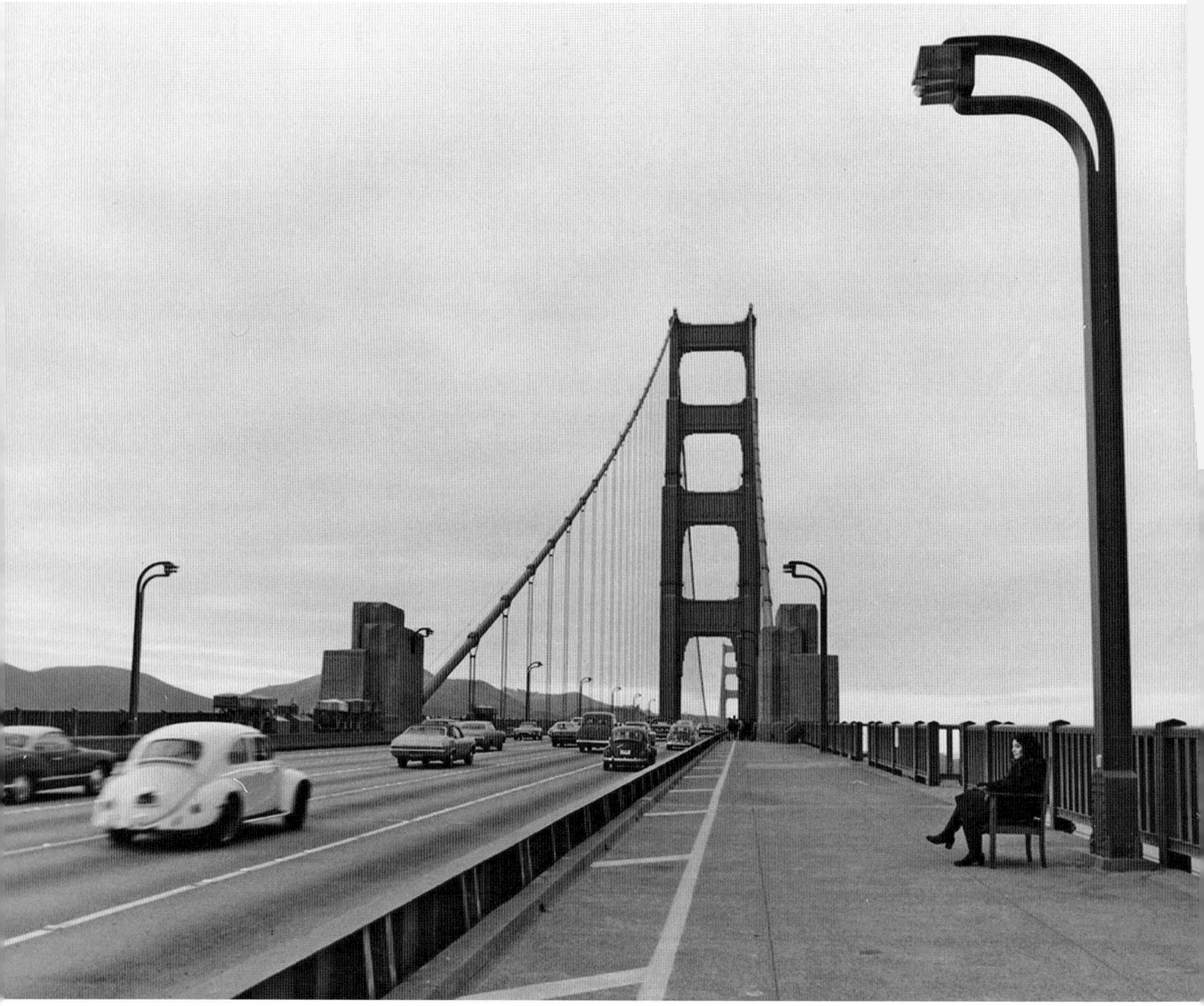

# The Artist in the Counterculture

## Bruce Conner to Mike Kelley and Other Tales from the Edge

THOMAS CROW

Princeton University Press

Princeton and Oxford

Published by Princeton University Press
41 William Street, Princeton, New Jersey 08540
99 Banbury Road, Oxford OX2 6JX
press.princeton.edu



**Jacket front** Jean Conner, *The Temptation of Saint Wallace* (detail), 1963, collage, 50.8 × 38.1 cm, Collection San Francisco Museum of Modern Art, Accessions Committee Fund purchase
**Jacket back** Bruce Conner, hand-painted lightshow transparency, c. 1967, 5 × 5 cm, courtesy Conner Family Trust
**Page ii** Bonnie Ora Sherk, *Sitting Still (Golden Gate Bridge)*, 1971
**Pages vi–vii** "Artists Against Escalation" protest at the Los Angeles County Museum of Art, 16 May 1965, photograph by Charles Brittin, Charles Brittin Collection, Getty Research Library, Los Angeles

**Library of Congress Cataloging-in-Publication Data**
Names: Crow, Thomas E., 1948– author.
Title: The artist in the counterculture : Bruce Conner to Mike Kelley and other tales from the edge / Thomas Crow.
Description: Princeton : Princeton University Press, [2023] | Includes bibliographical references and index.
Identifiers: LCCN 2022002244 (print) | LCCN 2022002245 (ebook) | ISBN 9780691236162 (hardcover) | ISBN 9780691236261 (ebook)
Subjects: LCSH: Art and society—California—History—20th century. | Counterculture—California.
Classification: LCC N72.S6 C76 2023 (print) | LCC N72.S6 (ebook) | DDC 701/.03—dc23/eng/20220709
LC record available at https://lccn.loc.gov/2022002244
LC ebook record available at https://lccn.loc.gov/2022002245

British Library Cataloging-in-Publication Data is available
Designed by Gillian Malpass
This book has been composed in Adelle and Adelle Sans
Printed on acid-free paper. ∞
Printed in Italy
10 9 8 7 6 5 4 3 2 1

# CONTENTS

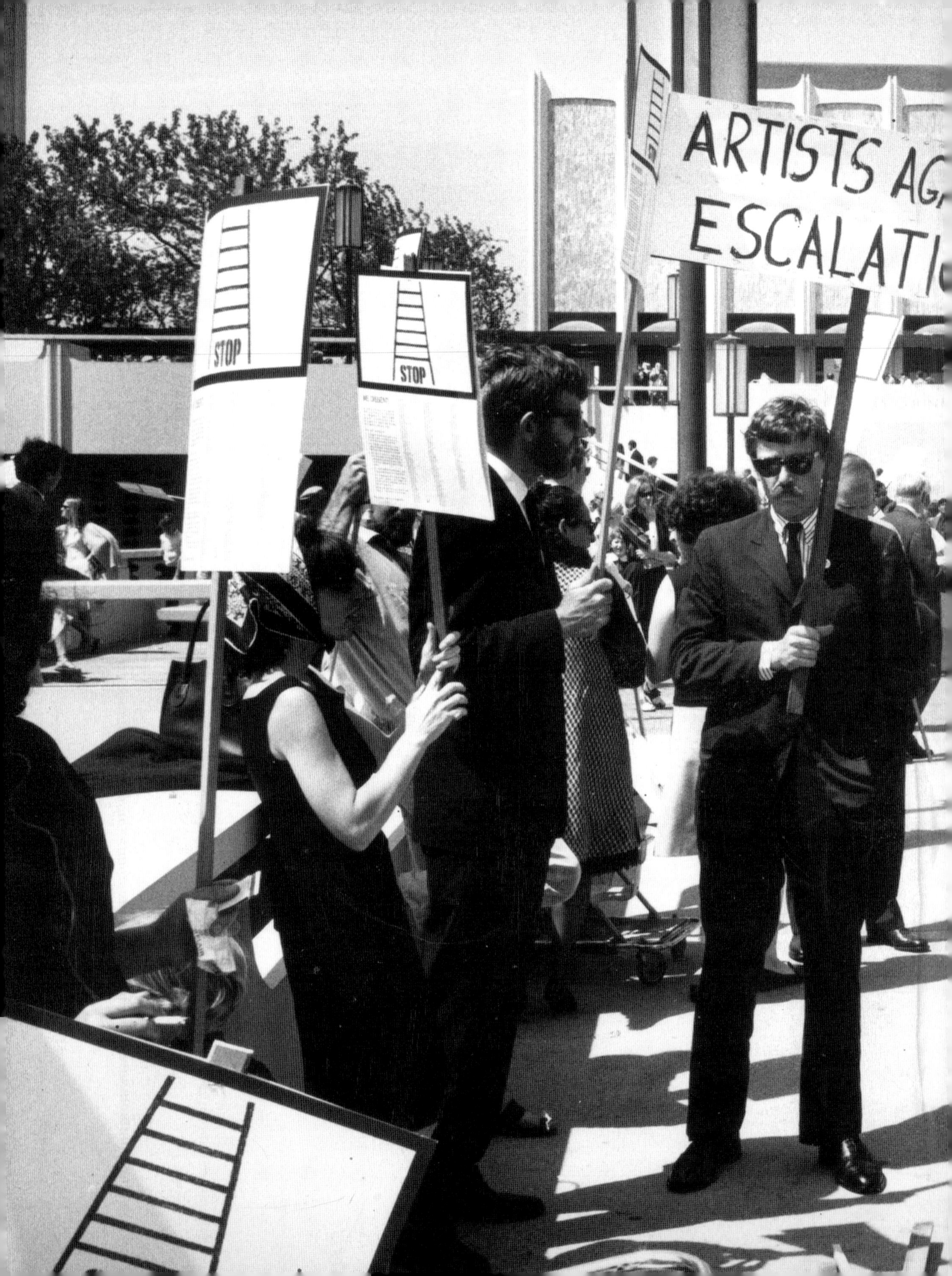
ARTISTS AG
ESCALATI
STOP
STOP

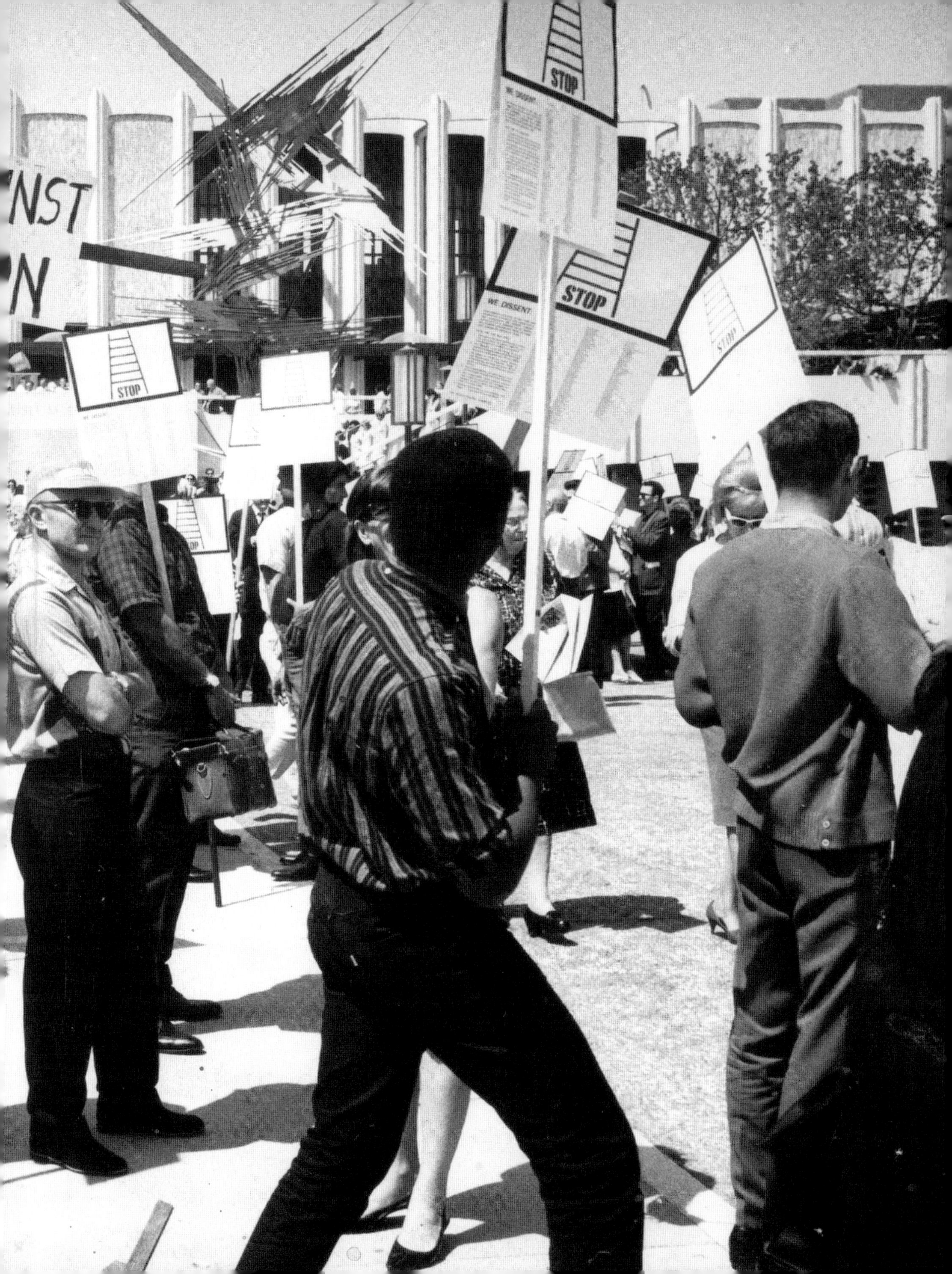
STOP
WE DISSENT:
STOP
STOP
STOP

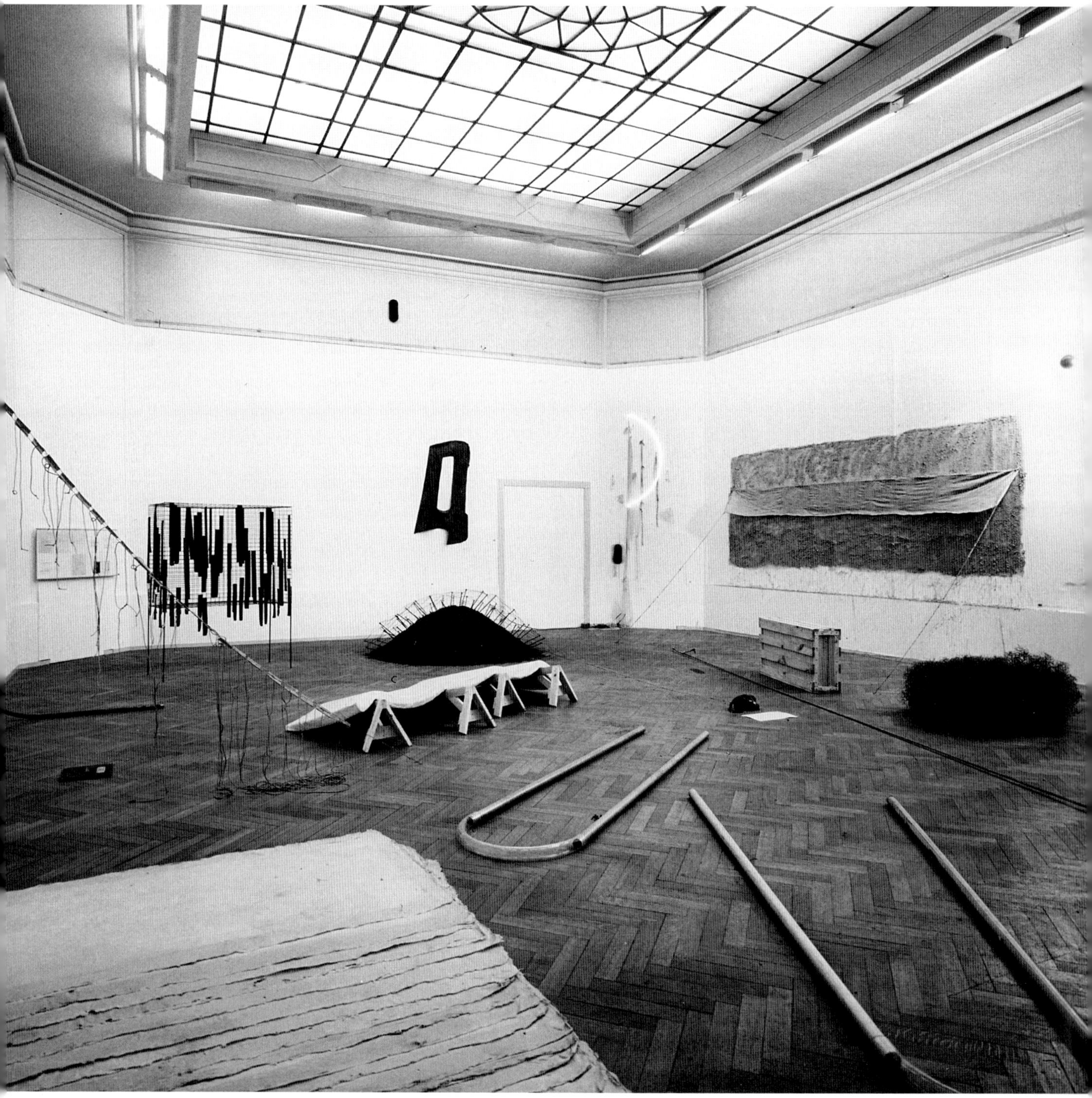

1 *Live in Your Head: When Attitudes Become Form* (Kunsthalle Bern, 1969), installation photograph, Harald Szeemann Papers. Photographs. Series IV.A. Projects, Getty Research Library, Los Angeles

PROLOGUE

# NEUROPLASTICITY

In the history of adventurously experimental art, the year 1969 is arguably marked by one event above all others. That year, the young curator Harald Szeemann, newly entrusted with the civic exhibition space in the city of Bern, sought to assemble evidence for a wave in art that he perceived but had escaped general recognition. To that end, he assembled works of sculpture by no less than sixty-nine artists from across Europe and both coasts of the United States.[1] His inclusiveness extended to inviting a significant share of the participants to gather in the staid Swiss locale in order to install work on site and engage in protracted discussion, as far as the polyglot crew could manage, in a colloquy over the fundamental character and function of art.

The invited artists ranged from Joseph Beuys, the established master of the Düsseldorf Academy and advocate for art's transformation into "social sculpture," to the largely untried Keith Sonnier, raised in the Cajun backwoods of Louisiana, who was inspired to try out neon light as a medium for the first time and so discovered his career-long signature material. Other participants, like the Californian Bruce Nauman and the Italian Mario Merz, had gotten to tubular illumination before him, which proved one of a number of rhymes and resonances that knit the show into a unified visual statement, one that amply confirmed Szeemann's intuition that some coherent tendency existed. Apart from scattered neon highlights and some shards of reflective glass, however, the overall look tended to a drab gray, ochre, and brown palette, the material textures rough and unrefined, their disposition sprawling and unconstrained by any expected definition of formal integrity (fig. 1).

Their curator attempted rationalizing the ensemble with this run-on list of attributes: "the obvious opposition to form; the high degree of personal and emotional engagement; the pronouncement that certain objects are art, although they have not previously been identified as such; the shift of interest away from the result towards the artistic process; the use of mundane materials; the interaction of work and material; Mother Earth as medium, workplace, the desert as concept."[2] Albeit disjointed, this list can stand for what has become the consensus view of this moment of "process" or "anti-form" in western art, down to the contemporaneous excursions into large-scale land art by Michael Heizer, Walter De Maria, and Robert Smithson, who were all three represented in the show by cognate, gallery-scaled contributions.

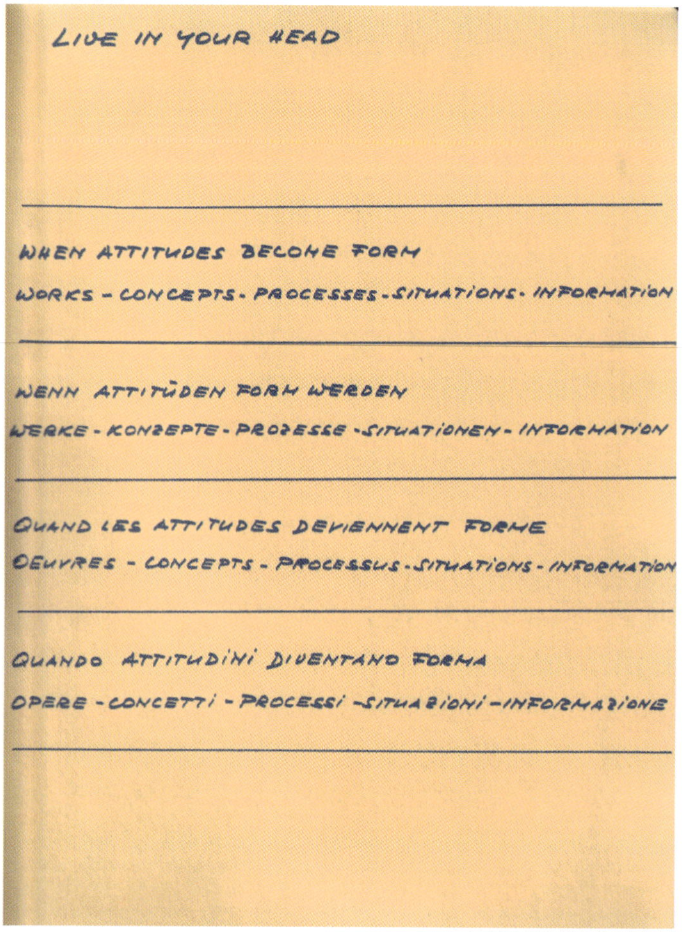


**2** Cover of the exhibtion catalogue for Harald Szeemann's *Live in Your Head: When Attitudes Become Form* (Kunsthalle Bern, 1969), collection of the author

Indeed, Szeemann's exhibition has retained landmark status for what seems to have been an uncannily moment-defining prescience.

The only element that has failed to survive in received wisdom is the actual main title of the whole exercise: *Live in Your Head*. Those four words had been proffered by the young, long-haired Sonnier, to be happily adopted by Szeemann, who bannered them on the cover and title page of the catalogue (fig. 2). But in historical recollection, it is the latter's subtitle, *When Attitudes Become Form*, that is invariably cited, sometimes along with the sub-subtitle, *Works-Concepts-Processes-Situations-Information*. Reasons suggest themselves as to why Sonnier's pithy exhortation has effectively been erased in some collective act of willful forgetting. "Live in Your Head" evokes raptly inward meditation or mind-expanding fireworks, both being hallmarks of the incorrigible counterculture in enclaves like the Haight-Ashbury in San Francisco, as opposed to emphasizing reasoned reappraisal of fine-art aesthetics, which the more decorous subtitles can be taken to imply when held up for scrutiny in a graduate seminar room.

Which set of connotations would Szeemann have preferred? One answer lies in the rarely quoted follow-up to the list above: he posits by way of explanation that "hippie philosophy, the rockers and the use of drugs should eventually affect the position of a younger generation of artists." The weightier German compounds used in his original Bern text, "Hippietum" and "Rockerexistenz," lend these countercultural references heightened status as conditions of life—from which, he proposes, the art on view had emerged. In an interview for Swiss television at the time of the opening, Szeemann repeats the same points with greater emphasis. He declares to his interviewer, speaking in French, that his desire is to transmit via the exhibition a certain "prise de conscience" (awakening or coming to awareness) born on the American West Coast: hippies, rockers, and drugs again, alongside eastern thought and an "anti-société," all of which have formed, he maintains, an entire youth movement in need of new means of expression. States of mind heretofore diffused over this "existential expanse" now assume—he gestures implicitly toward the contents of the exhibition—condensed artistic "form."[3]

It can, of course, be wondered how the outwardly unprepossessing look of the art materials on display accords with the rainbow-hued accoutrements of the counterculture in its flamboyant hippie phase. But the latter was never the whole of the phenomenon by any means; retrospective fascination with the gaudier displays by 1960s free spirits has obscured the Zen-inspired agrarian stream, with its ethic of voluntary poverty and plain self-sufficiency, present since the earliest manifestations of countercultural life. Intensity of mental transformation, Szeemann was implicitly arguing, actually increases as the gap widens between inward vividness and outward modesty of means. On the side of the spectator, perceptual acuity heightened by meditative centering or psychotropic substances might transform the least prepossessing matter into a riveting object of visual attention—that is, if one could really, REALLY see into that piece of felt or pile of sand.[4]

■

Defining and periodizing "the counterculture" remains an endlessly vexed arena for debate, nor will its parameters ever be definitively demarcated. As a place to start, Szeemann's rumination—an awakening born on the West Coast of America, drugs, hippies, eastern mysticism, an existential landscape—arose from first-hand observations on his scouting expedition to both San Francisco and Los Angeles, presciently introducing the neologism "anti-société" to stand for the newly minted term *counterculture*. The latter term came into its currently common usage only in the later stages of the phenomenon it names, courtesy of *The Making of a Counter Culture*, the popular book by the Bay Area historian and peace activist Theodore Roszak, published in 1969, that is, in the same year as *Live in Your Head*. But Roszak's still impressive treatise nowhere offers a capsule definition of its object, emphasizing instead the conditions of American postwar abundance and the consequent loosening of the old family discipline born of Depression and wartime privations. Accelerated by the Cold War expansion of public higher education, these changes opened the necessary space for the ferment of youthful discontents and active rebellion against the surrender of personal autonomy demanded by the new technocratic order. As he wrote in a later appraisal, "We will never know how many people belonged to the counter culture. It may be wrong to speak of it as having a membership at all. Rather it was a vision, that to one degree or another, drew the attention of passing many. More important than the size of the dissent was its depth. Never before had protest raised issues that went so philosophically deep, delving into the very meaning of reality, sanity, and human purpose."[5]

Roszak's capacious emphasis on process suggests that the best way forward would be to posit the counterculture (generally rendered as one word in more recent usage) as a spectrum or continuum over which certain traits will emerge more strongly or recede into the background depending on the chosen moment, location, and angle of observation. As with any emergent cultural formation, its inception will have been gradual, such that its first readily evident manifestations will arrive only after a considerable period of underground preparation; just as its waning and supersession will likewise be relative and likely never be entirely concluded. Szeemann's statements in 1969 are enough to establish that the relationship between the counterculture and the advanced art of the 1960s constitutes an inviting area for inquiry. But the repression of his preferred exhibition title in subsequent accounts, systematically forgotten along with his explication in terms of "hippie philosophy, the rockers and the use of drugs," demonstrates that even this most explicit document of a link has not been enough to shake conventional wisdom that LSD-consuming, motley-garbed, guitar-bashing wastrels could never have had significant bearing on the serious enterprise of advanced visual art.

Concentration on California in this book carries with it a certain intellectual argument that bears on how the art of our time might open itself to fuller interpretation. New York-centered art practice and criticism of the 1960s assumed a secure, confident sense of command over the experience of art: disabused, pragmatic, unmoved by anything but verifiable observation: "My painting is based on the fact that only what can be seen there *is* there. . . . What you see is what you see," in the famous 1966 pronouncement of the abstract painter Frank Stella, meaning banishment of all literary allusion, romantic conjecture, or emotional reading-in. By the turn of the decade, however, a powerful theoretical skepticism had arisen in other intellectual spheres, questioning whether the unified, self-aware subject fundamental to this outlook could be said to exist, whether taken as sole creative author of a work or as sovereign judge in its reception.[6] In our time, both these ideal types have come under withering attack in the name of diversity, as both makers and viewers from heretofore excluded ethnic, gender, and postcolonial communities have insisted that hybrid heterogeneity constitutes the ethical norm—as indeed it always has done.

Looking to California, however, reveals that a systematic dismantling of the putatively unified, autonomous, not to say "bourgeois" subject had already taken place, pursued with rigor by early adopters of psychedelic drugs. These were credentialed psychiatrists in Los Angeles and San Francisco during the years around 1960. Their view was that the inhibited, self-policing, materialistic individual produced by the prevailing postwar norms was inherently ill and condemned to misery. Psilocybin or LSD therapy, with the right setting and skilled therapist, offered the least stressful, even pleasurable path to overcoming this psychic impairment, as opposed to the years of halting, painful confrontation with repressed memories entailed in psychoanalysis. By scrambling "the mazeways of behavior we utilize," in the words of the UCLA psychiatrist Sidney Cohen, a way was opened to a reintegration of the subject with its previously inaccessible true self. His colleague Michael Agron, a psychiatric clinician at the UC San Francisco, outlined the therapeutic schema: a sufficient LSD dose initially disorganizes the ego and its defenses, with oppressive internalized precepts breaking down. Anxiety at this onset of defenselessness for a time disables sensation and affect, a temporary phase that gives way to heightened acuity of the senses, intense rapidity of association, and the feeling of god-like awareness, in the course of which previous anxiety and confusion yield to a suddenly clear consciousness of the subject's secure place in a boundless universe.[7]

Over the few years before this book came to be written, there arose a thoroughgoing revival of an analogous approach to psychotherapy in new centers established across a dozen major research hospitals in North America. Heralding this development in 2018, the science journalist Michael Pollan wrote with fervor for a wide audience that "LSD truly was an acid, dissolving almost everything with which it came into contact, beginning with the hierarchies of the mind (the superego, ego, and unconscious) and going on from there to society's various structures of authority."[8] No early enthusiast of the 1960s could have put the matter more succinctly. And no less an establishment voice than the *New York Times* was extolling in 2021 the power of psychedelics to induce "neuroplasticity, the brain's ability to change and reorganize thought patterns, enabling people with psychological disorders to find new ways to process anxiety, depression or deeply embedded trauma."[9] To cite just one undertaking founded in 2018, the resonantly named Center for Psychedelic and Consciousness Research at the Johns Hopkins Medical Center, is pursuing just such a mission. The background to this newly adventurous respect for the potential of psychedelic therapies, these researchers say, are the seemingly intractable components of an American mental health crisis as evidenced in suicide rates, prevalence of PTSD, alcoholism, and opioid addiction.

The dispiriting corollary to these excited reports is of course the intervening half-century of suppression and criminally lost time suffered on account of the fierce political counter-reaction and legal proscription that erupted the minute that this prospect of transformed consciousness escaped the confines of supervised medical practice. The early California centers of research in psychedelics had included the veterans hospital in Menlo Park near Palo Alto, where the novelist Ken Kesey first experienced LSD as an experimental volunteer.[10] That encounter led in fairly short order to the renowned Acid Tests staged by his entourage, the Merry Pranksters, careening from venue to venue up and down the West Coast in their famously decorated bus—a prime catalyst for growing numbers submitting themselves to these chemical solvents of their inherited parental culture. Instrumental to this escape of LSD from medical discipline (publicly decried by Cohen among other practitioners) were the labors of the young chemist/engineer Augustus Owsley Stanley III, who pioneered the large-scale, unauthorized production of the drug in the Bay Area to a high standard of quality. Despite the subsequent celebrity of latecomer Timothy Leary as the preeminent acid guru, his East Coast base offered nothing like the same availability or mass of adherents.

Concomitant with this countercultural accelerant were the abundant occasions for communal partaking in LSD or other mind-altering agents, the key being the explosion of new rock music (Szeemann's admired "Rockerexistenz"), rewarding for both physical release and stoned contemplation in venues accessible to young, liberated spirits far away from psychiatrists' hushed treatment rooms. Even though acts like the Grateful Dead, Jefferson Airplane, the Byrds, and the Doors were to achieve enormous celebrity, at the beginning their performances were accessible and cheap—the Dead often for free. A milder climate doubtless had a contributing effect—the famous Human Be-In that brought tens of thousands to Golden Gate Park in 1967 took place in January. There was greater familiarity and comfort with esoteric religious ideas imported from Asia, while San Francisco and Los Angeles had always been cities where new arrivals came to remake themselves. Thus, a broad community, though not without casualties among the unprepared and unlucky,[11] came to enact and explore on an organic level in one giant experiment—stoner hedonists alongside searching psychonauts—what remained elsewhere a matter of recondite philosophical debate.

For all these reasons, the mother ship of the California counterculture predominates in these pages, with one conspicuous detour to the axis of Detroit and Ann Arbor, Michigan. That regional scene mounted its own smaller but potent musical explosion, yoked to a special brand of political militancy joining hippies and activists. Why that matters for visual art was that the young Mike Kelley—later to become a quintessential Los Angeles artist—had seen all this at first hand. And it led him to the following observation, which bears directly on the guiding thesis of this book: "Contemporary American art history," he reflected in 1992, "is spookily aligned with Reagan/Bush ideology. By excising artworks from the 1960s that mirror the social and political upheavals and countercultural activities of the period, or focusing on works primarily in the formalist tradition, an unspoken alliance is forged with the conservatives: both agree that these unsavory issues are not appropriate for art, and thus for society."[12]

■

In lamenting this exclusion, Kelley was certainly speaking for his personal commitments, which he brought to California while still a student in the 1970s. He started late, but there exists in the person of Bruce Conner an artist of the first rank who participated unreservedly in the whole carnivalesque surrender of normative selfhood as it unfolded from the beginning. By his own testimony: "I did everything that everybody did in 1967 in the Haight-Ashbury in 1958, '59 and '60. I painted my windows. I painted my shoes. I would take peyote and walk out in the streets and realize that there was absolutely nobody in the whole Bay Area that was taking such a strange substance to alter their consciousness."[13] It will surprise no one that he, in fact, had plenty of company in consumption of peyote during the late 1950s, but his main point remains valid, that the counterculture identified with the Haight-Ashbury District and the 1967 "Summer of Love" had been anticipated by at least a decade, albeit in more underground guise. He also participated in the systematic use of psychedelics in psychiatric therapy under the aforementioned Michael Agron, while the much-admired assemblage sculptures he fashioned between 1958 and 1964 served, in his estimation, as "reports" of rewired associations and mental dislocations from inside psychotropic episodes. The hyper-kinetic blizzard of impressions conveyed by his films, careering from one thought-image to the next faster than normal cognition can follow, offered a glimpse into the mental acuity of a psilocybin high. Much the same can be said of his work at the other end of the temporal spectrum, mandala drawings that exhibit fascinated, near-obsessive attention to texture and the minutest detail. They demanded days on end of meditative concentration to make and encouraged a cognate state of mind in their viewers—or, conversely, ecstatic release when rendered as transparencies to be splashed over the walls of the Avalon Ballroom, as Conner's main artistic occupation became light-show projections behind the music, at the same time indulging his deep and longstanding immersion in the blues-based popular music that others were only just discovering.

As this book means to situate the practice of art within the California counterculture from the late 1950s to the end of the following decade, it thus finds its armature in the life of an artist of undisputed stature most fully implicated in virtually every realm of countercultural resistance to the expectations of the dominant straight world. As a younger poet acquaintance of Conner aptly phrased it, Conner gave "the so-called 'counter-culture' its, well . . . culture";[14] and it will be the task of the first five of twelve chapters to put flesh on the bones of that assertion.[15] To the extent that this amounts to a biography, it addresses a subject hyper-resistant to the ordeal of living inside of one. Conner billed his first solo exhibition in San Francisco, held in 1959 at the hole-in-the-wall Spatsa Gallery, THE LATE BRUCE CONNER. For years into the 1960s he refused to be photographed, during which time he followed Agron's therapeutic dismantling of the superficial self.[16] He sought at one point to disperse his singular identity among other Bruce Conners culled from phone directories and responded to an inquiry from *Who's Who* in the early 1970s with another declaration of his death, which was duly printed in that reference work. He described the prying and presumption of curators as a "weapon" trained against his well-being. But wariness of self-definition went hand in hand with a brand of irascible charisma that drew others to him, such that tracing his manifold activity brings a much larger, extra-individual field into view. Hence the marquee names of the sixties who make their appearances in these pages: Michael McClure, Allen Ginsberg, Jay DeFeo, Bill Graham, Ken Kesey, Norman Mailer, Timothy Leary, John Lennon, Richard Brautigan, Roger Corman, Toni Basil, blues virtuoso Paul Butterfield, the Diggers and their parent, The San Francisco Mime Troupe, Dennis Hopper and the other principals in *Easy Rid*er, all alongside less heralded women and men, intimates and allies, in whose company Conner's existence unfolded.

All of this occurred, it must be said, a long time ago, its first stirrings now six or seven decades in the past. But the folk memory of the long 1960s nonetheless appears to persist unaided and unabated. James Meyer had no difficulty filling the pages of his recent book, *The Art of the Return: The Sixties & Contemporary Culture*, with ambitious works of art largely conceived since the turn of the current century in conscious reference to countercultural era.[17] But folk memory is highly selective in its emphases and occlusions; so, indeed, is any form of history, but more formal, documentary approaches to narrating the counterculture allow for some degree of considered self-correction and refinement. Nor does any existing history, formal or folk, place a visual artist at its heart. Those present-day artists drawn to memorializing the period can here observe one of their number, a practitioner eminently worthy of their esteem, turning the drive toward self-liberation and the defiance of oppressive norms into compelling aesthetic statements—attitudes become form indeed.

■

Conner's path may have ranged across the United States and beyond its borders to Mexico City and London, which properly enlarges the subject; but the consistent core of his identity—as Szeemann asserted for the counterculture as a whole—remained in California. And so will be the core of this book, its first half leaning hard if not exclusively toward San Francisco and the north, the second toward Los Angeles and the south. Once its initial, Conner-aligned trajectory reaches 1969, the date of *Live in Your Head*, the next, essential task will be dropping back, in order to trace the risk-laden witnessing by other artists on the West Coast to America's catastrophic military incursion into Indochina, public manifestations of political dissent that Conner largely kept to an interiorized, elliptically expressed turbulence—for all the undoubted vehemence of his pacifist convictions. These next two chapters (6 and 7) bracket the decade of the 1960s, datable from James Turrell's astonishing 1960 adventures as an anti-war conscientious objector channeled into the secret campaign by the CIA in Southeast Asia and closing in 1970 with the second of two trumped-up trials endured by the Black Panther Bobby Seale, an enormity that dovetailed with the campus explosions set off by Richard Nixon's invasion of Cambodia in the spring of that year. Where anti-war fine art tended toward the path of principled refusal (Turrell and Wally Hedrick), graphic communication came to the fore, urgent issues of racial injustice coming to intersect with fierce opposition to the war across a broad phalanx of designers joining the famous cloistered nun Corita Kent, whose intransigent silkscreen statements put at risk her entire religious vocation; the radicalized former airman Rupert García, who returned from Indochina to be plunged into the maelstrom of Third World Liberation movements sparked by the student rebellion at San Francisco State; and Emory Douglas, the young Minister of Culture and poster artist for the beleaguered but defiant Panthers.

To enlarge the focus beyond painting, sculpture, and experimental film opens the way to major female, Black, and Brown artistic voices in California, as the chapter shifts from its opening attention to the vestigial fine-art "objects" of Turrell and Hedrick to the reproductive media of silkscreen prints, posters, and newsprint. Following Szeemann, it could be said that acknowledged fine artists mounted a credible reckoning with the new imperatives of social dissent only toward the end of the 1960s. An American document of this late arrival and its consequences comes courtesy of Philip Leider, then the editor of *Artforum*, who confronted the collapse of the established critical authority in fine art that his own journal had perhaps done most to put in place. That authority had established itself in service of the sheltered and recondite character that had overtaken self-consciously advanced art, the logic of which, as adduced above, depended on a mode of technocratic reasoning consistent with the dominant regime of expedient calculation against which the counterculture arose.[18]

So Leider intuited in a moment of intellectual crisis, explored in Chapter 8, seeking his remedy chiefly in the outsized excavated land art of Michael Heizer and Robert Smithson, which occasioned a Beat-style ecstatic road trip through the western American deserts to witness them (see Szeemann on "Mother Earth as medium, workplace, the desert as concept").[19] Both artists' compulsion to create new landscape features nonetheless lies open to present-day suspicions over cults of masculine mastery and sensitivities to intricately fragile ecologies. But something of an antidote to those domineering ambitions had already made itself felt in Leider's native Bay Area, not beyond the built-up urban core but straight through it, especially by taking on, as did Bonnie Ora Sherk and Terry Fox, the threats presented by ruthless forces of development to the compactly interwoven fabric and metaphysical aspirations of countercultural life.

Such locality dependence, however, made the work both non-portable and remote from the awareness of outsiders. Contemporaneous artists in Los Angeles faced quite the opposite problem in their having to connect over considerable distances across a dispersed urban complex. Serious artists throughout the region, as their numbers grew, organized themselves within a sprawling constellation, at the nodes of which were institutions of higher education. Predispositions toward irreverent iconoclasm and the cultivation of personal autonomy in the face of constituted authority had long taken root in California's extensive network of colleges and universities; indeed, they lay at the heart of the Free Speech Movement that erupted at UC Berkeley in 1964, arguably launching the overtly public phase of the counterculture across the board. After a lag, these proclivities became central to art making in and around Los Angeles, with the occupants of the separate clusters performing them for one another, then cross-fertilizing their counterparts elsewhere as artistic ideas and energies migrated from place to place within the system.

The fact that two primary foci—the new, exurban campuses of UC Irvine to the south of the city and California Institute of the Arts to its north—architecturally resembled bastions of technocratic enterprise may well have exacerbated the contrarian impulses of the artists, both faculty and students, housed therein. Recruited from an even more distant outpost, the Navy town of San Diego on the Mexican border, John Baldessari galvanized the fledgling program at CalArts by his brand of understated conceptual irony, pursued with one eye always on latest developments in the larger world encompassing New York and Europe—catalyst for the subsequent renown achieved by Michael Asher, Bas Jan Ader, Jack Goldstein, Lewis Baltz, Allen Ruppersberg, Chris Burden, and Baldessari himself.

The initial phase of this emergent formation occupies Chapter 9, with Chapter 10 tracking a diagnostic shift in theme strongly correlated to the pervasive criminality ascribed to Los Angeles in the disabused crime fiction of the 1940s by Raymond Chandler and James M. Cain, a genre that provided a reading public, whether local or far-flung, with its most vivid pictures of an elusive metropolis mined with hidden malfeasance. Criminals and victims alike vanish from sight, leaving their discovery to the detective, a fictional figure embraced in this period as an alter ego by more than one Los Angeles artist. The term *noir* arose, courtesy of some French aficionados, to categorize the Hollywood films into which these stories were quickly adapted, often by European expatriates, with their characteristically crepuscular lighting, tense sexuality, and enigmatic plots. For artists undergoing withdrawal from the moral clarity and enfranchisement of youth conferred by the anti-war movement, they would find that the ills of pollution, over-development, and environmental destruction presented more ambiguous targets and resisted decisive solutions. A pervasive, sinister, and largely hidden array of forces seemed always to prevail, such that dissent becomes a bleaker, more lonely witnessing to inhuman conditions largely impervious to principled resistance.

Enter the *noir* sleuth—or his fugitive quarry—as artist surrogate, a figure lent vivid immediacy by the thoroughgoing revival of this sensibility in the brooding period film *Chinatown*, released in 1974, written by Robert Towne and directed by Roman Polanski. Towne's lament for the lost Los Angeles of his childhood made the city as much a character as Jack Nicholson came to embody in the role of the detective protagonist feeling his way from one fatal misunderstanding to the next. The mid-1970s also saw the dispersal of the university-trained artists who had revived the *noir* coloration of the city, but that development left the field more open for the entry of previously excluded aspirants (the subjects of Chapter 11), who made the actual streets and alleyways of Los Angeles into their medium, some assuming an intentionally collective character in pockets of the segregated city: the four gifted young artists who composed Asco (Patssi Valdez, Harry Gamboa Jr. Willie Herrón III, and the shapeshifting Gronk) on the Latin Eastside; the Brockman Gallery and Studio Z (think David Hammons, Senga Nengudi, and Maren Hassinger) in Black South Central. Disaffected young whites with meager prospects brought a richly unsavory aesthetic vitality to the punk venues of Hollywood and San Francisco in both musical and visual style, sending out waves that drew Bruce Conner back into action in parallel with the young Jenny Lens as photographers of record.

The punk scene, into which Conner threw himself at the advanced age of forty-five, naturally integrated a raw approach to music with its aggravating performance and style, reawakening with new urgency his longstanding desire to lend his art a musical dimension. Much the same can be said of Mike Kelley, whose abbreviated career closes the book in a more compressed complement to the opening exploration around Conner. Attention to this Irish-American artist will also have the unexpected effect of opening to question one consensus boundary long placed around the counterculture: "Black Power never made up part of the counterculture," one recent attempt at a synthetic history is pleased to pronounce, a view surprisingly anticipated by the otherwise more latitudinarian Roszak.[20] Kelley, however, before assuming his place at the center of Los Angeles art, gained his first countercultural experience in a place where this exclusion did not apply, owing to the one musical genre not normally in evidence in accounts of the counterculture: namely, jazz.

The free, experimental music evolved by Black players like John Coltrane in the mid- to late 1960s, called the "New Thing" at the time, moved its Black audience as an authentic voice of liberation. Serving as something of elder statesman to this tendency was the Afro-Futurist visionary Sun Ra, in whose Solar Arkestra younger talents like Pharaoh Sanders came to their hard-blowing maturity. As the cosmically mystical imaginations fostered by the West Coast counterculture waxed over the course of the 1960s, Sun Ra had already staked out a rich province of that territory in the name of Black experience. Nor did the presumed eclipse of counterculture's transformative aspirations slow him down, as he kept the faith in participatory ritual as the reason for musical performance. Nengudi and her Studio Z cohort never missed what she called the "total theater" of a Sun Ra performance in Los Angeles, just as some years earlier, under the aegis of the poet and rebel ringleader John Sinclair, the Detroit–Ann Arbor radical axis had provided an especially receptive home for the bandleader's unpredictable extravagances in sound, movement, costume, and philosophy. Kelley, one more besotted University of Michigan hippie, recalled: "The stage was filled with tons of equipment and many musicians . . . The aesthetic was a mix of African music, exotica, big band, science fiction, Greek chorus, and political rally . . . unlike anything I had ever seen or heard. . . . It was the most intellectually and physically demanding show I have ever seen."[21]

So deep did this memory penetrate that Sun Ra remained a constant touchstone, a horizon of aspiration for Kelley's art until the end of his grievously shortened life in 2012. His art was flourishing at an exceptional level during the same period that the artists surveyed by James Meyer in his *Art of Return* were staging their re-imagined 1960s; but Kelley had personally experienced one crucial, only slightly belated flare of actual countercultural intensity, the imprint of which never left him. If anything, the full measure of memories and identifications he carried had become only more salient to his sense of mission and artistic decisions, thus confounding any sense that the last period of generalized rebellion in the west could safely be consigned to the past.

3 Bruce Conner, BRUNETTO LATINO, 1956,
ink on paper, 20.32 × 17.15 cm,
Collection San Francisco Museum of Modern Art,
Gift of Robert and Lynne Dean in memory of
Larry Secrist

ONE

# PEYOTE FRONTIER

THE YOUNG BRUCE CONNER HAD BEEN UNABASHED in sizing up the prospects for his art career in both New York and San Francisco. On a first foray to the art capital in 1953, he had gone so far as to cold-call Robert Motherwell, securing a studio visit and conversation with this admired senior figure. Two years later, on the strength of a term scholarship to the art school then housed in the Brooklyn Museum, he arrived with portfolio and slides under his arm, his perseverance and his tolerance for the expected rejections yielding the prize of long-term affiliation with the estimable Charles Alan Gallery on Madison Avenue. The restless young artist, still in the midst of graduate studies at the University of Colorado, next traveled to San Francisco, where he stayed for a month with Michael McClure, the poet who had been his closest school friend from Wichita. As he had sought out Motherwell in New York, he approached Richard Diebenkorn as a comparable doyen of the local scene. Nearly two decades afterward, his choking experience on first seeing Diebenkorn's art in person remained vivid enough to prompt this rich analogy: "it was like too much icing. It was like eating sweet and sour pork for the first time and then having a banana split afterward. The only way I could think about comparing them was it was like a little too much at one time for me to take."[1]

It would not then appear to have been the city's reigning style of painting that prompted Conner and his wife, the artist Jean Sandstedt Conner, to opt for San Francisco in 1957, but he at least knew he would no longer fear the life of the friendless outcast he had felt himself to be in New York—despite all the professional encouragement he had received: "When I was in New York it was like a maze, a rat maze, going from one little box to another little box and passing through passageways to get from one safe haven to another."[2] Perhaps his most trenchant work from his last stay in the city during 1956 meditated on the epic poetry of incarcerated torment to be found in Dante's *Inferno*. Already skilled as a printmaker, he crafted a dense drawing with pen, brush, and ink that emulates the fine hatching and border of an etching in order to bring into visibility the head of the poet's Florentine mentor Brunetto Latino (fig. 3), in life a distinguished writer and civic official, suddenly encountered in the parched, scalding sands traversed by the elliptically characterized "Sodomites," as rendered here in the widely read English translation of the 1950s by John Ciardi:

And I, when he stretched out his arm to me,
searched his baked features closely, till at last
I traced his image from my memory

in spite of the burnt crust, and bending near
to put my face closer to his, at last
I answered: "Ser Brunetto, are you here?" (*Inferno*, 15.25–30)

With simultaneous density and economy, Conner's drawing translates both the blackened features of Brunetto's bulbous, scorched-bare skull and the effort entailed in discerning the revered likeness beneath it, a shadow shadowed by the abyss that lies just beyond the rim of scalding sand and raining embers on which the narrator and Virgil at that moment find themselves. Their alternatively halting and hectic movement among the damned could well be described as "passing through passageways to get from one safe haven to another," always encircled, as Conner characterized the city, by an enclosing rim that blocked out the world: "I could rim as long as I wanted to and I still would not be able to see the horizon."

No such problems awaited him on the hillsides of San Francisco. The fact that McClure and his poet-spouse, Joanna, were already established there, living in the Western Addition building with compellingly unorthodox visual artists like Jay DeFeo and Wally Hedrick, another sympathetic married couple, doubtless played a large part in their choice. Conner nonetheless acknowledges that "most of the people that I knew or knew about here were poets . . . And all of the people that moved out here were more involved in literary things than the visual arts."[3] McClure had, in fact, first migrated to the city wanting to study abstract painting with Clyfford Still at the California School of Fine Arts. Discovering that Still was no longer in residence, he found his life-long vocation on joining a poetry workshop at San Francisco State College with Robert Duncan (who enjoyed close ties to the art world via his partner, Jess Collins, and the social hub they made of their shared, four-story Victorian house in the Mission District).[4] Nor was the most pressing reason for Conner's move to San Francisco a matter pertaining to either art form. Having left higher education, his Boulder M.F.A. unfinished, Conner was now subject to the military draft and determined to fail the medical examination. Here the liberal environment of the Bay Area, its receptiveness to eccentricity and wider allowance for psychiatric anomalies, made it more likely he would strike an examining physician open to the playacting he had in mind—in the service of which he transformed himself into the just the sort of forlorn outcast he had felt himself to have been in New York.

He turned up on McClure's doorstep in this willfully derelict condition, as the poet recalled: "Here was Bruce, whiskers growing in different directions, his face smeared, his clothes tattered and torn, dishevelment that would make Hamlet at his worst look like a sartorial exclusive."[5] According to McClure, Conner completed his disheveled appearance with "the first Rat Bastard that I ever saw. It looked like a canvas with a handle on it . . . feathers sticking out, dolls heads in it, peyote buttons in it." That recollection appears to conflate

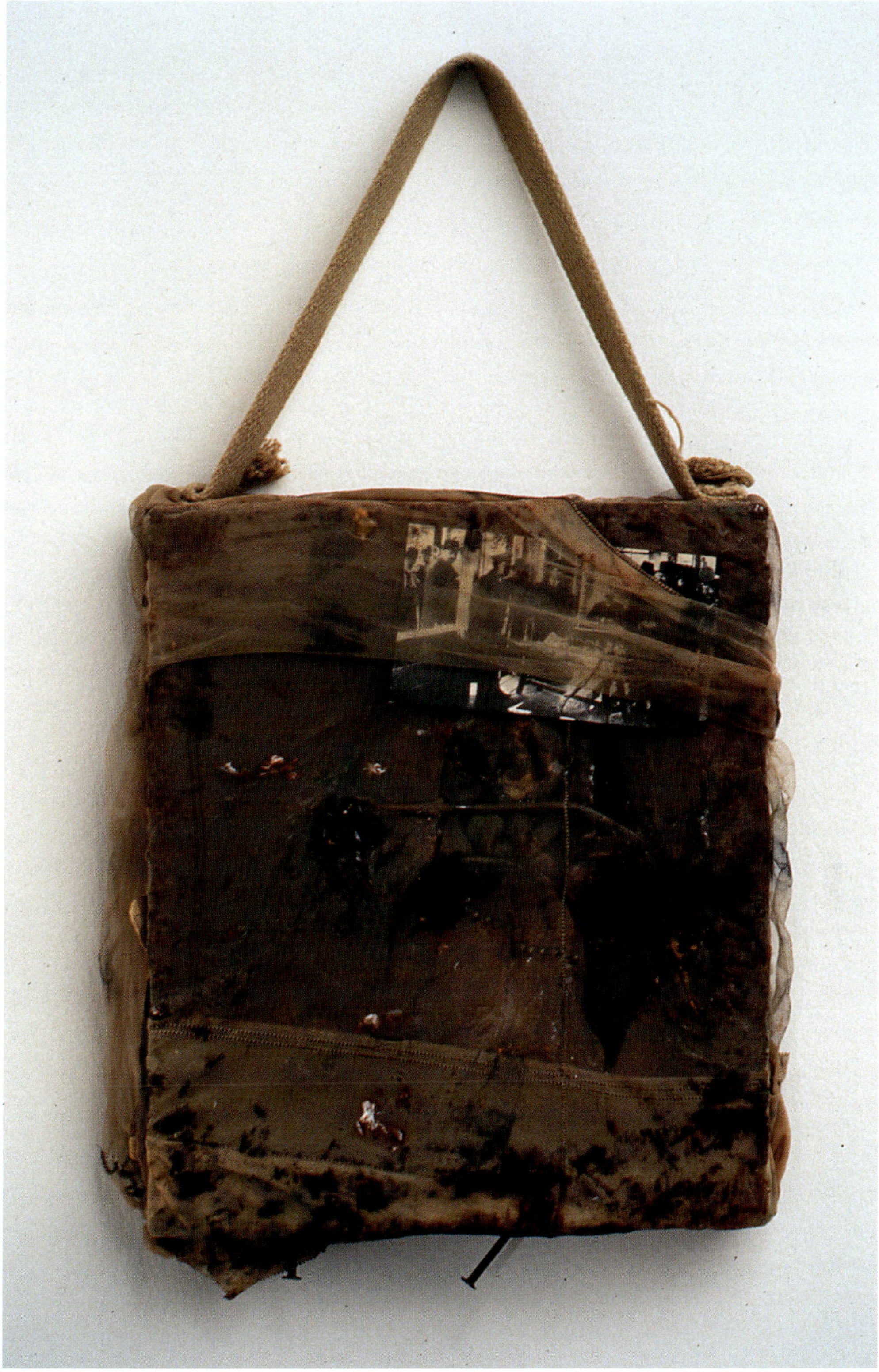

4 Bruce Conner, RAT BASTARD NO. 1 (front), 1958, wood, canvas, nylon, newspaper, photographic reproduction, wire, oil paint, nails, bead chain, etc., 42 × 23.5 × 7 cm, Collection Walker Art Center, Minneapolis, Gift of Lannan Foundation, 1997

this inaugural prototype with one or more that followed (no doll's head nor actual peyote buttons).[6] For his part, Conner described the object (fig. 4) as taking on its own "persona": a "wounded" painting that he had attacked and then bandaged with nylon stockings, affixed with "a picture of a cadaver on an operating table . . . with wire and wood representing bones and structure."[7] From these operations emerged a spell-casting fetish-object crafted to defeat the morbid powers of the war machine.

One way or another, Conner achieved his goal of exemption from the draft, and RAT BASTARD NO. 1 came to engender dozens more in a similar vein.[8] But there is much bound up in this episode that goes beyond colorfully self-interested behavior. The date of Conner's draft resistance, which is what it was, came nearly a decade before the escalation of American draftees being sent to Vietnam, when such evasion became understandably widespread. The peacetime American military of the late 1950s was a largely non-lethal proposition. At the same moment, for example, the future novelist Robert Stone, who would become a Kesey-aligned countercultural figure during the mid-1960s, was willingly serving aboard a naval transport in the South Indian Ocean. Future light-and-space master James Turrell, who figures in the following chapter for his efforts to shield others from conscription, was then preparing to serve as a CIA pilot in Southeast Asia in order to fulfill his lawful military obligation as a conscientious objector. Irving Petlin, who will likewise emerge in that chapter as a key figure in bending art toward indictment of the Vietnam War, was at that moment leading a secret life as an Army intelligence non-com at the Presidio, all the while taking as full a part in the same San Francisco art scene as was Conner. In the context of the late years of the Eisenhower administration, Conner's actions stand out for their fierce anti-militarism and intention to subvert the law, deemed by him a force inimical to his personal survival. In the service of this subversion, he resorted to the artificial cultivation of extreme states of mind and body, self-transformation projected onto an uncomprehending world with extravagant outward dramatics: key traits in any definition of the counterculture.

RAT BASTARD NO. 1, bearing its charge of spleen and painful imaginings of authority and military discipline, bolstered his cause as he faced down the draft board's medical exam. Its contents are obscured from the front by dark nylon wrapping, but the other side offers a ragged newspaper clipping (fig. 5), its subject the staged photographs made by one William Langley of Dallas, in which costumed models posed for *tableaux vivants* re-creating ancient forms of torture. The featured example, its naked male figure in a crucifixion pose, is captioned: "The original 'Hot Foot' was the so-called 'Boot' in which the feet of prisoners were destroyed by ladles of molten metal."[9] Nor was he finished with this line of analogy, the next year amplifying it in a far more public fashion when a more immediately urgent parallel to the moral case against the Cold War militarization had emerged in the campaign against capital punishment.

For more than ten years Caryl Chessman, imprisoned at San Quentin on northern San Francisco Bay, had been fighting a sentence of death for robberies and sex crimes that met no plausible legal threshold for execution. His memoir of confinement and plea for justice,

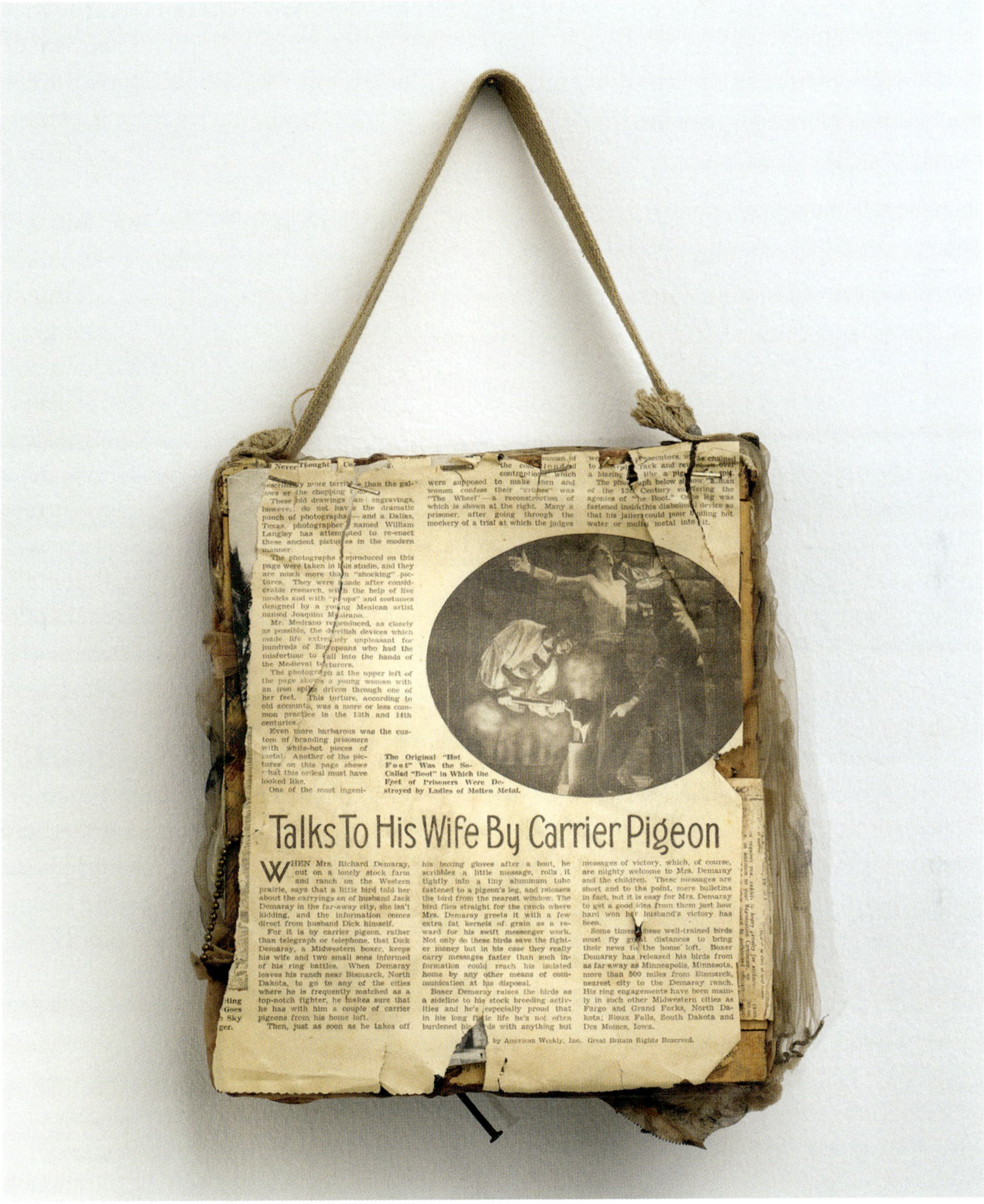


**5** Bruce Conner, RAT BASTARD NO. 1 (back), 1958,
wood, canvas, nylon, newspaper, photographic reproduction,
wire, oil paint, nails, bead chain, etc., 42 × 23.5 × 7 cm,
Collection Walker Art Center, Minneapolis, Gift of Lannan Foundation, 1997

smuggled out of the prison, became an international bestseller and an enormous impetus for the cause of abolition.

The cause and the uproar around it drew Conner for the first time into the topical arena of politics. Using a cast-off high chair as a support, he began sculpting an agonized stand-in for Chessman out of black wax, a figure that transformed itself as he worked it into a tortured and mutilated victim, gagged and bound with torn nylon (fig. 6). He called it CHILD, and for once such a gesture had an immediate public impact, sending visitors away horrified from the annual exhibition of the San Francisco Art Association, perhaps shocked as much by the adult genitals as by the ravaged face—or so reported the censorious critics, relishing the prospect of scandal from the "beatnik" fringe.[10] Much is made in the literature on Conner of the later destiny of CHILD after he sent it to New York as part of his solo exhibition at the Charles Alan Gallery.[11] From there it passed to the collection of the august Museum of Modern Art, but not before an interim, private purchase by one of MoMA's trustees, Philip Johnson, as a buffer to absorb its rebarbative character, much as Johnson had done a short time before with Jasper Johns's 1956 *Flag*, out of apprehension over its putative mockery of the national symbol. Unlike Johns's soon-to-be-celebrated work, however, Conner's CHILD, possibly damaged in transport and prone to deterioration, languished un-conserved in storage for many decades. During the interval between its two early moments of exhibition in the confines of art, however, Conner found another use for CHILD, one that made the most of the work's saturation in talismanic ritual and torment, thus to be wielded like a power-object akin to RAT BASTARD NO. 1.

Chessman had finally been sent to the gas chamber in May 1960, following a signal failure of courage on the part of California's liberal governor Edmund Brown. Thousands of students from San Francisco, Berkeley, and the surrounding area staged mass protests at the prison. Two months later, many of the same students were among the two thousand demonstrators protesting hearings in the city by the Un-American Activities Committee of the United States Congress, which had for more than a decade deployed its powers of subpoena to hound deviants from America's anti-socialist orthodoxy, ruining careers and jailing witnesses on contrived charges of perjury and contempt of Congress. In a confrontation that turned the event into "Black Friday," riot police beat two hundred protesters on the steps of the city hall. On the following day, when the demonstration swelled to five thousand, Conner joined the protest, carrying the heavy, awkward CHILD on his shoulders, with a sign affixed reading "Stop Police Brutality." One smartly dressed young organizer confronted him over the repulsive character of the sculpture, complaining that it violated the high-minded decorum his committee wished to maintain and unnecessarily provoked the police.[12]

It has been too easy to split the New Left off from the counterculture, as capacity for moral witnessing and protest remained inseparable from the latter's larger collective dissent from conformity and obedience. But an undeterred Conner had nonetheless provoked, at an early stage, what would become a persistent tension between the reasoned ethical appeals proffered by much of the New Left and the non-rational powers conjured by the counter-

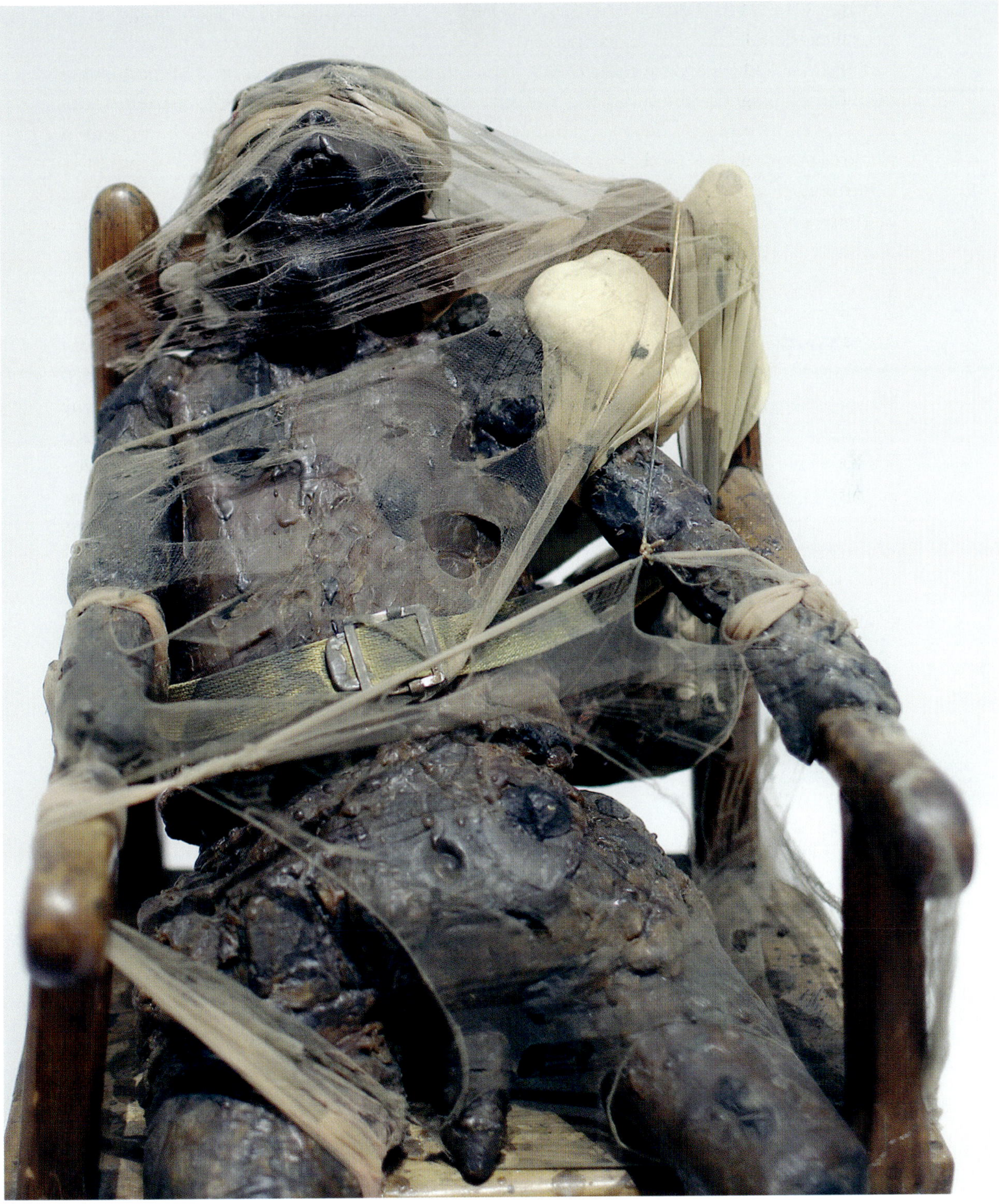

**6** Bruce Conner, CHILD (detail), 1959, mixed media, 87.7 × 43.1 × 41.7 cm, The Museum of Modern Art, New York culture—even when their basic sentiments were aligned. Looking back in 1968, in conversation with the *Rolling Stone* magazine critic Thomas Albright, Conner would reflect that he had "always been involved in mysticism—Zen, alchemy, magic, all that stuff."[13] In the enlightened museums of the present, power objects revered by the traditional cultures that made them are kept from the view of the uninitiated public. In the long sequestering of CHILD in the MoMA storerooms, there may have been some unconscious perception of its inherent curse on the compromises with corrupt forms of authority (for example, the youthful record of Philip Johnson as a fervent Nazi sympathizer) on which the institution depended.

■

Analogous themes manifested themselves less overtly but just as profoundly in a large assemblage of the same year to which Conner gave the title TEMPTATION OF ST. BARNEY GOOGLE (fig. 8). The titular character was the furthest thing from saintly on the menu of popular culture, a timeworn newspaper cartoon of a tattered, bug-eyed, racetrack tout that was first launched in 1919. But that comic indirection served Conner as a disingenuous alibi for his taking on the theme of demonic temptation in its most sublime artistic manifestation. In the legend of Saint Anthony, the desert hermit of the early Church overcame both the sensual enticements sent by Satan and the deathly blows of bestial creatures in a rocky, Egyptian cave. Among the many authoritative representations of the saint's ordeal, the configuration of Conner's assemblage points to one in particular: *The Temptation of Saint Anthony* by Matthias Grünewald on an inside wing of his testament to ultimate torment, the Isenheim altarpiece (fig. 7). Not for the last time, Conner would dispose his apparently improvised concatenations of disparate flotsam and nylon mesh into a composition that rhymes with the arrangement of an old-master painting. In the early literature of the Church, God was said to have observed Anthony's mortal struggles from afar, only later praising him for his stalwart resistance to the swarming personifications of sin and evil. Grünewald places his divinity inside a loosely solar aura at the pinnacle of the composition, to which Conner responds with a shrouded lunar disk filling in the altar-like arch at the top of the

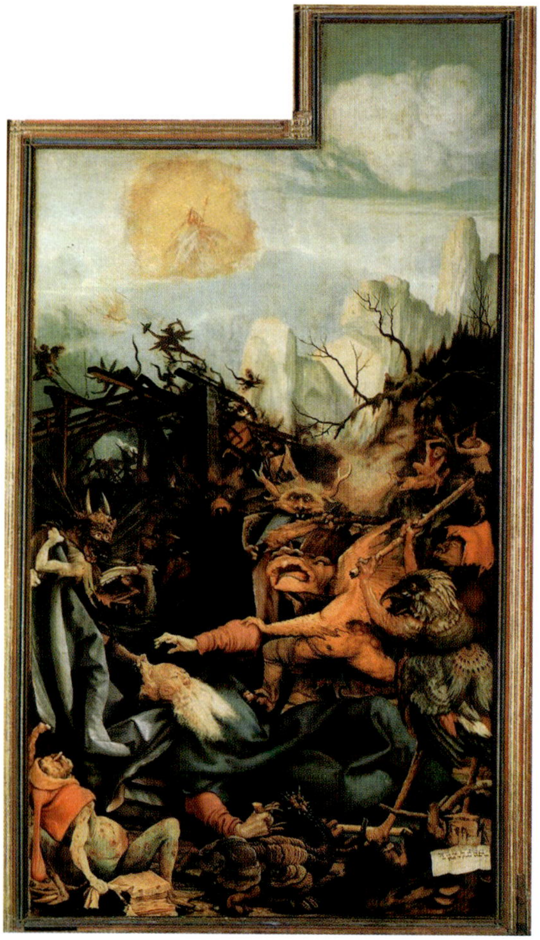

7 Matthias Grünewald, *Temptation of Saint Anthony*, 1512–16, oil on wood, 265 × 141 cm, Musée d'Unterlinden, Colmar

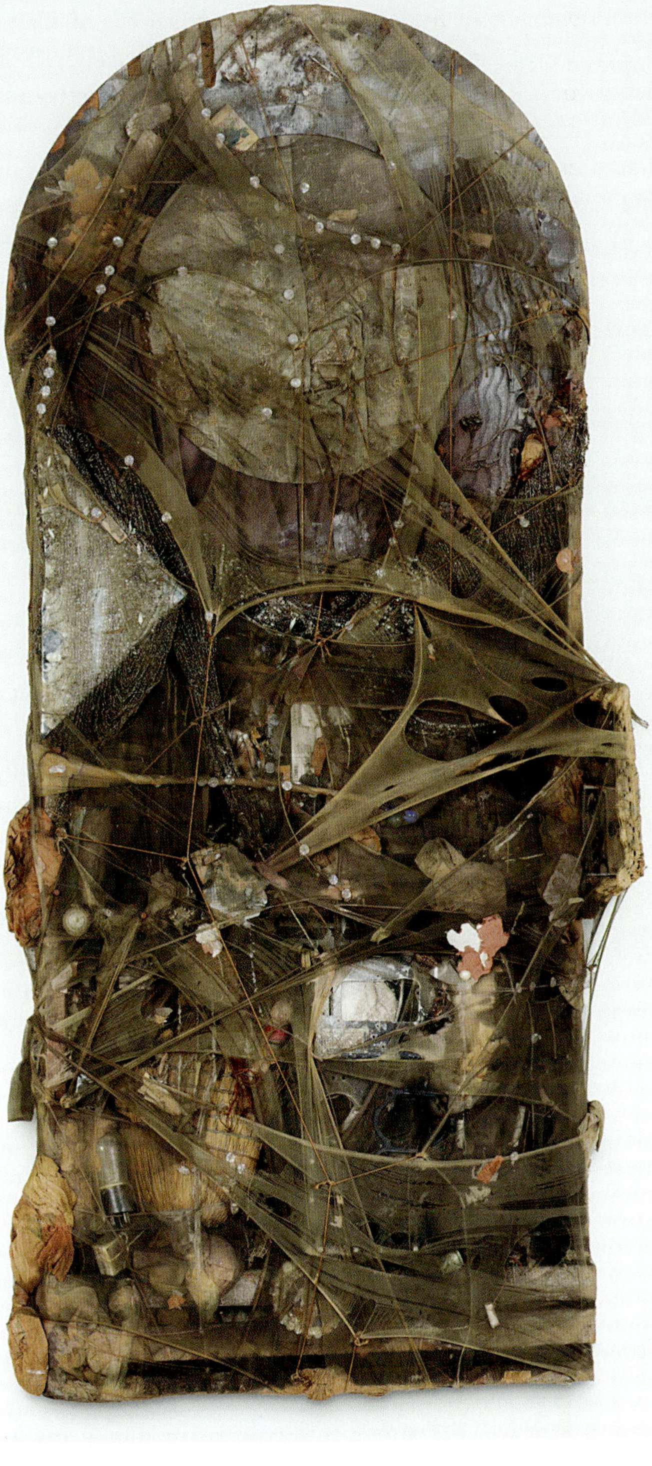

**8** Bruce Conner, TEMPTATION OF ST. BARNEY GOOGLE, 1959,
mixed media, 21.1 × 42 cm,
Museum Moderner Kunst Stiftung Ludwig, Vienna

panel. One skein of stocking, stretched to a point from right to left across the center, echoes the arms of two creatures reaching toward the bald pate of the hermit, while the shallow curve of a skein below tracks the prominent fold in the cloak of the saint. A collection of bundles with an old vacuum tube occupy the place in the lower left occupied by swollen, diseased body of a peasant in the Grünewald panel.

It is an art-historical commonplace to note that the complex altarpiece, housed in what was a monastery hospital in the Franco-German Alsace, is dedicated to the healing of "Saint Anthony's fire," a debilitating ergotism induced by a mold on grain. Hence the prominence of skin sores on this peasant figure and on the body of the crucified Christ himself in the principal tableau. Centuries later, this same substance would yield the refined hallucinogen LSD, lycergic acid being the molecular core of ergot. While the Swiss pharmaceutical researcher Albert Hofmann had long before synthesized what he named LSD-25 in 1938, it stayed largely out of view until shortly before Conner composed his TEMPTATION OF ST. BARNEY GOOGLE. At the initiative of the Beverly Hills psychiatrists Oscar Janiger and Sidney Cohen a select coterie of wealthy celebrities, Cary Grant among them, were being administered the drug in therapeutic sessions; Aldous Huxley first obtained the drug from the same source.[14] None of this was likely a secret from Conner. As will emerge in detail below, a friend and clinician, the psychiatrist Michael Agron at the University of California medical campus in San Francisco, as noted in the Prologue, had already embarked on his own use of psychotropic drugs for therapeutic purposes.

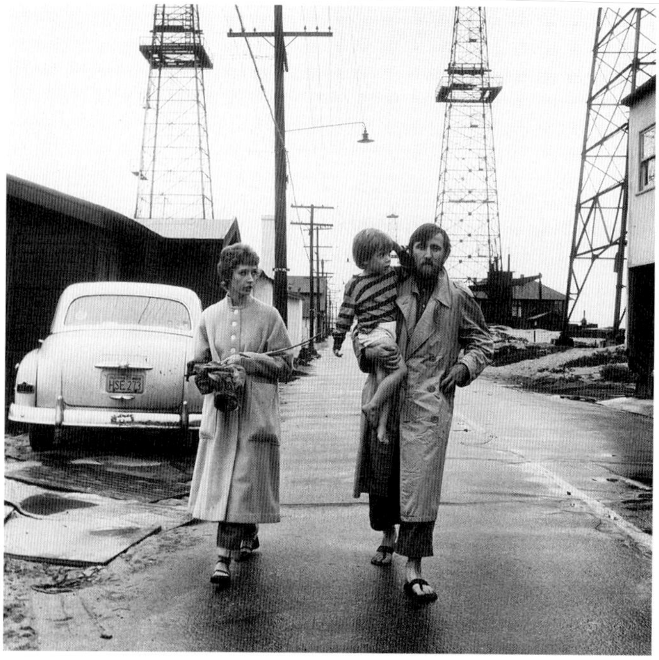

9 Shirley, Tosh, and Wallace Berman, c. 1957, photograph by Charles Brittin, Charles Brittin Collection, Getty Research Library, Los Angeles

At that juncture, adventurous spirits among the San Francisco bohemians favored more organically derived hallucinogens that had the imprimatur of Native American ritual sanctity. Michael McClure, harking back to 1958, writes at length about his introduction to the mescaline-bearing pulp from the buttons of the peyote cactus, describing its preparation and sacramental ingestion "for joy, for consciousness, for spiritual elevation, for what the Romantic poet Keats called 'Soul-making'." It is probably safe to correlate "joy" with getting high to an ecstatic degree beyond the pleasures of marijuana, which moreover brought, for that moment at least, no legal jeopardy. This mind catalyst came to McClure from the recent Los Angeles transplant Wallace Berman (fig. 9), whom he called a "mystic painter and photographer" and his "peyote father."[15]

Berman had been a long-admired leading light in bohemian circles, a tireless disseminator of experimental writing and graphics via *Semina*, his finely printed, unbound journal of poetry and prints that he assembled and mailed to friends at irregular intervals starting in 1955. An exhibition of his sculpture in 1957 had led to his arrest and conviction on a far-fetched charge of public obscenity; at the announcement of the verdict, he had compounded his punishment by writing on a courtroom chalkboard: "There is no justice, only revenge." His fine paid by a friend, the actor Dean Stockwell, Berman then fled the city with his wife, Shirley, and their young son, Tosh, for the more tolerant environs of San Francisco, where they first established themselves at the end of 1957 within blocks of both the McClures and the Conners in the Western Addition.

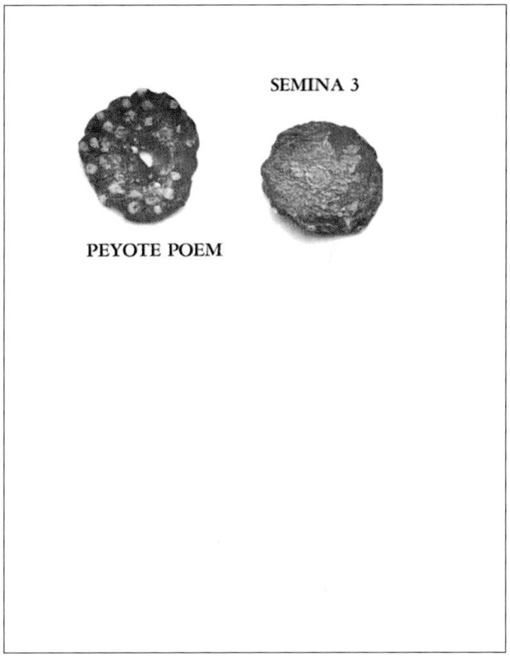


**10** Wallace Berman, *Semina* 3, 1958, cover sheet, Metropolitan Museum of Art, New York

The publication of *Semina* came with them, the old circle of free spirits like Stockwell sporadically augmenting their new, like-minded community in San Francisco. When *Semina* 3 appeared in 1958, its cover sheet announced McClure's poetic translation of the transforming experience, his "adventure of consciousness," induced by ingesting peyote, the title juxtaposed with cropped photographs of a peyote button as an isolated disc from the front and back (fig. 10). The poem reads in part, "My eyes won't focus but leap. / I see I have three feet. / I see seven places at once! / . . . Flashes / of light / and meldings. I wait / seeing the physical things pass."[16]

And that psychedelic bond encompassed Conner, who matched McClure's forthrightness on more than one occasion, proposing his sculpture as visual and tactile correspondences to the peyote experience. He confided to Albright, "I had a lot to do with psychedelics up till the time I stopped doing assemblages—I thought of myself like George Catlin traveling across the country into a new territory, then coming back and making a report. But I decided this represented a kind of arbitrary role-taking, communicating something that couldn't really be communicated."[17] The ethnography of peyote ingestion as a Native American rite very likely prompted his thoughts turning to Catlin, the nineteenth-century explorer-painter who specialized in Native-American subjects. And his regretful confession of untranslatability may parallel a tactful unwillingness to presume entry into that culture, however extravagantly the mythic Native American would be admired and aped within the 1960s counterculture.[18]

Conner's remark nonetheless fully acknowledges that the much-admired assemblages he fashioned between 1958 and 1964 were, indeed, apart from anything else, "reports" of rewired associations and mental dislocations from inside psychotropic episodes. Allen Ginsberg offered a cognate account, pithier than McClure's, of sharing peyote with his companion Peter Orlovsky in San Francisco during the writing of *Howl*, a few years before. As they stood at the main traffic intersection of North Beach, he recalled, "I looked into Peter's eyes, and I couldn't find anyone there . . . It was shock when we looked at each other and perceived two phantom ghosts with empty eyes, laughing fiendishly."[19] And Conner's recollection of one peyote voyage accords with Ginsberg's shocking encounter with the self as a stranger:

> I experienced myself as this very tenuously held-together construction—the tendons and muscles and organs loosely hanging around inside—and it seemed like at any moment disaster could strike and you could fall apart. I mean, you were just held together by this thin skin and strings of flesh. And shortly after that I started working on a number of named pieces, but the first one was SNORE, which has all these organ-like lumps of things.[20]

Though relatively small at three feet in height, the hunched, upright configuration of SNORE (fig. 11) approximates a human shape, its chest and cranium hollow voids in which space and substance change places. For matter analogous to this stretched, frayed, barely holding encasement, Conner's brilliant choice was the torn and laddered nylon stocking, a manufactured material he had tried out as the bandages in RAT BASTARD NO. 1 and as the restraints in CHILD. Its fragility, transparency, and web-like patterns when stressed all suited the theme of incipient physical disintegration; but it inescapably carried disturbingly uncanny, perversely eroticized associations with the epidermis to which it normally clings.

▪

Conner was at the time disciplining himself to produce one new piece in some medium every day, using a studio space adjoining the storage of props and costumes maintained by the San Francisco Mime Troupe.[21] It is more than telling that Conner would have been so linked to this acting ensemble almost from its inception, as the Mime Troupe's trajectory runs like a bright thread through the entire saga of the San Francisco counterculture. Founded in 1959 by Ronny Davis, the group's name derived from the fanciful grotesqueries of the bygone Italian *commedia dell'arte*, which had dominated popular entertainment in Europe from the sixteenth through the eighteenth centuries. In a kind of pastoral return to a putatively simpler but more vivid time, Davis embraced the highly stylized artifice, cross-dressing, and disguise that characterized the genre, its broad comedic types, and declamatory acting style, along with its itinerant mode of production: rough platforms set up in public parks, a hat passed round after performances.

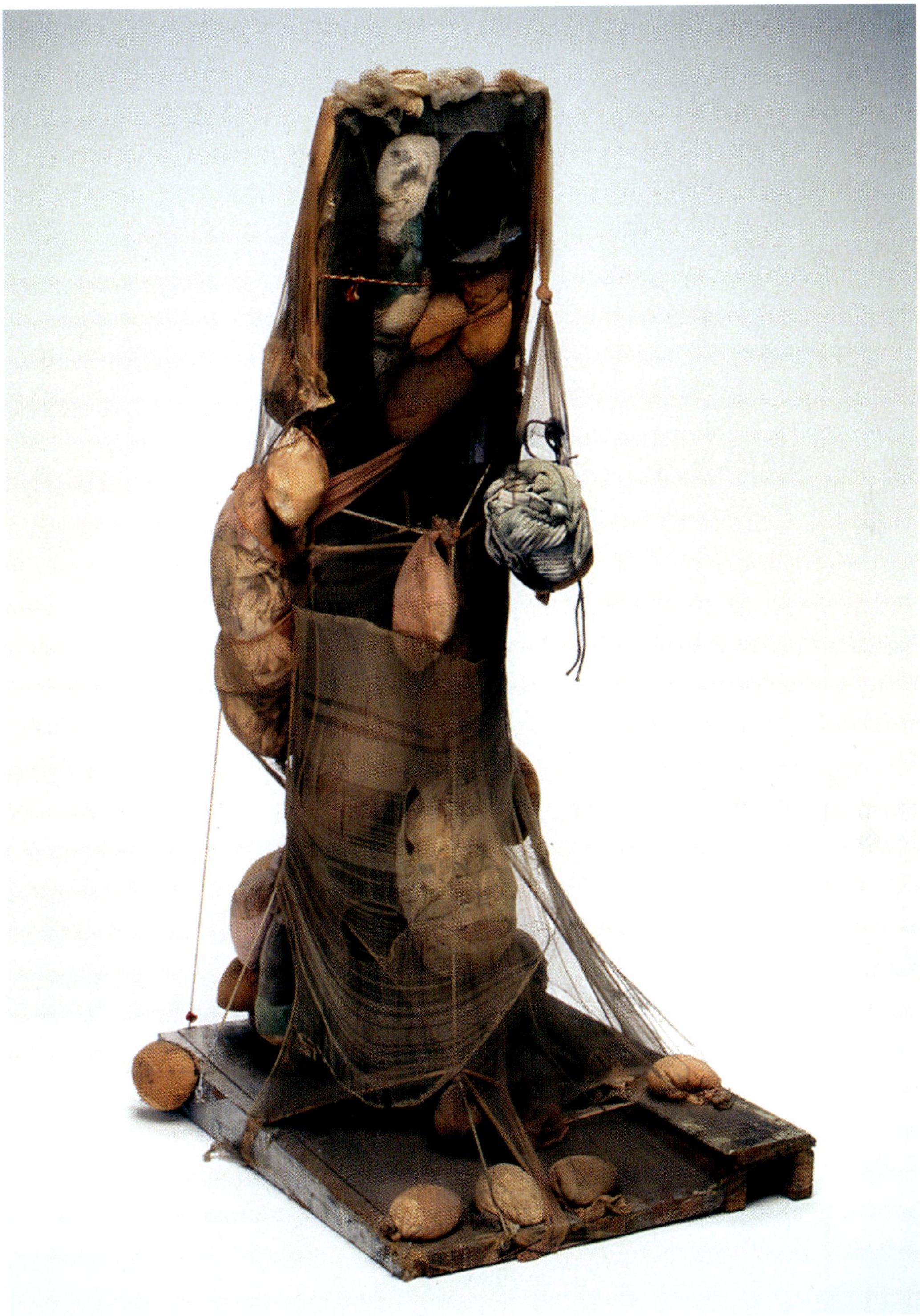

**11** Bruce Conner, SNORE, 1960,
mixed media, 92.7 × 44.5 × 54.6 cm,
Fine Arts Museums of San Francisco

It merits a pause in this account to note in definitional terms the salient place of the Mime Troupe in the development of the San Francisco counterculture, at this juncture barely visible but due to borrow much of its outward aspect and attitudes from Davis's company. The Troupe itself offered a model for communal, self-organized, and self-sufficient survival on one's own terms. Perhaps less obvious but central was the practice they pioneered of freely appropriating the city's public parks as places for group assembly, play, and growing self-recognition. More overt were the eclectically fanciful costumes, which members of the audience began taking up themselves as templates for rebelliously out-of-time self-fashioning. Turning the irreverence inherent in his chosen theatrical tradition toward intransigent Leftist agitation, Davis began regularly clashing with Parks authorities, confounding the usual bifurcation between hippies and militants. These legal imbroglios hastened the development of an intensified community consciousness, as San Francisco musicians rallied behind the group with benefit concerts, these then setting the pattern for the burgeoning ballroom scene to follow. A breakaway group of Mime Troupe actors, eager to turn their energy and personal charisma toward a utopian social project, became the fabled Diggers, who proved the most inventive and bold organizers of alternative institutions to feed and clothe the hippie influx.

In that most of these developments lay in the future, however, what can be drawn from Conner's early bond with Davis and his incipient project of "guerilla theater"? He offered a possible answer to a later interviewer who was quizzing him about his work of this period in relation to that of other assemblage artists: "How would you distinguish or separate your own work . . . ?" asks his interlocutor, "Does it have to do with sculptural considerations? The use of unusual materials per se?—is that the content?" Conner's answer cuts through the confusion: "It has to do with the theater. Theater in the sense of an image, an environment that's made privately. Somebody makes an altar in their house, or they set up objects on tables, or they organize objects in windows (like a real theater with curtains). A church is another kind of theater; a museum, is another kind of theater."[22]

Davis aimed to clothe in light-hearted, fancy-dress farce the stark, uncomfortable truths of social oppression by the rich and powerful. Conner likewise conceived his static theater as exposure of internalized structures of oppression, most pointedly the character and effect of what today would be termed toxic masculinity, exemplified but not monopolized by the military ethos he so despised. The bits of female finery he placed inside his assemblages signaled in his mind a woman's self-abnegating submission to the unequal regime of power between the sexes; he likened these adornments to Christian saints depicted holding the instruments of their own martyrdom. In perhaps the most discussed of Conner's assemblages, BLACK DAHLIA (fig. 12) of 1960, he again used nylon stockings as the basic matrix, here deployed as a sack or envelope around the black and white photograph of young female figure, nude except for stockings, standing and viewed from the rear. A burlesque-show panoply descends from her discreetly naked torso—sequins, feathers, fringe, and tinsel—so as to fill and distend the base of the nylon envelope, one set of tendrils extending itself, hovering between touch and disguise, to cover the cleft between her buttocks. The profile

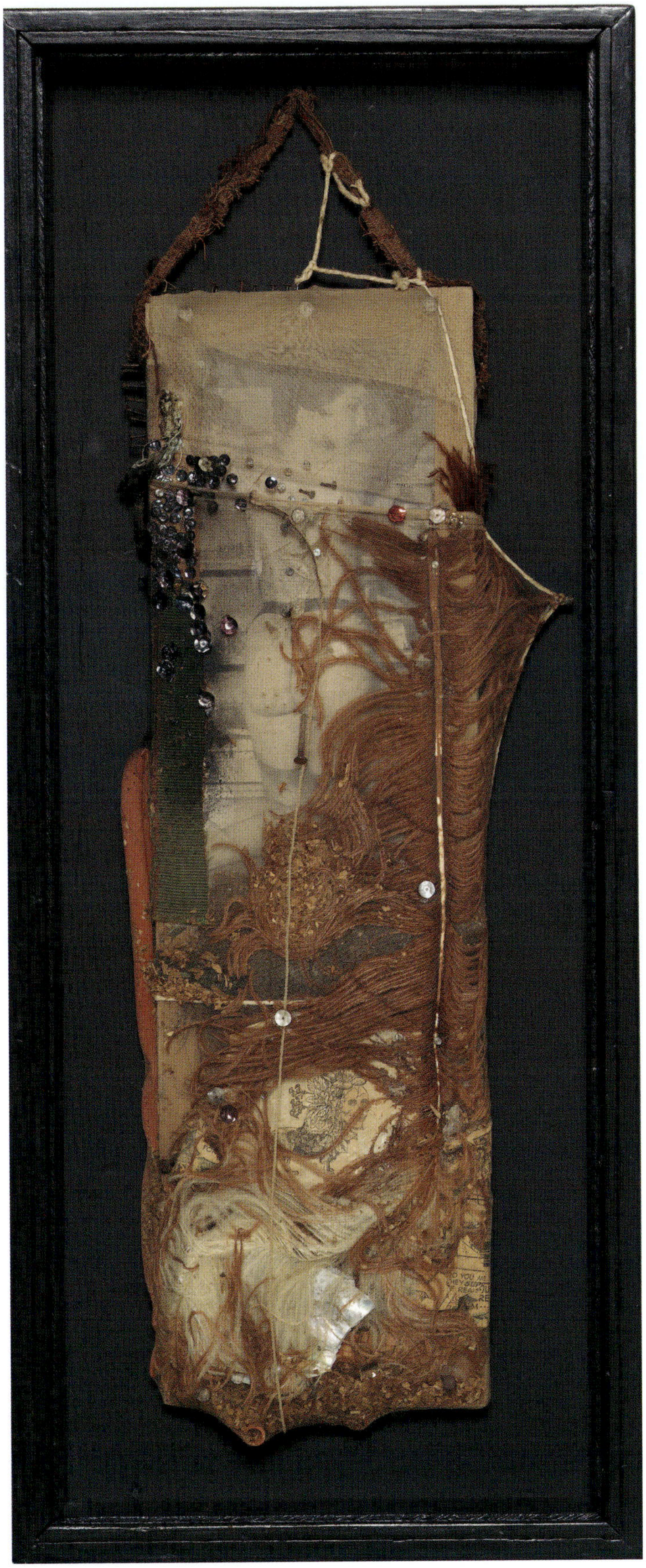

**12** Bruce Conner,
BLACK DAHLIA, 1960,
mixed media, 67.9 × 27.3 × 7 cm,
Museum of Modern Art,
New York

**13 and 14 (FOLLOWING PAGES)** Bruce Conner,
BLACK DAHLIA (details)

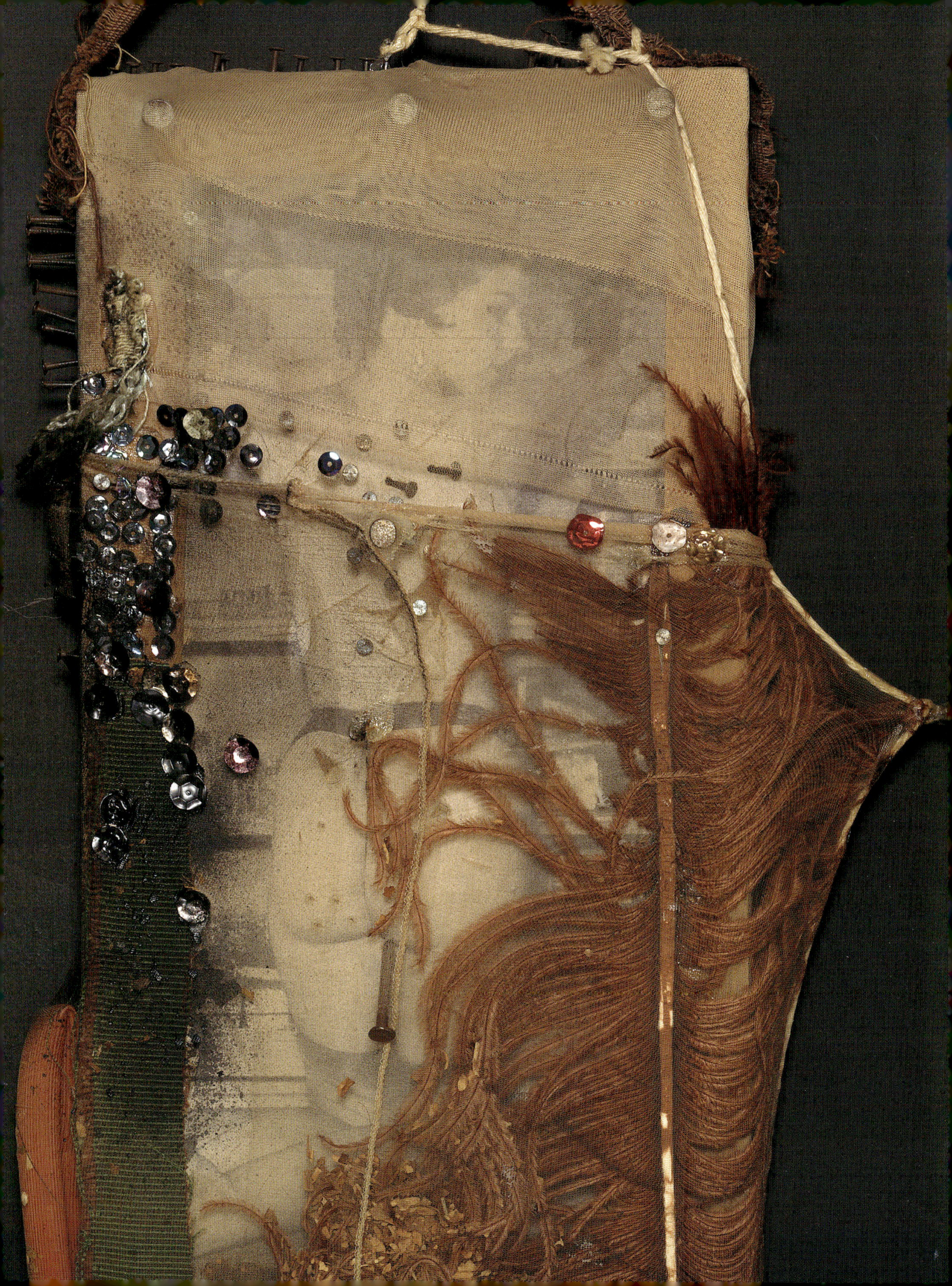

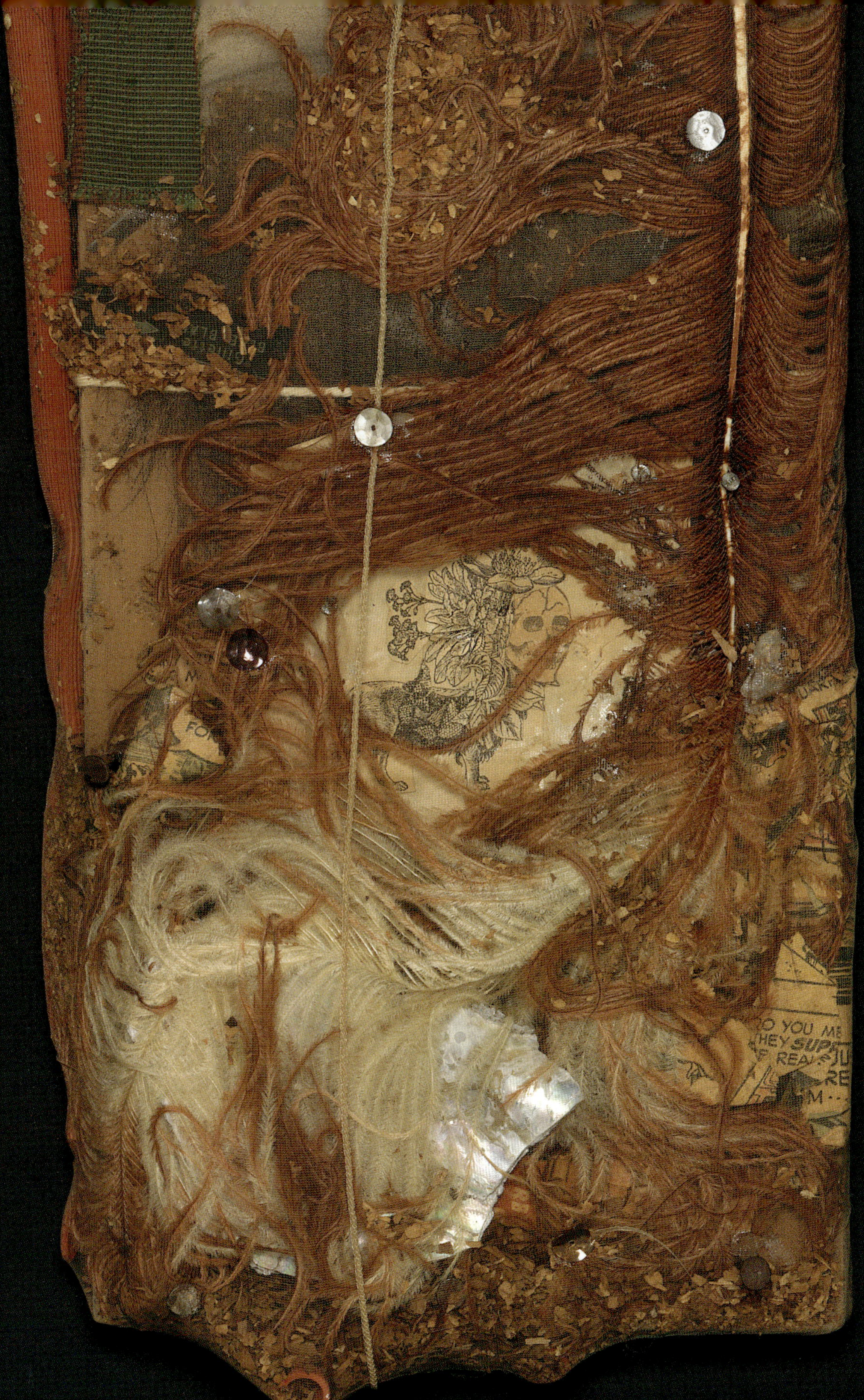

turn of her face reveals little feeling, but the flowing luxuriance around her, notwithstanding its origins in feathered hats and threadbare, sequined dresses from the Salvation Army store, supplies the furniture of a recumbent, dreaming state. Amidst the flotsam hangs a pattern for a Japanese death's-head tattoo, in keeping with the morbid connotations of the work's title, the Black Dahlia having been the name pinned by the newspapers in 1947 on the victim of a horrifying murder in Los Angeles. The case became a sensation under that name because the body of a young newcomer to the city named Elizabeth Short had been dismembered and left to be discovered in a revoltingly gruesome display—and because her murderer was never found.

Despite Short's lack of any acting credits, an appetite for perverse glamour fed the legend that she had been an aspiring actress, so one wonders whether the erstwhile entertainment-industry apprentice Wallace Berman might have played a part in Conner's choice of subject. Before adopting his earthy, alternative mode of life, the young Berman had been a magnetic figure on the margins of Hollywood show business. In the recollection of Sidney Felsen, a Fairfax High School friend (who would co-found the lithography workshop Gemini G.E.L), "Wally hung around with Sammy Davis Jr. quite a bit, and you'd regularly see them at Herbert's Drive-In with a crowd of hot young dancers . . ."[23] In the striking photograph from the year of the murder (fig. 15), Berman poses with his regular dance partner, Loree Fox, on Hollywood Boulevard in flamboyant zoot-suit trousers, his hair styled in a dramatic pompadour. Consistent with his frequenting the jazz clubs of South Central Los Angeles, his studied look partook of both Chicano and African American style cues. Short's remains had been discovered in the district of Leimert Park, just to the west of the Berman's favored Black neighborhoods. Having occured at the fringes of Berman's way of life in the years just after the war, the Black Dahlia case would likely have been far more present to the mind of Berman than of Conner, who had been a Kansas teenager at the time of these events.

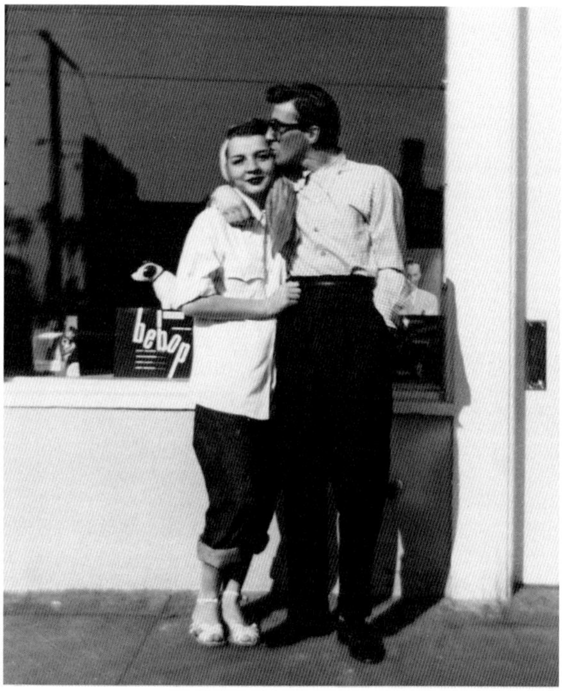


15 Loree Fox and Wallace Berman, at Tempo Records, Hollywood Boulevard, 1947, photograph by Lee Wilder, Charles Brittin Collection, Getty Research Library, Los Angeles

So might it have been conversations with the Bermans, along with their own sense of martyrdom at the hands of what Berman called the "city of degenerate angels," that brought Elizabeth Short so vividly into Conner's imaginative universe? Conner referred to fake finery of the kind enfolded into his assemblage as "demonic devices," objects of martyrdom akin to "the chains and the locks and the crowns of thorns," just as in the scenography staged by the provincial fetishist William Langley that he had inserted into RAT BASTARD NO. 1. Not exempting himself, Conner said of the work, "I might project or assume the character of a personality, like the person that's producing this is the Black Dahlia, and it's also the person that killed the Black Dahlia. Instead of there being individual actors before me, I'm using objects and characters that aren't defined as separate performing characters. Mental attitudes. The relationship of victim to assassin."[24] In Conner's mind, then, his macabre *guignol* was not so much about transposing the multiple roles in the drama as it was about subjecthood that never settles, the fluid substitution of one potential self for another and another in an agonistic scene of inner conflict.

Laboring daily in the studio adjacent to the Mime Troupe, with the wages of sin in his mind's eye, he sought some compensatory stability via two pieces grounded in the west's core narrative of redemption, CRUCIFIXION and RESURRECTION, thereby completing the thematic arc of Grünewald's altarpiece.[25] The former (fig. 16), at more than two meters in height, towers over upright works like CHILD and SNORE.[26] The blackened figure suspended from the cross, trailing wisps of nylon hose wrapped and stretched from crossbar to base, artfully adapts to three dimensions any number of devices from painted Renaissance representations of Christ's agony, while the amputations of the lower limbs bring into visibility the victim's dismemberment, which had only been implied in the BLACK DAHLIA (into whose figure cruel nails had nevertheless been driven). The pendant RESURRECTION (fig. 17) reverts to his customary size, the shreds of sheer nylon now transfigured into the torn burial shroud falling away from the rising figure suggested by wooden sticks crossed in an *X* configuration, the chest achingly hollow, with its just previous recumbent position enveloped in a cocoon-like body bag at its feet.

These were wholly serious works, no other artist having brought the theme so fully into a contemporary arena of torment this side of Francis Bacon. In the exchange with Thomas Albright noted above, having asserted his attachment to various forms of esoteric mysticism, Conner pointedly added, "there's no reason to reject the Christian mysticism," while Albright notes that Conner kept at hand his own typewritten concordance to the New Testament. And that scriptural application came through in a later interview from the mid-1970s, where he offered forthright testimony to the moral seriousness with which he invested the cycle of RAT BASTARDS: "The society which we have . . . expresses power and violence and death and that's its main structure. And the signs of that are in the symbols that we see around us in the arts, in the clothes, in the roles that people play in the society. That people have to deal with this kind of crucifixion of the spirit all the time; and that how well they shine through that is the triumph of those individuals."[27]

Conner's thoughts anticipate in their own way the sophisticated reckoning by the philosopher Mark Johnston with the incomparable import of the Crucifixion as the ultimate indictment of our general human regime of competitive self-love and punitively orthodox righteousness. "There is nothing noble or 'humanly redeeming' about it," he avers,

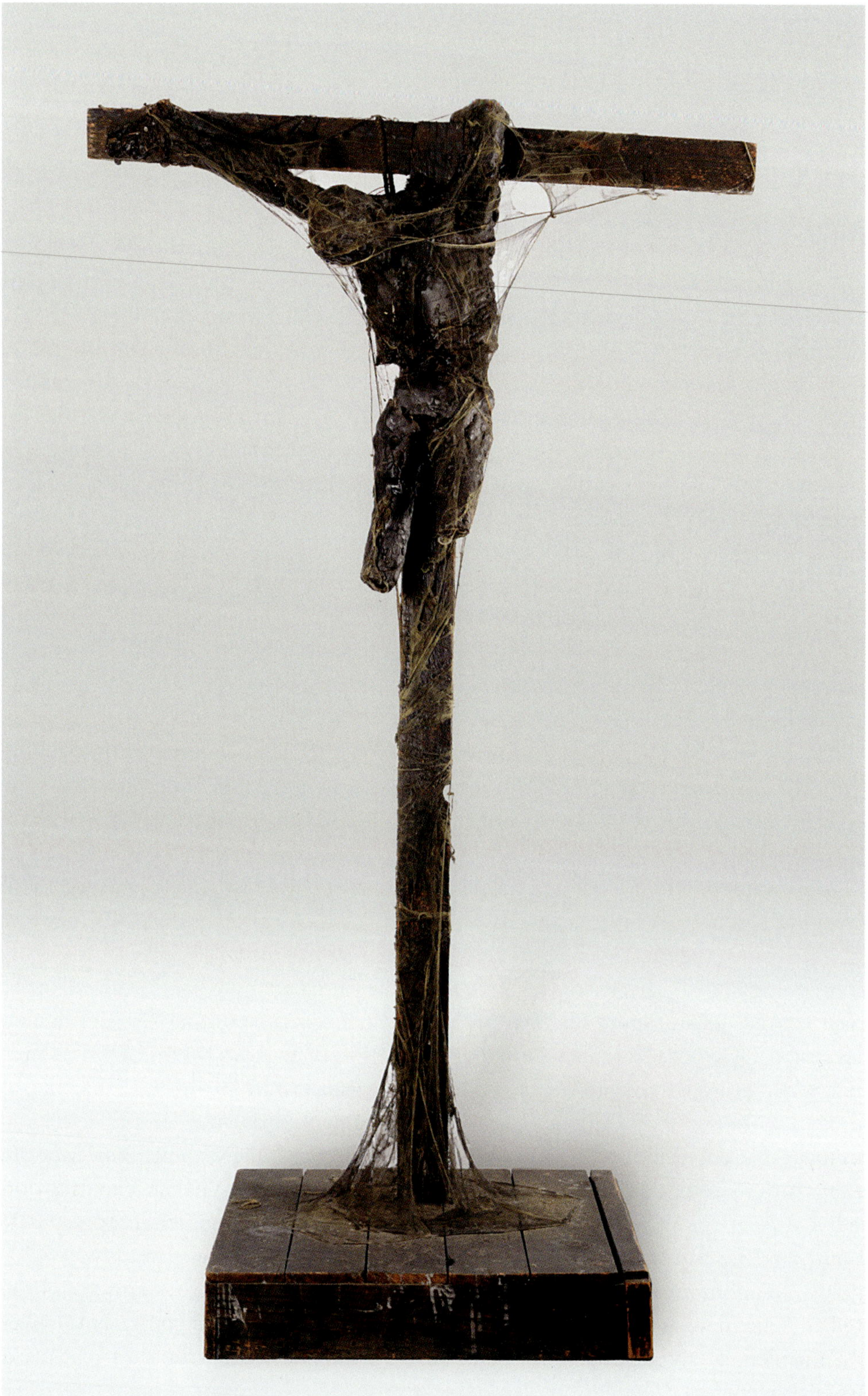

**16** Bruce Conner, CRUCIFIXION, 1960, mixed media, 215.9 × 119.4 × 69.9 cm, di Rosa Collection, Napa

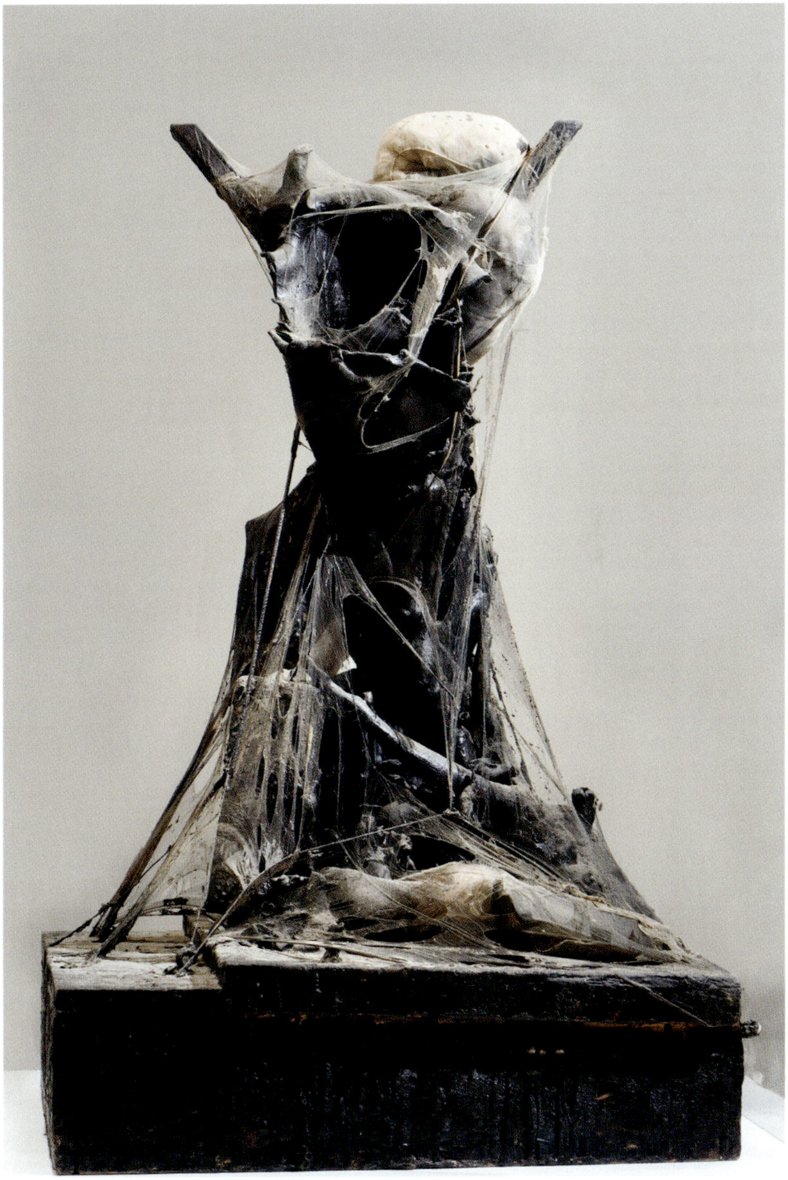

**17** Bruce Conner,
RESURRECTION, 1960,
mixed media, 91.4 × 61 × 58.4 cm,
Museum of Contemporary Art,
San Diego

"beginning as it does with his desperation in the Garden and ending with his despair on the Cross. It is not a cathartic tragedy." He shares with Conner the recognition that "Victimization, sacrifice, and religious violence have been forever unmasked as illegitimate strategies by which our murderous envy of each other is temporarily discharged, and yet preserved as an ongoing psychological orientation."[28] That last phrase about "murderous envy" might be re-stated as "crucifixion of the spirit all the time," and Conner came to a point in 1961 when he felt compelled to escape entirely the realm of the American war machine and the social sickness engendered by it.

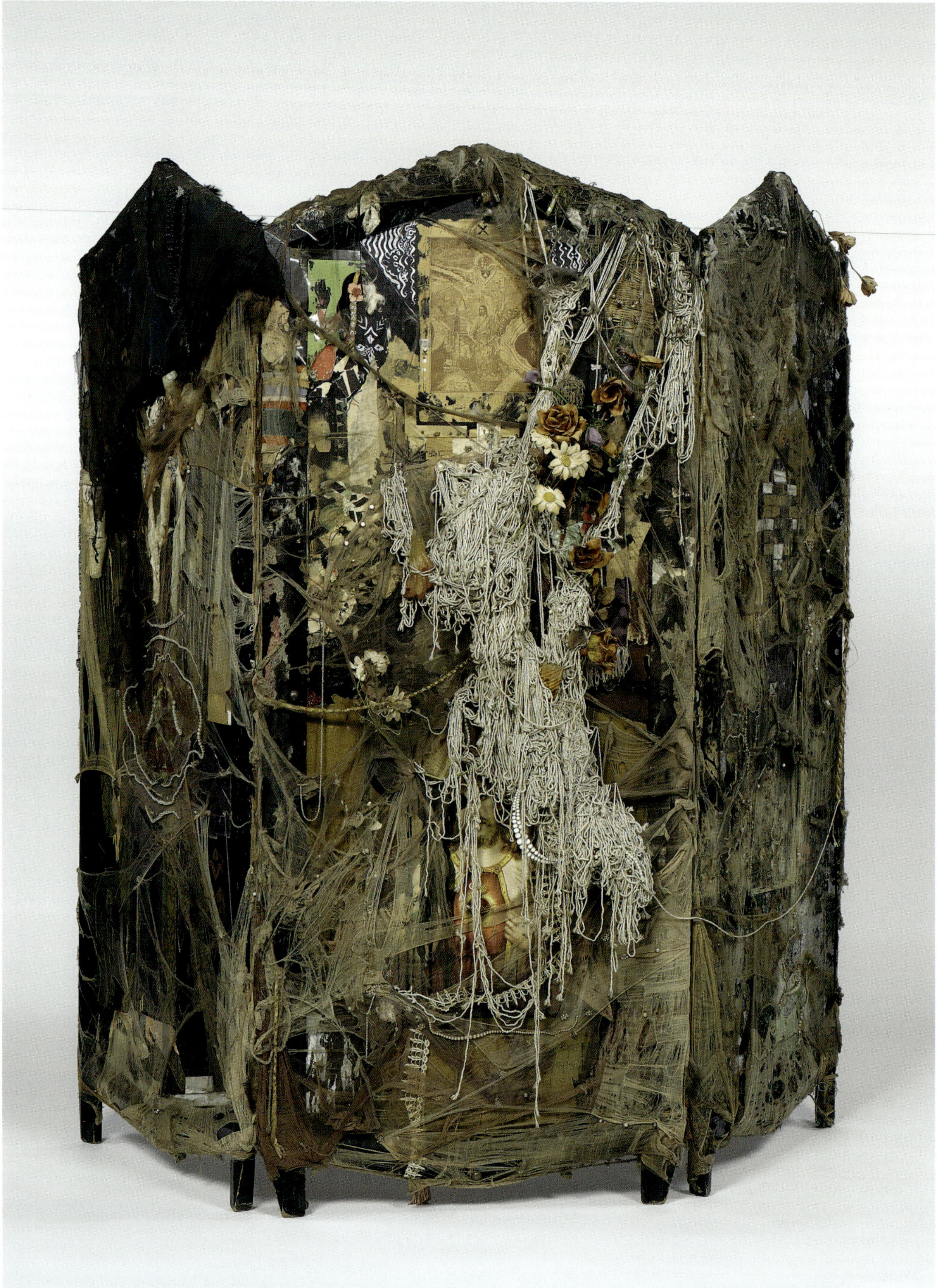

TWO

# MOVIES AND MEXICO

ALL THE WHILE THAT CONNER WAS PURSUING his daily routine of sculpture production in his studio on the Mime Troup premises, he was already embarked on the second of the justly celebrated films he had undertaken after arriving in San Francisco. The fact that he would be pursuing another art form in parallel with his assemblages fits easily with his generally restless appetite for adventure and his impatience with boundaries. But his decision to make A MOVIE in 1958, the most influential early instance of an independent filmmaker composing from found footage (and one of the most consequential first films ever made), came on the heels of his close contact as a student with not just one but two of the key figures in American experimental film: Harry Smith and Stan Brakhage.

It is a curiosity of our intellectual culture that Harry Smith, as often as not, still needs to be introduced to many otherwise cultivated adepts of advanced art. In the annals of abstract film, there was probably no one more significant, but his manner, appearance, and mode of life all worked against him, his outsider persona reinforced by his diminutive, hunchbacked frame, bottle-glass spectacles, and high-pitched voice. Smith's first efforts in the medium arose from his immersion in the San Francisco jazz scene, as he sought to create kinetic visual counterparts to the frenetic tempi and harmonic complexity of bebop players like Dizzy Gillespie and Charlie Parker. The painted, dyed, and scratched patterns he painstakingly deposited on actual film stock bore sufficient correspondence to prototypes in European abstract painting to catch the attention of Hilla Rebay, the artistic confidante to the magnate Solomon R. Guggenheim and co-founder of the museum that would eventually bear his name.[1] She offered Smith a grant in 1950 to continue his efforts under her eyes in New York, but the stipend provided no more than the minimum required to establish himself in the city, so he lived as he would always do, by availing himself of the generosity shown by friends and acquaintances, bartering what he did possess, strategic non-payment of rent, pawning borrowed equipment, and forswearing all attachments to conventional domestic life, so appearing always a shape-shifting drifter with barely a trace left behind him.[2]

Conner, nonetheless, remembered him well from his first foray into New York at the age of twenty. He had found his way to the social circle of Lionel Ziprin, a poet of Cabalistic leanings, and his wife, Joanne Eashe, whose esoteric interests ran from bebop to Buddhism. Their

**18** Bruce Conner, PARTITION (back), 1962,
mixed media, 181.9 × 73.7 cm,
Musée national d'art moderne, Centre Pompidou, Paris

apartment provided a gathering place for the vagabondish likes of Smith and Conner; what was more, they could offer employment to both of them designing offbeat greeting cards under the name Inkweed Studios.[3] After his return to the University of Nebraska, Conner regularly sent them dozens of cleverly accomplished drawings over the ensuing years, leaving no doubt as to his graphic talent and his eye for the stylish drolleries of the *New Yorker* cartoonist (and, later, Shrek creator) William Steig (fig. 19). "They were totally disorganized as business people," Conner said of the Ziprins; "They were not a business. They were very much involved in cabala and magic theory, and Tibetan mysticism as well. They would tell me stories, fantasies. Lionel gave me a book of cabala that was all in Hebrew. I could not read it but he said it was good for me and it was good luck to have. And it has a mandala image in it."[4]

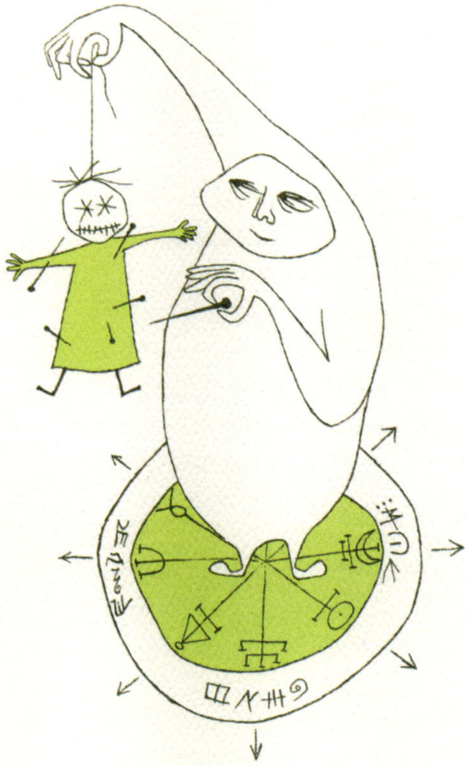

**19** Bruce Conner, "Thinking of You," c. 1954, greeting-card design for Inkweed Studios

"Harry Smith," Conner continued, "was very much involved in that" (along with designing "totally unpopular" three-dimensional Christmas cards for the Ziprins). Indeed, Smith believed the purpose of all his endeavors in art making and specialist collecting (among the latter, string figures and obscure southern recordings that helped spark the folk-music revival) was to recover the universal harmonic relations encoded in the lore of esoteric knowledge cultivated by the Ziprins. Not long after establishing himself in New York, Smith turned away from his handmade abstractions to a form of collage animation, building on, in the words of P. Adams Sitney, the master scholar of underground film, "Tarot cards, Cabalistic symbolism, Indian chiromancy and dancing, Buddhist mandalas, and Renaissance alchemy."[5] Young as he was, Conner came to these abstruse preoccupations with some familiarity. While in high school, he recalled, "I was borrowing books out of the Wichita Public Library on witchcraft, alchemy, with all those drawings that were used as illustrations in the alchemical works. I thought the illustrations were just fascinating."[6] His not unsophisticated apprehension of Dante has already come up in these pages

Conner's impetus to follow Smith in putting this fascination to use in film took another five years and arguably exposure to Stan Brakhage's distinctly different approach to the medium, which sacrificed all other concerns to the personal eye and intimate human experiences of the filmmaker. Brakhage shuttled between his base in Denver and both San Francisco and New York, where in 1955 he had memorably collaborated with the assemblage artist Joseph Cornell on *Wonder Ring*, a lyrical homage to the imperiled elevated trains of Manhattan.[7] In the next year, Conner enlisted him as a sponsor for a student society at the University of Colorado called the Experimental Film Group. Brakhage, says Conner, "brought his films and showed them. He told me I ought to make movies. But I didn't want to." That changed after Conner arrived in San Francisco and got to know Larry Jordan, a friend and former student of Brakhage. The two started another film society, and Conner, in his words, "was able to get into a position where I would be encouraged and actually have the equipment and learn how to splice film. It depended on me and Stan Brakhage and Larry Jordan."[8]

His first film, A MOVIE, channels Conner's two mentors in opposite terms. If Brakhage insisted that the eye of the camera was deeply aligned with his own, Conner would maximally distance the film imagery from his own authorship by relying on existing commercial footage, then being repackaged and sold for home entertainment. "I had virtually no money," Conner reflected on that moment, "I was working as an usher in a movie theatre for a dollar an hour. My wife was working with me at a hot dog stand. It's really a poverty film: it was made from footage from newsreels, documentaries, sports events, movies, everything. They were films condensed down into two-and-a-half minute silent reels, which were actually cheaper than buying black and white film and processing and printing it."[9] A silent Hopalong Cassidy western dominates the first minutes of A MOVIE, followed by intercut clips from newsreels, documentaries, soft-core eroticism, and thrills-and-spills novelties, interrupted by out-of-place titles and a countdown leader familiar from the educational films screened in the classrooms of the period.

During the first two-thirds of the film's twelve-minute running time, Conner extracts from all this flotsam a symbolic rubric that reaches back to the alchemical occultism as espoused by Harry Smith, a four-part scheme based on the prescientific elements: Earth (clouds of dust raised by covered wagons and pursuing Hollywood Indians, a charging elephant, and careening motor vehicles); Air (dirigibles and aerialists); Water (mishaps on waves and water skis); and Fire (the crash of the Hindenburg, exploding fighter planes, the Bomb). The instances noted here are not exhaustive but indicative of the kind of found fragments Conner grouped under these tacit headings. In the final third of A MOVIE, the four categories repeat themselves, but in shuffled confusion, as another, somber theme emerges in instances of mayhem and death not played for amusement: executed wartime criminals hoisted into the air, for example, or heaps of corpses spread over the earth. When the soundtrack, lifted from the *Pines of Rome* by Ottorino Respighi, grows louder and more urgent, the moral artist who would soon be fashioning CHILD makes his appearance in bleaker material that retroactively casts the seemingly lighthearted tumbles and accidents from before as diagnostic of cruel voyeurism—taking pleasure in the pain of others—which permeates everyday entertainment. But there is a final coda involving Water, taken from a scuba-diving documentary, whereby descent into a black abyss gives way to radiant light suffusing an upward gaze toward the surface and air.[10]

Conner did not begin work on his second film, COSMIC RAY, until 1960, and the editing of the project extended into the following year, a protracted gestation seemingly belied by its extremely short running time of roughly four minutes, though it is composed from significantly more pieces of film than the first film had been. Its markedly accelerated pace called for a different approach to its musical soundtrack. Harry Smith had on occasion screened his abstract animations to the live accompaniment of bebop jazz, his first love, but, as he later observed, viewers were unconsciously adept at synchronizing the movement on screen with just about any music he might supply. Conner took matters much more tightly in hand by borrowing his soundtrack from Ray Charles's up-tempo R&B hit of 1959, "What'd I Say" (which shifts the significance of the title away from spacey radiation to transcendent soul music, that is, "Cosmic" Ray Charles, who sees without being sighted). Conner's choice bears multiple meanings consistent with the outlook evident in his other work at the time. It had been only a few years since Charles had scandalized a good portion of the Black community by adapting the gospel music of the church (a lifelong love of Conner) to secular, even carnally erotic themes. For Conner, as his contemporaneous assemblage works make plain, such interplay between the sacred and profane—stripping away the one yields the other and vice-versa—lay at the heart of both his artistic and his moral imagination.

His choice of music was even more discerning in that he rejected the tinny AM radio version of Charles's hit in favor of the more soulful and full-bodied performance released on the transcendent live album *Ray Charles in Person*, the product of a miraculous 1959 recording on a single microphone in a Georgia baseball field—still relatively little known but one of the greatest rhythm and blues albums ever made. Conner enlists the stadium announcer's breathless send-off ("Ray Charles! The great Ray Charles! The High Priest! Ray Charles himself! What a show! What a show!) as the audio closer to the film. To call the music merely driving or propulsive is to substitute linguistic cliché for the qualities that Conner translated into pulsing bursts of white light exactly keyed to the arrangement of the music, percussively picking up and reinforcing the beat. Over the next few years he would begin reciting in public verses extracted from the New Testament on the theme of light: one such, which seems especially pertinent to COSMIC RAY, runs, "The light of the body is the eye; therefore when thine eye is single, thy whole body is also full of light; but when thine eye is dark, the body is also full of darkness (Luke 11:34)." As the body of Ray Charles is full of light, so is his eye, however blind it might be to the stumbling blocks of this world.

In addition to the greatly enhanced number and precision of his edits, Conner undertook more advanced processing by layering sequences of live footage he shot himself—of Beth Pewther, a fellow artist from Wichita, dancing in various states of undress—into the abstract matrix. As with the BLACK DAHLIA (a "body full of darkness"), Conner vehemently refuted charges of salacious voyeurism, invoking instead the fragile life principle at perilous risk under the destructive regimes of the Cold War. The interpenetration of ecstatic sensuality and metaphysical yearning had been the hallmark of the *Semina* circle around Berman, and COSMIC RAY compresses that conjuncture into perhaps its consummate artistic realization.

The intensity of Conner's engagement with Charles's music, along with his obsessively labor-intensive process of construction, similarly followed from his own initial psychedelic experiments with peyote. But the film's pell-mell rapidity of optical transitions (making the pace of A MOVIE seem relatively languid by comparison), its rapid-fire jumps from one thought-image to the next, faster than normal cognition can follow, coincided with the arrival of another psychotropic agent. Conner later put a question to an interviewer, "Haven't you turned into pure light at some time or another?" Then answered it himself with an air of authority: "Some people do that when they take mushrooms."[11] Psilocybin, the active agent of the Mexican *teonanactl* fungi, was new to just about everyone in the scene, and among its delayed effects was to launch the then little-known psychology researcher Timothy Leary toward his notorious leadership of a mind-expansion movement.

■

In his first memoir, Timothy Leary offered an extended account of his sojourn during the summer of 1960 in Cuernavaca, Mexico, occupying a palatial, rented villa and searching out these mushrooms among the surrounding Indigenous villages. A Mexico-based academic associate succeeded in winning over the local *curandera*, a practitioner of folk medicine, whom Leary chose to call Señora Juana, to supply his group with a generous bag of the sacred fungi.[12] In the course of recounting these events, Leary notes, "Bruce Conner came with us shooting movies, dancing around filming the sides of meat hanging in the butcher shops and the swarms of black flies and the piles of fruit, the sidewalk displays of cloth woven in red and yellow seed and cell designs."[13]

Conner later recalled his time with Leary with vivid if disabused force: "We would go into a village; it would be all—almost all—Indian, or part-Indian. Sometimes there would be few people there that could even speak Spanish. . . . We would be these obvious, obnoxious, barbarian gringos coming in over the dirt roads into this adobe village with no electricity or anything like that. And the first damn thing he does is say, 'Where are the mushrooms? And where is the *curandera*? . . . What happens when you take the mushrooms?'"[14] Conner marveled at the generosity of the villagers they encountered, considering the trouble that inquisitive outsiders always brought with them. Taking Leary at his word places Conner in Mexico late in the summer of 1960, shooting the Mexican portions of his evolving LOOKING FOR MUSHROOMS (fig. 20). But no other record attests to this chronology, and several firmly place the Conner–Leary encounter two years later, after Bruce and Jean Conner had left San Francisco in December 1961 to settle in the Juárez district of Mexico City, just south of the historic center, driving all the way with only two suitcases and a trunk in the back of their car (a film-editing console must have made the trip as well, in that Conner completed COSMIC RAY only after their move). In interviews some decades later both Conners describe Leary paying them a visit in June 1962. And Conner had written to his dealer Charles Alan on 25 June 1962, "I am traveling to magic mushroom villages with Tim Leary (Harvard Psychiatrist) and eating them and making movies of the villages."[15]

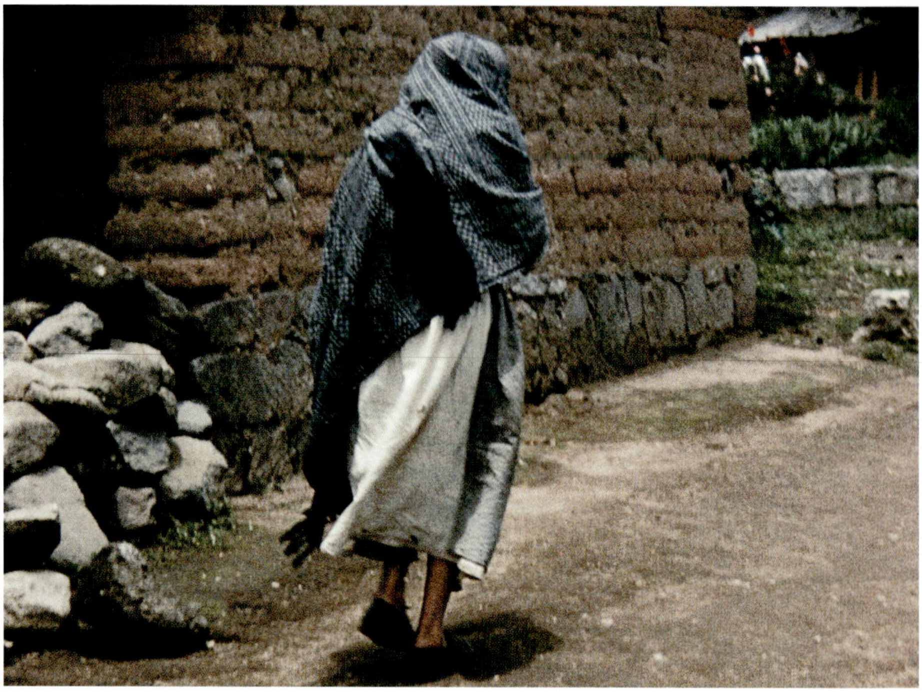

**20** Bruce Conner, still from LOOKING FOR MUSHROOMS, 1959–67, color film

Having been belatedly introduced to lysergic acid diethylamide in late 1961 (belatedly by comparison with the California psychiatrists noted above) through the roguish Englishman Michael Hollingshead, the "Harvard Psychiatrist" had largely put mushrooms aside, even abjuring the synthetic psilocybin that he had been using as the chief agent of mind expansion for his growing circle. By the summer of 1962 he had established a colony for LSD experiments in distant Guerrero, on Mexico's west coast. But Jean Conner recalls one unusual attraction, as she understood it, that drew Leary far away from his main Mexican enterprise to relive in Bruce's company his 1960 adventures with a substance no longer central to his project: "Jacqueline and John Kennedy came to Mexico [29 June 1962], and there was this huge parade. That's when we met Timothy Leary, who was there for the parade. He was very charismatic. I didn't know much about him, though we had heard of him. I believe Philip Lamantia introduced us to Tim."[16]

The crowds and hoopla surrounding the Kennedys' visit may have offered cover for some other mission, but the occasion helps place Leary in the Conners' vicinity that summer of 1962. Lamantia, an older poet and practiced peyote devotee, had been living with his wife in Mexico City, having for the most part withdrawn from the social side of the Bay Area scene

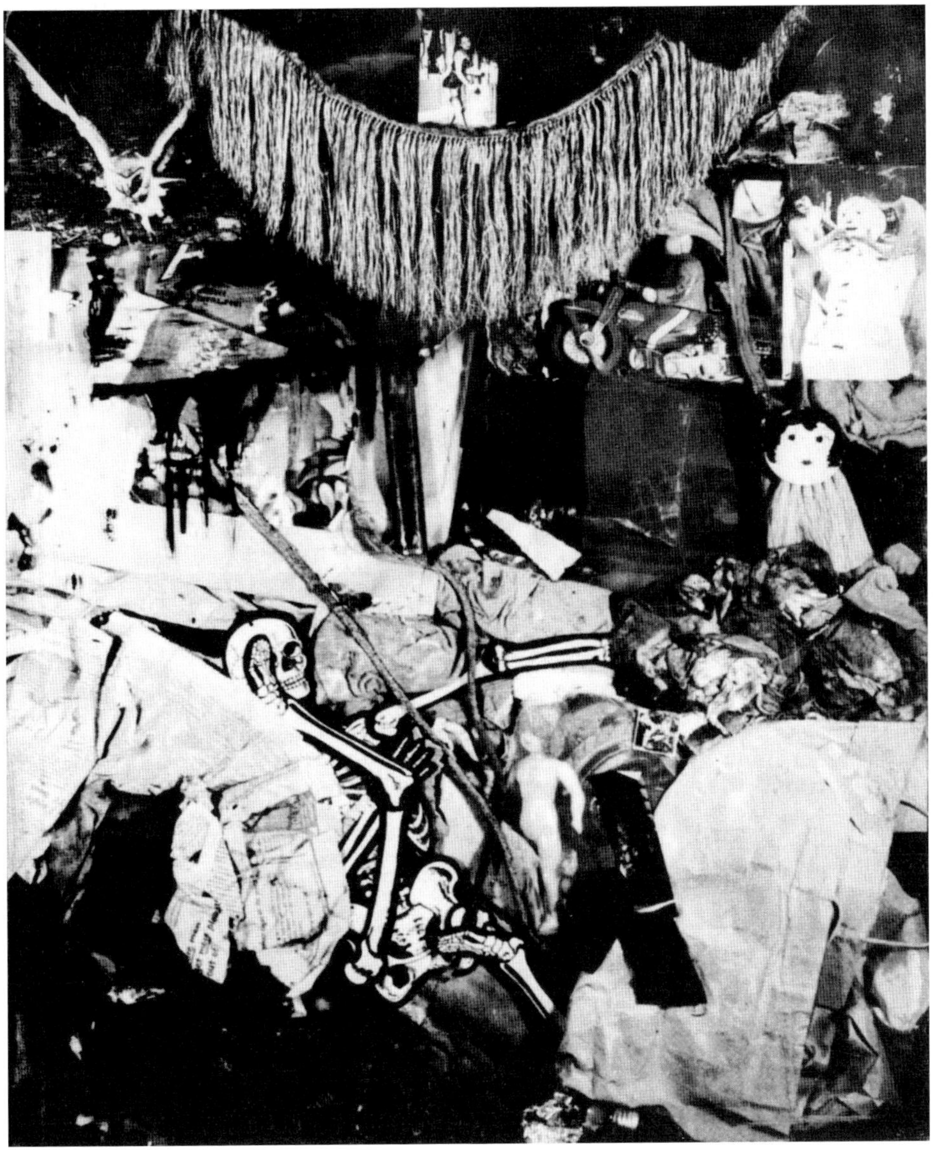

**21** Bruce Conner, SUPERHUMAN DEVOTION, c. 1960, mixed media, lost

for extended stays in the Mexican capital. "Philip was the main person I knew down there," Conner recalls,[17] the two having begun work in 1960 on a poetry collection titled *Destroyed Poems*, with Conner providing its extraordinary wordless cover image: a cropped photograph of the evolving assemblage he called SUPERHUMAN DEVOTION (fig. 21), all its component items squeezed between two panels of salvaged window glass with ornamented frame and candle holder, a garland of fringe suspended from the top edge, dolls in various states of repair and dress inside, along with a jointed, cut-out skeleton and *pistola* instantly evocative of Mexico's Diá de los Muertos.[18]

Further insight into the Conners' Mexican life comes via the recollections of a young free spirit from the Bay Area named Yvonne Bond. Having taken leave from her studies at Berkeley, she arrived in Mexico City in 1962 and secured a place sleeping on the floor of the Conner apartment, where she remained for the next six months:

> This was an incredible scene. I was twenty-two. I barely knew them. I had seen them at a few parties, right? . . . I knock on their door in Mexico City and say, "Hi! Do you think I could stay here for a while?" . . .
>
> Without saying a word, Bruce grabs a roll of heavy plastic stuff like you'd put on your windows. He cuts off a swath of it, crunches it all into a big mass, gets a staple gun and throws this plastic down and staples it into the wood floor. Throws a blanket on it and puts a pillow on it and says, "There you go."[19]

Bond also offers a close-up account of one way that Leary came to resume his mushroom affinity in the Conners' company. "It was one of those magical moments," she relates: "There's a knock on the door and there's a very diminutive Mazatec Indian man with a hand-woven bag over his shoulder, campesino clothing, who very softly and humbly says in Spanish, 'I hear there are some people here who would like to have a mushroom ceremony.' . . . And that was our first mushroom ceremony with Don Isauro Nava."

"How he got our address I'll never know," she marvels, though Leary's presence on the occasion may offer a clue, and all partook in the night-long session. While she and some friends then made the pilgrimage to Huautla de Jiménez in the mountainous Mazateca of Oaxaca, Don Isauro's home and the center of the Indigenous mushroom cult, the Conners stayed behind. On Bond's return to her nailed bed on the Conners' floor, her report from the Huautla mushroom ritual likely resembled her later recollection:

> I lifted up out of my body and I said, "Oh wow, gee, I died so young. That's kind of a shame." I went higher and higher up in the sky and was flying alone among the planets and stars. I thought, "You know, it's not that bad to have died here at this time. It's good to have died here in Mexico." . . . I kind of hear this little voice that says "Come back, come back," . . . So I gradually drifted back there and settled into my body . . . a thousand-year journey in ten minutes or something.

Bruce Conner had a line of his own in such pursuits, having embarked on another excursion into the native spirit world when Walter Hopps, the owner of the Ferus Gallery in Los Angeles, paid them a visit the same year. The gallerist possessed a long family history in Mexico; he had lived there as a child and was still almost universally known (despite his imposing height) by the nickname Chico. His grandfather had come to the port of Tampico in 1880 to get in on the mineral boom, and Hopps had relatives with land to the south near

Puebla. When some ruins were discovered there, he and Conner went down to explore them, finding only a few artifacts but one human skeleton. They slept in a stone structure on the site, but Hopps's rest was fitful, as he attests to his friend's continued partaking of psilocybin: "It wasn't always easy to get a normal night's sleep with Bruce around," he relates; "Stoned, he had visions and thought strange things were going on in the night sky, winged beings coming after him and so on."[20] When a later interviewer asked him, "What did you do in Mexico?" Conner's reply begins, "A lot of drugs and pyramids and . . . ," but the questioner infuriatingly interrupts and stops him from finishing the thought, wanting to get straight to "the art."[21]

The most often cited of Conner's stated reasons for the move to the Mexican capital was a desire to escape American violence and the threat of Cold War nuclear annihilation, a level of dread that drug experiences could only have heightened and to which CHILD and CRUCIFIXION had lent agonized personification. "Mexico is a wonderful place to go if you're running away from death, because they celebrate it with bells and parades and everything else," he later observed to an interviewer.[22] The abundant sensory and affective stimuli abounding in their everyday surroundings absorbed the Conners, whether stoned or sober. Jean speaks of their unsurprising fondness for Mexican churches with their elaborately embellished reliquaries, shrines, and altars attended by costumed effigies of the suffering Christ, the celestial Mary, and myriad saints, often of mixed Indigenous and European provenance.[23] By Bruce's testimony, the penetration of such ritualized accumulations of objects bore intimidating resemblances to his own artistic impulses, particularly to his habitual commingling of the sacred and profane: "I would go by an auto-repair garage and in the midst of the greasy tools and objects on the wall would be a shrine to the Guadalupe. A picture of the Virgin. Right next to it would be a monkey wrench and an electric lightbulb, and plastic flowers, and a pinup of a half-naked girl. Pictures of family, souvenirs, all sort of objects there."[24]

Conner referred to his own work as an "extension" of the symbolic accumulations he saw all around him. He had made a similar observation before, when he described a San Francisco second-hand shop, idiosyncratically curated by its African American proprietor, as the real "art of assemblage."[25] But in Mexico City, the authority of such vernacular expression was far more pervasive. He abjured vying with the intimidating local complexity, instead simplifying his assemblages with broader textures and colors than had been the case in his previous work. One of his recorded remarks—made to the same obtuse interviewer—recurs in virtually every commentary on his Mexican period: he opined that his work had been impeded by the fact that he could no longer rely on discards left in the streets, since any refuse would instantly be scooped up by real scavengers. In that he had always relied as much on other, more sanitary sources, such as thrift shops and the Mime Troupe's leavings, this state of affairs seems less decisive than usually assumed. Where local rubbish is concerned, a 1995 piece, *The Seven Lives of Garbage*, by the Belgian artist Francis Alÿs is instructive. While living in the historic center of Mexico City, Alÿs dropped seven small bronze figurines of snails into trash bins, later to find two of them for sale on the streets. He bought one of them back as a permanent record, the others presumably continuing along other circuits of

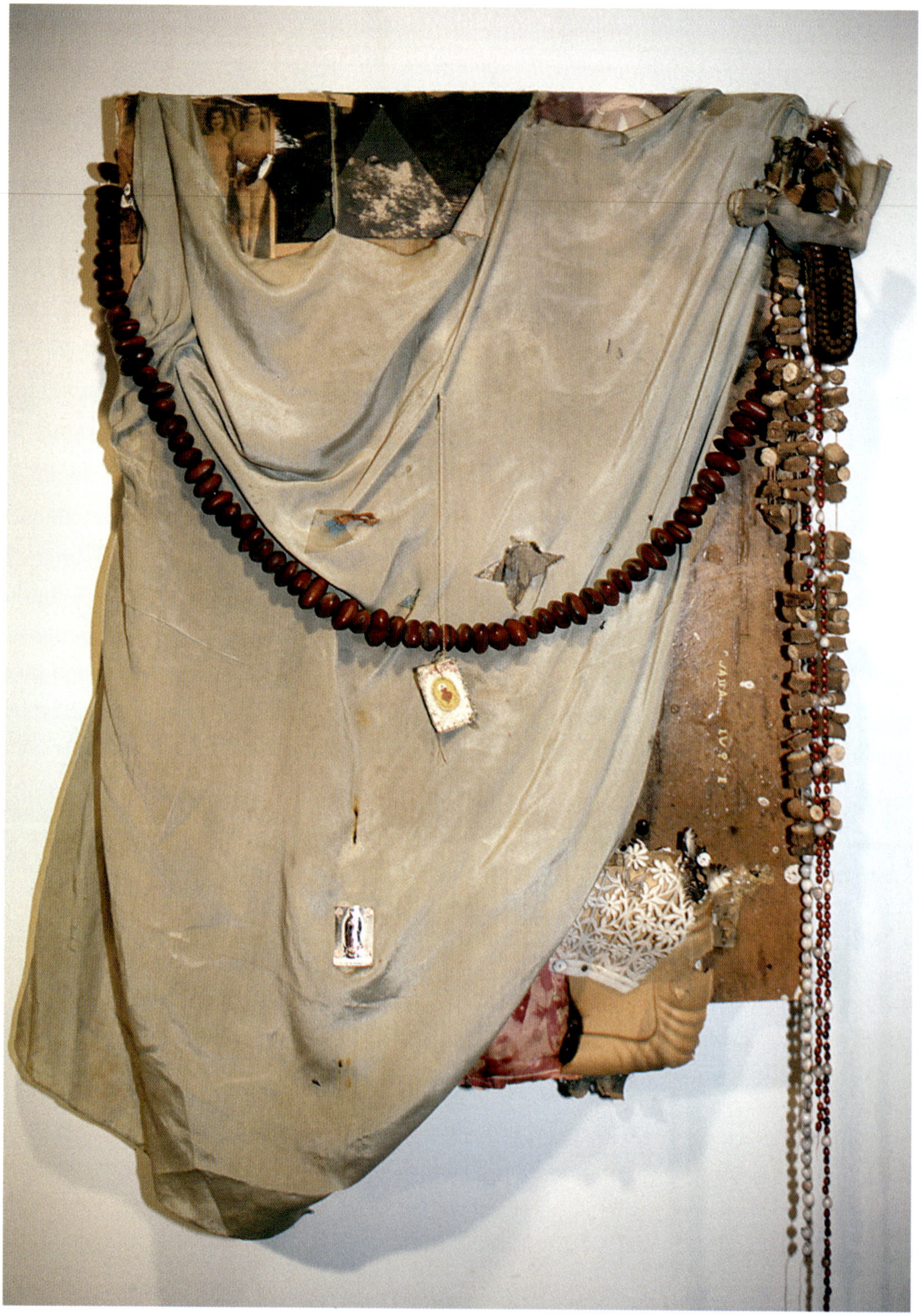

**22** Bruce Conner, GUADALUPE, 1962, mixed media, 68.6 × 50.8 × 12.7 cm, private collection

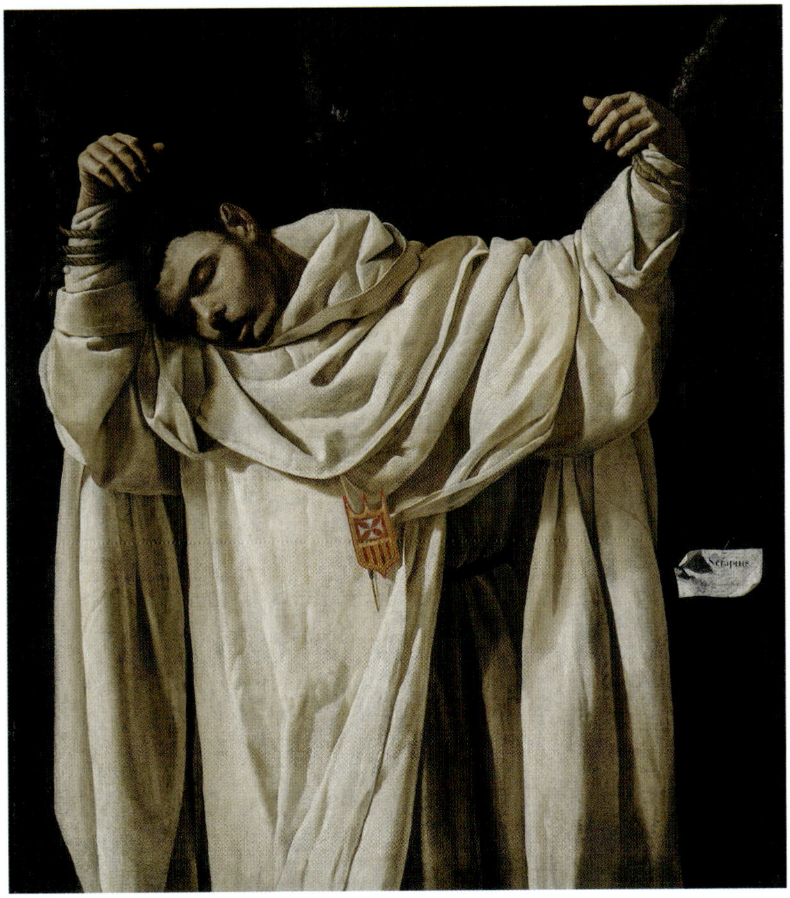

**23** Francisco de Zurbarán, *The Martyrdom of Saint Serapion*, 1628, oil on canvas, 120 × 103 cm, Wadsworth Atheneum, Hartford, Conn.

exchange.[26] Opportunistic vendors and peddlers, along with market stalls selling foodstuffs, trinkets, jewelry, textiles, lace mantillas, the lace-like patterns of *papel picado*, even wigs, left Conner with no shortage of material, nor does his plentiful output of assemblages in this period appear in any way deficient in richness of substance.

Under the group title "Hecho [Made] en México," he tended to align the component parts more in parallel to the wall; but this observation should not incite pointless discussions as to whether this makes them more like "painting," though they certainly reach toward beauty and desire for transcendence. GUADALUPE (fig. 22) of 1962 relies on a large diagonal sweep of torn bed linen, mimicking the white robe worn by the martyred Saint Serapion, famously shown suspended from ropes, as though crucified, by the Spanish baroque artist Francisco de Zurbarán (fig. 23). Much as he had transformed Grünewald's *Saint Anthony* in 1960, he arrays his found materials in a pattern that approximates this canonical work of historical fine art. Among a profusion of cleverly apposite correspondences, a garland of dried beans (the indigenous staple food) traces the edge of the monk's cowl; and where

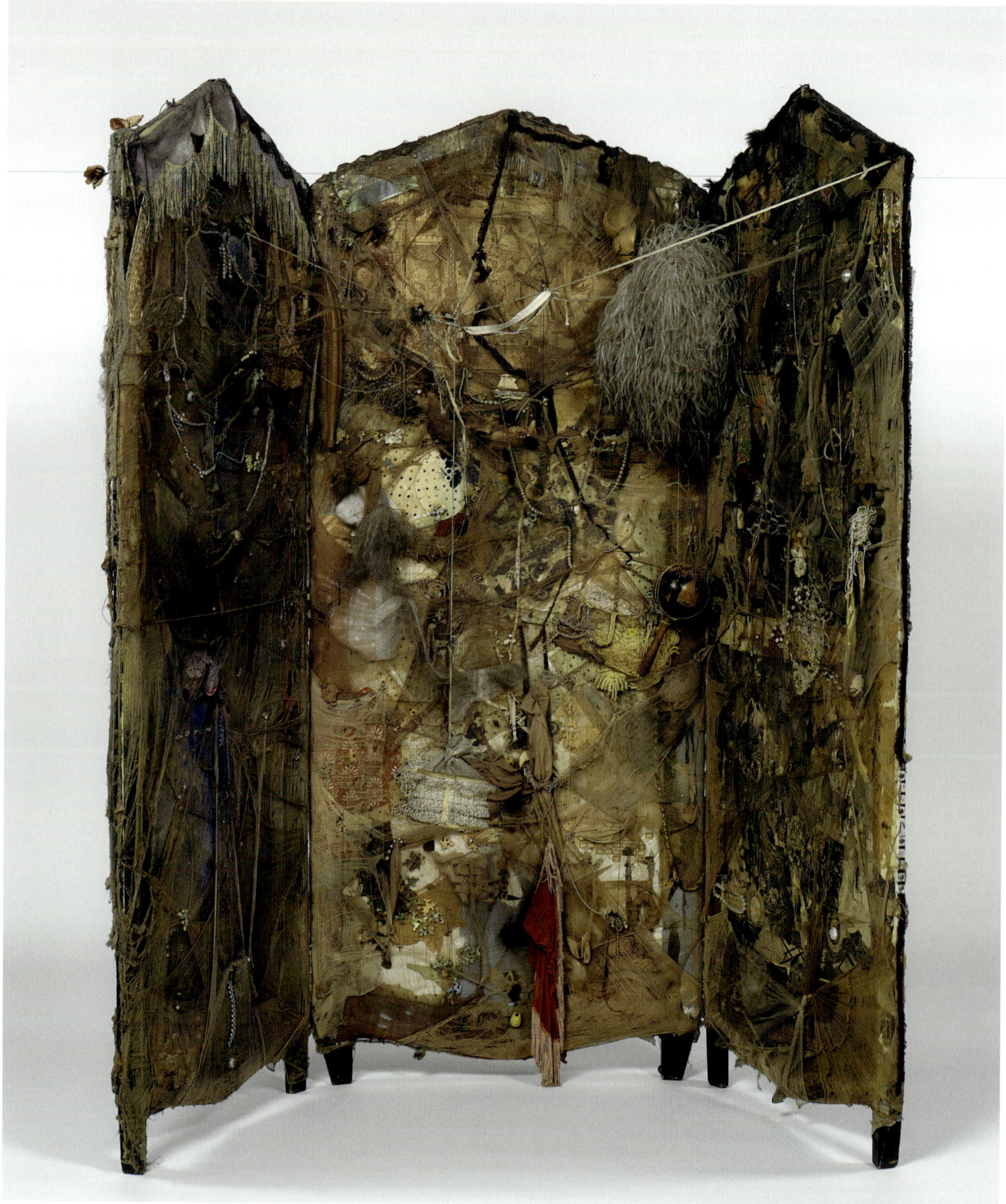

**24** Bruce Conner, PARTITION, 1962,
mixed media, 181.9 × 73.7 cm,
Musée national d'art moderne, Centre Pompidou, Paris

Zurbarán positioned the medallion of the martyr's order, Conner hangs a medallion of the Virgin of the Guadalupe at the same angle and in similar colors. Just how thoroughly and uncannily his rough, found materials remake the prototype offers a window onto the subtlety of the decisions that went into every one of his assemblages

It is a commonplace among sophisticated Mexicans to foreswear any allegiance to Catholicism but proudly declare themselves Guadalupanos, that is, devotees of the miraculous image of Mary, Nuestra Señora de Guadalupe, witnessed and rendered in legend by the Indigenous Juan Diego in 1531 and housed in the enormous pilgrimage shrine on the outskirts of Mexico City where the apparition is said to have occurred (the most visited such site in the world). The success of the cult of the Guadalupe, now as resonant a symbol of Mexican identity as any other, proved a crucial instrument in reconciling the subjugated population to Spanish colonial rule. But the leader of the Mexican independence movement, Miguel Hidalgo, marched under her banner, as did Emiliano Zapata during the Mexican Revolution a century later. Considering Conner's own sophistication, GUADALUPE might be said to strike a late anti-colonialist blow against the hegemony of European art in received art history, where Zurbarán loomed large and Mexican art barely figured at all. What is more, far from being an homage to baroque painting, the force of Conner's transpositions from Zurbarán depends on their being reconceived in concretely Mexican terms, where the time of bloody Spanish conquest, pestilence, and dominion (Zurbarán's time) finds itself enmeshed in millennia of pre-Hispanic time.

Alongside the unforced elegance of his reliefs, a parallel, more familiar aspect of Conner's approach to assemblage also emerged during the Mexican sojourn. Inside their apartment, furnishings and other domestic items, including a conga drum, attracted more the maximalist, encrusted accumulation of material reminiscent of his past San Francisco proclivities—in particular the tripartite, floor-standing screen that goes by the title PARTITION (fig. 24), where even nylon stockings make a spectacular reappearance, and Christ baring his sacred heart peers from beneath a fringe on the opposite side (fig. 18). Now a prize possession of the French National Museum of Modern Art in the Centre Pompidou, it seems a miracle in itself that the sculpture survived the vicissitudes of all their various moves over the next few years, such is the sheer profusion of items and articles applied with equal liberality to all sides of the head-high screen. It stood as a practical divide between the sitting and eating areas of their apartment and most probably was elaborated bit by bit over the course of their stay, PARTITION amounts to an epic summation, beyond descriptive paraphrase, of the artist's sculptural preoccupations to that date and beyond, as the still incomplete piece accompanied the Conners during the next significant phase of their lives, which entailed an even longer absorption into a drug and music counterculture far from their California home.

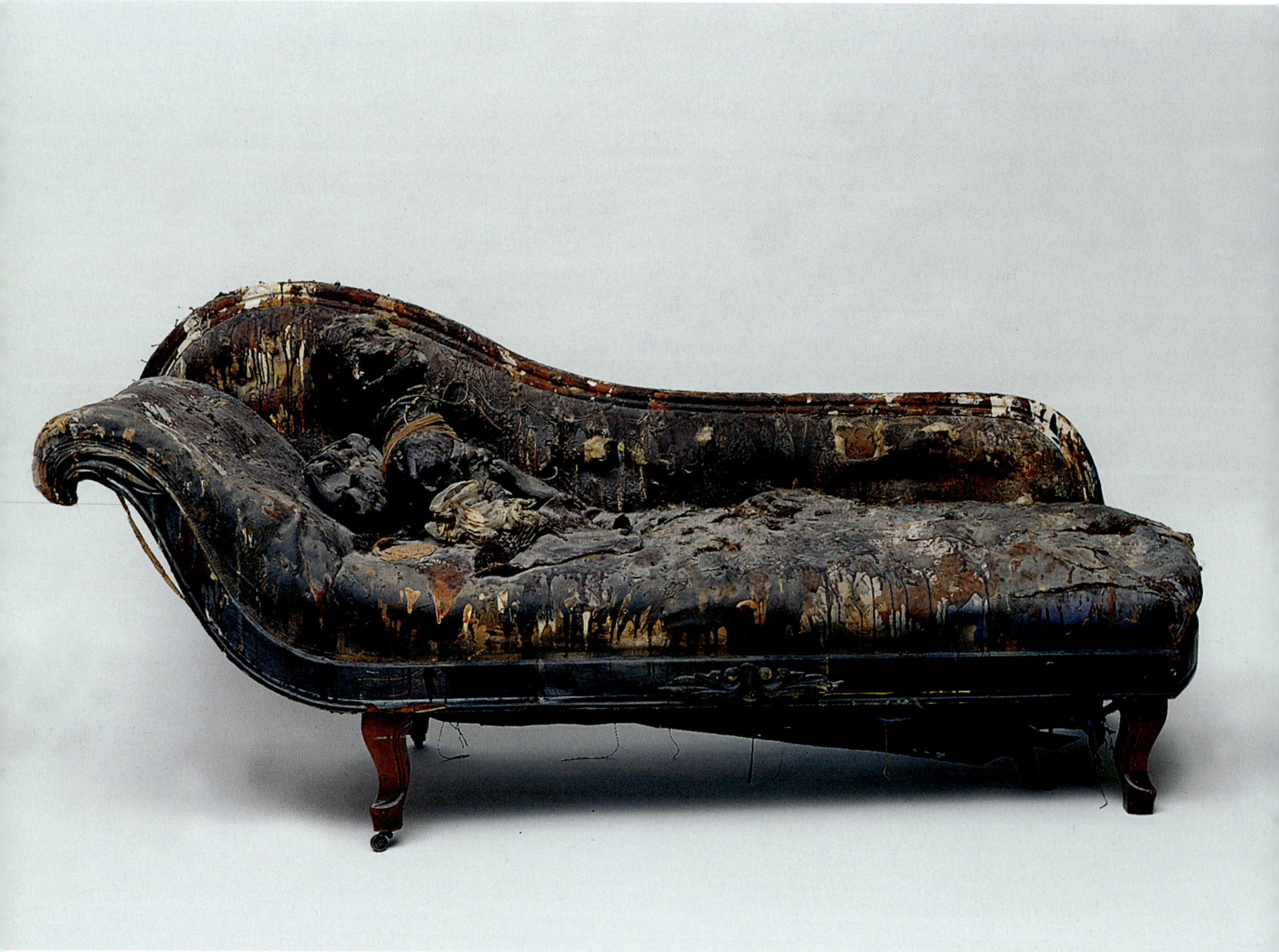

**25** Bruce Conner, COUCH, 1963, mixed media, 81.3 × 179.7 × 68.6 cm, Norton Simon Museum, Pasadena

THREE

# BOSTON AND THE LEARY LURE

Not long after the birth of their son, Robert, at the end of September 1962, the mounting practical difficulties of life in Mexico sent Bruce and Jean Conner back to Wichita, Kansas, an understandable berth where relations and friends could offer support as they coped with both a new infant and their depleted funds. After having established themselves there in the early months of 1963, word arrived that they were welcome to join a communal residence in a capacious, nine-bedroom house outside of Boston in the leafy, prosperous suburb of Newton. The invitation came from Bruce's old Mexican companion (and Mexican headache) Timothy Leary. The two must have kept in touch either at first or second hand, such that Leary would have been aware of the couple's straitened circumstances and chafing Midwestern exile. Traveling in late April to the University of Chicago, where work of his was being shown in its annual Festival of the Arts, Bruce continued on to inspect their prospective Newton quarters; in short order he was able to return, gather family and belongings, their car bulging with artwork, and make the move to the residential cell of Leary's International Federation for Internal Freedom.

This episode is noted in every published study of the artist but most often dropped in a blandly incurious manner, as if this kind of thing—being ushered into the intimate midst of the most ambitious, educated, emotionally entangled explorers of expanded consciousness to be found on the planet—could be taken in stride as an unremarkable turn of events. There generally follows a narrative rush to move the couple out of there and into more seemly surroundings in Brookline, another well-off, close-in suburb, where they had established themselves in their own apartment by November 1963. From there the story turns toward Conner's fashioning of REPORT, his filmic meditation on the incomprehensible finality of death, demeaned by the voyeuristic indecency with which broadcast television had exploited the Kennedy assassination.

The present account will attempt to fill in some of what has been passed over too quickly in accounts of the Boston-area phase in the Conners' lives, a task that properly begins with his first stop on Bruce's journey to Newton. As he later recounted, "Some students at the University of Chicago were having a festival of the arts. They wanted me to be an artist-in-residence and show my movies and have a collage show. . . . They had some balloons and circus

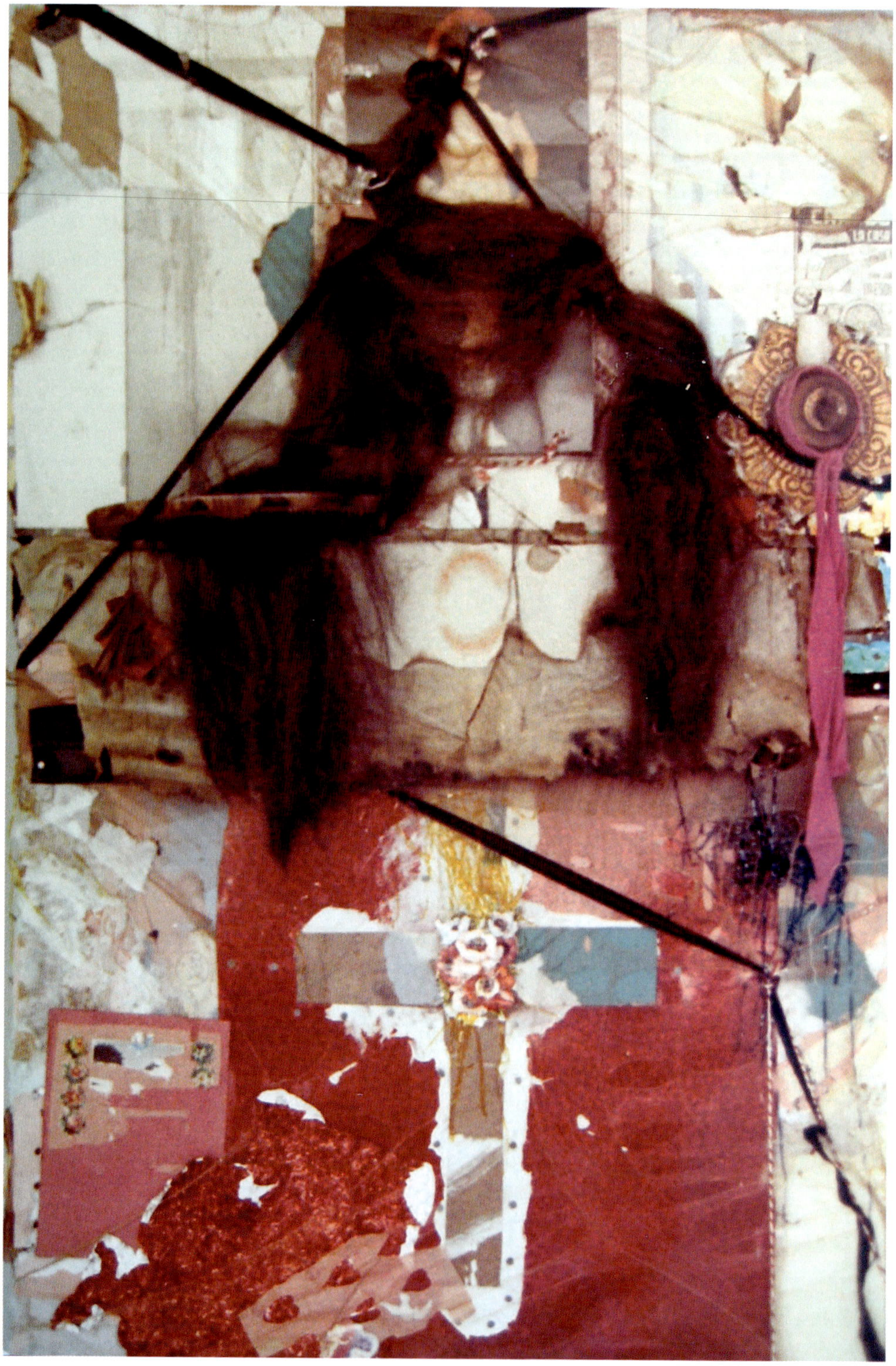

**26** Bruce Conner, SENORITA, 1962,
mixed media, 86.4 × 59.7 × 16.5 cm,
Museum of Contemporary Art, Los Angeles

posters inviting you to the Bruce Conner Circus on the Midway [the Midway Plaisance, a wide, grassy esplanade originally created for the 1893 World's Fair]." He added that the invitation was necessarily unsanctioned by the institution: "No college," he reflected, "would ever invite me to do anything if it were officially part of the college."[1] His exhibition opened on 27 April 1963; its enthusiastic student sponsors put out an accompanying publication with the Mexican assemblage SENORITA—its shank of hair holding a comb in place over a cubist grid of fancy paper—on the cover (fig. 26), enclosing a text patched together from remarks that Conner had made in his correspondence with them. Claes Oldenburg had just been there in February to stage a Happening, a multipart sequential portrait of the artist's Chicago hometown, which he called *Gayety* after a venerable burlesque house on South State Street. The involved, multipart event concluded with a large, soft airplane sculpture lowered onto the audience.[2] Plainly excited by the experience, Conner's student sponsors, possibly hoping for something similar, tried out the term with him. He sidestepped the prompt, however, with the same expansive, deflecting proviso he applied to the term *assemblage*: "They should happen anywhere, at any time, with audience or no audience, police sirens, naked ladies, flashlights, strawberry shortcake, feathered elbows, dead mice, rolled up sidewalks, smoked turning head inside out, growing fingers, sleeping in trees, sitting in pianos, happenings happen all the time."[3]

Under that fanciful brief, Conner arranged his sculptures and drawings, also screening his films, in the same space where Oldenburg had lately orchestrated his Happening extravaganza. As artist in residence for the festival, he sportingly entered into its other activities, serving as a juror for the student art exhibition.[4] When Norman Mailer made a campus visit to speak at the festival, Conner accompanied the celebrity writer's hosts when they met him at the airport. Asked to be driven straight to Conner's show, Mailer bought on the spot a drawing and the hanging sculpture 4$^{TH}$ DIMENSIONAL NEO-FUNKY BOX (now lost). More consequentially, Conner also met and heard during his stay the young Southside blues singer and harmonica player Paul Butterfield. In an interview with Paul Cummings in 1973, he revealed, "I got involved in music when I had a show at the University of Chicago in 1963. At that time there was a band playing once every week on campus. It was called the 'Twist Band,' and the man who was running it was Paul Butterfield. Played amplified harmonica. I had never heard anything like that before."[5] Then twenty-one, Butterfield was a white child of privilege who had attended the august Laboratory School attached to the university but had stepped outside the expectations of his class under the spell of the Black blues clubs in the adjacent neighborhoods of Chicago's Southside. At that moment Butterfield was moving from the campus entertainment that Conner recalls to leadership of the Paul Butterfield Blues Band, composed of stellar players, white and black, and destined for an incandescent if abbreviated career on stages like the Fillmore Auditorium and the Woodstock Festival.

COSMIC RAY offers sufficient testimony that Conner had always been "involved in music," to say the least, but he had been denied or had resisted formal training and recoiled from mastering musical notation. In the Chicago style of electrified blues, exemplified by "Big"

Walter Horton, "Little" Walter Jacobs, and Otis Rush, the player cups the instrument up close to a microphone, amplification cutting through the electrified instruments and drums. Even though the brass reeds of a diatonic harmonica come tuned to a single major key (as opposed to the chromatic instrument played most famously by Stevie Wonder), these adepts achieved the flattened thirds and sevenths of the blues scale, along with a vocal-like melisma, by playing in the key a fourth below, thus drawing in rather than blowing out on the most important notes. They and their acolyte Butterfield could project with a power and soulfulness that struck Conner like a revelation. It seemed something of a miracle that such musicianship could emerge from a "minor" instrument so small and simple it seemed a virtual toy. "Playing harmonica was something you didn't have to tune," Conner marveled; "You wouldn't have to learn notes. You could carry it around in your pocket." A chronicler of avant-garde film complained a few years later, "He prefers playing the harmonica to speaking about his work . . ."[6] The San Francisco poet Daniel Abdal-Hayy Moore wrote that he seldom heard Conner speak, but "often heard him play the harmonica, at Be-Ins, at Acid-Tests, which he seemed to do in lieu of speaking anyway."[7]

Despite the brevity of the two-week Chicago Arts Festival, Conner bonded with the decade-younger Butterfield to a sufficient degree that they would contemplate working together on an ambitious, unrealized 35-mm film in collaboration with the noted independent director Shirley Clark, a "musical comedy" to be titled THE BRUCE CONNER STORY.[8] When his show closed on 11 May, Conner set off for Massachusetts and the communal house at 23 Kenwood Avenue in Newton, clearing the way for the entire Conner family later to join the twelve residents, including three children, already housed in the property financed by Leary's younger Harvard associate Richard Alpert, the heir to the New York and New Haven Railroad fortune.[9]

■

Owing to their association with the LSD therapist Michael Agron, going as far back as 1960 in San Francisco, the Conners probably assumed they had some kind of handle on what they were signing up for. But they were moving in during a time of high drama in the affairs of the fledgling International Federation for Internal Freedom, founded only in the previous January, but already attracting a relative fortune in funds from dues-paying applicants for membership. Under a complicated set of circumstances, both Leary and Alpert had separated themselves from Harvard, making the IFIF their sole professional vehicle. Leary decamped in May for Mexico on two missions: one in Mexico City aimed at contracting with a pharmaceutical company for a regular supply of the drugs they required; the second entailing a return to the coastal village outside Zihuantanejo in Guerrero state, seeking to create a permanent summer headquarters for the IFIF. This time around, however, Leary's courting of notoriety in the press had caught up with him, and even the Mexican president took part in the action to expel him from the country. By the middle of June 1963, he was back in Cambridge, in his words, "our reputations and credibility forfeited. Suddenly we were outcasts. It was lonely on the frontier."[10] The Conners would, nevertheless, see him only intermittently over the rest of the summer, as he turned back toward the Caribbean in order to find a new location for a headquarters to house the eager subscribers to the IFIF, a quest that ended in his being expelled by August from both Dominica and Antigua in turn. Then the whole situation was put right by three siblings, heirs to the Mellon fortune, who had been drawn to Leary's cause. Among their assets was 2,500-acre estate outside the small Hudson Valley town of Millbrook in New York's Duchess County, distinguished by an enormous if somewhat dilapidated manor house and a half-dozen subsidiary dwellings, all of which they put at the group's disposal. In short order, the principals at 23 Kenwood Avenue decamped for Millbrook, and soon the Conners were living independently in Brookline.

A young artist named Charles Giuliano, who had just graduated from Brandeis in nearby Waltham, paid visits to 23 Kenwood Avenue and recorded some rare direct observations of Conner during that summer. Giuliano spent time in the basement of the house, which Conner used both as a studio and a storeroom for various of his assemblages, CHILD among them. Although nominally the property of Philip Johnson, the twisted figure in the highchair figured in a series of Conner's exhibitions between 1961 and 1968, so it made sense that he would keep it with the others during the intervals between them. COUCH (fig. 25) was in the works, "a shabby old Victorian couch with candle wax dripped over it," as Giuliano remembered it.[11] The intermediary in ushering the young artist into Conner's orbit had been Giuliano's Waltham housemate, the folk musician Mel Lyman, whose instruments were banjo and harmonica. "Mel was one of those people who just came in and out," Conner relates, "He was living with a bunch near Brandeis, all students and dopers. This guy in Anthropological Review had just written about morning glory seeds and how they got you stoned, and Mel was there three or four nights a week at the coffee grinder, grinding up seeds from this 500-pound bag we had in the kitchen."[12]

The background to this prodigious activity in mid-summer 1963 lay in the critical shortage of LSD that had overtaken the commune. The previous January the Food and Drug Administration had begun insisting on an import license for the mescaline, psilocybin, and LSD that the Sandoz pharmaceutical company had been supplying from Switzerland, and the Learyites were in no position to secure one. Until sufficient clandestine sources could be found, the morning-glory seed experiment was a way to fill the gap.[13] Whatever highs were available, Conner found his films in demand as a supplementary stimulant: "I remember once," he goes on, "Mel called up and said, 'I got 12 people, I want to bring 'em over, we've all taken the seeds.' I said no, but he came anyway. All these people showed up and he said, 'I want to see your movies.' And I ran A MOVIE. And in the middle of it, somebody just exploded over the place, threw up all over the place. And Mel thought that was great. 'It was so much for him he just had to throw it all out,' was the way he saw it."[14]

Giuliano recalls the screening of A MOVIE, along with COSMIC RAY, in less dramatic terms, but attests to "a lot of head games going on and I viewed this as the playful mischief of psychedelic Zen monks." He recounts that on another occasion, "Bruce told me he had an old Underwood typewriter he wanted to give me. I thanked him but explained that 'I'm an artist not a writer so perhaps you can give it to somebody else.' He listened, then left, and came back with a baseball bat. Without a word he smashed the typewriter with a ferocious blow. I vividly recall the ribbon popping out and unrolling as it traveled across the floor." All he could say was "Mind blowing."[15] Later in life, Conner looked back with considerable spleen on that period, disgusted in retrospect by Leary's profligacy and self-promoting opportunism. "I thought I got damaged from the thing," he reflected, "and there were other people who got even more damaged." It was not the drugs in themselves, but Leary's cavalier irresponsibility toward the many people who trusted him, Conner speculating that his whole approach was to induce bad trips as a kind of dominance ritual, if not out of sheer perversity. But that skepticism did not seem to have dented pursuit of his own drug experiments. He told Giuliano that he "had dragged all of that work from San Francisco to hang out at IFIF and take part in those acid tests." Asked whether he had experienced bad trips himself, Conner gave a noncommittal answer, relying on artful circularity: "I think that's a matter of how some people define it. I don't know what that represents but, you know, there were usually some stressful situations in almost every situation."[16]

■

Conner's artistic energies, over their recent months of peripatetic existence, had gravitated to the most portable of all media, simply drawing, which in his hands lent itself to channeling the other side of the psychedelic equation, from rapid-fire careering between flashing, instantaneous thought-images to a slowed, fascinated, obsessive attention to texture and minute detail. Two drawings made early in the Boston sojourn testify by date and by location to his place in Leary's psychedelic milieu. An untitled sheet bears the subtitle AUGUST 31, 1963 (fig. 27); large at nearly two feet square, its dense field of staccato marks, reminiscent of Van Gogh's pointillist graphic style, counts in the thousands individual touches, each of which is broadly fluent in its own right. The comparably scaled 23 KENWOOD AVENUE (fig. 28), which pays tribute to the address of the Alpert–Leary house, multiplies the number of touches by an order of magnitude. Where the former drawing trades in large rhythms of compression and release across its composition, 23 KENWOOD AVENUE concentrates similar episodes into tighter contiguous areas, suspending these roiling visual events within a set of nested rectangles on the outer perimeter that frame mandala-like circles in the central core. Both works testify to unremitting concentration and deep meditative absorption (Conner reportedly working ten hours a day, for weeks at a time), allowing his close-up immersion in the micro-process to guide the creation of larger form.[17] "Sometimes I start at the top left-hand corner and go across. Images are continually changing all the way through the process becoming silhouettes and shapes, figures," he explained with impeccably stoned logic, "It's like watching a whole—you know, it's watching a river, it's watching a movie, it's watching a thousand different drawings all happening . . . If I cover the whole page there isn't any room any more, it's finished."[18]

To call the logic of such drawings stoned is in no way to condescend to them; heightened senses and affect reveal possibilities in graphic articulation that forgo superficial resemblance in order to approach the genuinely dynamical, emergent processes of natural flows and growth. In light of Conner's persistent cultivation of such mental states, the question can be asked why he and his wife did not themselves move on with the group to the estate at Millbrook; there was certainly no shortage of room for them there. But the rural Hudson Valley, as they must have recognized, would have been a desert as far as their other interests were concerned. Despite the demands of caring for an infant under chaotic conditions, Jean Conner was not inactive as an artist. The San Francisco Museum of Modern Art possesses a 1963 collage by her of truly alarming, not to say nightmarish character, all of a piece with the fear and panic she would have been witnessing around her: a vortex of botanical and insect fragments centered on a hollow eye socket; Titian's abducted Europa from Boston's Gardner Museum joins the swirl; a pair of hands emerges from a cloud above, cradling an upturned urn that is both mushroom and phallus (fig. 29). She called it the *Temptation of Saint Wallace*, likely a reference to their friend Berman, perhaps ascribing to him Saint Anthony's capacity to face down demonic forces. Or she might have had in mind comparable forces swirling around her forbearing person right where she was.

Excesses of intemperate and self-indulgent behavior became commonplace over that autumn within the social circles into which Lyman would have introduced them. A musician of impressive skill, he carried a romantic backstory of having hoboed his way from the West Coast picking up his skills from deep rural folk musicians along the way. The aggregation at the heart of the burgeoning Boston folk scene, the Jim Kweskin Jug Band, recruited Lyman first as their banjoist and then to play harmonica, which carried chief melodic duties in the band's chosen genre. As developed on the streets of Memphis during the 1920s and 1930s, jug bands were named for the expedient of generating a bass line by blowing over the open top of a jug with pursed lips, controlling the pitch via speed and direction of breath. Along with string-band instruments, dime-store noisemakers like kazoos could approximate brass; guitar picks on washboards served for high percussion, while a washtub bass with a single string might substitute for the jug. The volume and combined strength of the rhythm section made for superior accompaniment to dancing over any solo performer. And it had been the jug bands that had first brought the harmonica into its own within the broader blues tradition.[19]

As unlikely as it may sound to those unfamiliar with old recordings of Gus Cannon's Jug Stompers or the Memphis Jug Band, such ensembles were capable of surprising subtlety across a wide spectrum of styles, absorbing nearly every genre of American vernacular music. For anyone familiar with Bruce Conner it should be plain that the jug-band approach to music would suit him down to the ground. He would surely have been aware that most 1960s enthusiasts for the originals had first heard them on the collection of transcribed 78 rpm discs compiled by his old acquaintance from the Ziprin circle, the filmmaker Harry Smith, and issued by Folkways Records in 1952 as the hugely influential, 6-LP *Anthology of*

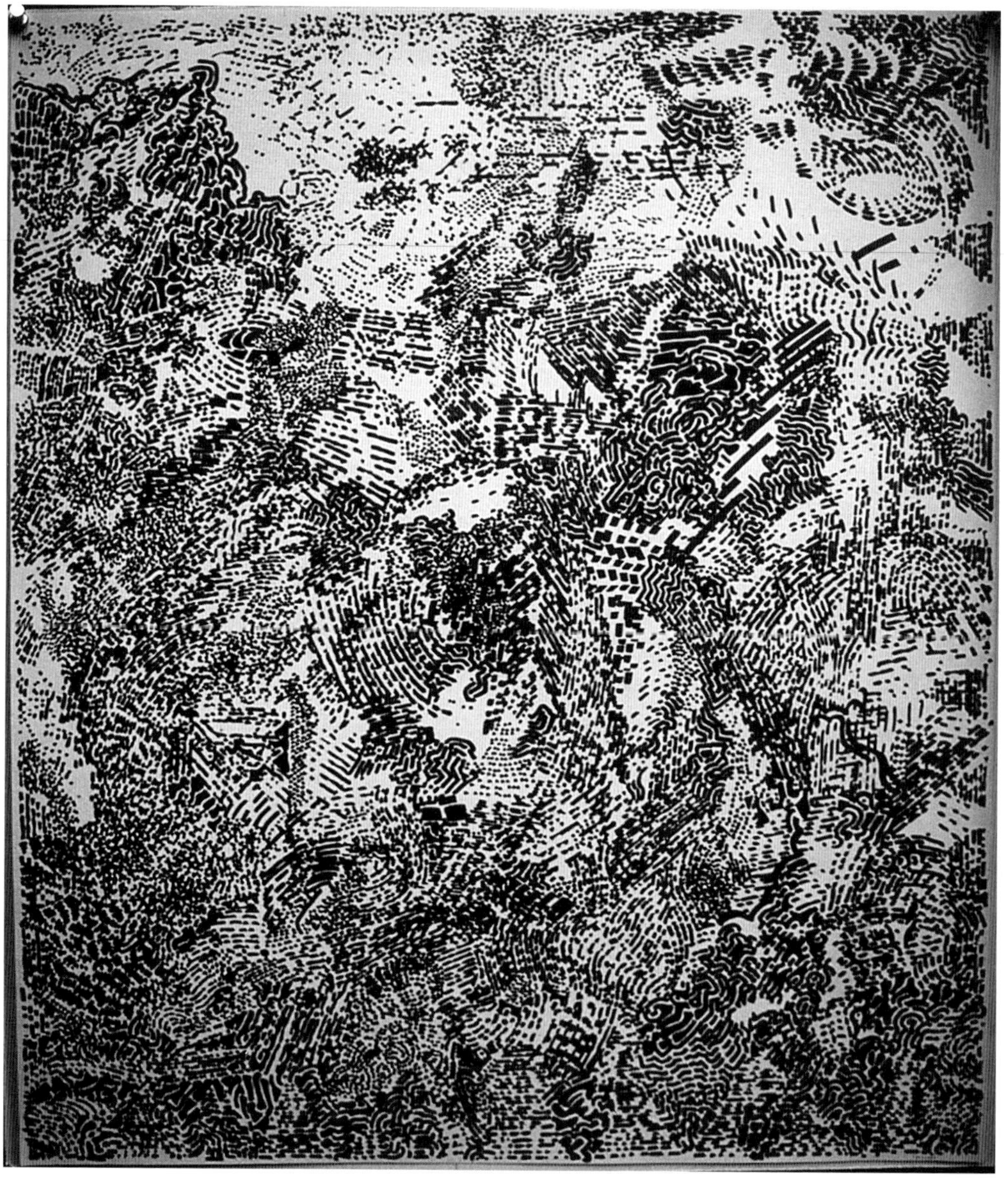

**27** Bruce Conner, UNTITLED: AUGUST 31, 1963, 1963, ink on paper, 60.6 × 50.8, private collection

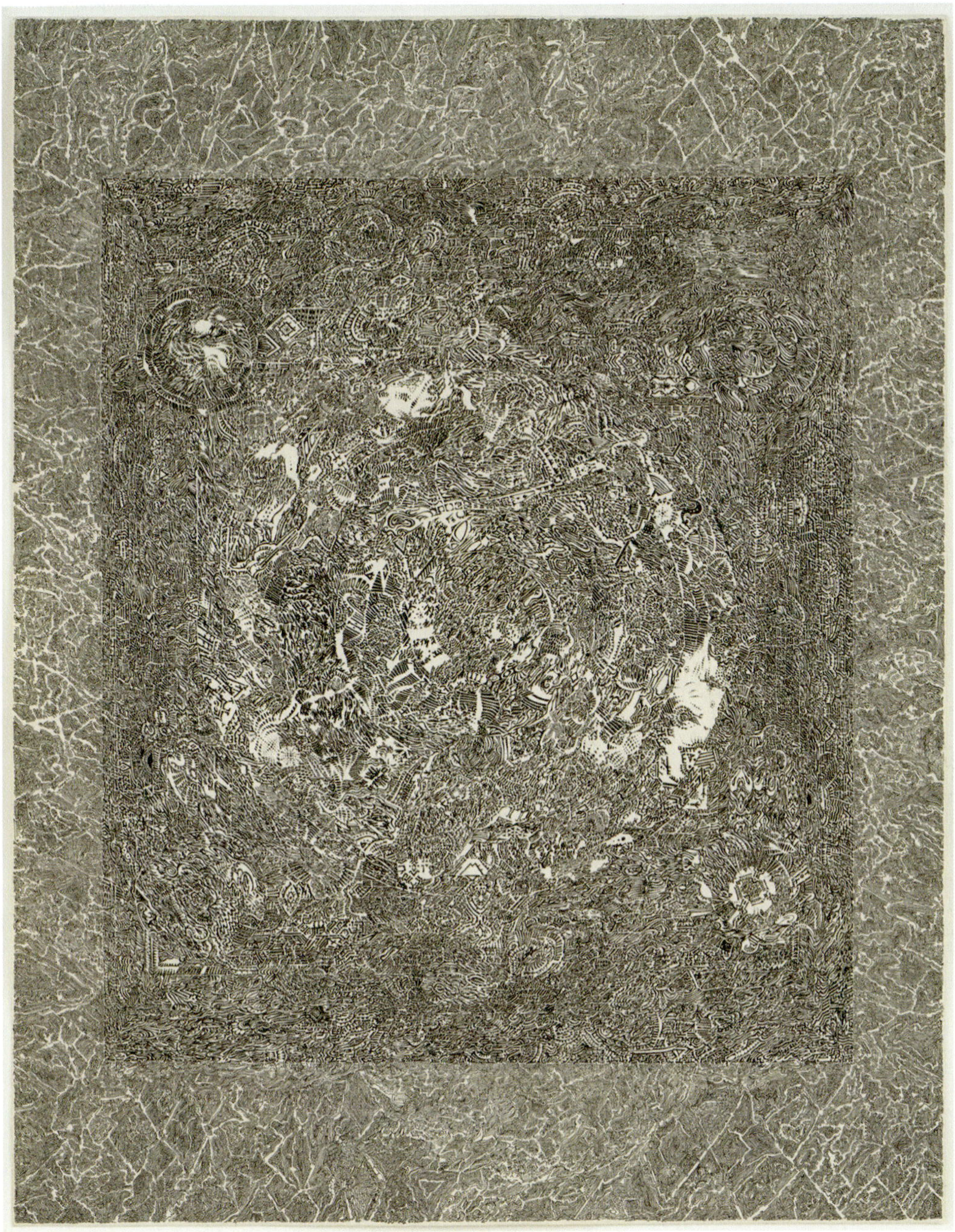

**28** Bruce Conner, 23 KENWOOD AVENUE, 1963,
ink on paper, 66 × 50.8 cm,
The Museum of Modern Art, New York

*American Folk Music*.[20] Despite his versatile mastery of folk idioms, Lyman exhibited one very Conner-like musical obsession. Having let him stay in the attic of his house, Kweskin marveled that "he stayed up in that little room and listened to Ray Charles, nothing but Ray Charles. I asked once why he never listened to any other kind of music, he said, 'Ray Charles contains all music'."[21]

On stage and in the bars of Cambridge the Kweskin Band offered an antidote to the earnestness and high-minded moralism that attended much of the folk-music revival, all without surrendering the essential mantle of fidelity to their recondite sources. They could use their multifaceted sound to expand the traditional repertoire into early jazz and novelty ragtime, which had been Kweskin's original enthusiasms, also shared by the second lead vocalist, multi-instrumentalist, and arranger Geoff Muldaur, a renegade, Loomis School preppie, with whom Conner became especially close.[22] Muldaur's vibrato-rich, upper vocal register gave the group a poignant blues timbre unknown this side of the otherworldly Mississippi bluesman Skip James. But the almost ethereal quality of his singing did not preclude his taking lead on harder, up-tempo material, nor did it coincide with any inhibition in his appetite for earthy experience: "the Jug Band never stopped," he marveled, "We'd go out and have a major shoot-out before the show and of course after the show. All day we'd go around looking for markets, find a Greek restaurant, have a gigantic meal, whip on over to the gig, tear everybody up, including ourselves, and go and party all night."[23]

Conner, in Muldaur's memory, moved in and out of this scene, his immersion in the Kweskin Band's music going up a notch when he purchased a compact Swiss tape recorder with funds provided by an unexpected filmmaking grant from the Ford Foundation. He began climbing up on stage, indulged if uninvited, to record their music, though tending to disappear, says Muldaur, when the all-night party commenced: Conner's focus on work, he remembers, was nearly "unbearable," and the recording, it became clear, belonged to that category rather than to recreation.[24] Muldaur also recalls another recording, a two-minute sound work (now lost) that conjured thunderously harmonic sonics from the rush of a continuously flushing toilet. In terms of Conner's musical education, it was doubtless with Muldaur and company that he saw the electrifying James Brown revue in Boston;[25] they likewise shared and informed his abiding devotion to African American gospel music. But the artist had much to impart in return, so much so that Muldaur calls him his "mentor," as Conner would set about exposing him—with next to no words but a sure sense of where the younger musician's knowledge needed enlarging—to some unknown film or a music recording in one more esoteric set of scales.

The purpose of the Ford Foundation grant had been to advance the work on REPORT, and Conner felt it all the more appropriate, even necessary, to be living in Brookline, where Kennedy had been born and where he had originally intended to be buried. In the midst of all his vocational and avocational activity, the Boston gallery of Hyman Swetzoff was able to mount an exhibition in October from Conner's drawings and store of sculptures extracted from the basement at 23 Kenwood Avenue. That relationship was important to the artist

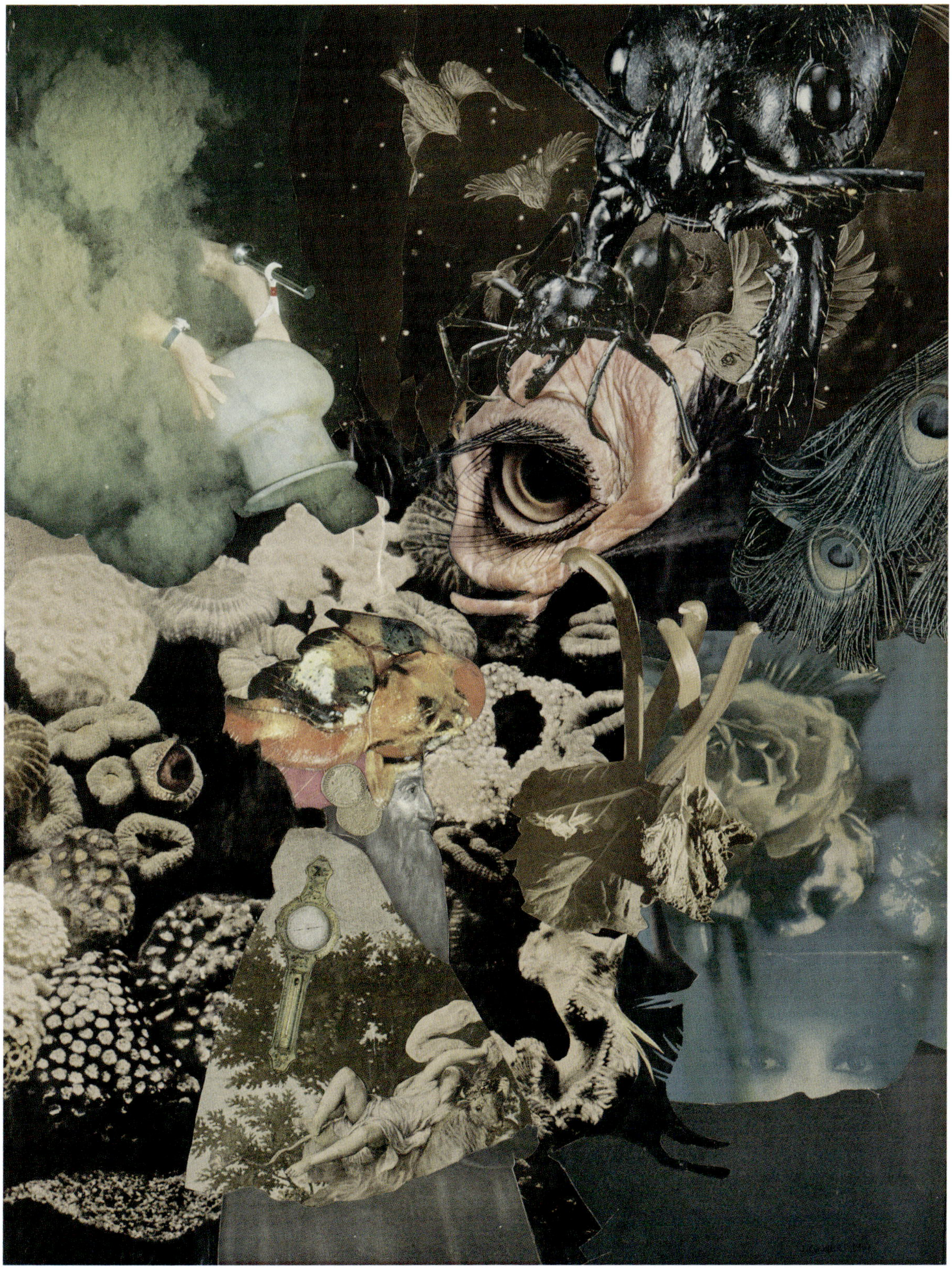

**29** Jean Conner, *The Temptation of Saint Wallace*, 1963, collage, 50.8 cm × 38.1 cm, Collection San Francisco Museum of Modern Art, Accessions Committee Fund purchase and another reason to carry on in Boston (he deeply mourned Swetzoff after the dealer was murdered in 1968). The day of Kennedy's assassination, Giuliano relates, Conner made an assemblage and put it in Swetzoff's window on Huntington Avenue—speculating that this might have been the earliest public response to the tragedy in art.[26]

While the grant kept paying the bills, Conner further undertook his most ambitious plan to date for an exhibition at the Charles Alan Gallery in Manhattan. Between his own stock and Alan's, they possessed enough work for Conner to mount in April 1964 what he regarded as a representative, ten-year retrospective, emphasizing assemblage and collage. The reviews were strong, including a large notice in the Sunday *New York Times* by the artist/critic Brian O'Doherty, but one that made him regret he had tied himself to an identity as a filmmaker: "With the Ford Foundation grant, all of a sudden instead of being an artist that had made a couple of short films, I became a filmmaker who dabbled in the arts."[27] The headline on O'Doherty's review brought the point home: "Conner and His Films: The Artist as Director, Performer and—Occasionally—As Artist."[28] Most of the review, to the artist's intense chagrin, was about A MOVIE and COSMIC RAY, which the critic had asked to see but were not part of the show: "People came to the gallery and said, 'Where are the movies? What's this junk on the walls?' I was very proud of the show. I wanted people to see what I had done. This kind of notice was something that I had always wanted. It meant some attention was going to be paid. But it was totally diverted and twisted around. The gallery sold two things out of the show. Didn't make enough to pay for the announcements."

It is received wisdom in critical and scholarly commentary on Conner that he revels in presenting a shifting, inconsistent identity to the world. But this episode makes plain that he has had this anti-persona imposed upon him by self-interested observers incapable of processing all the facets of his artistic activity into a coherent subject. When he endeavored to present a consistent autobiography in exhibition form, perhaps as a way of restoring a more whole sense of self amid the competing enticements of Boston drugs and music, no one was prepared to take it in. It was at this juncture, in the wake of his crushing disappointment, that he swore off making assemblage sculpture, even threatening, in a letter to Alan, to destroy those he still had in his possession.[29] The lesson he appears to have taken from the experience was that his next show would constitute an identity free from conventional presuppositions, one as far as possible under his own control.

■

The Conners would not resettle in San Francisco until 1965, but the opportunity for a staged re-entry presented itself the year before, one in which he could consolidate the lessons and heightened experiences of both Mexico and the Newton-Cambridge-Brookline axis but with no illusions about mounting a conventional retrospective. The destination was familiar ground, the well-appointed Batman Gallery, which Conner had helped to locate and fit out back in 1960 on behalf of its affluent founders, Billy and Joan Jahrmarkt. Its opening exhibition had been devoted to his assemblages, the announcement bearing a photograph of the BLACK DAHLIA. Michael McClure had supplied the gallery's slightly sinister, slightly comic name, along with authoring its grandiosely ambitious press announcement, and Conner had painted its interior black, burning candles during the show to enhance the installation's grotto effect.

Owing, Conner attests, to Billy Jahrmarkt's heroin addiction, management was erratic;[30] and the Jahrmarkts had sold Batman early in 1962 to another kind of proprietor altogether: Michael Agron, in partnership with his spouse Hazel. Along with Oscar Janiger and Sidney Cohen at UCLA, who had been treating well-off clients with psychedelics for the better part of a decade, Agron believed fervently that LSD, administered by a trained, attentive therapist, could enable neurotic patients to retrieve repressed traumas without the usual pain entailed in excavating psychically threatening memories, but instead with pleasurable affect and better outcomes (though with findings on suggestibility during initial stages of anxiety that reveal why the CIA was taking such an interest in the drug).[31] Yvonne Bond, the Conners' houseguest in Mexico, shared their link with Agron: speaking of the juncture around 1960 when correspondence between the Conners and Agron began, she observed, "The pure LSD that came along first was very good. I was fortunate to have some of the first doses of that with friends and then psilocybin from Mike Agron, the psychiatrist, who gave it to volunteers and then recorded our experiences."[32]

Conner's chief grievance with Leary would be that his self-dramatizing antics had provoked the outlawing of mind-altering agents with legitimate purposes, thereby putting an effective halt to the work of clinicians like Cohen and Agron.[33] As scholar Anastasia Aukeman reports, the Batman Gallery came to pursue "an exhibition program that explored states of consciousness."[34] The Agrons assumption of ownership took place just after the Conners had arrived in Mexico, but there was correspondence throughout their absence from San Francisco, which suggests a longstanding relationship.[35] For Conner to arrange for a show at the Batman that summer of 1964 was to stage his return to San Francisco via an exhibition that proved more a therapeutic intervention than anything resembling the recently closed "retrospective" at Charles Alan. There is a way in which his accumulated store of material on the East Coast carried on without him as a surrogate self to be represented at future exhibitions mounted by the Rose Museum at Brandeis University (1965) and the Institute of Contemporary Art at the University of Pennsylvania (1967). His show with the Agrons, by contrast, reconstituted another, reborn artistic self in advance of the Conners' permanently returning to the West Coast the following year.

The exhibition posted some remarkable firsts on any art-historical scorecard. Years before Michael Asher, the premises were open to visitors around the clock; years before Chris Burden, the artist inhabited the installation, putting himself on display as an exhibit; years before Joseph Kosuth, texts in mechanical type applied to uniformly pristine monochrome canvases hung on the walls. But little injustice is actually entailed in these oversights, in that the arena of competitive avant-garde feats was not one in which Conner had the slightest investment. Nor did any of these innovations of his stand alone; each gained its salience from its interrelation with the other components of the installation, all of them coordinated

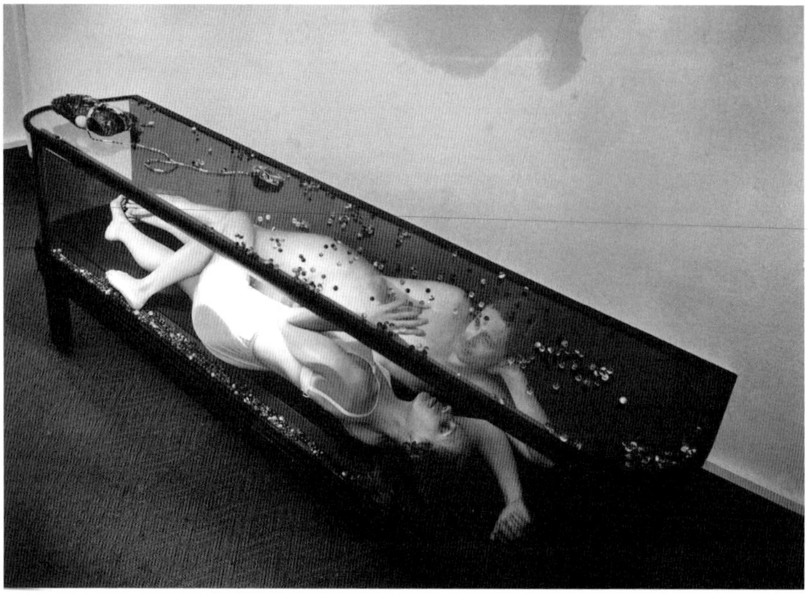

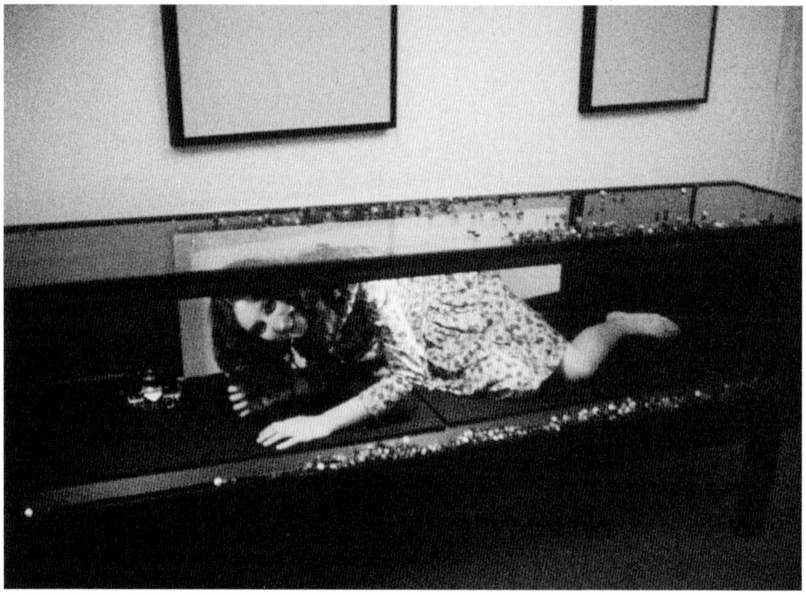

**30 (TOP)** Jean and Bruce Conner inside the jeweler's case at the Batman Gallery, 1964, photograph by Edmund Shea,

**31** Vivian Kurz inside the jeweler's case at the Batman Gallery, 1964, still from Bruce Conner, VIVIAN (black-and-white film, 1964)

in such a way as to strip away the artist's defenses, prerogatives, and disguises: a goal very much in the vein of the contemporaneous human-potential movement, with which Agron's Freudian-based rhetoric, nonetheless, had a great deal in common.

To achieve personal transformation, so ran the consistent credo of the movement, an emotional and mental ordeal had first to be overcome. For an artist who persistently likened his sculptures to dramas, the Batman exhibition allowed Conner to mount one in real time, complete with human actors. He occupied the space for the entire three days the show was open; during one twenty-four-hour period, anyone could walk in the door. Prominent in the installation was a horizontal jeweler's vitrine, large enough to hold two people—and on one occasion holding Bruce and Jean Conner, who rendered themselves open to visitor's scrutiny in vulnerable undress (fig. 30).[36] Red marbles were said to have rolled like jewels inside and outside the glass case. The physical and psychological discomfort occasioned by this exposure can only be imagined, especially for Jean, who had made the trip from Boston for this three-day event. So had a woman named Vivian Kurz, who likewise would take her place (alone) inside the tomb-like vitrine (fig. 31).

At an earlier point, back in Boston, both Charles Giuliano and Mel Lyman had been courting Kurz. She had avoided both men by joining the Conners at their new residence in Brookline, a pattern perhaps anticipated by Yvonne Bond's long stay with them in Mexico the year before.[37] Lyman, bereft at the departure of the lover who had brought him to Boston, fled back to Kansas after a bad experience with LSD and the Leary entourage.

Conner left an exceptional record of the Batman exhibition by shooting a large part of his three-minute film titled VIVIAN on the occasion of the show, capturing the actual appearance of the evanescent exhibition, the contents of which functioned as much as apparitions from the Conner past as they did as current objects of aesthetic contemplation. Most apposite to the Christological three-day duration was a reinstallation of the 1960 RESURRECTION (fig. 32), set on a pedestal that raised it to head height. Its parallel counterpart was THE BRIDE (figs. 33, 34), made in the same year, a collapsed and decayed cascade of dusty nylon stockings with other flotsam, hung over a shrouded humanoid armature. The latter signals the theme of marriage, to be sure, but in a moribund condition that Conner once likened to the aged Miss Havisham of *Great Expectations*, sitting in the rags of her wedding gown amid the uncleared setting of the banquet decades after being left at the altar: all this while Kurz roamed the gallery in all her youthful insouciance.

A note of redemption, however, stood altar-like at the center of the room in the shape of a collage he had fashioned from a suitcase in Mexico, to which a mystical folk image of three Christs was affixed within a lozenge of fringe and inside of which was a resumé of the Conners' life there in the form of a chair cushion and an infant's mattress (fig. 35). Centered on a pedestal in the middle of the gallery, candles burned like an offering along the top of SUITCASE throughout the three days of the exhibition.[38] To one side, on a pedestal scaled to match the others in the room, he placed an embellished pair of Mexican shoes, tied into a bundle with a single beaded garland descending nearly to the floor. Along each flanking wall marched a uniform sequence of new quasi-paintings (fig. 36). As he told a local reporter as

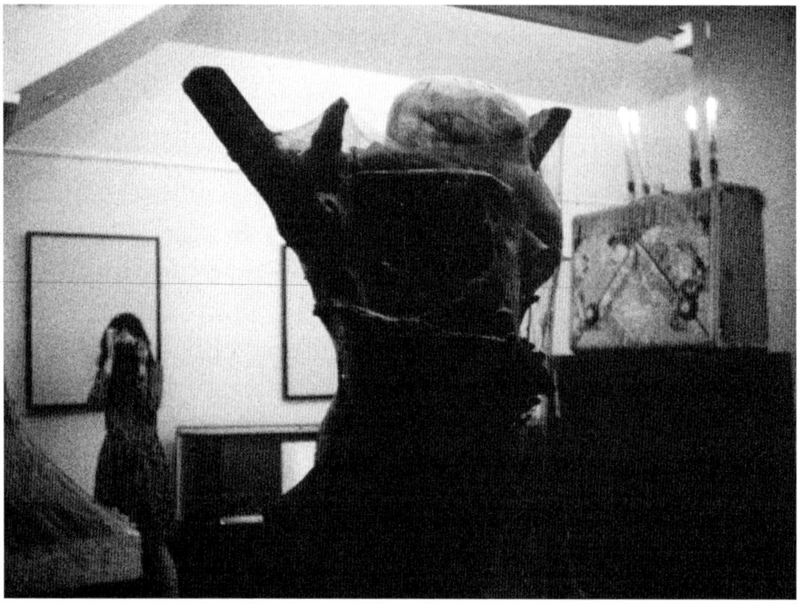

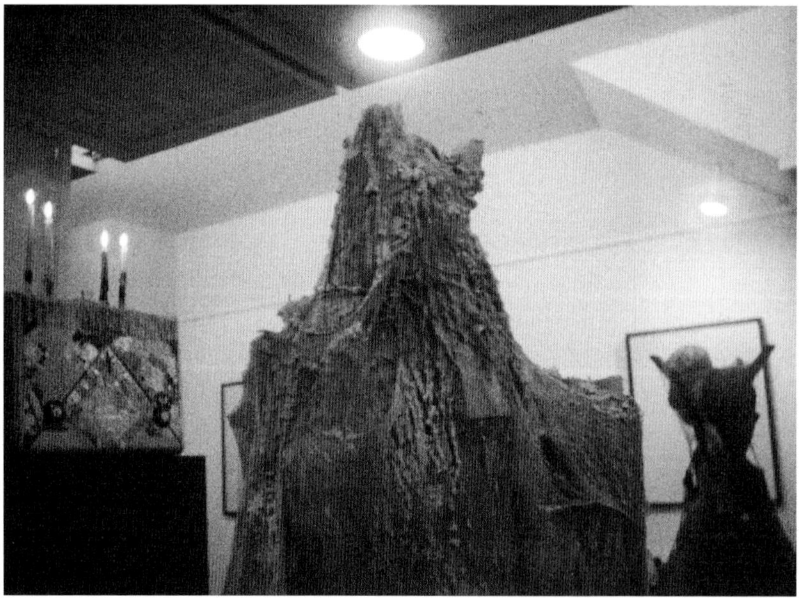

**32 (TOP)** Bruce Conner, RESURRECTION (foreground) and SUITCASE (rear) at the Batman Gallery, 1964, still from VIVIAN (black-and-white film, 1964)

**33** Bruce Conner, THE BRIDE (foreground) with SUITCASE and RESURRECTION at the Batman Gallery, 1964, still from VIVIAN (black-and-white film, 1964)

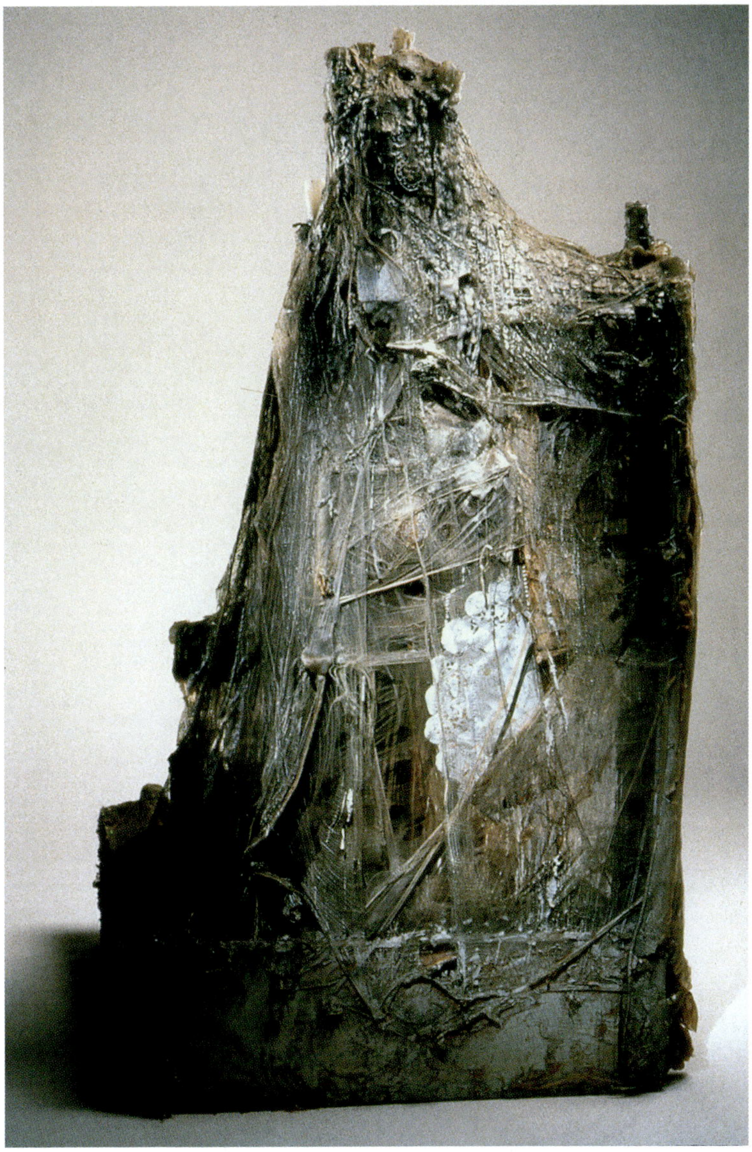

34 Bruce Conner, THE BRIDE, 1960, mixed media, 92.7 × 43.2 × 58.4 cm, Walker Art Center, Minneapolis, Braunstein/Quay Gallery and T. B. Walker Acquisition Fund, 1987

they stood in the gallery, "They're big canvases that I bought pre-stretched, primed and white. I never handled them at any time even when the gallery hung them. Someone else printed the words on them that I supplied: 'Do not touch!' But the 13th canvas, bought and delivered in the same way, I did handle myself. I myself printed on it the word, 'Touch!' Then I covered it with glass."[39] Divided into two groups of six, the DO NOT TOUCH panels lined a processional path like a gallery of saints leading to the blocked admonitory injunction TOUCH.

In the presence of the likewise glass-clad display case, not to mention Kurz in person, a subtheme of the show became not just what could be touched or not touched, but who. Imprecise but inescapable biblical resonances hung in the air, the forbidden fruit of Genesis that made

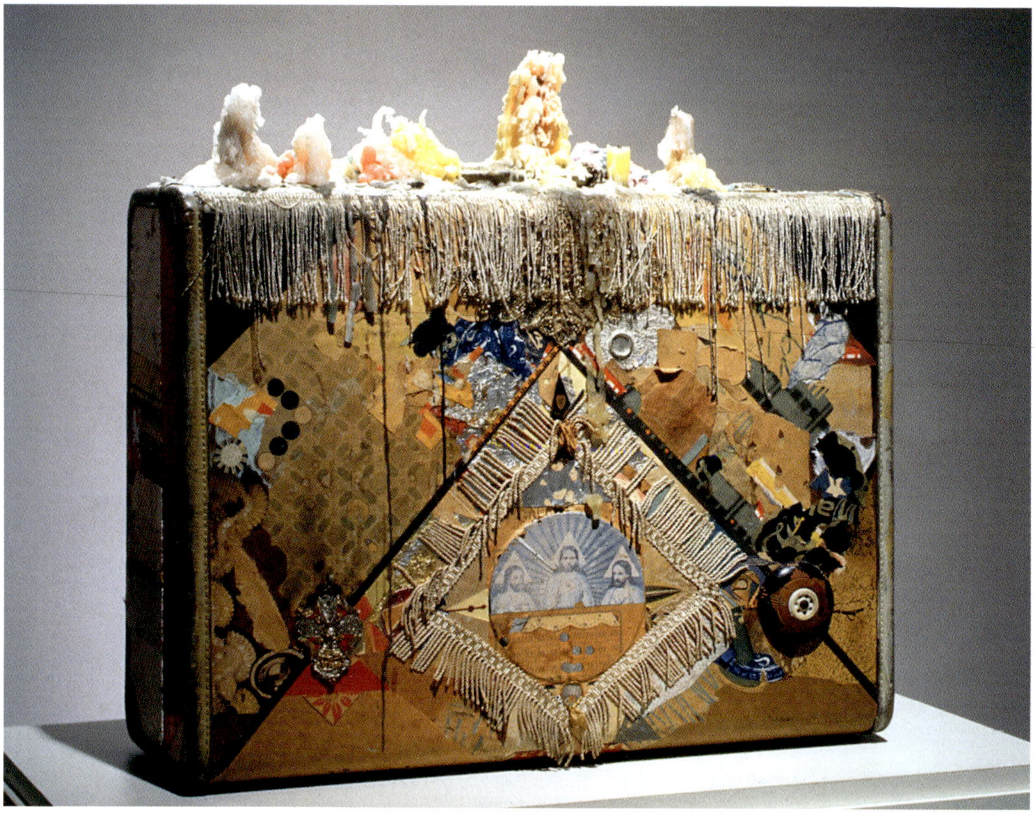

35 Bruce Conner, SUITCASE, 1962, mixed media, 55.9 × 61 × 22.9 cm, Frederick R. Weisman Art Foundation, Los Angeles

Christ's sacrifice necessary and the do-not-touch admonition, Noli Me Tangere, the warning of the risen Christ to Mary Magdalene that his resurrected, heavenly body was an entity apart from the physical one he had previously occupied. Confirming the inevitable analogy to the entombment of Christ, Conner stated, "After three days the stone was rolled away and I walked out."[40] But the psychodrama did not appear to be over even after their return to Massachusetts. He later spoke elliptically of what sounds like a therapeutic contract, but one to which he did not entirely adhere. Life, he said, "became very difficult with Vivian and became very difficult with my wife. It was decided that I would not see Vivian for about a month and during that month when I could not see Vivian I made that film. I looked at Vivian every day."[41] His choice of soundtrack—typically subtle in its apprehension of the ambient culture—was an up-tempo cover of Nat Cole's 1950, Oscar-winning ballad "Mona Lisa," recorded in 1959 by the southern rockabilly singer Conway Twitty. One sees Kurz climb into the glass coffin while bright sequins rain onto its lid (fig. 37); the lyrics of the song reinforce the interplay between life and death, the association of art with morbidity, that had saturated the Batman outing: "Are you warm, are you real, Mona Lisa? / Or just a cold and lonely, lovely work of art?"

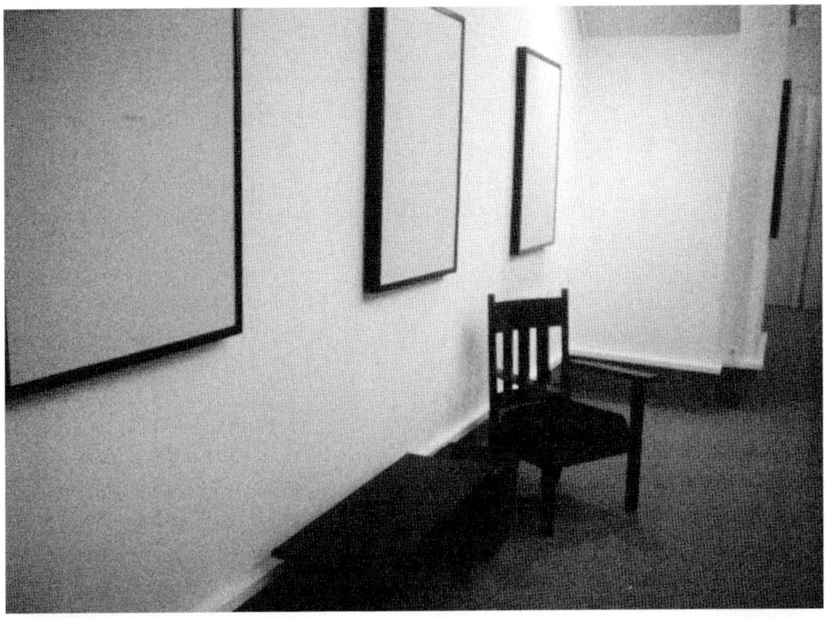

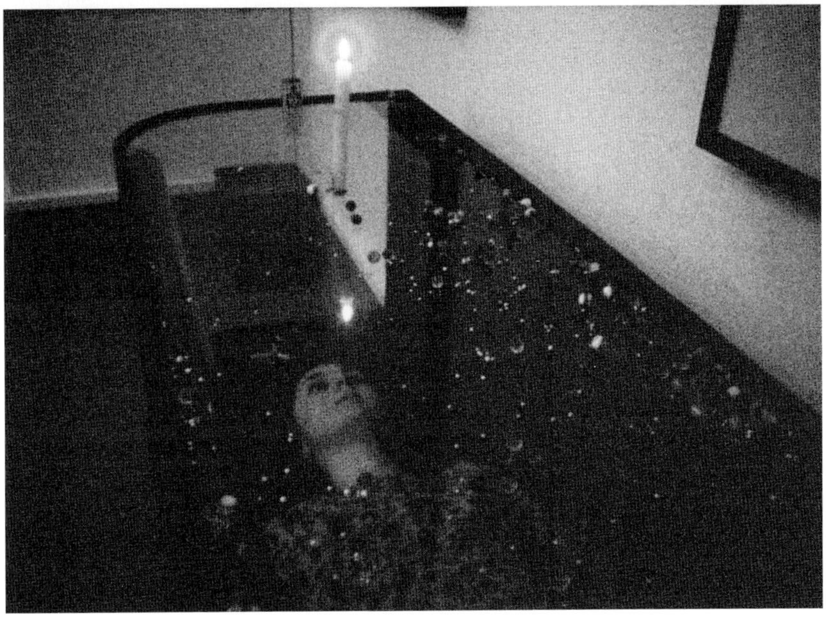

36 (TOP) Bruce Conner, TOUCH/DO NOT TOUCH (detail)
at the Batman Gallery, 1964, still from VIVIAN (black-and-white film, 1964)

37 Vivian Kurz at the Batman Gallery, 1964,
still from VIVIAN (black-and-white film 1964)

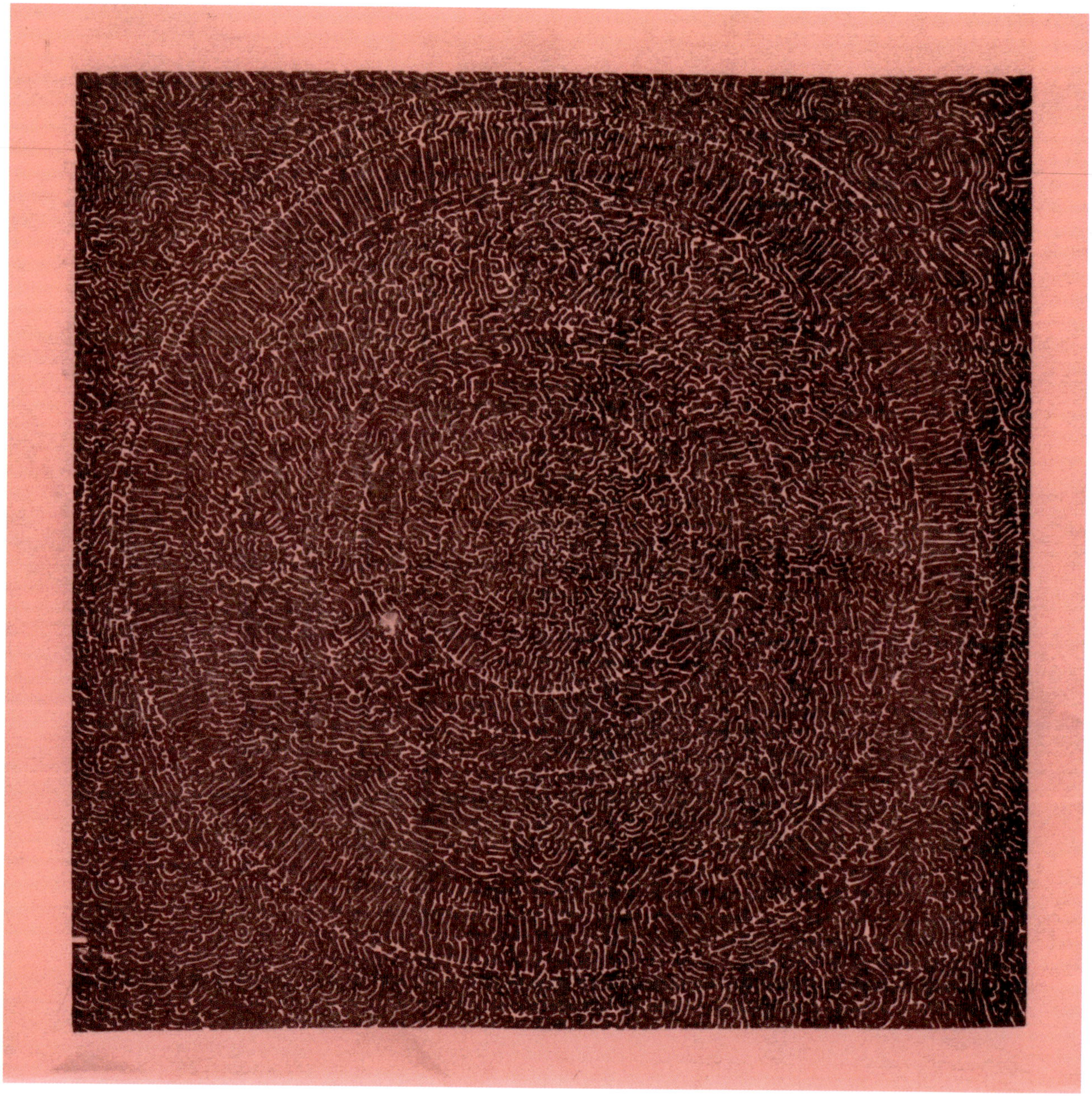

38 Program cover for the Trips Festival, San Francisco, January 1966, after a drawing by Bruce Conner given to Michael McClure

FOUR

# PSYCHEDELPHIC ORACLE

DURING THE COURSE OF THE BATMAN EXHIBITION, old friends from the Conners' early days in San Francisco, Wallace Berman and artist George Herms, drove up from Los Angeles to lend their support in a kind of vigil, sitting in the space while Conner projected films on the wall. With adventures of self-transformation pervading the mindscape of the West Coast, whether via disciplines of meditation, artificially induced mind expansion, or soul-baring, encounter-group therapies, it had to be asked, what relationship existed between a transformed self and the one that existed before? After his installation-experiment with Michael Agron, Conner launched a project of canvassing all the individuals in America named Bruce Conner, simultaneously magnifying and diluting the chief marker of his identity, artistic and otherwise. Taking out an advertisement in perhaps the most obscure location he could have found, a literary journal called *Joglars* put out by a group of Harvard undergraduates, he tabulated an initial list, organized by the prospective service advertised by each of the Bruce Conners (with the implication that he, too, was no more than another service provider).[1] This exaggerated reticence had as its complement that same year in his beginning the long-term exchange of identities he would pursue with the most notorious figure of young Hollywood, that being Dennis Hopper. Only three months after closing the Batman show, Conner was already back on the West Coast, now in Los Angeles, cultivating bonds with Hopper and a group of demi-celebrities for whom fame unimaginable to an artist was no more than a staple of their livelihoods.

Conner would have been intrigued by the close formal parallel between his and Hopper's surnames; while Hopper would have reciprocated by his eagerness to be recognized and accepted as an artist himself. In 1964, indeed, those aspirations prevailed over the humdrum television roles he was relying on. Despite evident talent, looks, and reputation as the spiritual heir to the late James Dean, he had not been cast in a studio film since 1958. His exaggerated method-acting pretensions had so put off the veteran director Henry Hathaway that feature-film offers dried up until 1965 when Hathaway relented and gave him a part in a John Wayne vehicle, *The Sons of Katie Elder*. Hopper's income, nonetheless, dwarfed that of any artist, and he had married into wealth as well. Having lost a remarkable collection of Abstract Expressionist and early Pop works to the Bel Air fire of 1961, Hopper had kept up as a collector, befriending Andy Warhol, continued his efforts as a painter, and developed an impressive portfolio as a photographer. It was in that last capacity that Conner enlisted him to lend visual support to his Bruce Conner quest.

One of the Bruce Conners listed in the *Joglars* directory provided "Physical Services" at his gymnasium on the West Side of Los Angeles, so the artist Conner enlisted Hopper, along with female friends from show business, to document the sexual innuendo inherent in this particular "service" on location (fig. 39). There was more than joking irony to this gesture, in that Conner was breaking his personal embargo against being photographed at all, one that he had breached only a few times in his early career.[2] That he should choose to do this in the guise of a mock-lothario, surrounded by professional television dancers, casts further doubt on the resolution of his home-life difficulties, as does his protracted absence from Brookline. Much later, he referred to the image as "a satire of the star system," but that seems a weak alibi.[3] Where he had earlier mocked cheesecake-posing in A MOVIE, now he appeared to bask in its proximity, exhibiting his incipient proclivity for the Hollywood slumming that Hopper was more than ready to provide. But there was a deeper dimension to this playacting, in that the two more prominent of the posing women, Toni Basil (dancer, choreographer, singer) and Teri Garr (dancer, actress), joined Hopper, Dean Stockwell, and Russ Tamblyn, among others, in wanting to identify as artists as an escape from the cookie-cutter roles, studio surveillance, and industry philistinism they endured in their professional lives. Seeking a share of countercultural authenticity, all had come into the orbit of Conner's old mentor, the show-business escapee Wallace Berman.[4]

Two years earlier, Berman had ended his self-imposed, Bay Area exile and returned to Los Angeles, as had George Herms. Both of them became artistic mentors to these part-time Hollywood refugees, who eagerly tried their hands at assemblage, which presented a low bar in terms of technical skill but plenty of expressive scope. Tamblyn (the Jets leader "Riff" in the film of *West Side Story*) speaks in rapturous terms of Berman's effect on them: "I had already begun to turn away from show business, because it had begun to seem empty to me. . . . I've met a lot of movie stars, and I was friends with lots of them, but I never met anyone with the aura Wallace had. He had a way of inspiring people to channel their energies into something creative without telling them to . . ."[5] Another Berman adherent was the erstwhile child actor Billy Gray, famous for playing the teenage son in the family situation comedy *Father Knows Best*. But Gray had lost his wholesome image and most of his acting career when arrested for marijuana possession in 1962, retreating to the Topanga house bought at the height of his fame, where he, too, joined the group.

Berman reported in a letter to a friend a visit that year by Conner, who memorably "did the twist to Screamin' Jay Hawkins."[6] In his choice of dance material, Conner again manifested his taste for the harder edge of contemporary rhythm and blues, with a touch of the hyper-theatrical, in that the voodoo-drenched Hawkins often sang his signature hit, "I Put a Spell on You," after rising from a coffin to open his act. References to Conner's dancing follow him throughout the recorded observations of his acquaintances, beginning with Timothy

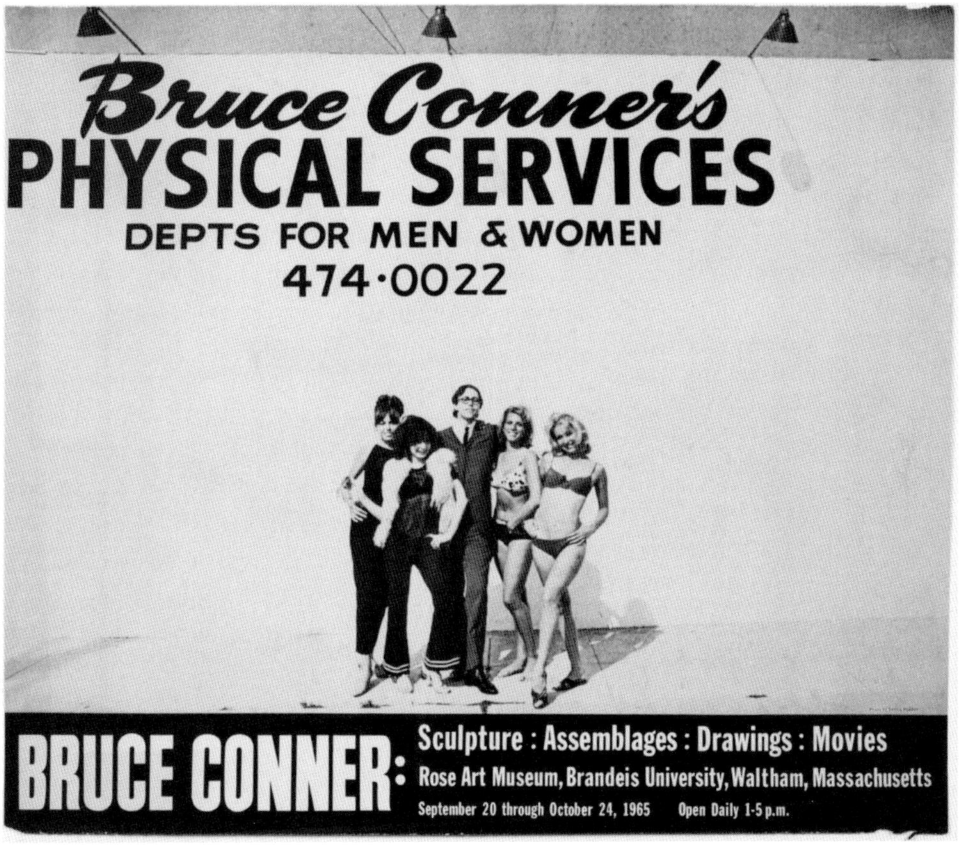


39 Bruce Conner, untitled poster featuring Conner with Toni Basil, Teri Garr, and "Hullabaloo" dancers in West Los Angeles, 1964, photograph by Dennis Hopper, courtesy the Kohn Gallery, Los Angeles

Leary's characterization of Conner "dancing around filming" in Mexico in 1960. During his 1964 stay in Los Angeles, he not only posed with dancers, but set about filming his own paean to the body in movement to rock music: BREAKAWAY, with Basil as its central subject, keyed to her energetic, non-hit recording of the same title. In October 1964, however, the recorded song did not yet exist. When he gathered with Basil and a group of friends in an apartment above the picturesque carousel on the Santa Monica Pier, his goal was to amass sufficient raw footage to be cut and spliced precisely synchronized to the beat of a hypothetical piece of music. For the moment, it was Conner improvising with a new set of Hollywood peers. Basil was then living with Dean Stockwell, the actor who had stood bail for Berman after his bogus arrest for obscenity in 1957 (the traumatic event, as noted in chapter 1, that propelled his self-exile to San Francisco). As Conner was filming her, Stockwell was filming them. In his dancing, as with his harmonica playing, he did not let absence of polished technique (Geoff

Muldaur affectionately recalls it as a "robotic shuffle") deter him from confidently stepping forward, even in the company of consummate professionals. Thus one sees Conner demonstrating to Basil a little sideways shuffle step he wants her to do. When the first day of filming yielded little that was usable, a second, Hopper now assisting with lighting, went better.[7] The episode announces, *in nuce*, the oscillation of Conner's point of reference between the metaphysical aspirations that prevailed in San Francisco, where he would edit BREAKAWAY, and the pervasive commercialism of Los Angeles, where the film's repertoire of slick and practiced moves originated. And Conner would regularly move in and out of the manic Hopper orbit over the next half-decade, to the point that he almost possesses two post-1965 biographies, one for Los Angeles and one for San Francisco, the founding scene to which he and Jean made their return within a year—and doing so in time to be on hand as the rough beast of the counterculture, in the eyes of its many detractors, was manifestly slouching over the horizon.

▪

In the meantime, Conner had one stop to make that promised to equal or surpass the starry ambience of his Hollywood circle. In mid-December 1964, the Pop-identified London dealer Robert Fraser mounted a show of his assemblages. Conner was on hand in good time to collaborate with Fraser on what he happily called the "beautifully done" hanging. And the opening, he recalled, attracted a satisfying complement of everyone who counted in the London art world, eliciting a highly favorable review by John Russell in *The Sunday Times*. "Remote holes, bags and pockets, half-hidden in the assemblage like the dark mouth of a cave in the woods, tempt the spectator to explore," the critic appreciatively opined, going on to reassure his readers of the larger significance conveyed by these exotic accumulations: "Yet in spite of the multitude of objects used, each work is not a heap of treasure but the comment of a man obviously involved in the world today."[8]

Fraser would go on to gain his most lasting fame by orchestrating the famous album sleeve for the Beatles' *Sgt. Pepper's Lonely Hearts Club Band*, assigning principal design duties to his gallery artists, the married pair Peter Blake and Los Angeles-born Jann Haworth. Conner visited them at their disconcertingly Southern Californian flat, but reported that, for the moment, Fraser did not yet know any of the Beatles—a shame, in that one or two of the Liverpudlians might well have rescued the artist when he found himself in a state of awkward isolation at the party for his exhibition. "There seemed to be a certain hipness" to Fraser's well-connected friends and clients, as he ruefully recalled, but it proved to be "just stuck on top" of glacial class-consciousness. Falling back on his old dancing, soul-loving persona cut no ice: "I was playing Ray Charles very loud and expecting everyone to party and jump around [but] I was comparable to a visiting aborigine."[9]

Some who attended Fraser's screening of Conner's films might have been forgiven some such impression, as he chose to project REPORT with his own blood caked onto the celluloid:

"I had the blood taken out of me by syringe, then put it on the film. It was sticky, my hands kept sticking to the film. It dried very quickly. Every time the film was shown, some blood would flake off and the projector would have bits of blood on it." Adding that dimension of gothic ritual to each screening might be understood in light of Conner's acute involuntary internalization of external violence, undiminished since his acting out over RAT BASTARD NO. 1 and CHILD: "The film had a strong effect on me as well as other people. Even after years, I'd sometimes have to leave the room."[10]

After these chastening experiences abroad, the Conners seem to have slipped away from Boston quietly in mid-1965, but with one characteristic gesture on Bruce's part. Friends attest that he found ways surreptitiously to enter their apartments in order to deposit with each of them a work of his own art.[11] Their next stop lay at the center of a world set to rival the London of Fraser and the Beatles for innovation in music, style, and otherworldly aspirations: the Haight-Ashbury District of San Francisco. Already in 1962, Michael and Joanna McClure had resettled in what was then a somewhat bypassed neighborhood, where wooden houses of Victorian style, large if often in poor repair, could be had inexpensively. Its proximity to the old campus of San Francisco State College had already attracted a distinctly nonconformist and youthful population; rising rents and commercialization around North Beach began a migration of poets and their cohort to the same destination; while the landlord of the apartment building that the McClures had shared with their artist friends in the Western Addition had evicted the lot of them. One of the chief attractions of the new neighborhood lay in its adjacency to the vast green spaces of Golden Gate Park; what was more, a narrow spur of the park called the Panhandle extended for eight blocks parallel to Haight Street at the foot of the sloping neighborhood, a natural place for gatherings and semi-impromptu events featuring the rock bands resident in the surrounding blocks. As they had on their first arrival in San Francisco, the Conners settled into an apartment a few blocks from the McClures, but with the difference that their new, shared neighborhood was already taking on a heaving, seething life of its own, as it galvanized into an over-publicized destination for would-be free spirits.

Bruce's return had been heralded by the inclusion of his Boston mandala drawing, 23 KENWOOD AVENUE (fig. 28), as endpapers to the *Psychedelic Experience* by Timothy Leary, Richard Alpert, and their Newton associate Ralph Metzger.[12] In their free adaptation of the Buddhist "Tibetan Book of the Dead" (the fourteenth-century Bardo Thodol), the book's authors offered their idealized account of an LSD-induced passage from a defensively incomplete existence through ego disintegration and discovery of a whole self within (that being very much Michael Agron's construct as well). Conner had, of course, implicitly mocked the cliché of "finding yourself" when he sought out the other Bruce Conners, but there he was on the page, splendidly represented in the reigning psychedelic tract of the time, one then going through printing after printing.

Conner had transformed the mandala motif itself from an exotic diagram into an evolving, creative form, and he kept on making more of them. He had given one to McClure, which turned up early in January 1966 on several thousand programs (fig. 38) printed for an event called the Trips Festival, to be held in the cavernous Longshoreman's Hall at Fisherman's Wharf.[13] Conner's handiwork is credited on the last page, with McClure listed as its owner, but the artist's participation is billed more prominently in the central spread (as "illustrious film maker") accompanying the challenge:

> Can YOU pass the Acid Test? There's no way to think about it or read about it. There's no other way to know than go ahead on it. Can you die to your corpses? Can you metamorphose? Can you pass the 20th century? What is total dance?

As the first line made plain, the San Francisco Trips Festival followed on from the Acid Tests staged at various locations around California by the novelist Ken Kesey and his obstreperous entourage known as the Merry Pranksters. At these events, staged as far away as Portland and as close as San Jose, Kesey's group would roll up in their wildly patterned school bus and proceed to serve an LSD-laced brew to anyone who attended, as everyone's senses were assaulted by an array of light and sound equipment. Musical accompaniment came courtesy of a former jug band called the Warlocks, local to Palo Alto, down the Peninsula, where Kesey's psychedelic odyssey had begun back in the early 1960s.

That saga has famously been told at length in Tom Wolfe's 1968 *Electric Kool-Aid Acid Test*, a work of underestimated depth of research, published so soon after the events it recounts as to become a countercultural phenomenon in itself.[14] Much of its narrative would have been unfamiliar to the Conners, as they had begun their Mexico-to-Massachusetts itinerary just as Kesey was getting started on his parallel course as acid *animateur* in the west to Leary's in the east. To join in the Trips Festival would have been a way for Conner to claim a rare place in both narratives. A rock journalist registered his presence, unknowingly reporting an early screening of REPORT: "It turned out as another sort of rock dance plus Acid Test. . . . Kesey was writing on the overhead projector . . . A film of a repeated loop of Jackie Kennedy reaching for a door handle after her husband's assassination was on the screens."[15]

Conner's longstanding antipathy to state persecution must have been aroused by Kesey's accumulating legal troubles at the same moment. Recently given a reduced sentence for a marijuana bust the year before at La Honda, his woodsy Peninsula home, the writer was rearrested for the same offense, in the company of a minor, on the rooftop of Stewart Brand's North Beach building. That violation threatened to send him back for a full sentence on the first conviction and to add one much worse as a second offender.

The first concept of the Trips Festival, organized in Kesey's support, had been to invite the non-initiated to a sensory re-creation of an acid trip without need of the actual drug. But soon a large sack of doses began circulating on the floor, courtesy of Augustus Owsley Stanley III, who had inaugurated the era of mass illegal manufacture of LSD when Sandoz pulled back from supplying the incorrigible new psychedelic movement and legal prohibition loomed. Over the course of the recent Acid Tests, the folkie Warlocks had re-emerged as the electrified Grateful Dead, who effortlessly dominated the Trips Festival even without the state-of-the-art amplification that Owsley would shortly be able to provide, thanks both to inherited wealth (he was the grandson of a Kentucky senator) and to his growing drug proceeds. For Conner, as one can only surmise, the music of the Dead was like witnessing a melding of the power projected by the Paul Butterfield Blues Band and the folk eclecticism of the Jim Kweskin Jug Band (one of the Dead's signature songs, "Cold Rain and Snow," had originated with Mel Lyman's North Carolina mentor on the banjo). Many others in the Longshoreman's Hall over the long night were witnessing the onset of the San Francisco ballroom events to come.

In the ensuing weeks, rock dance-concerts began sprouting across the Bay Area in every kind of available accommodation. But within a few months, two players had emerged with the best venues, the Fillmore Auditorium and the Avalon Ballroom, old, second-story, big-band dance halls, each with a balcony running around the perimeter, just eight blocks separating them. Controlling the Fillmore was the clipboard-wielding Bill Graham, a New York transplant and relative square, who had lately served as the business manager for the impecunious Mime Troupe; staging benefit concerts to pay the group's continual legal bills had gotten him started as a promoter. Overseeing the Avalon was Chet Helms, with a supporting collective called the Family Dog, whose members were already self-presenting in the Hippie mode of extravagant vintage clothes and long male hair. By April 1966, Graham and Helms fell out over rival bookings of audience favorite, the Paul Butterfield Blues Band (in October, the Kweskin Band would headline at the Avalon).

Part and parcel of this rapid evolution was the visual component of projected light and images on slides and film. The sources of this development are many: one strong lineage arose from the rich tradition of experimental, abstract filmmaking in the Bay Area (where Harry Smith got his start); the visual and aural pandemonium contrived by the Merry Pranksters, both at Kesey's La Honda compound and on their road-trip Acid Tests, provided another. In short order, following the Trips Festival, various companies like the Joshua Light Show and Head Lights took shape, their names emblazoned as attractions on the concert posters. So integral had the light shows become that the Grateful Dead met with consternation when they unveiled the enormous stack of amplifiers that Owsley had built for them in that spring of 1966; their black color was deadening the lights, so the community-minded band promptly had them painted white. It is unclear whether Conner followed up immediately on his contribution to the Trips Festival illuminations, but his major project for 1966, editing BREAKAWAY, is difficult to imagine apart from the weekly spectacle on view in the ballrooms of freeform dancers moving under eye-dazzling light displays: the exact subject of his film.

■

Conner could have set the footage he had taken of Toni Basil back in 1964 to any suitable piece of dance pop, as he had freely matched his previous films to music of his choice. But the opening title, her given name, Antonia Christina Basilotta, makes plain that the film belongs to her, which extended to the soundtrack alongside her constant presence on screen.

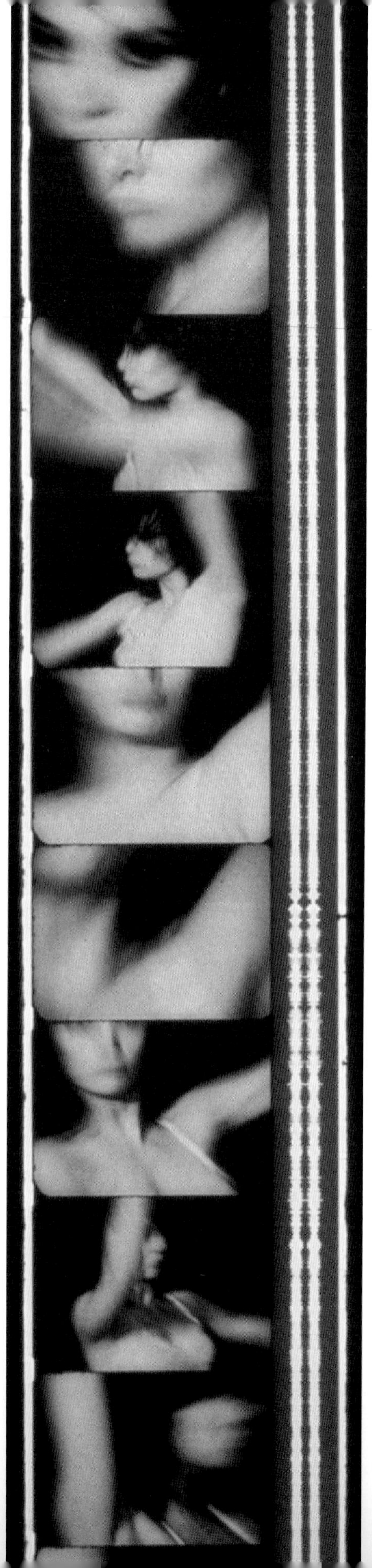

For that to happen, she needed to make a record, and her first single appeared in February 1966, at which point Conner's path was clear.[16] The A-side, that is the song promoted for radio play, is a mid-tempo, folk-rock lament, titled "I'm 28," about (of all things) aging and life passing you by. The B-side, the titular "Breakaway" is not much faster but boasts an emphatic, not to say pounding dance beat and a theme, entirely congenial to Conner, of liberation from all the envious voices enforcing conformity and mental imprisonment. Johanna Gosse puts it well: "Conner's camera dances with her, punctuating her movements with rapid cuts and frenzied zooms that render her body an ethereal streak of white light against a black void, a spectral apparition that threatens to 'breakaway' from visibility entirely"[17] (fig. 40).

Certain of those effects had been achieved inside Conner's Bolex camera, derived from Basil's own approach to movement and costume. As Gosse discovered, she cut out the polka-dot holes in her black tights that correspond so well to the exposed perforations in film leader that were already one of Conner's trademarks.[18] Nowhere better than in BREAKAWAY is the white light emitted by the projector incisively revealed as the fundamental condition of film, to be defined as successive interruptions of a pure state of illumination—a recognition he had long been intimating through other means. Absent from Massachusetts in 1964, Conner had sent his young friend Henry Moss (the Harvard undergrad who published the Bruce Conner services advertisement) to impersonate him at a screening of his films held at the Worcester Museum of Art.[19] In the course of the event, Moss was instructed to read marked verses from the Bible on the metaphysics of light, passages like the one quoted above apropos COSMIC RAY: "The light of the body is the eye; therefore when thine eye is single, thy whole body is also full of light; but when thine eye is dark, the body is also full of darkness (Luke 11:34)." While BREAKAWAY does without explicit theological allusion, flashes on screen from the leader perforations and the open gate of the camera carry intimations of an infinite beyond, viewed through the agency of his female subject, the contingency of life at its highest vitality made evident by light that stands in for what cannot change.

**40** Bruce Conner, stills from BREAKAWAY (black-and-white film, 1966)

Such a proposition—even so stated in a manner infinitely more heavy-handed than the film does—would not have seemed exceptional among San Francisco adepts of *zazen* and psychedelic revelations. Conner's way required weeks of labor demanding the most painstaking precision, the process a meditative discipline in itself as he cut and spliced the hundreds of edits required to synchronize the fractured moments of Basil's performance to her rhythmic anthem of release from the chains of fallen human existence. Having achieved that, he appended to his edit a mirror image, doubling the length of the film by running the first two and a half minutes (the duration of the song) backward, the music turning into unintelligible groans, yelps and bleats: the beginning is the end; the departure, the return. And such aural experimentation possessed as solid a grounding in the avant-gardism of the city as did BREAKAWAY's flickering imagery. Overlapping with the abstract filmmakers' world was the San Francisco Tape Music Center, founded in 1962 by the composers Morton Subotnik and Ramon Sender to serve as a laboratory and concert venue for electronic music. Coincident with the European Fluxus festivals, the launch of the Tape Center inaugurated an international hub for advanced art music of the kind that Paul McCartney and the Beatles would later absorb as they sought to exceed the pop formulae on which their first fame was based.[20]

The Beatles' initial use of purely electronic sounds, including tape loops and recorded instruments played backward, arrived in August 1966 on the last track on their album *Revolver*, "Tomorrow Never Knows." John Lennon, its principal composer, had consciously been seeking to channel into music the Leary/Alpert/Metzner *Psychedelic Experience*. "Play the game of existence to the end / of the beginning" goes the concluding chorus, a fair description of the reversed temporality in BREAKAWAY. When Lennon intones at the start, "Lay down all thoughts, surrender to the void / It is shining," such an aspiration would not have been lost on Conner, as this was the musical score he close to accompany his 1967 cut of LOOKING FOR MUSHROOMS, timing his edit to its length. One question remains as to whether he had done this before or after he sent the film to Lennon in London. All he wrote in a note later published by his distributor, Canyon Cinema, was: "Once I sent a print of LOOKING FOR MUSHROOMS to John Lennon and some cards that Mike McClure and I made."[21]

The cards he mentions merit attention in themselves. Fashioned sometime in 1966, they take up where the Trips Festival cover left off, but in a miniaturized form that seems to elude rather than court visibility. On twenty-five tiny sheets of paper, only two inches square, the pair printed a dense mandala drawing by Conner on one side and four words on the other, themselves configured as a square—the invitation being to arrange and re-arrange them, *Semina*-like, in grids of spontaneous verbal-visual poetry (fig. 41). They packaged each set in a simple stationer's envelope, the flap with the authors' names and the date, the front imprinted with ten words "leftover" from the one hundred printed on the cards. Their Wichita friend David Haselwood, likewise relocated to San Francisco, executed the fine printing.[22]

In return for his gifts, Conner received a reply from Lennon (fig. 42), likely in June 1967 (the date reads, "June, Moon, Spoon"). The first portion of the typewritten missive assumes the voice of a besotted female fan named Vera Button, a CONNERMANIAC prone to misspellings and professions of undying devotion. Dominating the lower portion of the sheet is a drawing by Lennon's son, Julian, a sunflower face with a dark insect-shape for a mouth, signed "J L 4," indicating his age in 1967, while in between is a succinct message bearing Lennon's personal signature:

Thank for films
Thank for cards
THANK FOR YOU.

The Beatle signs off with a matey "must think ob [sic] beatle production that is when we're through a small cycle" (*Sergeant Pepper's Lonely Hearts Club Band* had only just been released at the end of May). In the mention of a "beatle production" might lie the sign of a Conner–Beatles collaboration never to be; but it might rather indicate a preceding bond over the semi-definitive, decidedly trippy cut of LOOKING FOR MUSHROOMS, set to Lennon's "Tomorrow Never Knows," that Conner made in that year. It made a definite impression: Robert Fraser wrote to him independently on 24 June 1967, "John Lennon was knocked out to receive

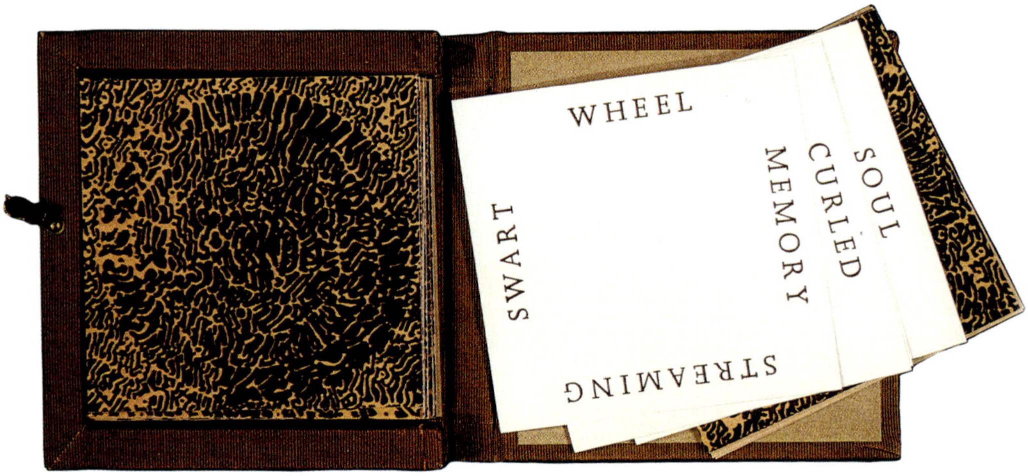


**41** Bruce Conner and Michael McClure, cards with case, 1966, printed by David Haselwood

LOOKING FOR MUSHROOMS. If you'd be kind enough to send five further copies of the movie I'd be grateful as apart from the three other Beatles there's me and another fanatical admirer who would be eager paying customers." [23]

The astute Beatles interpreter Ian MacDonald made considerable claims for that Beatles track along lines that make equivalent sense when applied to Conner's world that year.

June Moon Spoon
Weybridge englander.

)ear Bruce Conner,

You dont know me but Iknow you and you are my fave raveand I'd like a fab gear photo of you and your family and all your hogs and cats you must keep being such a world famous and Im not just saying that bacaz you are so as I said knownand dont just think of me as some little well you know CONNERMANIAC Im a truly inverted admimmeror and Its my sister what likes the monkees even though you are old and hairy . Ilove you evn though you are married tell your wife not to worry its not a deep down motherfuckinggreasyknickerskindoflove its awarmhighkneeholddaveclarkkindoftrue Bluesort of thing.Ilike hocking cricketwheels as you might have gathering.

Even though you are finished Iwill love you till the end of time-

Yours in a fishnet legiron

Vera Button.

say high to the dog wil

2636 558586585 8 6 69 7 6 tu 96 96 96i 97u yj-fgx ho tuf o-yit yuykg½-fg sjli 1hk khkj hkgj-t8yiyd

Thank for films
Thank for cards
THANK FOR YOU.

must think ob beatle production that is when were through a small cycle

LOVE FROM

John Lennon.

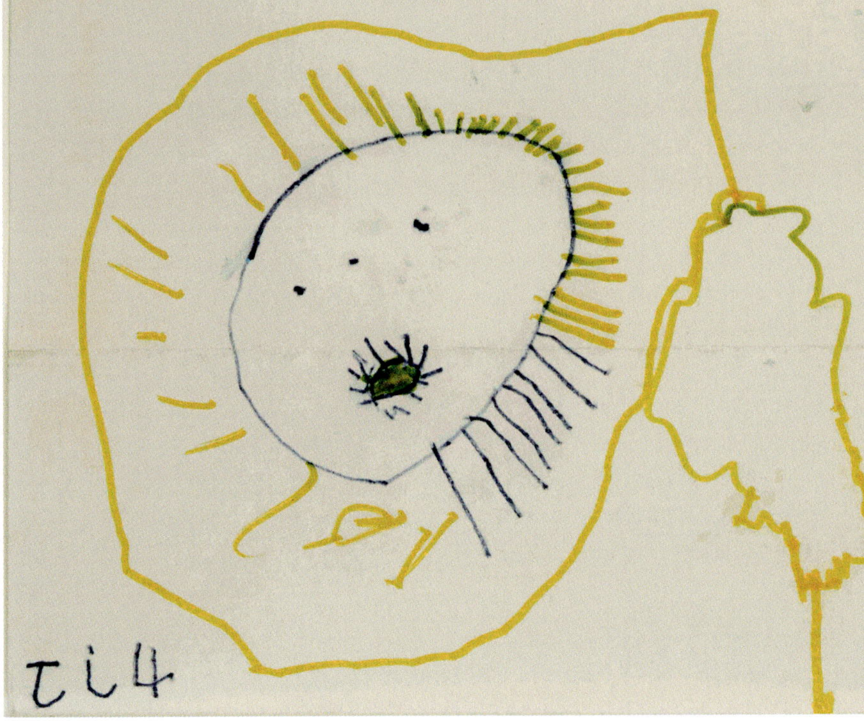


**42** Letter from John Lennon to Bruce Conner, June 1967, Bruce Conner Archives, Bancroft Library, University of California, Berkeley

"Tomorrow Never Knows," he writes, "launched the till-then élite-preserved concept of mind-expansion into pop, simultaneously drawing attention to consciousness-enhancing drugs and the ancient religious philosophies of the Orient, utterly alien to Western thought in their anti-materialism, rapt passivity, and world-skeptical focus on visionary consciousness." Though published in 2007, the late MacDonald's somewhat outmoded diction could readily belong to a later 1960s milieu and catches key components of the artist's particular personal ethos. The drone of Indian music as borrowed by the Beatles, MacDonald continues, "serving notice that the ensuing music will contain no tonal 'progress'—no change of key or chord," thus evoking the necessarily unchanging chord struck by the creator: "the Sound that is God," in the words of avant-garde drone composer La Monte Young.[24]

One shudders to think of the result had Conner taken a parallel approach to playing the harmonica; but his drawing had found its way to a profoundly cognate refusal of varying emphasis and legible development in a work of visual art. While he emphatically lacked the instant mass audience that Lennon enjoyed, there was an emerging circuit of communication in which his efforts on the page found their following. The events and activities that made the counterculture what it was remained nearly invisible to the established organs of news and publicity (with the exception of Ralph J. Gleason's forward-looking music column in the *Chronicle*). Access to vital information depended on word of mouth channeled via hubs like the Psychedelic Shop on Haight Street or Moe's Bookstore in Berkeley, hand-distributed posters, and mimeographed efforts like the Trips Festival Program, which resembled a poet's homemade chapbook. In the summer of 1966, Conner joined a group of floating membership, including members of the Progressive Labor Party, making a stab at starting a regular publication, to be backed by the Thelin brothers (Ron and Jay) who owned the Psychedelic Shop. The first effort, which appeared on 2 September 1966, was called *P.O. Frisco*, the initials standing for Psychedelphic Oracle: "That name was suggested by Bruce Conner," Ron Thelin attests, "which I always dug very much and fought for very hard."[25] But the harder political element dominated the single number to appear under that name, with the inaugural number of *Oracle of the City of San Francisco* coming out on 20 September. Signaling a move away from what Thelin called "a student, civil-rights, newspaper orientation," the October issue of the new monthly featured a Conner mandala drawing as its centerfold.

The *Oracle* continued until 1968 under its editor, Allen Cohen, with flamboyant, neo-art-nouveau graphics emerging by issue 3, as the paper established a central niche for itself in the practical and symbolic economy of the Haight and the archipelago of head communities across the entire Bay Area. In Cohen's exalted recollection,

> The Oracle would go from hand to hand and mind to mind in the evocative states unveiled by marijuana and LSD. It was a centering instrument for that intense, aesthetic, and expanded perceptual universe. . . . To achieve the oracular effects we wanted we would give the text, whether prose or poetry, to artists and ask them to design a page for it, not merely to illustrate it, but to make an organic unity of the word and the image. Most of the artists would conceive and manifest their designs in a state of expanded awareness.[26]

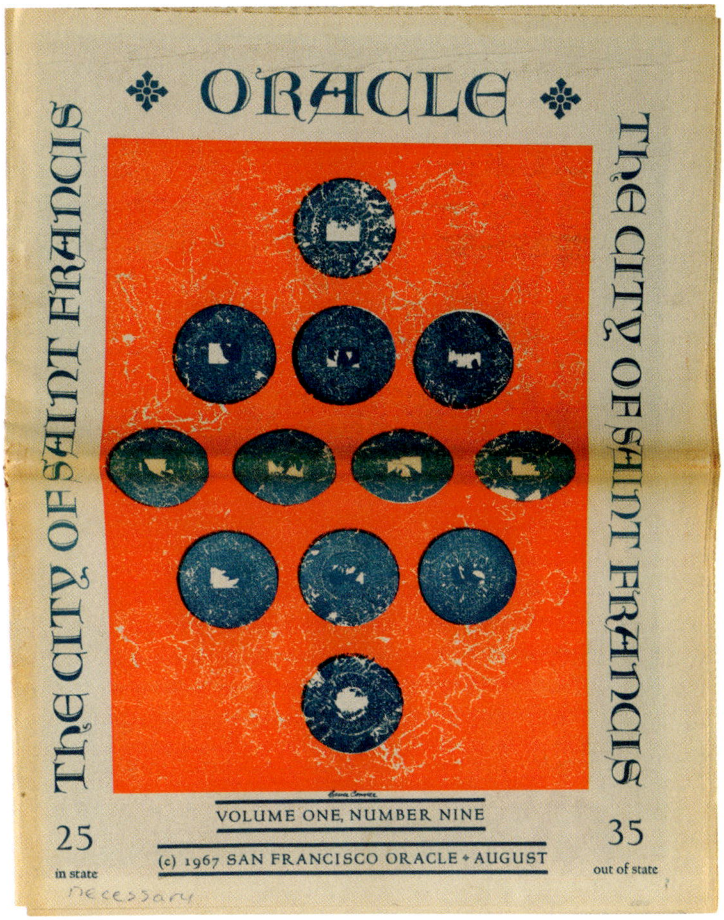


**43** Bruce Conner, cover illustration for *The City of Saint Francis Oracle* (August 1967)

Conner's next contribution to this enterprise did not arrive until issue 9, August 1967, but it graced the cover in several different pairs of contrasting colors: a drawing of twelve mandala circles arranged in a cruciform pattern, each of them composed of his signature intricacies of curvilinear pattern, irregular openings at the center and sometimes the edge of each disk (fig. 43). The surrounding field is just as densely articulated, such that it may well have taken him the entire ten months between his two *Oracle* contributions simply to finish the composition. Its slowed effect of disorientation, at least for Cohen's minds "in evocative states," complemented the kinetically disorienting impact of BREAKAWAY, the exacting labor on the two projects just following if not overlapping with one another. The impact of each thus depended on weeks and weeks of solitary, exacting concentration. It would not have been lost on Conner that each orbited the spontaneously immediate experiences of the ballroom concerts, ecstatic surrender to sensory surfeit and disorder being the reason so many attended them.

A younger San Francisco State filmmaker, Ben Van Meter, had started a new light-artist company early in 1967, forging a regular relationship with Chet Helms's Avalon. Van Meter's own films had carried an evident debt to Conner's, and he succeeded in recruiting the past master, now thirty-four years old, to join him as an active presence on the psychedelic scene: "I worked at the Avalon Ballroom up through 1967," Conner recalled with evident pleasure,

> That was three or four nights a week with a light show called the North American Ibis Alchemical Light Show. It more or less culminated all my work with motion pictures. Because I was working with two or three sixteen millimeter projectors in the same way. There was a whole bank of slide projectors with sixty slides in each: there were a dozen of those. And three strobe lights, and overhead liquid projectors. There were five or six other people who were working with me on this. It was like working in a rock band. People would improvise. We were improvising off the music and the music would improvise off us. It was like a 200 degree screen.[27]

This new vocation prompted a dramatic adaptation of his intricate drawing style in both macro- and micro-dimensions. He took his capacity for taking pains to a new level by filling in with vibrantly multicolored patterns the two-inch-square acetate surface of clear 35-millimeter slides (fig. 44), a labor to match the labors of Harry Smith on his hand-painted films. And, likewise, he was then able to witness those miniscule patterns assume a pulsating size thousands of times larger as they played over the walls and bodies assembled in the Avalon Ballroom.

The totality of the ballroom sensorium depended on the light-show artists expanding the spatial, kinetic, and chromatic dimensions of projected light beyond the capacity of film in ways that challenged Conner's ambivalent allegiance to that medium: "Most of my movies prior to that time dealt with sound and a more or less visual mime to the music (or sound)," he reflected; but the light show was doing all that at an exponential gain in intensity and, what was more, entering the real-time dimension of performance that had been the province of music. His harmonica skills, however enthusiastically expressed, were never going to win him a place at the front of the stage. As he finished up his outstanding film commitments, however, he found his place behind it: "Since my films were extensions of music, or music in relation to image, what more perfect way to improvise and create at the same time it's happening and to have it immediately consumed rather than going through the long delaying tactic of working for months and months and then trying to coerce people into a little room to look at this sort of thing."[28]

Conner is well known for his laments at this same moment concerning his career as an artist and the fate of his works as they passed though the conduits of dealer's storerooms and collector's living spaces, shuttling on and off museum walls, his frustrations building to such a breaking point that he resolved to stage his own disappearance: "I wouldn't answer correspondence. I quit teaching. I quit exhibiting. I quit reading about art shows. I stopped going

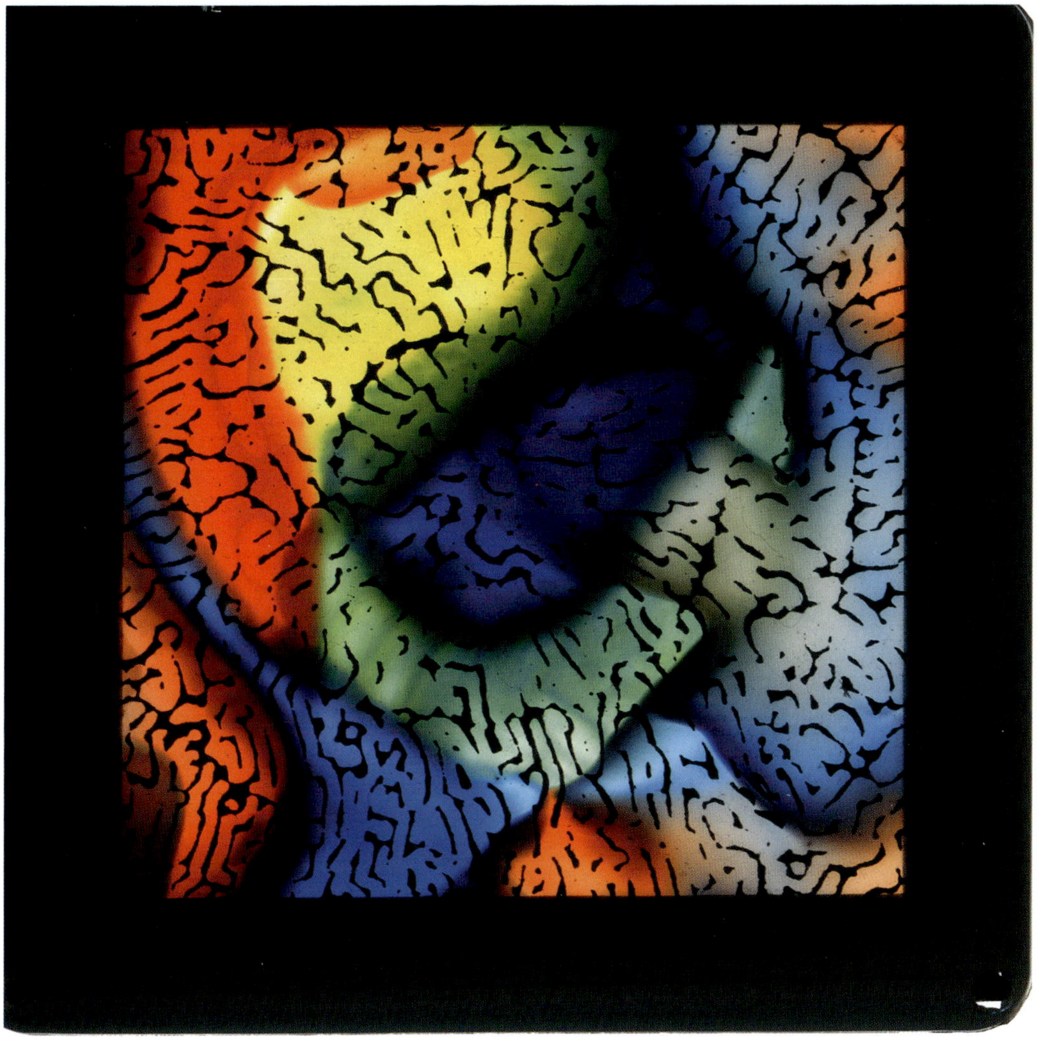

44 Bruce Conner, hand-painted lightshow transparency, c. 1967, 5 × 5 cm, courtesy Conner Family Trust

to museums and galleries. I supported myself as a janitor and a salesman in a knickknack shop and selling tickets at a movie theater."[29] Light-show artists worked in the shadows behind the spotlights, their individual, dark silhouettes undifferentiated. While serving his lifelong infatuation with blues and gospel-based music, Conner's role in the North American Ibis Alchemical Company, which he largely directed over its last year of existence, eminently suited this retreat. The rise and eclipse of the counterculture could stand as the American epic of our times, and every epic can use its wily Odysseus, the hero who declared, "No-man is my name, No-man do they call me."

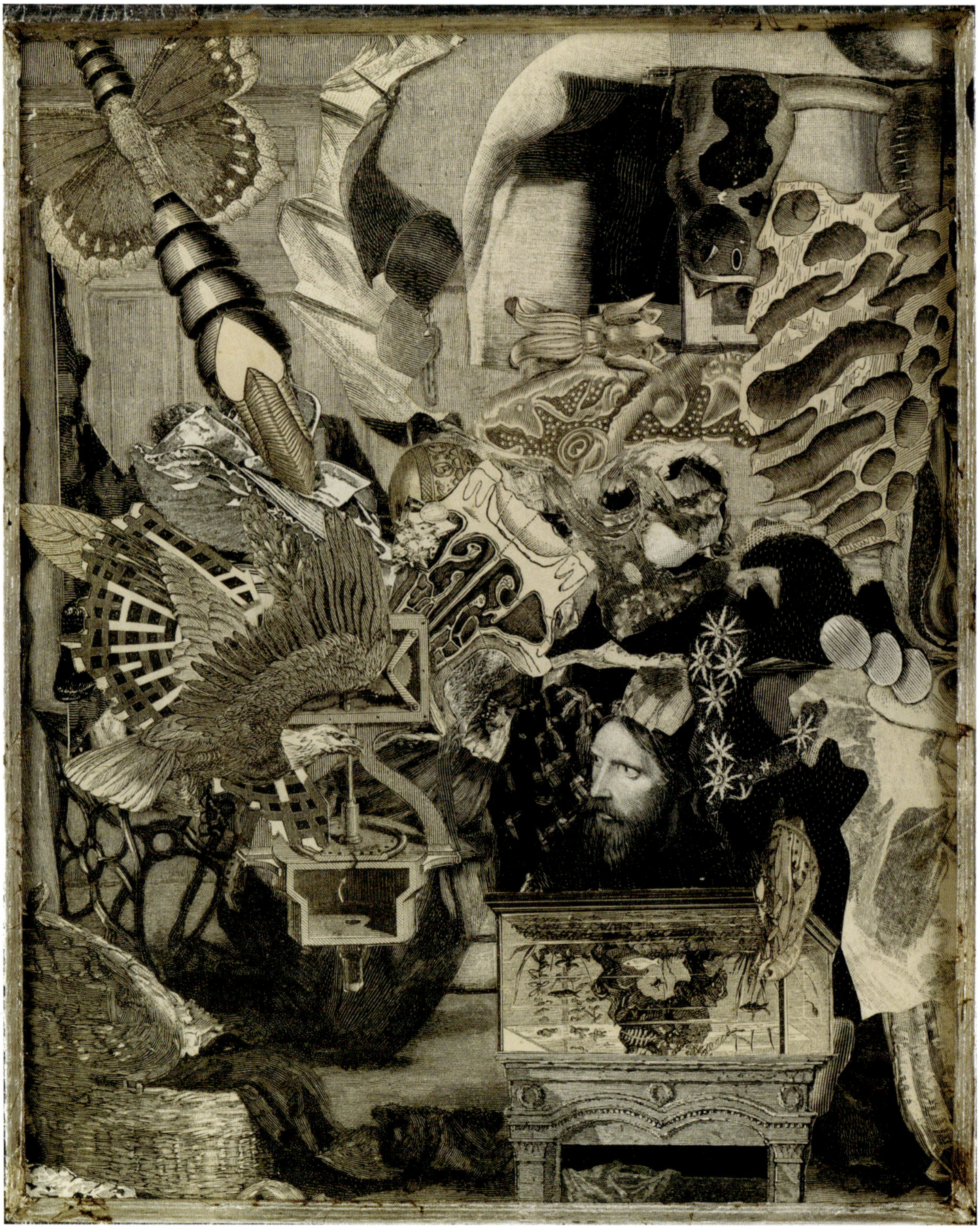

45 Bruce Conner, UNTITLED (DENNIS HOPPER ONE-MAN SHOW), 1960–65, collage, 18.4 × 15.2 cm, private collection

FIVE

# LIVING UP TO THEIR REPUTATIONS

Conner's countercultural immersion in the *Oracle* and the Avalon, seemingly so Haight-centric, was not as straightforward as his own recorded testimony might make it seem. There was another counterculture nearby in Los Angeles in which he was an active if less frequent participant, one that had coevolved with the San Francisco scene in the early stages, but now was taking on a markedly distinct character. And prominent in that development was his boon companion Dennis Hopper.

In Hopper's mind, his gradual rehabilitation within the film business would not be restricted to featured acting roles: he had it in mind to direct. Like a number of his contemporaries and friends, the necessary apprenticeship proceeded though the production company of Roger Corman, the venerable master of quick production in genre categories: horror, bikers, beach parties, but with more elevated aspirations than the B-movie norm. His loose way of working allowed the likes of Hopper, Peter Fonda, and Jack Nicholson access, alongside acting, to scriptwriting, producing, and second-unit directing. By 1966, the counterculture had surfaced in Los Angeles to the point that it, too, could be exploited for quick cinematic profit. The result was Corman's producing and directing a film titled *The Trip*, written by Nicholson and starring Fonda, with Hopper both in a featured role and directing the second-unit footage of the tripping Fonda wandering the Sunset Strip.

Conner had followed the Dead, the Airplane, and Big Brother into the down-at-heel ballrooms in unfashionable neighborhoods where the San Francisco concert scene took off. There were, of course, new bands in Los Angeles, led by the former folkie Jim McGuinn's Byrds, likewise channeling folk and blues into danceable rock. The Mothers of Invention, Buffalo Springfield, Love, and the Doors would follow, musically equal if not superior to their counterparts in San Francisco. But the social geography and entertainment history of the metropolis to the south meant that their venues and interface with audiences were qualitatively different. Lying outside the reach of the city's jurisdiction, the Sunset Strip had its own particular history of license and excess. The shells of what once had been glamorous nightspots catering to the movie colony and the local mafia—Ciro's, the Mocambo, and the Trocadero among them—lined this unincorporated mile or so of Sunset Boulevard approaching Beverly Hills from the east. From the mid-1960s, young bands and dancers found one another in these repurposed venues. As Conner trailed after Hopper during the filming of *The Trip*, he would have swum along this brightly lit commercial corridor, overtopped with colossal billboards, heaving with teenagers from across the basin, while coursing with cruising cars packed with more. The Sheriff's Department and State Police would be out in force, and famous clashes occurred in November 1966 when the county attempted to close down a club that catered to patrons under the drinking age.

Conner appears near the beginning of *The Trip* in a non-credited, non-speaking part but filling the frame as he takes a hit and passes the joint in a crowd gathered by Hopper's character and where Fonda's arrives to connect with his LSD guide (played by an over-bearded Bruce Dern). The short, quickie production was released at the end of August 1967 (just catching the Summer of Love, as Corman must have calculated). Are Conner's fingerprints anywhere visible in the production? Early in the film, projected moiré and kaleidoscopic patterns play over lovemaking bodies in the dark, but that device had become by then a commonplace stand-in for hallucinatory sensations and would not have required his particular expertise. Utterly alien to him would have been the jejune, medievalized dream sequences (though with amusing quotations from Ingmar Bergman's 1957 *Seventh Seal*) that Fonda and Hopper were left free to film as a second unit in the Southern California backcountry.[1] But the Conner touch appears more than evident in two short sequences, hardly two minutes each. Distilling down hours of street footage, following the wandering Fonda character from every angle, yielded the sort of hyper-kinetic blizzard of impressions pioneered in COSMIC RAY, the mental acuity of a psilocybin high hopefully conveyed by a moving image. The conceit of *The Trip*, like the pretext for the 1966 Trips Festival in San Francisco, was to convey the experience of LSD without the drug. It defied the alarmist norms of the exploitation genre by portraying LSD therapy, much as Michael Agron had attested, as positive and life affirming. And there turned out to be a considerable audience for this message, the film taking in some forty times the cost of its production.

That success, crucially for what was to follow, validated Hopper's instincts in the eyes of the studio moneymen—instincts in part instilled by emulation of Conner's. And the latter, taking this identity-transfer in stride, sought to reinforce rather than contest it. Since the early 1960s, Conner had pursued an artistic sideline collaging together bits and pieces of nineteenth-century steel engravings in a way that inevitably recalls Surrealist works in a similar vein by Max Ernst (fig. 45). The derivation is apt to the degree that Surrealism sought via art to mirror if not induce expanded faculties of mind, a project arguably abandoned too soon. Conner began this series during his extended stay in Mexico, the time of what he referred to as "lots of drugs and pyramids."[2] Alongside the beginning of his abstract drawings, he used the joins and splices of these collages, most of them barely bigger than postcards, to generate visionary architecture and deliriously convoluted Baroque interiors that rivaled in absorbing intricacy the sort of densely packed mazes he achieved in 23 KENWOOD AVENUE (fig. 28). This particular example embeds a three-quarter portrait head of a long-haired, bearded figure with a marked resemblance to Hopper. Whether intended at the time or not (the two are said first to have met at Ferus in 1962), it found new purpose in 1967 when Conner sought to exhibit the series in Los Angeles as the DENNIS HOPPER ONE-MAN SHOW.

His hoped-for venue, Nicholas Wilder's prestigiously advanced West Hollywood gallery, balked over the confusion that the show's title and false attributions were likely to engender, all the more because Hopper had been doing his own visual art, which carried certain evident debts to Conner's example. As Conner was aware, his friend's approach to film montage took the debt to another level, which made his "gift" of a fully realized art project a highly ambivalent gesture. But it also entailed Conner's assuming an alternative identity distinct from the one he occupied in San Francisco, as he had begun to operate in Los Angeles in ways that were largely invisible to his networks to the north and where the threadbare, voluntary poverty of the janitor and ticket taker was far less conspicuous.[3]

■

Through all of Conner's numerous interviews (which became something of a métier for him), he rarely speaks about Los Angeles. In one, referring to a certain work only in passing, he notes, "I had this in a garage down at Thousand Oaks at Janss. Larry Janss."[4] Laconic the statement might be, but it opens onto a wide landscape of wealth and artistic privilege. Lawrence Janss, then a teenage aspiring photographer, was descended from a family of property magnates who had developed vast tracts of the Los Angeles basin, including the UCLA campus and surrounding Westwood Village—Thousand Oaks, the renamed Conejo Valley at the far northwest of the county, being just the latest of their projects. His father, Edwin Janss Jr., was also one of the premier collectors of contemporary art in the region and particularly close to Walter Hopps. Alongside his collection of recent objects, the elder Janss possessed one artifact that joins the family with the earlier common pursuits of Conner and Hopps: a stone mushroom with a figurated stem representing a crouching jaguar with a human head, its type most commonly associated with the proto-Mayan center of Kaminaljuyu in the Guatemalan highlands (largely beneath present-day Guatemala City). Students of ritual psilocybin use among Indigenous Mexicans insisted on the continuity between these current practices and the evidence of a sacred-mushroom cult in the first millennium BCE. Albert Hofmann, the pharmacologist who discovered the effects of LSD in 1943, kept a similar figurine on his desk at the Sandoz offices in Switzerland.[5]

One of Conner's undertakings in May 1967 brought his more recent young-Hollywood connections together with Janss family patronage. The mainstream director Blake Edwards (of *Pink Panther* fame) needed a "psychedelically" painted, live elephant for a forgettable Peter Sellers vehicle called *The Party*. Conner carried out the assignment, presumably a lucrative one given the lavish studio budgets of the period, and he played along when William Wilson, the art critic for the *Los Angeles Times*, showed up for an interview, describing him as "a bespectacled Rhodes Scholar gone cowboy" in a silver-studded denim jacket

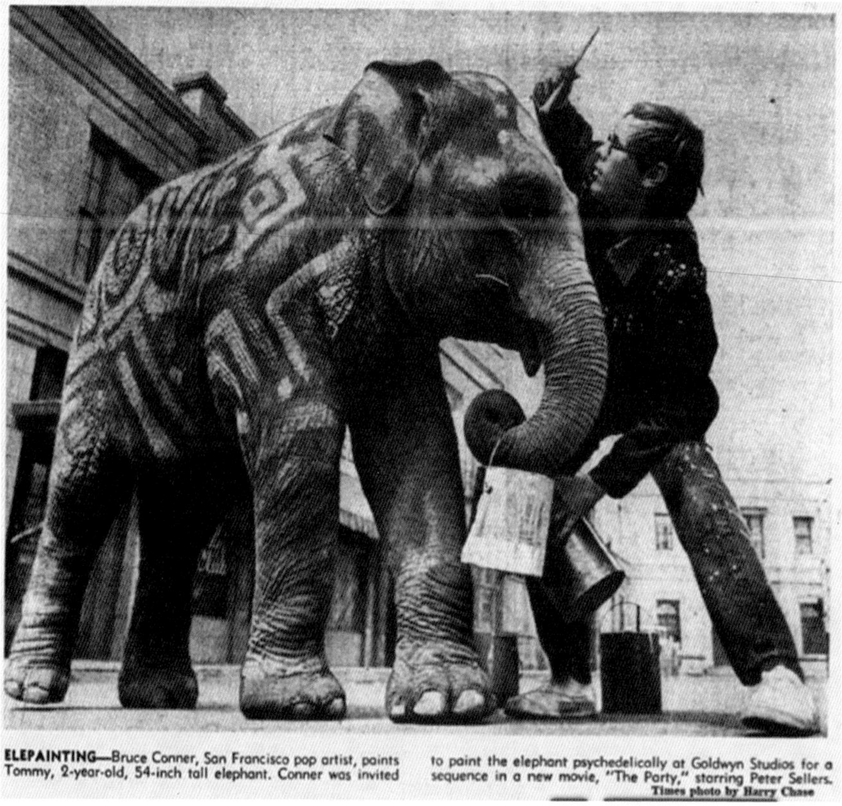
ELEPAINTING—Bruce Conner, San Francisco pop artist, paints Tommy, 2-year-old, 54-inch tall elephant. Conner was invited to paint the elephant psychedelically at Goldwyn Studios for a sequence in a new movie, "The Party," starring Peter Sellers.
Times photo by Harry Chase

46 Bruce Conner painting an elephant, photograph by Harry Chase, *Los Angeles Times* (May 1967)

(fig. 46). As Wilson reported, affecting the self-serious manner of the art historian, "The paint surface had been prepared with an underground of green spray. The artist applied his paint with a large round-headed brush, working primarily in orange and red. His style was largely geometrically abstract although he did employ certain recognizable iconographical symbols: the word 'Love' . . . a large red heart, and a circular symbol enclosing a 'Y' shape which has been prominently displayed at love-ins and peace marches."[6] A pack of photographers were in attendance, one among them Dagny Janss, Larry's sister, who presumably had accompanied Conner to the movie lot.

Though his effort did not appear in the final film (which was fortunate, given its stereotypically racist character), Conner brought to bear all his experience, gained from living in the Haight, of the dumbed-down popular translations of the counterculture on the verge of overwhelming that community. Just as he played it straight with the *Times* reporter, how-

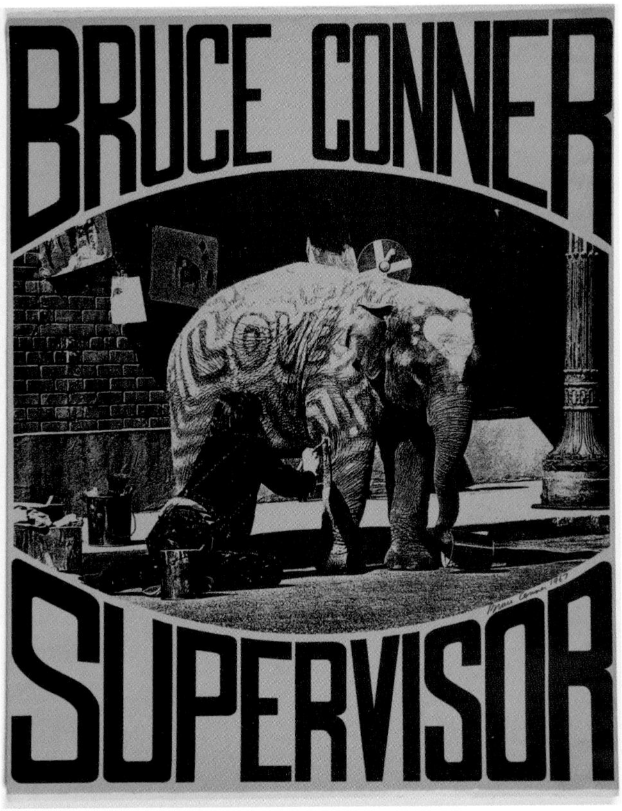


47 Dagny Janss (photograph) and
Edmund Shea (design), 1967,
screen print, 60 × 58.2 cm,
Collection San Francisco Museum of Modern Art

ever, he deployed the photograph taken on the day by Dagny Janss in a campaign poster (fig. 47) when he ran for the San Francisco County Board of Supervisors in the fall of that same year: with his back to the camera, he unfurls a fun-house Southern-Californian mirror held up to the Summer of Love. It has been all too easy to diminish episodes like the DENNIS HOPPER ONE-MAN SHOW, the elephant painting, or the run for office with words like stunt or prank, by which the interpreter arrogates from the artist a capacity for judgment as to what counts as a suitably significant endeavor. Kevin Hatch makes a worthy effort to resolve the dilemma by invoking the folkloric archetypes of the Clown or Fool, proposing that these types "have a common ancestor in the individual under possession, . . . inspired by ancient sacred wisdom."[7] Following this lead, it might make greater sense to call on Conner's own adept coinage: "the Psychedelphic Oracle," by which he embedded Apollo's conduit at Delphi into the parlance of the drug cults. Oracles speak only with gnomic indirection, shifting responsibility for choosing one path over another, whether to salvation or to catastrophe, from speaker to supplicant. And oracles also issue their pronouncements from a seat of authority, a place that Conner attained for a time, in form if not in substance, via his political candidacy.

The nature of the office itself may escape many unfamiliar with the arcana of California administrative statutes. County supervisors typically preside over expansive patchworks of municipal jurisdictions. The city and county of San Francisco, however, are unique in the state by being coterminous with one another. The county oversees only one compact city with no hinterland, and, at that time, prospective supervisors, of whom there were six, all ran at large, that is, competing for the votes of the population as a whole, just as a mayoral candidate would do. Availing himself of the automatic channels of publicity that came with his candidacy, Conner could count on the widest possible hearing for his series of decidedly oracular pronouncements.

It is misleading, however, to imagine Conner's semi-serious run for this powerful post as his idiosyncratic action alone. In fact, it had not been his idea to begin with, and it enlisted the efforts of several close companions from his Haight-Ashbury-based network. The photographer Edmund Shea had originally hatched the idea but had had to bow out after a drug arrest. Shea and Conner shared a close colleague in the poet Richard Brautigan, each of them being closer to him than to one another. Brautigan was at this point on the verge of publishing his fragmentary, elliptical novel *Trout Fishing in America*, which would bring him both a fortune and national celebrity. In the interim, however, he had been living his typical hand-to-mouth existence, holed up in a run-down apartment that boasted a sculptural work by Conner. The writer had, moreover, accumulated so many eccentric possessions around it that the apartment had become an outsized, walk-in assemblage in its own right. Conner referred to it as "the Museum" and was so fond of the place that he insisted, if Brautigan ever gave up the lease, that it be passed on to him as a studio.[8]

Brautigan's mode of life might have seemed shambolic, but he was acutely conscious of his cultivated visual image as a tool in achieving literary success. Towering in height, he accentuated his stature with a white, tall-crowned Stetson, which topped a forty-niner's mustachioed visage and outfit to match—though mellowed with hippie beads. So he appears in the subsequently famous cover image of *Trout Fishing*. Its photographer, Erik Weber, had taken off for India, so Brautigan had lined up Shea to take his place. Via this same circuit, Conner decided to take up Shea's candidacy for Supervisor, with more of the Haight network in tow. That meant, among others, the Diggers, the Mime Troupe offshoot of radically anarchist social activists, whose aim, in service to what they called "life theater," was to make the Haight over into something as close as possible to a currency-free gift economy. Taking their name from the agrarian communists of the English Civil War, the principals of the group—Peter Berg, Emmett Grogan, and Peter Coyote among them—kept out of view as much as possible, their shadowy existence behind the potlatches of free clothes and free food adding to the immense community prestige they enjoyed.[9]

Berg and Conner together plotted how to bring the issue of peace to the fore. This core motivation for the campaign "stunt" has received much less attention than it merits: "We were discussing this about the end of the war," said Conner (anticipating John and Yoko), "and the thing to do was to *end* it and tell everybody it's ended and to celebrate its end and put into people's minds the concept of the war is over."[10] That visionary approach would have cut little ice with the Berkeley-based activists, and the event that Berg and Brautigan organized at the Straight Theater proved elliptical to a degree. The latter came up with idea of photographing the words 'DO NOT TOUCH' from the artist's 1964 canvases and reproducing them on hundreds of small file cards. Having taken the cards up to the theater balcony, Brautigan waited until Conner finished his speech, then threw them all over the heads of the audience so they covered the floor like a paper blizzard. There they lay, the audience largely obeying the printed admonition, with Conner being as puzzled by the gesture as was everyone else: "It was sort of a mystery to me why he had chosen to do that."[11]

Though perhaps no more mysterious than Conner's own pronouncements as a candidate. In his printed pamphlet, under "occupation," Conner listed "Nothing," later explaining to the curator Joan Rothfuss that this meant "an empty space that becomes whatever fills it." Under the heading of qualifications for office, he returned to the full biblical passage from Luke extolling the light that fills the body, adding a prophetic ending from an unconnected verse: "For there is nothing covered; that shall not be revealed; neither hid that shall not be known."[12] His place on the ballot also brought exposure during the candidates' forum on public television, where he again read from the sayings of Christ, this time on love, mercy, and war.[13] That Conner also wrote a speech composed as a list of desserts would likewise fall under the oracle's remit of permitted obscurity. Shea pitched in on the two memorable posters, one centered on a studio portrait of a beatifically posed toddler (out of the mouths of babes); the other based on the painted elephant, on which Shea bestowed the antique look and old-timey design of the Avalon Ballroom poster style associated with Alton Kelley and Stanley Mouse (fig. 47). The pattern on the elephant's hide in its central image had sent up the media version of the Haight, but its new context recast "LOVE" from a Hollywood hippie cliché into a solemn injunction consistent with Conner's elliptical quotations from scripture, a diametrical shift in meaning that depended on the divide of his persona in San Francisco from the one he occupied in Los Angeles, along with the wall of obscurity he maintained between the two countercultural scenes.

■

The divine or diabolical madness that surrounded Dennis Hopper was of another order than the deceptively elliptical interventions of the Psychedelphic Oracle. The trio of younger principals involved in *The Trip*—Hopper, along with Peter Fonda, and Jack Nicholson—reassembled in 1968 to make a new film that Fonda had conceived as an update of the biker genre, a Roger Corman staple in which all had acted in the past. This time, however, the bikers would be cut loose from gang identities and criminal menace; instead, they would be seekers and free spirits, just as the creators saw themselves and their countercultural friends. Fonda would produce and Hopper would direct, while they also played the two chopper-riding leads, Wyatt and Billy (after the archetypal Western hero and anti-hero), setting off from California and intent on arriving in New Orleans in time for Mardi Gras. Having recruited the veteran satirist Terry Southern to produce a script, the pair eventually found their way to Nicholson for the part of a straight, small-town lawyer who falls in with their quest, first to his delight and then to his doom. The success enjoyed by *The Trip* made the project an easier sell, though the new venture bore faint resemblance to the actual hip, drug-infused milieu around them. Ken Kesey, a small-town Oregon bruiser at heart, had brought the Hell's Angels into the margins of the Bay Area counterculture, but hippies did not on the whole ride motorcycles (both Fonda and Hopper were themselves shaky on them). *Easy Rider*, as Southern christened it, was a genre mash-up from the start: among other things, a buddy road trip with precedents going back decades, while ostensibly catching the moment of the psychedelic era at its peak. For all these reasons, *Easy Rider* was as much a business proposition as it was an expression of cultural rebellion, one designed to touch multiple ages and audiences. Hopper never tired of crowing openly that it would overthrow the ossified old Hollywood of the established studios.

Obliged to begin filming in New Orleans, so as not to miss the 1968 Mardi Gras festivities, Hopper's firmest early idea was to reprise his overtly Conneresque segments of *The Trip*, this time with improvised filming in 16 mm among the revelers on Bourbon Street and then in the deserted gothic alleyways of Saint Louis Cemetery No. 1, where the emotional culmination of the film was to occur. Conner does not appear to have been among Hopper's party, but Toni Basil was there to play one of two prostitutes who accompany Wyatt and Billy to the parade and the cemetery, where the characters drop acid together. Without much sense of the preceding story, Hopper opted to heighten the intensity by hectoring his fellow cast members into distressing psychological and physical self-exposure, creating a nightmare version of the confrontation with self that the LSD therapy of a Michael Agron was intended to induce. So extreme had Hopper's abusive volatility become that Fonda called his co-star's wife, the actress Brooke Hayward, in Los Angeles, warning her to take their children and leave the house before the actors and crew returned.

She delayed taking that drastic step, and one evening some weeks later, as Hayward later relayed to writer Peter Biskind, "Dennis came striding into the house accompanied by underground filmmaker Bruce Conner [who] sat down at the Victorian organ and started to play." Husband and wife faced off, Hopper full of threats, "Conner still pounding at the organ like a mad Phantom of the Opera, refusing to look up." Taking Conner aside, she pleaded, "Bruce, I want you to get Dennis out of here now, far away." He replied, "I don't want to get in the middle of this," to which she hissed, "I'm not asking you to get in the middle of this. I want you to get him out of the house. On some excuse, go down to Malibu, go see Dean Stockwell, so I can get myself together."[14] After their departure, she seized the opportunity to pack up and leave with the three children they shared, but Hopper and presumably Conner never made it to Malibu. From the house perched above the Sunset Strip they had barely entered the main thoroughfare on the journey westward before Hopper was stopped and arrested on suspicion of marijuana possession. The chief financier of the film stood his bail and spirited him out of town on the pretext of a lengthy expedition to scout locations, while his wife began divorce proceedings.

Amid this rush of events, Conner's name drops out of that story, but it remained one to conjure with, as Hopper later forged the unwieldy footage into something with a coherent feel and look, one built on abrupt cuts, indifference to conventional continuity, and technical "flaws," like lens flare left in—all wholly artificial, but carrying a documentary effect of unvarnished truth. Said Fonda approvingly, "It was Bruce Conner's influence on Dennis that got him to cut as wildly as he did, which was totally against the principles we had all studied, and it seemed free-form and abstract."[15] Only the thoroughly Conner-like proposal to run the credits upside down met with resistance. But Hopper's grandiose ambition to create a four-hour epic required removing him from the final edit; his collaborators eased him into a stay in Taos, New Mexico—the new home he had discovered on his scouting foray—to work exclusively on the New Orleans footage. Once again, the rapid-fire cuts are vintage Conner, his muse Toni Basil at the center of the proceedings. The claustrophobic passageways of the aboveground graveyard, an outdoor museum of florid ornamentation and statuary, echoed the atavistic look of Conner's collages from old engravings. And the murky original footage, which had dismayed everyone at its first screening, came out redeemed, bleached and grainy with apparent age, functioning much as originally intended

Was Conner there in Taos? His presence seems unrecorded, other than at one remove via Hopper's editing decisions. But it is nonetheless tempting to think so, given that he is documented as being on hand while the first edits were being applied to Hopper's next film, the portentously named *The Last Movie*. Its director now occupied the Taos adobe mansion once owned by the heiress and arts patron Mabel Dodge Luhan, purchased with the profits from *Easy Rider* and allowing for a large, rotating entourage. Hopper had not in any way moderated his substance intake or dangerously erratic behavior, putting himself in even greater professional jeopardy with an eccentric story, filmed early in 1970 at extreme altitude in Peru, about an American movie crew that leaves behind a lethal sort of cargo cult after departing a location in a small village. The chartered plane carrying crew and cronies—Conner, Basil, and Stockwell among them—filled with pot smoke the minute it left the ground, becoming the jet-propelled Hollywood version of the old Kesey bus.[16]

Once on the ground, Conner made himself useful by helping scout locations in the near-magical setting, though his presence has been submerged in subsequent accounts by such tales of drug intake and general misbehavior as to render countercultural liberation into a decadent parody of itself: the songwriter Kris Kristofferson, working on songs for the soundtrack and playing a small part, drily observed, "Suddenly you're 33, in Peru, with a gang of guys living up to their reputations."[17] The shoot nevertheless proceeded with reasonable efficiency, under the steady, gifted cinematographer László Kovács, yielding forty hours of printed film for Hopper to render into an releasable feature. Conner's particular gifts may not this time have been so apposite; but he remained at Hopper's side, traveling to Taos four times to offer his counsel. When Hopper married the singer and actress Michelle Phillips, who had a minor part in the film, on their return to Taos from Peru, Conner officiated at the double-ring ceremony, dressed for the occasion as an ordained reverend of the Universal Life Church (so ill-considered was the match, however, that a traumatized Phillips left the compound after eight days and immediately filed for divorce).[18]

Conner's steadfast presence in Taos, despite Hopper's benders, rages, and gunplay, shows laudable loyalty at a minimum, or something deeper, more like mutual possession in an uncanny sense, consistent with the occupation of an oracle's body by another spirit. For his part, Hopper, a fabled glutton for credit at the expense of his other collaborators, never hesitated to acknowledge his debts to Conner. The two found ways to stay in one another's orbit, the artist, in particular, falling into occasional occupations around Hollywood filmmaking, once appearing as an extra dancer in a club scene choreographed by Basil for a teen exploitation picture called *The Cool Ones*. Peter Fonda would employ him in 1971 as an associate producer on his own debut as director, a period western called *The Hired Hand*.[19] Hardly major but, nonetheless, a world away from the outward modesty he adopted in his San Francisco existence as janitor, shop assistant, and movie ticket taker—but not an artist, so far as he could help it: "When I would get letters regarding exhibitions, my work, etc., I would throw them away, sometimes sent it back saying DECEASED."[20]

*Rolling Stone* magazine had followed the notorious Hopper to Peru and to Taos, documenting the tortured saga of *The Last Movie*. One of its topline reporters, David Felton, also caught up with Conner in 1971. "The career of artist Bruce Conner is as unpredictable as his pioneer assemblages and films," he informed his young, rock-oriented readership; "For 15 years he has dabbled among the great and weird, the straight and near-straight around the country. He has produced light shows, played the harmonica and run for supervisor of San Francisco." But now the journalist finds him making his living "in that city as a minor box office attraction, collecting $2 per film buff at the Interplayers Theater near Aquatic Park. Thin and scholarly in a gray business suit, Conner sorted out change during a Von Stroheim twin-bill."

The main business of the piece, however, and the reason for this backstory was the career of Mel Lyman, he and Conner having crossed paths in Boston eight years before, when Lyman was playing harmonica in the Kweskin Jug Band. As noted above, Lyman had also been a fixture around the Alpert–Leary house, where he had observed and absorbed enough to leave the band and set himself up in Leary's absence as a local guru and life guide in his own right. Lyman's sway over a growing community of adherents, including Kweskin himself, became such that they formed themselves into an inner-city commune, one in which Lyman's words were received as near-to-divine revelation. Conner offered some clear memories of the first stirrings in this direction: "We'd talk about things. One time Mel was talking about morning glory seeds and how they put people to sleep sometimes, and I thought that was a real drag, you know, that must not really be enlightenment. And the conversation went into talk about rituals and exercises; and all of a sudden it started hingeing around what is God, what is Cosmic Consciousness and everything." He remembered, with a mock-acceptance of blame, proposing to Lyman that "mostly what people do when they talk about God is a projection of what they think God is, and it always comes down to a projection from a person. So the best way to find out what God is is to say you're God yourself."[21]

Felton had shared a Pulitzer at the *Los Angeles Times* for reporting on the Watts Rebellion and had written the bulk of *Rolling Stone*'s deep coverage of the Manson family. That effort, along with its saturation reporting on the deadly debacle of the Rolling Stones free concert at Altamont, established the magazine as a cultural bellwether beyond its rock-music roots. Felton's interview with Conner helped introduce another mini-epic of long-form journalism, which stretched over two issues, the journalistic hook being that Lyman was the east-coast Manson, with all the mind control and threatening aura if not the murders: one more elegy lamenting the descent of the counterculture into social dysfunction. In this regard, Conner served not just as a convenient informant for a San Francisco-based journalist, but also as a voice uncannily wise before the fact, not to say oracular, present throughout most of the counterculture's ascent and now its seeming crash. That narrative has always been a prop to the right-wing, Nixonian reconsolidation then already underway, however, and it is more than doubtful that Conner would ever have subscribed to it.

He would reconnect with Hopper when resurrecting the DENNIS HOPPER ONE-MAN SHOW as a portfolio of prints in 1973. On the occasion of their opening display, the two of them drolly acted out their exchange of identities, each posing in a director's chair emblazoned with the name of the other. But Conner's moment in the Hollywood counterculture had ended, in significant part because that moment was itself already flickering out. Hopper does not direct again for nearly twenty years. Wallace Berman dies in a road accident in 1976. The long cultural arc so well illuminated by the first phase of Conner's career finds itself, though far from extinct, scattered to the winds.

The implicit account of that arc offered here has, however, been missing its essential complement. Conner anathemized war and the war machine from the depths of his being, but the swelling movement that emerged in 1965 against the American war in Indochina has been largely absent from this record. That mobilization, along with the newly militant advocacy of rights and recognition for persecuted minorities into which it fed, occupies the first of the following two chapters. The scale and scope of events coming to a head in the late 1960s require, moreover, a wider view over the activities of multiple artists, so the gear and gauge of exposition that follows will undergo a shift. But the multiple countercultural forces that Conner's progress brought into focus remain a constant.

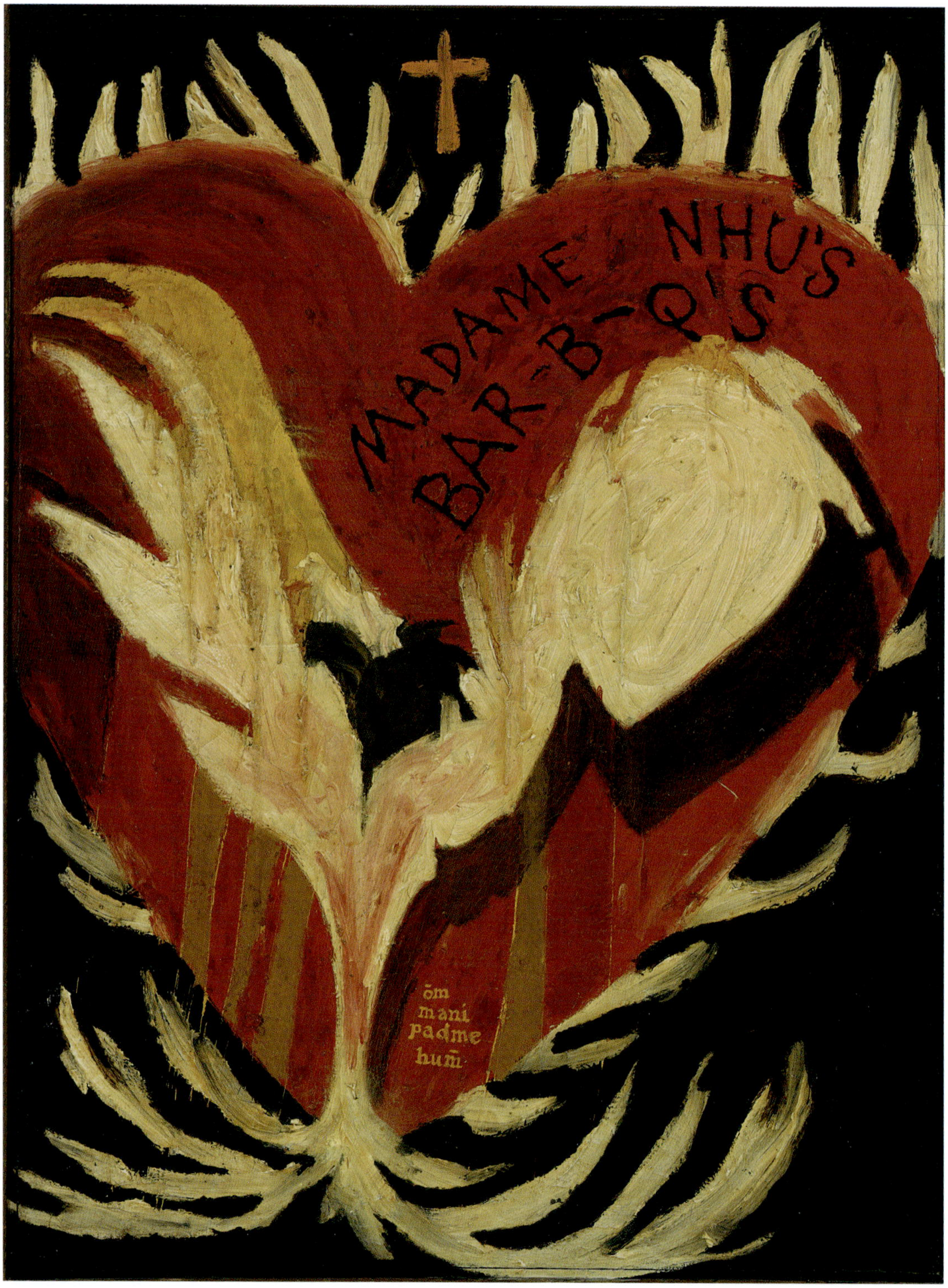


**48** Wally Hedrick, *Madame Nhu's Bar-B-Qs*, 1963,
oil on canvas, 167.6 × 121.9 cm,
Fine Arts Museums of San Francisco

SIX

# BEARING WITNESS TO WAR

WHEN BRUCE CONNER FIRST MIGRATED TO SAN FRANCISCO, determined, as his first priority, to avoid military service, one new friend would have been the first to affirm that course of action. While studying art in Pasadena, Wally Hedrick had enlisted in the Army reserves with the firm expectation of avoiding combat in Korea, but then found himself abruptly called up in 1951: "We replaced the 24th Infantry Division that had just been shot to pieces by the Chinese," he told an interviewer in 2009; "They gave us guns and told us to go into these bunkers. I don't want to talk about it."[1] The deaths and injuries he witnessed left Hedrick, always on the political Left, deeply antagonistic to any form of military adventurism. By 1957, the year of Conner's arrival, he would have been one of the few civilians even to notice the deployment of American advisors in support of the armed forces of South Vietnam. Certain that this presaged carnage comparable to the Korean conflict, he fashioned an assemblage sculpture under the title *Rest in Pisces*, empty tuna cans standing for the coffins to come.[2] And, by 1963, the alert Hedrick no doubt seethed at the presence of some sixteen thousand of these advisors on South Vietnamese soil, dispatched in support of South Vietnam's repressive, Catholic ruling family: Ngô Đình Diệm, his brother, Ngô Đình Nhu, and his glamorous sister-in-law, Trần Lệ Xuân, universally known as Madame Nhu, the aggressive public face of the regime.

In that year, a new round of discriminatory measures against the Buddhism practiced by the majority of the southern population was met with tragically spectacular protests, beginning in June, when Thích Quảng Đức became the first in a series of Buddhist monks to immolate themselves as the ultimate act of protest. On 20 August, the Ngô Đình clan compounded their vicious shortsightedness by staging a coordinated raid by special forces on pagodas across the country, wantonly murdering monks and imprisoning others by the hundreds. When university and high-school students turned out in protest, scores of them ended up in prison as well.[3] Unfortunately for the regime's international reputation, Thích Quảng Đức's horrific suicide and those that followed were thoroughly captured by press photographers, a harbinger of the heightened, unfiltered visual evidence of the war's atrocities, in print and on television, that would set the Vietnam conflict apart from its predecessors. When pressed to offer some sympathy or regret over the public suicides,

Madame Nhu was captured on film responding, "I would clap hands at seeing another monk barbecue show."[4]

On a canvas of the same year, Hedrick reacted by scrawling in capitals across a roughly painted, dark-red heart, "Madame Nhu's Bar-B-Qs" (fig. 48). Strokes of gold-colored paint inscribe flames curling below and arising from the heart, while a shadow-casting golden silhouette, at once fire and bird, rises to dominate the immediate foreground. It is likely that the painting had been in the works before the public suicides in Vietnam, as the phoenix-like creature and the cross at top center accord with Hedrick's eclectic interest over some years in matters of "the spirit."[5] But the specifically Buddhist import of the Vietnamese events makes a pointed appearance in Hedrick's carefully inscribing near the heart's downward point the most widely recited of Buddhist mantras, "om mani padme hūm," an invocation of the Bodhisattva of compassion. Both the relative delicacy of the inscription and its humane sentiment counterpose themselves to the heartless, Americanized vulgarity of Madame Nhu's remark as emblazoned in painted letters across the top.

The United States had installed Ngô Đình Diệm in 1955 as Prime Minister of the new republic in the South, an entity intended to stand against Hồ Chí Minh's hegemony in the North at a time when the forced retreat of Chiang Kai-shek's Nationalist forces from the mainland to Taiwan was still a fresh affront to perceived American interests. Hedrick's "Madame Nhu" painting has been cited as presciently "anti-war";[6] but that supposition needs some qualification—first of all, by the fact that no active American combatants had yet overtly entered the conflicts between the gathering forces of the Viet Cong and the Army of the Republic of Vietnam (ARVN). In his entirely justified disgust at the Catholic regime's persecution of Buddhist clerics, the paradox of Hedrick's invective lay in its alignment with the emerging official policy of the Kennedy administration and its newly dispatched ambassador, the patrician Henry Cabot Lodge. Arriving in Saigon shortly after the anti-Buddhist crackdown, Lodge took little time in deciding that the existing regime had so forfeited popular support that it would have to go, lest the ARVN's halting battle against the expanding Viet Cong forces be lost before it really got underway. Having brought President Kennedy around to the same conclusion, military plotters were tacitly encouraged to stage the successful coup that overthrew Ngô Đình Diệm, with the rest of his family, on 1 November 1963—perhaps as the paint on Hedrick's canvas was still drying.

Hedrick had recourse only to the modest, in-group premises of the New Mission Gallery to register his incandescent dissent from America's proxy war in 1963. But the route to higher visibility for the widespread hostility among artists toward American intervention in Southeast Asia also began in San Francisco. Its passage, however, proved to be a tortuous one, requiring the closest approach to espionage, while making even more evident the pervasive presence of the military and its allied defense industries looming over virtually every aspect of life in California.

■

During the first years in which Hedrick knew Conner, doubtless bonding over their shared disgust for the aggressive military mindset, both would have been acquainted with fellow artist Irving Petlin, another Midwesterner in his twenties newly arrived in the city. Most recently a student of Josef Albers at Yale, Petlin had earned his first degree at the School of the Art Institute of Chicago, where he had studied alongside Leon Golub and Nancy Spero. Like them, he hewed to an expressive figural vocabulary, indebted to Surrealism in its free departures from normal perception and to Jean Dubuffet's Art brut in its attraction to rough outcasts and contempt for academic decorum. The child of Jewish refugees, his mother having lost most of her family in the Holocaust, Petlin's incipiently dissenting politics were further energized by the discoveries that arose from his other, non-artistic occupation in San Francisco.

After failing to be declared unfit—for no lack of trying—at his draft-board examination in New Haven, he swiftly found himself in Army basic training, followed by assignment to the intelligence service. His first posting came in 1957, to the Army's installation at the Presidio near the base of the Golden Gate Bridge, after which he shortly secured a studio alongside a number of other artists in the century-old Monkey Block (a corruption of Montgomery Block), once a San Francisco financial center but latterly taken over as the city's headquarters for bohemian creative endeavors. Surviving on just two hours of sleep, Petlin worked through the night on his art, never staying over in his Army quarters, while forging friendships by letting friends use his space during the day. And during his workdays his anger built.[7]

He described his duties in a much later interview: "We often had to prepare the Generals of the Sixth Army for briefings with Defense Department officials. And our job was to prepare them with information and rehearse them . . . there were these corporals drafted from graduate schools yelling at these generals, 'No, don't say that! Say it this way!'" But the job also gave him time and access to top-secret materials which lent this sort of service comedy a profoundly sinister undercurrent. Among the materials he was able to review in the course of his days were items of correspondence and film footage concerning the Western allies' attitudes to the transportation and mass murder of European Jews. As he related to the same interviewer, "They were always turning down any effort to stop the transports . . . it was if the British generals and the American generals were working from a formula. 'Yes, we know. Yes, we could. But, you know, Mr. President, it would delay the end of the war. And mean more US casualties. And we don't have sufficient fuel supplies. And it would mean greater allied casualties.'" So, in the end, he bitterly concludes, "Nothing was done."[8]

This retroactive rage at callous official malfeasance assumed a more up-to-date dimension after Petlin took off for Paris at the conclusion of his service obligation. Again in the company of Golub and Spero, he became acutely aware of the French debacle in Algeria, which had followed the conclusion of its colonial presence in Vietnam. Petlin joined the massive Parisian demonstration in October 1961 on behalf of Algerian insurgents against French rule, which proved a turning point in weakening domestic support for continuing the war. He

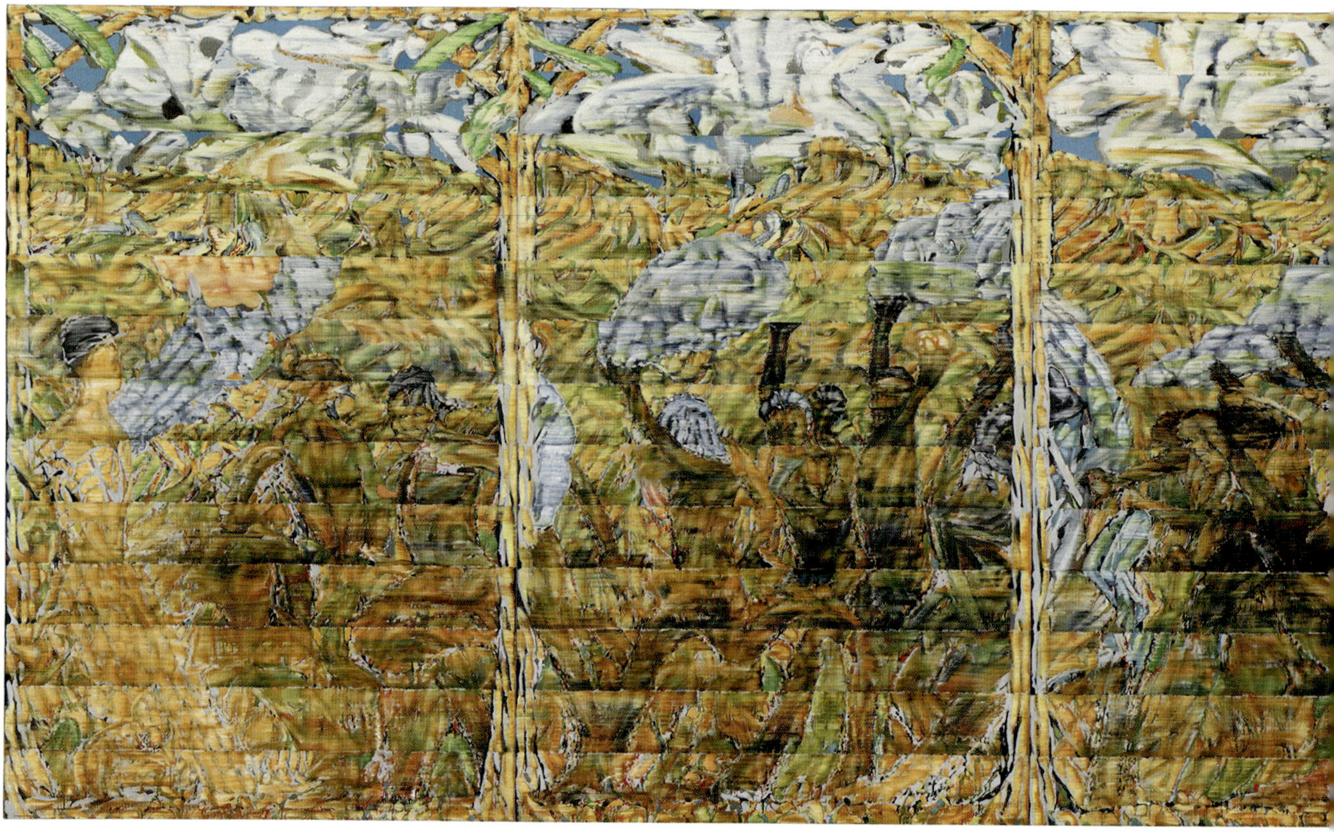

was badly beaten in the police attack on the march at the Charonne Metro station, reporting with justice that he had almost been killed in a rain of blows from lead-filed truncheons: several score of the marchers were murdered in a deliberate massacre ordered by the ex-Vichy chief of police. When reports surfaced of the dogs and fire hoses turned on young civil rights protestors in Birmingham, Alabama, in 1963, Petlin transposed his street experiences in Paris to a series of paintings on their American counterpart, then began making plans to leave a comfortable European life in order to confront the political emergencies at home: "Having experienced what happens to a country, when they fight an unjust war," as he recalled the moment, "I can [*sic*] see Vietnam coming, and I predicted to a lot of my friends . . . I said, 'What's coming to the United States is what happened here with Algeria, except it'll be worse. And I'm going back. And we better be aware that this is coming.'"[9]

Continuing West Coast connections led Petlin back to California in 1964, where Richard Diebenkorn had just moved south to join the studio art program at UCLA. Petlin followed him there to take up a visiting position, settling in the beachside suburb of Santa Monica and reviving friendships with the Los Angeles artists he had met in San Francisco, some of whom had slept on the floor of his old Monkey Block studio. The *bon viveur* part of him found an outlet in the clubs along South Central Avenue in Los Angeles, where he and his wife eagerly

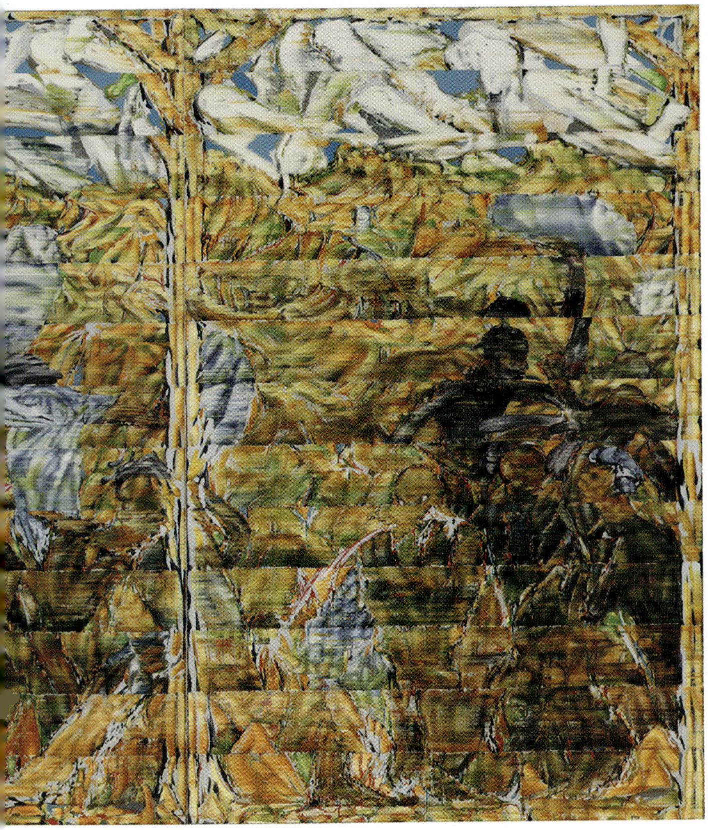

**49** Irving Petlin, *The Burning of Los Angeles*, 1965–67, oil on canvas, 243.8 × 609.6 cm, Fine Arts Museums of San Francisco

sought out opportunities for dancing.[10] Black American jazz was, of course, something close to a religion among the Parisian cognoscenti of the period, but the requisite inside knowledge likely came from Wallace Berman, newly returned from the Bay Area himself, who had haunted the local jazz and dancing milieux of the late 1940s and early 1950s. Walter Hopps shared the same passion (while the jive-dancing Bruce Conner, as noted in the previous chapter, was putting in the occasional Los Angeles appearance). The tensions that Petlin began to feel on their trips to the segregated South Central district gave rise to an enormous multipaneled painting he called *The Burning of Los Angeles* (fig. 49). Amid an overall tissue of striated, interwoven tesserae of complex colors, rippling masses of orange-yellow against cool clusters of white and blue, he embedded figures of African American men, their actions and gestures indistinct, as they seem to struggle against their entrapment in the densely braided matrix, arms defiantly extended above their heads.

Petlin presciently began work on this virtual mural, twenty feet in length and eight in height, months before the Watts Rebellion broke out late in the summer of 1965. For an artist of European descent (Polish Jewry in Petlin's case) to assume the burden of representation for the Blacks of Watts might grate on the sensibilities of the present moment. At that juncture, however, there were few rewards, little even in the way of moral prestige, to be gained in

American circles for overt dissent from any prevailing norms—still less with a finely wrought, expressive figuration that flew in the face of the dominant tendencies of abstraction and Pop. A good two years before Martin Luther King Jr. would endure widespread opprobrium, even from former allies, for linking the civil rights struggle to the cause of the Vietnamese anti-American resistance (about which more below), Petlin drew a bright line connecting the two in the early months of 1965.

■

It becomes fully possible to speak of anti-war American art once the American war in Vietnam begins in earnest during the first half of 1965.[11] President Lyndon Johnson and his war advisors began Operation Rolling Thunder, the sustained bombing of North Vietnam, in March; in the same month, two battalions of combat Marines landed àt Đà Nẵng airbase on the central coast in order to secure the launching point for the American aerial campaign. These watershed escalations of American involvement in the conflict elicited an almost instantaneous riposte from anti-war intellectuals and students galvanized into the Teach-In movement; the first major march on Washington likewise took place in March, with the early stirrings of regular peace vigils spreading through the liberal cities and university towns across the country.[12]

Visual artists, liberal-minded as most of them were, likewise heard the call, but their avenues for registering a protest depended to a great degree on the particular ecology of the local scene. The San Francisco Bay Area, the most historically free-thinking major metropolis in the country, its artists led by deeply anti-militaristic souls like Hedrick and Conner, would seem a natural forcing house for artists' action. In practice, the distribution of forces in the region rendered artists relatively marginal. The behemoth across the Bay, the flagship Berkeley campus of the University of California, staged its own teach-in on the war in late May on a scale that dwarfed its predecessors: some thirty thousand attended the event, convened on a university playing field in successive waves over a thirty-six-hour period. Its sponsoring body, the newly formed Vietnam Day Committee, would endure as a major engine of protest; the roster of speakers, including the co-organizer Jerry Rubin, the pediatrician Benjamin Spock, and the Yale historian Staughton Lynd, would remain among the anti-war movement's most prominent voices.

Los Angeles, by contrast, had been historically far more conservative, its major university campuses staying relatively quiet, while its defense industries were working around the clock in anticipation of a wider war. Against that backdrop, however, artists with a flair for visibility, like the handsome and gregarious Petlin, with his impressive mane of dark hair, could stand out more prominently. He had become friendly with John Weber, the chief assistant to Virginia Dwan at her gallery in the Westwood neighborhood adjacent to UCLA. Dwan had no northern counterpart in her ability to attract and stage art events of wide resonance and visibility. Those achievements, backed by an inheritance from the 3M Corporation, defy summary here; but her prescient sponsorship of the European *Nouveaux Réalistes* and American Pop and assemblage artists in the early 1960s had drawn energy from a formidable national and international network. So it represented a considerable boost to Petlin's cause that he was able to call a meeting in early May in the Dwan space, with the aim of establishing a coordinated form of artists' protest against the war. The scale of attendance revealed that he had tapped a hidden vein of discontent. Craig Kauffman and Larry Bell, both known for the gleaming perfection of their abstract sculptures, were enthusiastic participants; Walter Hopps, having moved from the Ferus Gallery to the chief curatorship at the Pasadena Art Museum, lent his imprimatur, as did the editor of *Artforum*, Philip Leider, and an important local collector, the real-estate scion Edwin Janss Jr, whose family had developed Westwood. The outcome of the gathering was an entity going forward that they called the Artist Protest Committee (APC).

Its first undertaking was an advertisement taken out the same month in the friendly pages of the local alternative newspaper, the *Los Angeles Free Press* (fig. 51).[13] It called out Lyndon

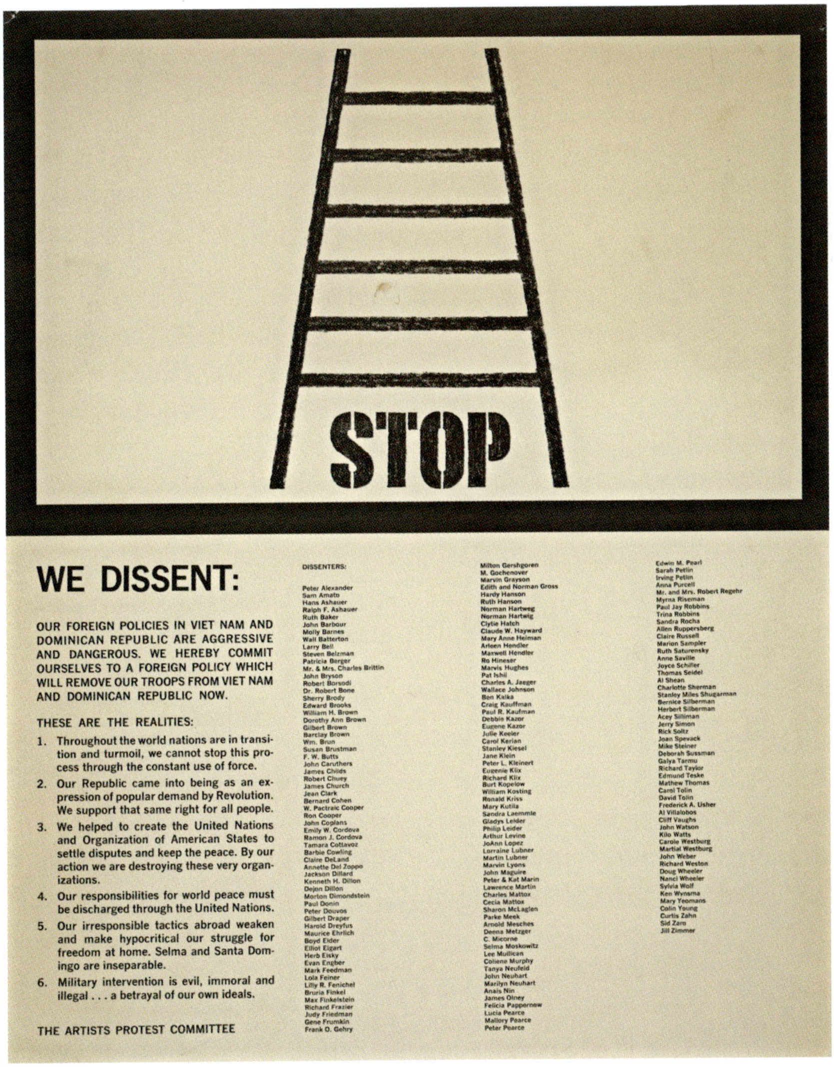


50 Irving Petlin et al., advertisement, *Los Angeles Free Press* (14 May 1965), 6–7, Getty Research Library, Los Angeles

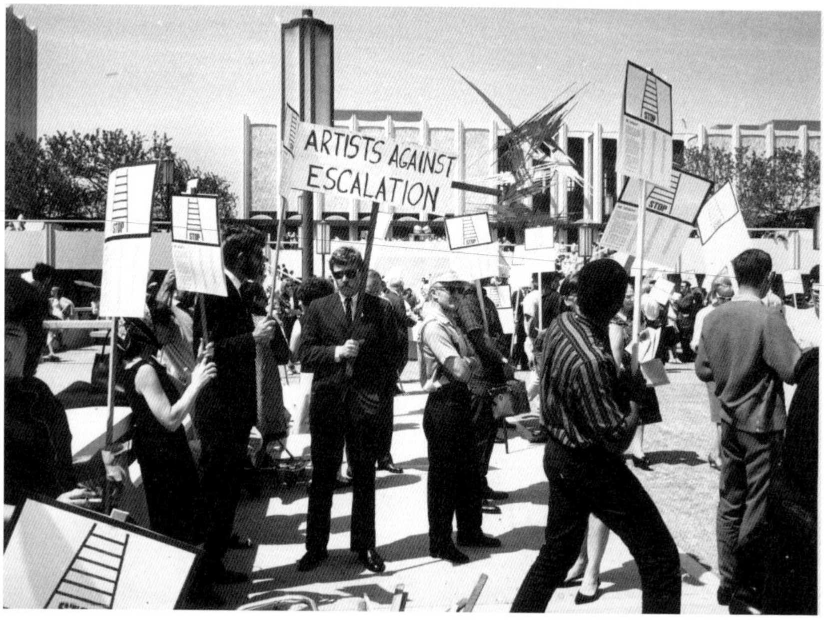


**51** "Artists Against Escalation" protest at the Los Angeles County Museum of Art, 16 May 1965, photograph by Charles Brittin, Charles Brittin Collection, Getty Research Library, Los Angeles

Johnson's recent intervention in the Dominican Republic along with the escalation in Vietnam. The ad was surmounted by the memorable symbol of a stark ladder as an ideogram for escalation, the word **STOP** in stencil block capitals beneath its lowest rung, with 174 signatories below.

Its message also included calls to action, visible protests in the mid-city art precinct, a vigil for peace at the Los Angeles County Museum (fig. 51) followed by a march up to the galleries along La Cienega Boulevard for a "white-out"—works on display being covered over in a suspension of business as usual. While the confinement of these public events to the circuits of the art world made them easy for the mainstream to ignore, Petlin was already hatching ambitions to take this solidarity-building exercise into enemy territory.

■

Petlin had caught wind of a disturbing undercurrent while out and about on the local art circuit. A good number of affable, educated gallery-goers, as he discovered, worked for an organization called the RAND Corporation, its blandly impenetrable headquarters located not far from his house in Santa Monica. It is a mark of the hegemony enjoyed by the defense contractors of Southern California that in 1948 the Douglas Aircraft Corporation would have set up RAND, its own quasi-autonomous, quasi-academic think tank, its mission to provide civilian analysis and policy proposals under contract to clients in the United States military. Relying in part on discreet conversations with a disaffected insider, Petlin deployed the acumen honed in Army Intelligence to grasp the extent to which US forces, primed with RAND recommendations, were pursuing lethal disruptions to life in the south of Vietnam as countermoves to the successes of the National Liberation Front.[14] As he put it, these articulate, outwardly liberal-minded neighbors "were planning and executing for the defense department—the safe hamlet concept, where you gather the peasants into a ring of barbed wire and then kill everything that moves in the country."[15]

Petlin resolved, as his first step on his artist's road of resistance, to bring this hypocrisy to light. Seeking the advantage of surprise, he relates, "We organized secretly. We never sent anything through the mail because we knew that we were already being watched." He had had earlier experience with being surveilled while living in Paris: having been enjoined against revealing any part of his prior work for Army Intelligence, he received a visit from a US State Department representative—suspicions having been aroused by his protest activities—with a tacit warning to remain buttoned up. Despite all his precautions in organizing meetings at Weber's Santa Monica apartment, two "red squad" sheriff's deputies burst in on one gathering, striking Petlin and photographing everyone present.[16] Even with this forewarning, however, the APC demonstration went on as planned: "We organized a demonstration by word of mouth, and hundreds came," Petlin relates, "We marched around the Rand Corporation holding up signs accusing them of genocide. They were so flustered, because they were all members of their communities and in various ways they wanted to be thought of as good people."[17]

His next step was a successful effort to maneuver four RAND functionaries into a debate, first with him and his friends—the amazing line-up of the artist Leon Golub, the gifted young critic Annette Michelson, and mainstay of the Bay Area counterculture, the poet Michael McClure—in a closed session inside the RAND building. There followed a public debate held on 3 August 1965 before an overflow audience in a studio screening theater on La Cienega Boulevard, hard by the gallery district. With a somewhat different set of participants, its aim remained one of alerting a somnolent public, via the twisted objectivity of the Randians, to the scale and level of violence likely to ensue in no more than six months or a year into the future. On both occasions, the artists' protest side of the argument proceeded with greater confidence, at the least exposing their opponents' reliance on blinkered conjecture uninformed by political or historical imagination. The theater audience, composed largely of students energized by the teach-ins and anti-war mobilization, naturally concurred, while the RAND Corporation permanently withdrew from any further self-exposure or public self-justification. But the exercise had largely remained within another self-affirming circle, leading to the next and most famous of Petlin's initiatives, which called on the Dwan Gallery to be more than a place of assembly.

■

Following his widening-circle strategy, the next phase would be taking artists' protest into the maw of a reactionary social order, soon nakedly to reveal itself in the election of Ronald Reagan as governor of California. For that to happen, however, imagination and expertise in working on a monumental scale would be required. In the fall of 1965, Dwan and Weber had been able to mount an exhibition of three mammoth sculptures by Mark Di Suvero, removing part of the gallery ceiling to do so. Di Suvero had first erected them on a beach at Point Reyes, north of San Francisco in far Marin County, where few could witness his inspired leveraging of the masses of trunks, spars, and timbers. After the warmly received exposure of his work in Los Angeles, the sculptor's sympathy with Petlin's APC made possible a multifaceted initiative by which he would direct the construction of a work destined to be witnessed by thousands: what came to be titled the *Artist's Tower of Protest* or, more commonly, the Los Angeles Peace Tower.

Collaborating with the architect Kenneth Dillon, Di Suvero designed a structure six stories in height, fabricated from steel bars that were held together, following Buckminster Fuller's principles of "tensegrity," in the stacked forms of an octahedron and a tetrahedron, into which a smaller, double tetrahedron was inserted to form its pinnacle (fig. 52). At the same time, the organization reached out to its membership and Dwan, to her international Rolodex, successfully securing four-hundred anti-war testimonials in paint, all the participating artists agreeing to work to an identical format: two-feet square and on a support hard enough to withstand the elements. At a highly visible junction halfway along the Sunset Strip, the nightlife center of the city, the committee wrangled a three-month lease on a prime vacant lot carved into the hillside so as to form an earthen amphitheater.

The twenty-score submitted panels were arrayed around the perimeter, at the center of which stood the Tower, painted in yellow and purple. An all-star, multiracial sculptural team of Eric Orr, Ed Burrell, Melvin Edwards, Judy Gerowitz, and Lloyd Hamrol assisted with the welding and rigging needed to raise the structure, their professional acumen supplemented by a local, self-taught sculptor-artist-engineer named Anthony Safiello. Having come upon the work site by chance, he decided to join in, eventually becoming—like the spiritual reappearance of the Watts Towers' creator, Simon Rodia—Di Suvero's chief assistant. Kurt Von Meier, a rare radical art historian of the day, who taught alongside Petlin at UCLA, wrote that Safiello "could be seen daily perched atop one of the beams, identified by a large red dot on his sweatshirt."[18] A feat of both sculptural engineering and daring physical construction, the Peace Tower's elegantly transparent geometry became a magnet for the attention of visitors and passers-by in the heavily trafficked precinct, weeks before its final completion.[19]

For the large majority of contributing artists, participation entailed no greater personal witness than signing their submissions. But for the artists and their supporters on the ground, commitment included confrontation and physical risk. Petlin boasted that a thousand visitors gathered around the tower each night after its opening at the end of February

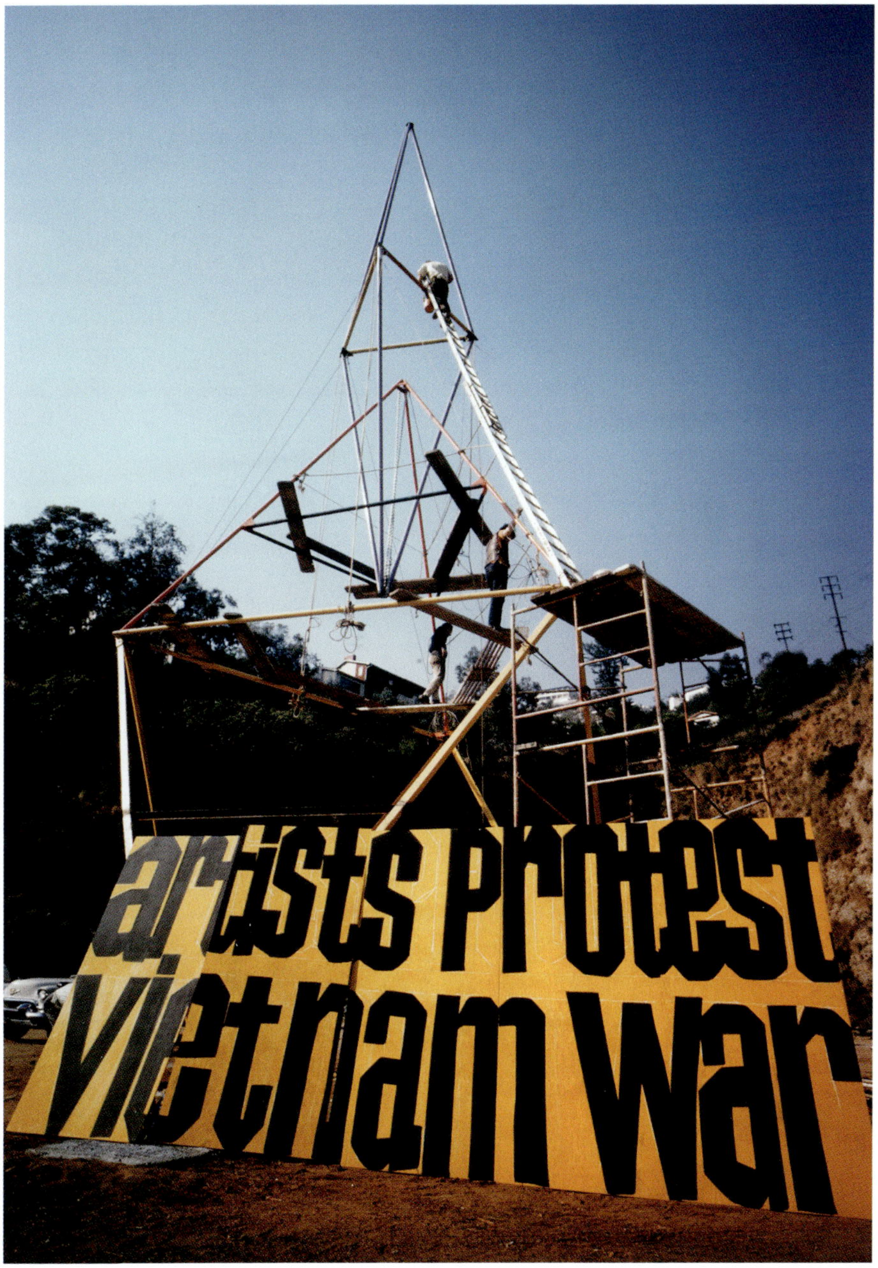


52 Peace Tower installation in Los Angeles, 1966, photograph by Charles Brittin, Charles Brittin Collection, Getty Research Library, Los Angeles

1966 (with the celebrated critic Susan Sontag, a graduate of North Hollywood High School, officiating). There is little reason to doubt the claim, with the necessary qualification, as recounted in the previous chapter, that a profusion of rock clubs along the Strip—these being the heady days of the Byrds, Love, Buffalo Springfield, the Mothers of Invention, and the Doors—had created a rare pedestrian district for nighttime congregation, the scene of continuous cruising by the young and car-proud. The authorities responded with relentless police harassment of clubs and club-goers, as well as a legal curfew for anyone under eighteen.[20] Wittingly or not, the APC had planted their grand statement right in the center of an already charged focus of the emerging counterculture, its effect heightened by drawing angry off-duty Marines and other right-wingers bent on verbal confrontation with "peaceniks," when not intending physical damage to the display. The latter threat resulted in fifteen to twenty volunteer guards being posted around the precinct on a twenty-four-hour rota. Young African Americans from the local chapter of the Student Non-Violent Coordinating Committee took part, instructing the other guards in their techniques of resistance.[21] When the artist Jim Gallagher was beaten and kicked by a sailor in civilian clothes, nearby Sheriff's deputies allowed the assault to go on, then pushed Gallagher against the car and arrested him for resisting arrest and disturbing the peace, letting his assailant walk free.[22] As with any effective installation work of the period, the Peace Tower enlarged its meaning by altering its surroundings over the four months of its existence;[23] but with the large difference that its size and subject matter brought along genuine risks that shared, if only slightly, in the massive violence it denounced.

■

The Los Angeles artist James Turrell, likewise in 1966, set yet a higher standard in accepting risk and absorbing punishment as witness to the enormity of the war. And his actions followed directly from the alternative civilian service he had performed in the Tibetan precursor to the anti-Chinese strategizing that drove the war planners of the 1960s. His strict Quaker upbringing led to his seeking conscientious-objector status as his draft age approached, while his precocious ability as a pilot—his late father had been a teacher of aviation—made him attractive to non-military actors in the national-security state. While still a teenager, between high school and college, Turrell spent months during 1959 and 1960 piloting aircraft over the treacherous escarpments of the Tibetan plateau on behalf of the Central Intelligence Agency. The planes were naturally not labeled as such, nor were his missions military in nature. Their goal was relief to Tibetans who had fled south in the aftermath of the failed rebellion against Chinese occupation in 1959, during which the Dalai Lama had gone into exile across the border with Nepal into India. Many had sheltered in the barren Nepalese kingdom of Mustang, while remnant bands continued acts of resistance from the inaccessible valleys just across the border with China. Throughout the 1950s, the CIA had fomented covert intrigues intended to frustrate Chinese influence, real or imagined, on its neighbors.

Among those ventures had been encouraging and arming the discontented Buddhists of Tibet to be a persistent thorn in the side of the People's Republic. Turrell has spoken about unlisted planes, whose pilots did not carry passports. "America has this shadow government," he told the gallerist Almine Rech; "It should stay in the shadows because it can't stand up in the light." Asked whether the Himalayan experience had been positive, Turrell replied, "It was nice in retrospect but we lost a lot of people. . . . The weather there is just capricious and tough. There are strong winds, and planes don't have a lot of performance at that altitude. The helicopters were a disaster . . . the crashes."[24] On his return, the perils and exhilaration of a teenager flying over the extreme altitude of the Tibetan plateau rarely, if ever, surfaced publicly, at least in the memories of his contemporaries at Pomona College, which he entered in 1961 at the customary age of eighteen. Tacitly, however, a link existed between the mental exertion necessary for a pilot to maintain a correct sense of orientation under conditions of dubious visibility—potentially a matter of life and death—and his decision to concentrate on perceptual psychology, then a particular strength of the Pomona curriculum. Indeed, Quaker strictures against objects of vanity restricted his art studies to the fashioning of ceramic vessels.

After finishing his psychology degree at Pomona, however, Turrell gave in to his artistic inclinations and entered the fledgling Masters of Fine Arts program at the new Irvine campus of the University of California. He still sought ways to sidestep the making of vain possessions, exploring evanescent flame and projected light as his exclusive media, while he renewed his Quaker commitments by becoming a regular congregant at the Orange Grove Meeting in Pasadena. Orange Grove stood out during these years by adding an extra measure of social activism to its open and spontaneous form of worship ("Conservative" in Quaker parlance). Among other forms of outreach, it became a regional focus for protest against the war in Vietnam. As a former conscientious objector, Turrell offered counseling to young men seeking the same status as an alternative to military conscription. Current law countenanced this activity, but drew a line against any explicit encouragement, which amounted to abetting draft evasion in the eyes of the authorities. While basing his art practice on a suspicion of false appearance, his alternative-service counseling brought home a further lesson in not taking appearances at face value.

"You might be surprised," he told David Pagel of the *Los Angeles Times* in 2007, "what you say over a period of six months. There was a couple. I took the woman to be the man's mother. She was not. She was an FBI agent." He went on to detail the consequences: "Everything [the couple] said was in truth a lie, and they just wanted to find me saying one thing—that I thought he should do this. I was positive I never had, I told my lawyer I never had, and then they had a tape of me out in the parking lot and apparently I said this is what he should do. And that was enough. I was arrested and served time in prison."[25] That ambush put his art, to say the least, on extended hold after his sentencing in March 1966: "As a result of things I said as a draft counsellor during the Vietnam War, I spent time in the penitentiary, and, to avoid being assaulted or raped, I would do things that got me into solitary. Solitary confinement was not a good thing, but at least there was safety, and I sought to get in there to be safe. Once you are there, it's tough because the cell isn't long enough to lie down or tall enough to stand up; it is meant to be physically confining."[26]

That Turrell took a lease on a Santa Monica studio in November 1966 suggests his actual time served would have been about six months, though the original sentence could have been longer. He found this new working space in the defunct Mendota Hotel near the Pacific at Ocean Park, then a down-at-heel neighborhood named for the adjacent amusement pier (since burned down). From that redoubt, he emerged into the public eye on one occasion. John Coplans, with whom Turrell worked at Irvine, had since moved to a curatorship at the Pasadena Art Museum, where he greeted his old protégé's return to freedom with a show of the first light pieces in October 1967.[27] But Turrell thereafter withdrew his light projections from any further public exhibition for nearly a decade—though not for any lack of encouragement. In 1969, the Museum of Modern Art in New York invited him to create an installation for a show they called *Spaces*, in which each invited artist was given the freedom of a solo gallery. Its curator wrote to her superior with some dismay and frustration at Turrell's indifference to the prospect of curating his own work in such a maximally prestigious venue: "On the trip to California I also approached an artist called James Turrell, whose work has never been seen here; indeed has hardly been seen on the West Coast. He consented, after much time and negotiation, to show me some pieces and I was enormously impressed."

The outcome of her approach provides some measure of how complete his withdrawal from the public art world had become in the wake of the Pasadena Museum outing: "Subsequently Turrell announced that he does not want to allow his work to be involved with the 'system,' meaning, I believe, the marketing and promotional system and therefore will never sell a piece or participate in any exhibition."[28] What he was pursuing instead consisted of a new series of non-portable (and eminently non-possessable) works based on the controlled release of ambient light, including street illumination and the lights of passing cars, onto the immaculate white walls of his darkened studio spaces. These ephemeral events, witnessed by only a few initiates, he came to call—with a nod to Marcel Duchamp's play of random events—the *Mendota Stoppages*. In keeping with this cultivated personal obscurity and his anti-war beliefs, he had also abruptly withdrawn from participating in the highly touted *Art and Technology* exhibition being prepared by the Los Angeles County Museum of Art, severing cooperation with his sponsor, the Garrett Corporation, a Los Angeles-based aerospace contractor, and leaving his erstwhile partner in the project, Robert Irwin, in the lurch. For all of Turrell's efforts to withdraw from view, however, his uncompromising stance attracted attention, even from the mass media. The art critic for the then popular *Newsweek* devoted an article in 1969 to "The View from Hill and Main" (the cross streets of the Mendota studio): "The 26-year-old Turrell . . . resists even the term 'artist,' together with the binding ties that the term inspires . . . 'The only coherent statement I got from him,' says one gallery official, 'was that he didn't want people to see his work in a context where they could be considered eligible for possession.'"[29]

■

Few artists of the Vietnam War period had seen as much of the regional conflict at greater physical peril, had staked as much on opposition to the conflict, or had sacrificed as much as a consequence. In virtually every other case, opposition to the war was a voluntary option.

Wally Hedrick's searing combat experience in Korea offers the closest comparison among artists of strong anti-war convictions, and, as noted above, he was the earliest and least compromising in his personal abhorrence of further American military intervention in Asia. Hedrick's actions, subsequent to his brief flurry of visible protest in paint during 1963, also offer the closest counterpart to Turrell's bearing witness by abstinence from the normal commerce of the art world, or, as Hedrick put it, "withdrawal of services." And parallel to Turrell's practice, the intensity of pacifism made a material difference to his art.

Hedrick was habitually vague in his explanation for the long series of black paintings, mounted in various formats, which he began in the late 1950s either by painting over existing works or covering canvases in black pigment from scratch, subtitling all of them "Vietnam Series." A few bore explicit titles: one in 1957 he called *Allen Dulles* after the director of the CIA; *Black and Blue Ideas* (1958–67) takes its name from a Louis Armstrong number beloved by this traditional-jazz-playing artist, transposing the musical title toward melancholy and bruising injury. His black canvases did not for him connote the funereal: it was not "so much that they were black, but that they weren't light. . . . Black to me is the absence of light."[30] The paintings would withhold their participation in any transaction with the viewer that entailed the stimulation of the optical faculties: to use one of his analogies, it would be like looking for one's face in a mirror when the room is entirely dark. Until the world rid itself of the stain of war, Hedrick would make a show of giving it nothing to look at. Between 1967 and 1968, he made that blackness more enveloping, assembling eight large black paintings into an enclosed, stygian *War Room*, a cube built of panels eleven feet square, with their black surfaces facing inward. One smaller black painting functioned as door allowing ingress and egress, Hedrick installing a strong spring so that the panel would slam shut with an entrapping sound once an entering visitor let go of it.

Such Buddhist-flavored witness against a regime of compulsive violence and dishonesty took the form, as had Turrell's, of masked light and withdrawn self-containment. In both their cases, the dates coincide closely with Bruce Conner's decision—as addressed in the previous chapter—to exit the normal circuits of visual art production, sidestepping the identity of artist in order to slip into such roles as light-show tech, mock-politician, and Hollywood jack-of-all-trades. When pressed by *Artforum* in 1970 to define the political responsibilities of the artist, Irving Petlin gave an answer consistent with these implicit positions of refusal: "where they are recognizable, artists should choose to withhold their work, deny its use to a government anxious to signal to the world that it represents a civilized culturally centered society while melting babies in Vietnam and gunning down kids all over the states. No."[31] All shared a visceral abhorrence of the ongoing war, for which each was prepared to sacrifice abundantly earned rewards. But oracular pronouncements and self-abnegation could go only so far, and the growth of the national movement against the American presence in Indochina was changing the terms in which an artist's witnessing against state violence could henceforth occur.

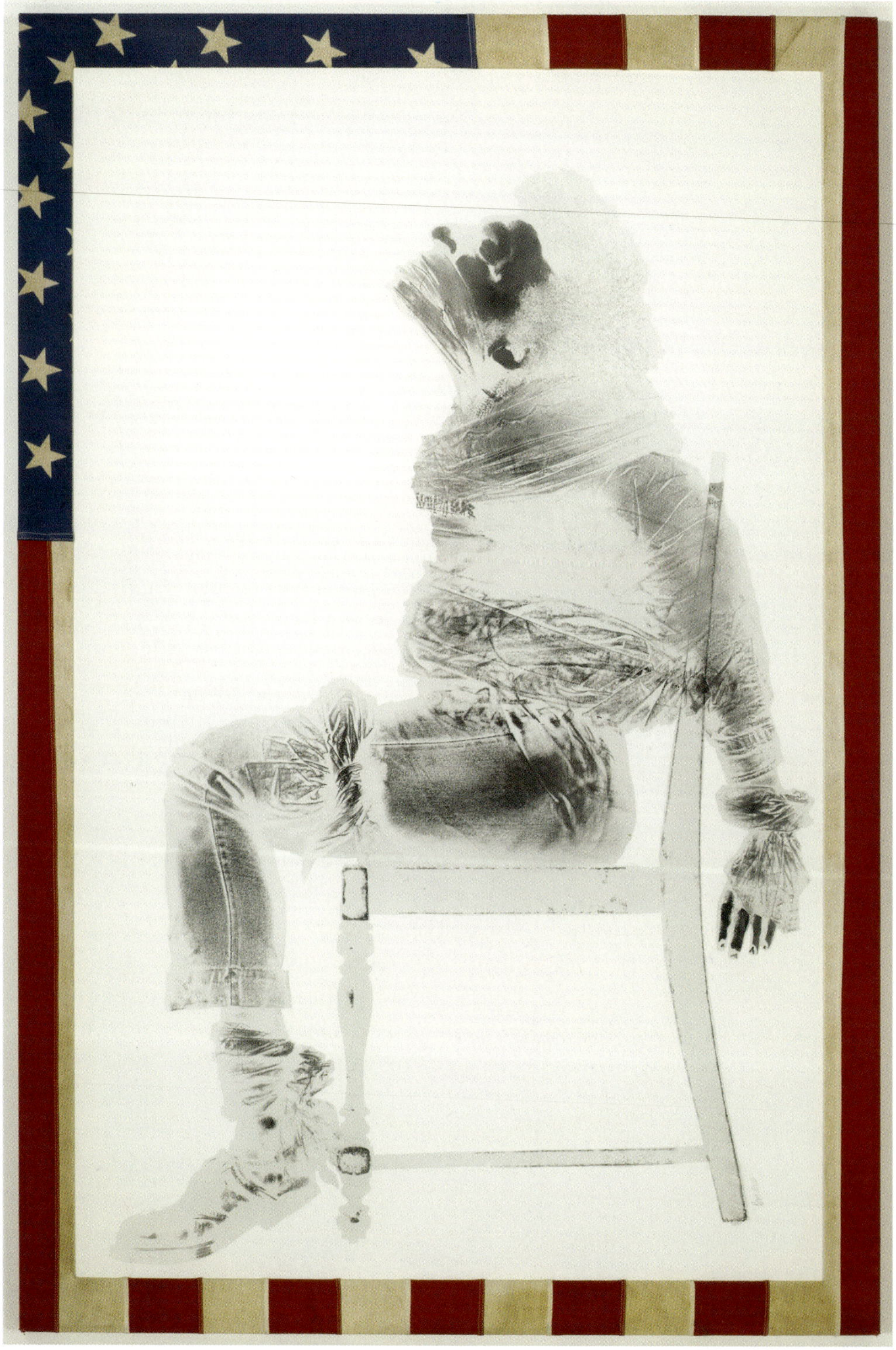

**53** David Hammons, *Injustice Case*, 1970,
margarine and powdered pigments on paper with textile,
175.3 × 120 × 5.7 cm, Los Angeles County Museum of Art

SEVEN

# FROM WAR ABROAD TO OPPRESSION AT HOME

ANTI-WAR MILITANCY ASSUMED A NEW LEVEL of intensity following the 1968 assassinations of Robert Kennedy, who had sought the presidential nomination as its charismatic standard-bearer, and Martin Luther King Jr., who in April 1967 had put his accrued prestige with white America on the line (and defied the caution of close associates) by linking the campaign for African American civil rights with opposition to the war in Indochina. He titled his bold address at the Riverside Church in New York, "A Declaration of Independence from the War in Vietnam."[1] At certain points he came close to the rhetoric used by those emerging black militants like Stokely Carmichael, who had both chafed at King's insistence on non-violence and expressly insisted on the link between racial oppression at home and the savage American oppression of national liberation movements abroad: "These are revolutionary times," King asserted, "All over the globe men are revolting against old systems of exploitation and oppression, and out of the wombs of a frail world, new systems of justice and equality are being born."[2] In Vietnam, King declared unequivocally that the American government had placed its young draftees, many of them African Americans, on the wrong side of such a struggle: "I knew that could never raise my voice against the violence of the oppressed in the ghettos without having first spoken clearly to the greatest purveyor of violence in the world today—my own government."

That convergence reached a watershed when a wave of demonstrations against the war took place at the Chicago Democratic National Convention in 1968, prompting a wantonly violent police riot that brought physical jeopardy to a far greater number of protesters than at any previous event. Richard Nixon's Department of Justice chose to exonerate the Chicago police by indicting a few for minor offenses, while charging a select group of prominent protesters (and two obscure young professors) with the felony of conspiracy and incitement to riot. The inclusion among the accused of Bobby Seale, the cofounder of the Black Panther Party for Self-Defense (about whom much more below), served the singular antipathy of the Director of the FBI, J. Edgar Hoover, toward any form of African American dissent, in that Seale had not even known the other defendants and had given only a single, last-minute speech. The Chicago Eight trial was assigned to the venomously pro-government judge Julius Hoffman, at whose high-handed rulings Seale regularly erupted, demanding that he be allowed to represent himself. Hoffman's response, in a breathtaking reversion to the bondage of slavery, was to have the Panther leader gagged and shackled to his chair over four long days of courtroom proceedings.[3]

Such a hideous spectacle might well have overwhelmed the capacities of representational art, had not David Hammons—an integral figure in the Black Arts Movement centered in the Watts neighborhood of south-central Los Angeles—already embarked on a series of "body prints." Coating his body with margarine, he could carefully leave a sticky configuration adhering to a large sheet unfurled on the floor, then cover those areas with powdered pigment. In a courtroom where photography was barred, the enormity of Seale's treatment lacked compelling public representation until Hammons placed himself physically in the prisoner's place to create what is rightly the most enduring of these works: *Injustice Case* of 1969 (fig. 53). The searing actuality of the event inspired a novel degree of actuality in the piece. Hammons set this supercharged Body Print against the slightly larger rectangle of a real flag, such that the national emblem both frames the event and bestows implied chauvinistic sanction upon it. When first displayed in 1970 at the Black-oriented Brockman Gallery, a second meaning of the title took literal form: *Injustice Case* appeared, as Kellie Jones explains, "not hung on the wall but in a seven-foot-high glass case with locked doors. The enclosure was lit and lined with black velvet like a fixture used for displaying jewelry or precious museum objects."[4] Inside, directly before the print, Hammons had placed a judge's gavel, both the instrument of Hoffman's authoritarian rule inside the courtroom and, more figuratively perhaps, the weapon with which the locked enclosing case might be smashed from the inside.

With the rush of intervening events, King's address at the Riverside Church no doubt seemed old news, and Hammons's attitude toward the martyred leader's legacy may have been ambivalent, but no work of art ever put so forcefully and memorably—with anything like its degree of personal witness—the argument by the civil-rights leader that the government of the United States had become the "greatest purveyor of violence in the world today." While many artists during this period produced works that denounced the American war in Southeast Asia, along with its effects on the home front, the criterion for attention here has been some personal sacrifice or assumption of risk in the pursuit of one's art. The personal jeopardy in this instance was of course Seale's, but Hammons, as a Black male in South Los Angeles, knew his own well-being to be in continual jeopardy from arbitrary harassments by the police and a hostile criminal justice system. In 1969, the year of the Panther leader's Chicago ordeal and Hammons's homage to his defiance, another implicit restatement of that thesis gained much wider visibility by virtue of its promulgation as an inexpensive print, likewise linking the agonies of war-torn Vietnam with the horrors of the slave's trade's Middle Passage.

Titled *news of the week* (fig. 54), after the Warhol-like reprinting of a magazine-cover image over an intensely red background of an American soldier in camouflage manhandling a half-naked Vietnamese male. Its headline reads, "Profile of the Viet Cong." Against a smaller field below, over a stingingly complementary green, appear two appropriated images: on

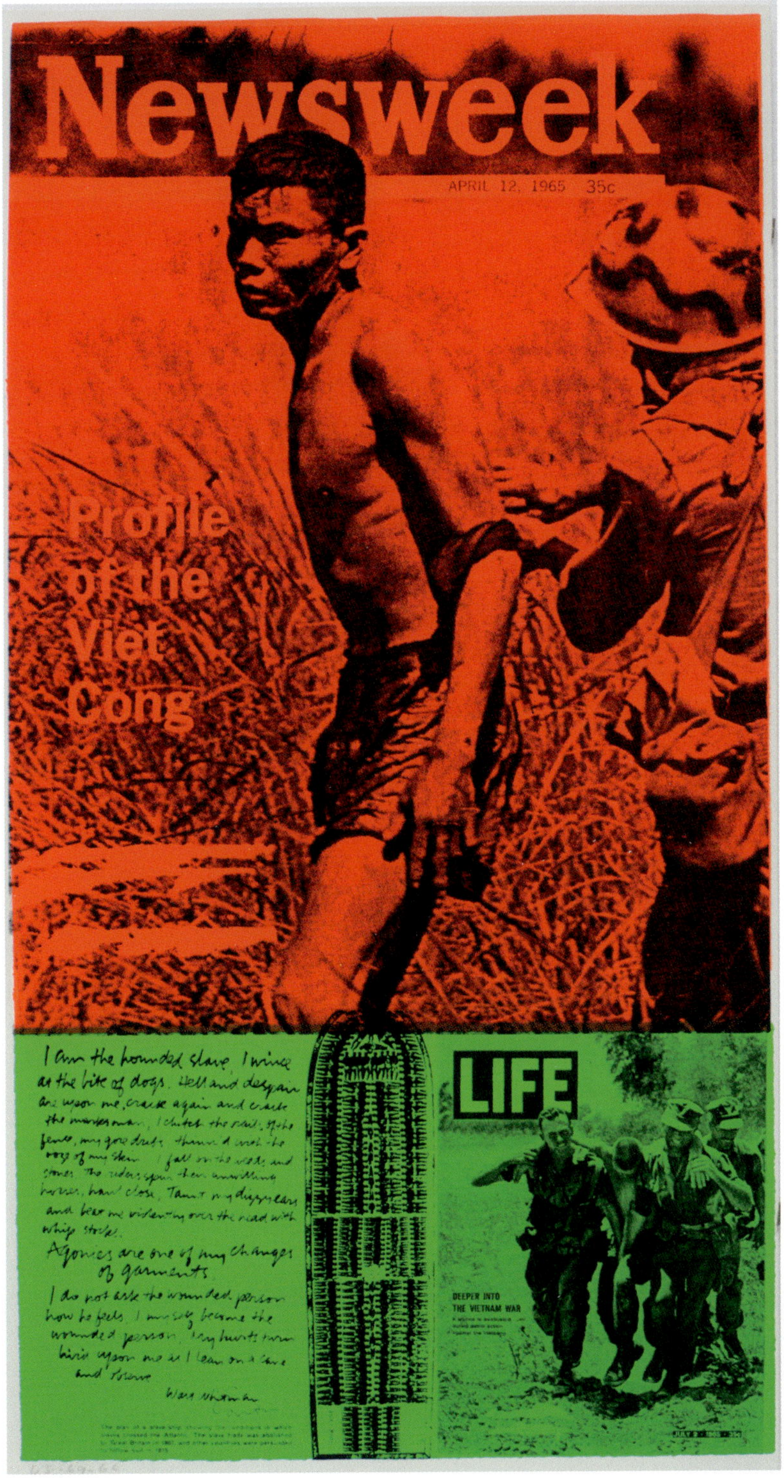


**54** Corita Kent, *news of the week*, 1969, screenprint, 57.2 × 29.2 cm, Corita Art Center the right, a cover from *Life* magazine featuring more American soldiers, a uniformed pair holding a shirtless wounded comrade between them; on the left, a famous diagram from the late eighteenth century of bodies arranged in the hold of the slave ship, juxtaposed to a hand-written passage of poetry from Walt Whitman, the first line of which reads, "I am the hounded slave." The artist was Corita Kent, a few years before widely known as Sister Corita and counted as one of the best-known artists in America.[5] But the moral outspokenness of her art came to be won only on the sacrifice of her cherished religious vocation.

In the Christmas season of 1967, *Newsweek* featured Kent on its cover under the headline, "The Nun: Going Modern." In that same month of December, the *Los Angeles Times*, a titanic civic power in those days, named her—alongside such national celebrities as Ella Fitzgerald and Billie Jean King—one of nine "Women of the Year." The reason for her celebrity appears all around her in the *Newsweek* photograph: the boldly colored combinations of text and abstract pattern she produced in the silkscreen studio of Immaculate Heart College, the East Hollywood institution where she had taught in the art department since the early 1950s. For all her fame and institutional achievement, however, Kent's position had been rendered precarious in the extreme. In 1966, the Cardinal-Archbishop McIntyre of Los Angeles had already written sternly to the Mother General of her order, ordering Kent to abandon her flourishing external career: "May I say further that we hereby request again that the activities of Sister Carita [sic] in religious art be confined to her classroom work and under your responsibility. You are reminded of the restrictions in this regard issued last year."[6]

Chief among the nun's offenses would have been her passionate and sympathetic response to the Watts Rebellion of 1965. Her print *my people* (fig. 55) deployed a simple but powerful transfer of the front page of the *Los Angeles Times* to instantiate the reality, rendered in terms of profound, incarnational immanence by the inscribed words of Father Maurice Ouellet, the Pastor of the Catholic parish in Selma, Alabama, where Martin Luther King Jr. had led the famous and deadly confrontations over voting rights just a few months before. Ouellet, a civil-rights advocate, took John XXIII's favorite collective term, "people of God," and translated it as Christ's body internally in turmoil, tortured all over again by inequality and oppression between the races.

Kent's transcription reads:

> The body of Christ is no more comfortable now than it was when it hung from the cross. Those who live in the well organized, well ordered, nourished, clean, calm and comfortable middle class part of Christ's body can easily forget that the body of Christ, as it now exists, is mostly disorganized, devoid of order, concerned with the material needs, hungry, dirty, not motivated by reason, fermenting in agonizing uncertainty and certainly most uncomfortable.
>
> Youth is a time of rebellion. Rather than squelch the rebellion, we might better enlist the rebels to join that greatest rebel of his time—Christ himself.

No sentiment could have been better calculated to enrage the reactionary archbishop, whose antipathy to any sort of civil-rights agitation was as intense and undisguised as that of

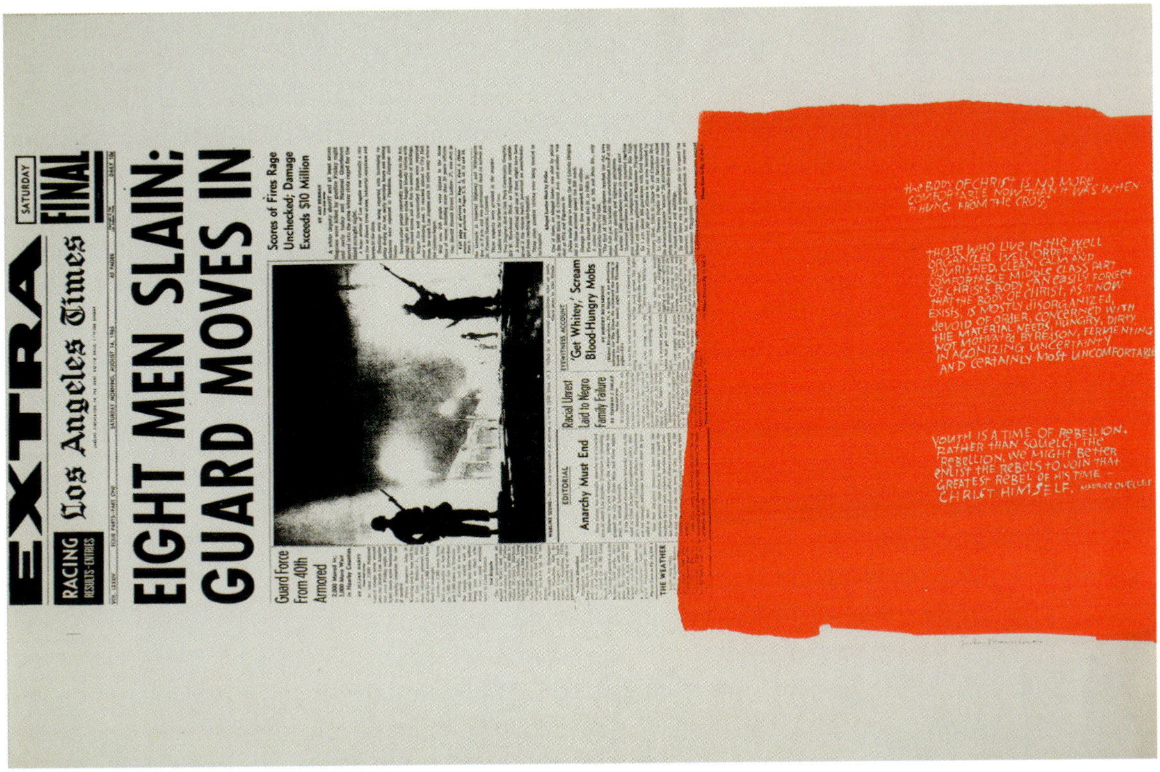


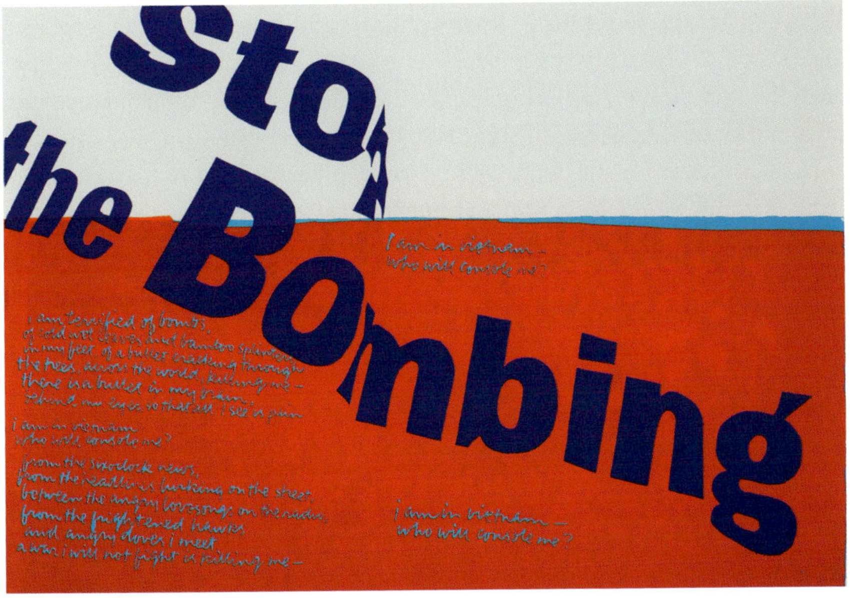


**55 (TOP)** Corita Kent, *my people*, 1965, screenprint, 58.4 × 88.9 cm, Corita Art Center

**56** Corita Kent, *stop the bombing*, 1967, screenprint, 39.37 × 58.42 cm, Corita Art Center

J. Edgar Hoover. Ignoring his efforts to discipline her artistic ambitions, Kent moved, like King, in 1967 to protest the war in *stop the bombing* (fig. 56), a flag-colored print in which the blue headline exhortation itself appears to follow a descending trajectory of jet-launched projectiles, burying itself in red earth surmounted by a sliver of paler blue. The inscribed verse by Gerald Huckaby—a 1950s fighter pilot, former *Time* journalist, and Catholic activist who taught literature alongside Kent at Immaculate Heart—sounds the repeated refrain, "I am in Vietnam. Who will console me?"[7] It will come as no surprise that McIntyre was an obdurate war hawk, like his former mentor Cardinal Spelman of the New York archdiocese, who lent a Christian imprimatur to Johnson's and later Nixon's determination to force North Vietnam into submission by relentless bombing attacks against civilians. Early in 1967, when some two thousand American religious leaders gathered in Washington to voice a collective statement of conscience against the war, not one the country's 250 Catholic bishops attended.[8]

Kent's speaking out against the war thus became a further offense in a lengthy bill of particulars against the Immaculate Heart sisters as a group. On 17 May 1968, Kent's close friend, the Jesuit priest Daniel Berrigan, along with his brother Philip and seven others, entered the offices of a draft board outside of Baltimore, Maryland, seized its records, and set them alight outside in a bath of napalm. After their arraignment, both the Berrigans then jumped bail for a fugitive life in the American underground (neither to be apprehended until 1970). Taking leave from her order in the summer of 1968, Kent travelled to Cape Cod to stay with her friend the art dealer Celia Hubbard. When autumn arrived, however, she remained in Boston, artistically active—and activist—but now religiously unaffiliated. The dominant motif in *news of the week* constituted Kent's farewell to the public person and cloistered nun she had been in her earlier cover profile in *Newsweek*, substituting Christ's "least of these" in place of her former prominence. In taking that path, she anticipated the decision her Immaculate Heart sisters in Los Angeles would make in 1970. When faced with the cardinal's draconian ultimatum that they return to strict orthodoxy and obedience, they disbanded their order and their college with it. Kent's losses and theirs—of community, sisters, and students—had been profound. As much as Turrell, she was made to pay a steep price for her testimony against the brutality and futility of the American War in Indochina.

■

Kent had not been alone in her resolute stand against the reactionary forces within her Church and in the larger political order; the dean of Immaculate Heart College, Sister Margaret Mary, and the Mother General of their order, Anita Caspary, were just as unwavering as their students. Compared with the wider landscape of California higher education, however, their small numbers and religious affiliation left them vulnerable to the suppression they soon suffered. But such was far from the case amid the vast complex of public universities and colleges in California, where the 1964 uprising fomented by the Free Speech Movement at the Berkeley campus had set the founding example for campus protest nationwide. Even the most beleaguered of the campuses proved able to sustain a radically critical culture in the face of vehement opposition from the predominantly reactionary culture that surrounded it. This was the freshly minted branch of the University of California at San Diego, then a medium-sized city at the absolute bottom southwest corner of the state: adjacent to Mexico but overwhelmingly white in both its demographic and outlook. Its region, moreover, was dominated to an exceptional degree by the Navy and Marine Corps, including the home base of the Pacific Fleet in the bay, a surrounding penumbra of hungry military contractors great and small, and a large population of buzz-cut, retired military personnel. Militantly conservative movements from the John Birch Society to the Goldwater and Reagan campaigns took root there early and virulently. In what seemed a calculated display of resistance to allowing the new enterprise in higher education from being identified with this right-wing context, the university administration brought in the German Neo-Marxist Herbert Marcuse to teach philosophy; shortly afterward, his student Angela Davis, an intransigent Black liberationist, followed him to continue her studies at his new seaside post. The faculty of the art department (as will be explored further in a subsequent chapter) filled up with free-thinking New Yorkers.

UC San Diego saw no militant, campus-wide disruption in this period, but the smallish circles of fervently anti-war dissidents did not lack for targets against which to demonstrate in the militarily fortified metropolis, a primary point of departure for the Southeast Asian theater (a good part of the campus itself rising on a former Marine Corps facility donated to the state as surplus land). The young artist Martha Rosler, nonetheless, found reasons to move away from her New York upbringing and earlier education in order to pursue her studies at UC San Diego, where she found sympathetic contacts in and around the university and to whom she brought in turn an unusually advanced feminist consciousness in concert with her anti-war commitments. Though admitted to the fine-art program as an already accomplished painter, her political priorities had turned her artistic energies in a dramatically different direction, toward the medium of collage from mass-produced photographs, engendering a series of twenty compositions, dating from 1967 to 1972, that she grouped under the title "House Beautiful: Bringing the War Home."[9]

Rosler's initial aim had been to counter the "text-heavy" handouts, "covered with slogans and paragraphs and arguments," prevalent at anti-war events but, as she saw it, out of keeping with the hectic pace of a street demonstration.[10] Her alternative approach instead emphasized immediate visual impact: she would clip out an idealized, sanitized interior from a home-decorating magazine, then insert vignettes of menace and violence from photographs of the war in Vietnam, generating an unfailingly jarring juxtaposition between clueless American affluence and the devastation being wrought in its name, purportedly in "defense" of that entitled prosperity. But such a bare descriptive formula does little justice to work done by the subtly composed intersections between her collaged elements. In *Balloons* (fig. 57), the titular element rises awkwardly in the corner of a double-height

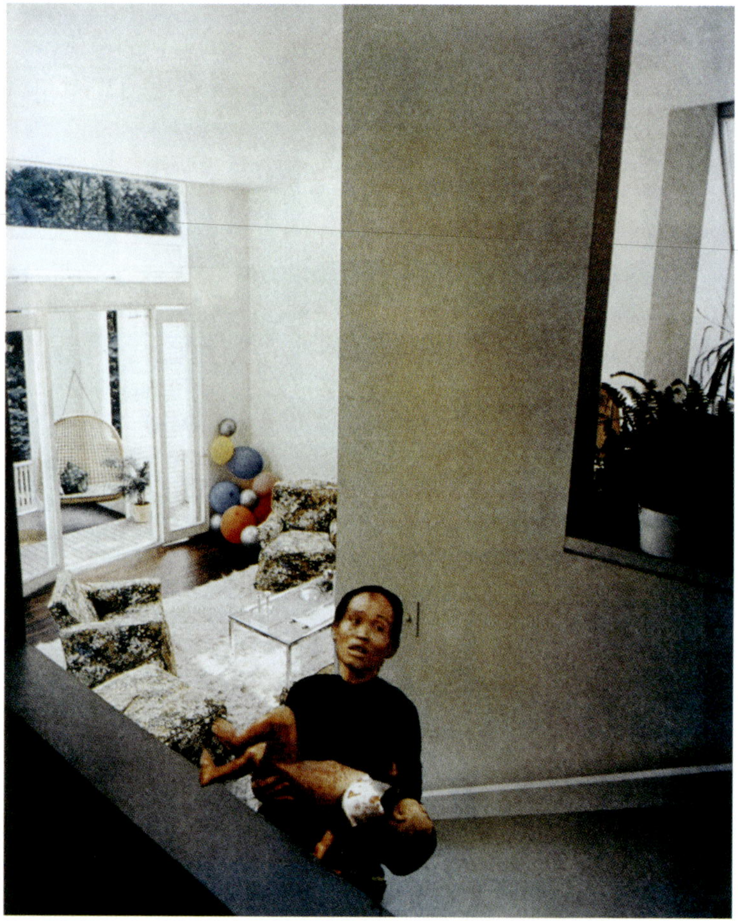

57 Martha Rosler, *Balloons*, from the series "House Beautiful: Bringing the War Home," c. 1967–72, pigmented inkjet print (photomontage), The Museum of Modern Art, New York

modern room, incongruously furnished in overstuffed chintz, while other angular walls confound the space in nightmare cubist terms. At the convergence of its vectors, she places a desperate Vietnamese woman holding a limp, wounded, barely clothed infant—no festivities likely in its life.

Though now widely known and admired, these works were never shown in a fine-art context during their period of production, serving instead as mock-ups for cheaply photocopied flyers to be handed out at the protest gatherings. Their disruptive internal divisions would not project themselves from the familiar, fine-art medium of pasted collage; rather they would have appeared all of a piece in black ink on cheap paper of this or that color, demanding an experimental form of non-linear reading on the fly. Her visual statements might have taken a moment to hit home, but no more than that for anyone who bothered to look, their economy an immediate stimulus to the requisite anger and protest spirit in an inhospitable setting that left little time to spare.

The evolving character of graphic communication within the anti-war movement depended on the local circumstances of protest and resistance. And it would prove only a matter of time before swelling discontent set off a conflagration somewhere in the system. Not surprisingly, it happened in the Bay Area, 500 miles from Rosler, the spark igniting in early May 1967, when six students occupied the president's office at San Francisco State College (now San Francisco State University) to protest the policy of providing male students' academic records to the Selective Service, that is, to the military draft. Loss of student deferment could, of course, lead to conscription and deployment to Vietnam. When the statewide chancellor refused to alter the policy, discontent grew to encompass other issues, primarily a drive to incorporate a spectrum of third-world studies into the college curriculum, beginning with a program in Black Studies. By spring 1968, a group calling itself the Third World Liberation Front had emerged to represent the full spectrum of minorities within the student body and speak to their frustrations. The campus remained in a state of continual disruption, with strikes and shutdowns, for nearly two years from that first sit-in over college complicity with the US war machine.[11]

Rupert García had entered SF State in 1966, resuming studies in studio art that he had commenced closer to his Central Valley roots at Stockton Junior College in 1960. Between 1962 and 1966, he had voluntarily served in the Air Force, at first in relative peacetime and latterly in logistical support of Rolling Thunder, the relentlessly punitive US bombing of North Vietnam intended, without success, to force concessions in the South. The young Chicano had found himself stationed in the uplands of Thailand, at a base from which sorties in the campaign were being launched in secret. As Turrell had been five years before, he, too, became entangled with the Central Intelligence Agency, García's role being to guard the clandestine airfield and occasionally set a perimeter around unexploded bombs jettisoned from returning flights. In a 1995 interview, he recalled both the unit's euphemistic name, "Military Assistance and Air Advisory Group," and the transparent subterfuge meant to obscure their national identity: "And so we were supposed to wear a kind of a hat and look like Australians, with these bush hats."[12] His awareness of deception and subterfuge in the war effort did not then entail anything like Turrell's Quaker pacifism; indeed, on first hearing of anti-war agitation back home, he felt an indignant desire to refute the war's opponents on his return. Once re-enrolled in college, however, doubt overcame him, as he imbibed the critical, left-wing subject matter so abundant in the SF State curriculum. Of his time there, he later recalled, "No one knows that I had ever served in the Vietnam War. I didn't tell anybody; I kept this close to my chest. So when I started to participate in critical discussions, reading leaflets that people were passing out, and studying philosophy and sociology and anthropology, taking special courses that were designed specifically around critical thinking and new theory about the commodification of everyday life—I began reading New Left theory and was exposed to the Black Panther Party and other Third World liberation thinking. And it began to make sense to me; it really made critical sense."[13]

García's early artistic efforts gravitated toward the fine-art print medium of etching and aquatint, picking up, it would have seemed, where he had left off in Stockton. But exposure to "critical thinking and new theory" made an almost immediate impact on his work. Without diminishing the softened textures and atmospheric qualities inherent to his chosen medium, he condensed and toughened it with an emblematic imagery of sociopolitical awareness. He based one series on a condensed vignette he called *Black Man with Glasses*—an isolated, bust-length portrait, the subject's expression hidden behind opaque shades, his pencil moustache and processed hair those of an entertainer. In some prints, the anonymous portrait appears alone; in *Black Man and Flag* (fig. 58) it replaces the stars within a caustically rearranged American flag, its direction reversed and black stripes running vertically like the bars of a prison cell: hipness caged.

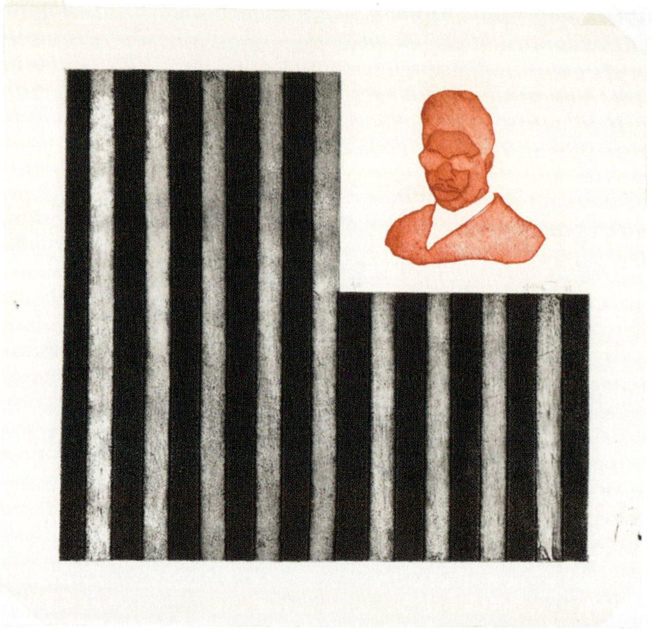

**58** Rupert García, *Black Man and Flag*, 1967, etching and collagraph, 55.4 × 58.9 cm, Fine Arts Museums of San Francisco

Dated to the fall of 1967, this print came into being some months after King's address at the Riverside Church, the moment that had firmly aligned protest against racial injustice with opposition to the war in Indochina. García sounded the latter note in his contemporaneous *The War and Children* (fig. 59), a vertically oriented, cruciform composition that likewise exploits the strength of compact, figural vignettes and stark tonal contrasts. During 1967, publicity of atrocities suffered by children in Vietnam, casualties of indiscriminate US bombing and shelling, had begun to chip away at the political timidity of conventional Americans unused to questioning the military actions and policies of their government. At the start of the year, another printmaker, Lorraine Schneider in New York, came up with a design that had arguably exerted the greatest impact on public anti-war sentiment of any piece of graphic art: *War Is Not Healthy for Children and Other Living Things*. Its disarming effect arose from her intentionally childlike (but not childish) calligraphy and floral embodiment of innocent life. In *The War and Children*, García took the theme toward a distinctly contrasting mode of graphic economy, which foregoes didacticism for more ominous disquiet and menace. The dark areas and shadows under the helmets convey the brooding presence of an implacable military force, like the Roman soldiers at the Crucifixion, with virtually no superfluous detail. The balancing dark shape at the base of the cross resists a literal reading, appearing simultaneously as a malignant flow from the mouth of the child or, conversely, a distorted hand gripping her throat and chin, one enlarged finger probing the same orifice.

The marks of traditional craft enhance rather than dilute the strength and clarity of García's motifs, which resemble the stylized, high-contrast conventions that contemporary San Francisco designers used to advertise the countercultural rock-ballroom scene. Another tributary of the same graphic current had flowed through Cuba to Paris, yielding in October 1967 the enduringly emblematic portrait of Che Guevara fashioned by the expatriate Irish designer Jim Fitzpatrick.[14] García reproduced Fitzpatrick's template in a 1968 poster over the slogan "RIGHT ON!" in stencil-patterned capitals. For him and his peers, the intimate and labor-intensive character of fine-art media like etching had become an unsustainable luxury in the face of the escalating political conflict at the college. When the campus-wide strike was called in November 1968, students in the art department—García in a leading role—organized themselves into a publicity arm of the strike action. He recalled that, the following year, a professor from England was visiting who was conversant with the silkscreened posters produced in Paris during the 1968 May Revolt by the Atelier Populaire, the workshop within the École des Beaux-Arts that blanketed the Latin Quarter with fly-posted invectives against authority and exhortations to altered states of consciousness. García described his activist role in translating the Parisian prototype to the local context of San Francisco:

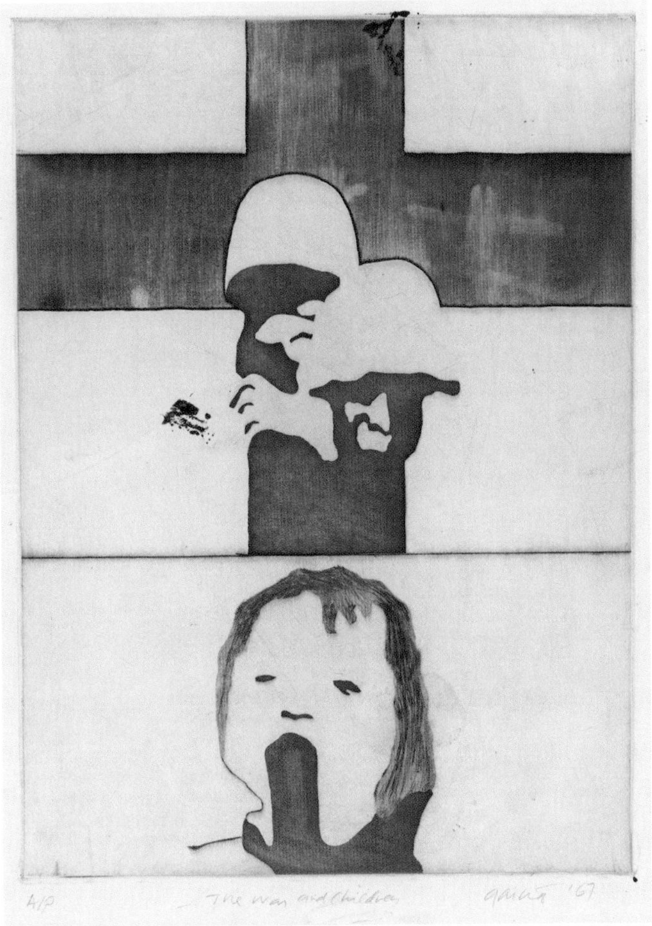

**59** Rupert García, *The War and Children*, 1967, etching, 40 × 28.4 cm, Fine Arts Museums of San Francisco

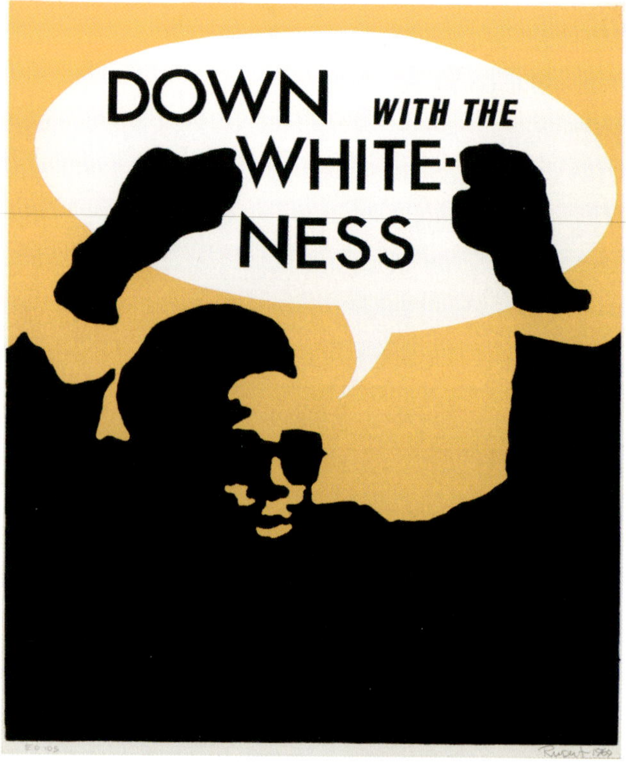


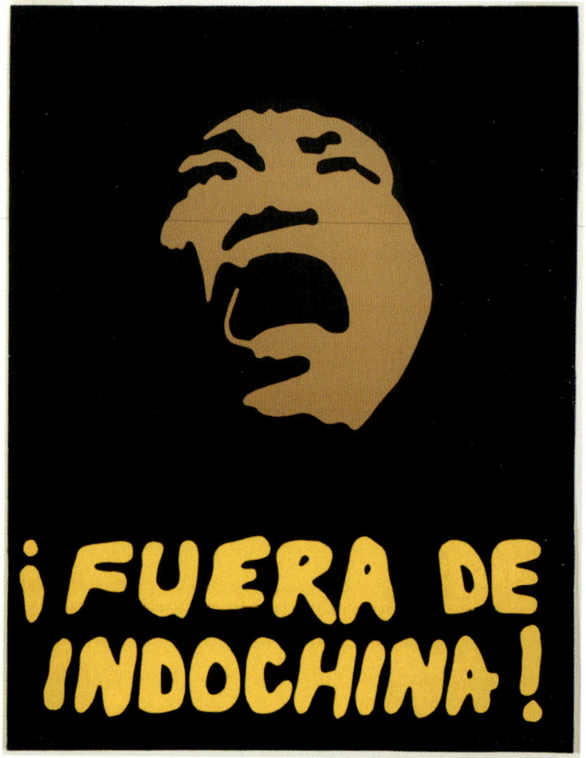


**60 (ABOVE LEFT)** Rupert García, *Down with the Whiteness*, 1969, screenprint, 66.36 × 51.12 cm, Fine Arts Museums of San Francisco

**61** Rupert Garcia, *¡Fuera de Indochina!*, 1970, screenprint, 60.7 × 45.6 cm, Fine Arts Museums of San Francisco

> I was a liaison between the art department and the other members of the Third World Liberation Front organizations. I would go talk to them and come back, and this kind of thing. And so we began to make posters dealing with the issues—issues from racism to better education to police brutality, antiwar, and much more. I mean, all the issues that were being addressed at that time made for a heady experience. Many of those issues were being dealt with in our poster brigade. And the posters were used in the demonstrations on campus, and some were used outside of campus, and some were sold to raise money to get people out on bail, people who had been arrested.[15]

One fierce outcome of his individual efforts was the incendiary 1969 poster *Down with the Whiteness* (fig. 60), in which he rendered a beret-wearing Panther in full oratorical flight, black-gloved fists isolated against the speech balloon that bears the poster's titular slogan. In its combination of energy with formal elegance, along with its transposition, via the definite article "the," of white identity into an abstract condition (as blackness inheres in the ink itself), García's design easily matches the best of his Parisian predecessors on both technical and conceptual levels.

The secret bombing and invasion of Cambodia in the spring of 1970 brought a renewed sense of crisis and urgency, sparking the most widespread uprisings on college and university campuses of the Vietnam era, including the retaliatory murders of student demonstrators by National Guardsmen at Kent State University in Ohio. That moment coincided with García's June 1970 exhibition marking the completion of his master's degree in fine art at SF State. The venue, however, was not on campus but at the Artes 6 Gallery in the city's Mission District—a cooperative Latino counterpart to the Brockman Gallery in Los Angeles, where Hammons had exhibited his *Injustice Case* the year before. García recalled that none of his teachers attended the opening, a possible indicator that the ascent of the Third World Liberation Front had opened a split in the earlier, strike-born solidarity between students and faculty.[16] As a graphic artist, his most forceful response to the 1970 crisis placed his ethnic identity at the forefront of his insistent anti-war message. "Out of Vietnam" became *¡Fuera de Indochina!* (fig. 61). No one needed to tell García that the theater of war in the region had always exceeded the notional boundaries of Vietnam, North or South. And his command of the high-contrast, international idiom of protest imagery had advanced to a level beyond the norm, significantly beyond his openly derivative take on Che Guevara. A minimal number of black intrusions into a terracotta field generate an elementally tortured visage that reaches from pre-Hispanic anguish over European conquest to the terrorized skyward gazes of Cambodian peasants under American onslaught.

■

At this time, another young graphic designer in the Bay Area was likewise linking the struggle for racial justice at home with resistance to American imperial overreach in Southeast Asia. Emory Douglas, then twenty-seven, stood high in the hierarchy of the Black Panther Party for Self-Defense, whose example, from the group's founding in 1967, had helped galvanize both the campus and off-campus causes to which García was committed. As the Party's Minister of Culture, Douglas had turned his considerable visual talent to making its newspaper, the *Black Panther*, a great success in visibility, circulation, and revenue, its distribution each Wednesday night providing an important occasion for group solidarity.[17] His signature style rendered shading into strong, lattice-like patterns in solid black, putting lots of ink onto eye-catching pages. By 1970, he was using the back cover of the paper as what was in effect a weekly poster, title at the bottom and explanatory legend across the top.

Douglas's back-cover graphic (fig. 62) for the issue of 31 May 1970 presented an up-close African American fighter, carrying an automatic rifle while wearing a broad-brimmed cloth hat and tropical fatigues in the style of a North Vietnamese soldier. Its title is "The Lumpen," and the legend reads in part: "The students focus their rebellions on the campuses . . . But the LUMPEN finds itself in the peculiar position of being unable to find a job and is therefore unable to attend the Universities. The LUMPEN has no choice but to manifest its rebellion in the University of the Streets."

It is true that the emerging California Panthers enjoyed only glancing exposure to the state's four-year universities, but the same is not true of its (in those days) well-funded and accessible community colleges. The Party's two leaders, Huey P. Newton and Bobby Seale, met at Oakland's Merritt College, where they both joined Black student organizations, imbibing some of the same philosophical sources that had first galvanized García, along with a prescient synthesis between understanding the status of African Americans as one of confinement in brutally policed internal colonies and recognizing the cognate neo-colonialist policies projected by American military and CIA interventions abroad, whether overt or clandestine. Douglas, for his part, having been impressed by Newton's and Seale's exploits in confronting police abuses, became an early recruit to the Party while still studying design at San Francisco City College.[18]

His early life had been punctuated by two stints in state juvenile detention, over the course of which he had acquired both an eminently useful vocational skill as a printer and the tough, street-level formation he extols in "The Lumpen." The cause that brought the first small Panther cell to wider attention, early in 1967, was the gratuitous murder by sheriff's deputies of a young Black, Denzil Dowell, in the East Bay ghetto enclave of North Richmond. The brother of the victim (and future Panther) found the body abandoned in the street, only for it to emerge that that he had been shot down by officers who claimed that they had justifiably intervened in a liquor-store robbery. Despite the predictable exoneration of the officers involved, all of their justifications were patently fabricated.[19] Protests were mounted, with Newton and Seale organizing an armed phalanx to prevent violent retaliation by the Contra Costa County sheriffs, who held jurisdiction over the impoverished, unincorporated community.

It is sobering, to say the least, that more than a half century of no change separates the murder of Denzil Dowell from the deaths at police hands of George Floyd, Breonna Taylor, and Rayshard Brooks (to name only a few). The immediate response of the Reagan-era Republican establishment to the display of armed community resistance, however, was head-spinningly different from our present-day realities. The state assemblyman representing a wealthy, Oakland-adjacent suburb introduced a bill to make illegal the carrying of loaded firearms in public. The Richmond events having drawn a wave of new recruits, the Panthers traveled en masse to the State Capital in Sacramento in May 1967 to protest the law, entering the legislative chamber fully armed, taking advantage of Newton's exact reading of current California law pertaining to carrying weapons. Douglas was one of the Panthers able to stand in with authority as part of this potent symbolic display, which made the group internationally famous—and notorious to a vengeful white power structure.

That authority and renown, augmented by the panoply of free social services organized by the Party in Oakland, provoked the now well-known, ruthlessly lawless campaign, driven by J. Edgar Hoover, of extra-judicial executions suffered by Panther leaders over the course

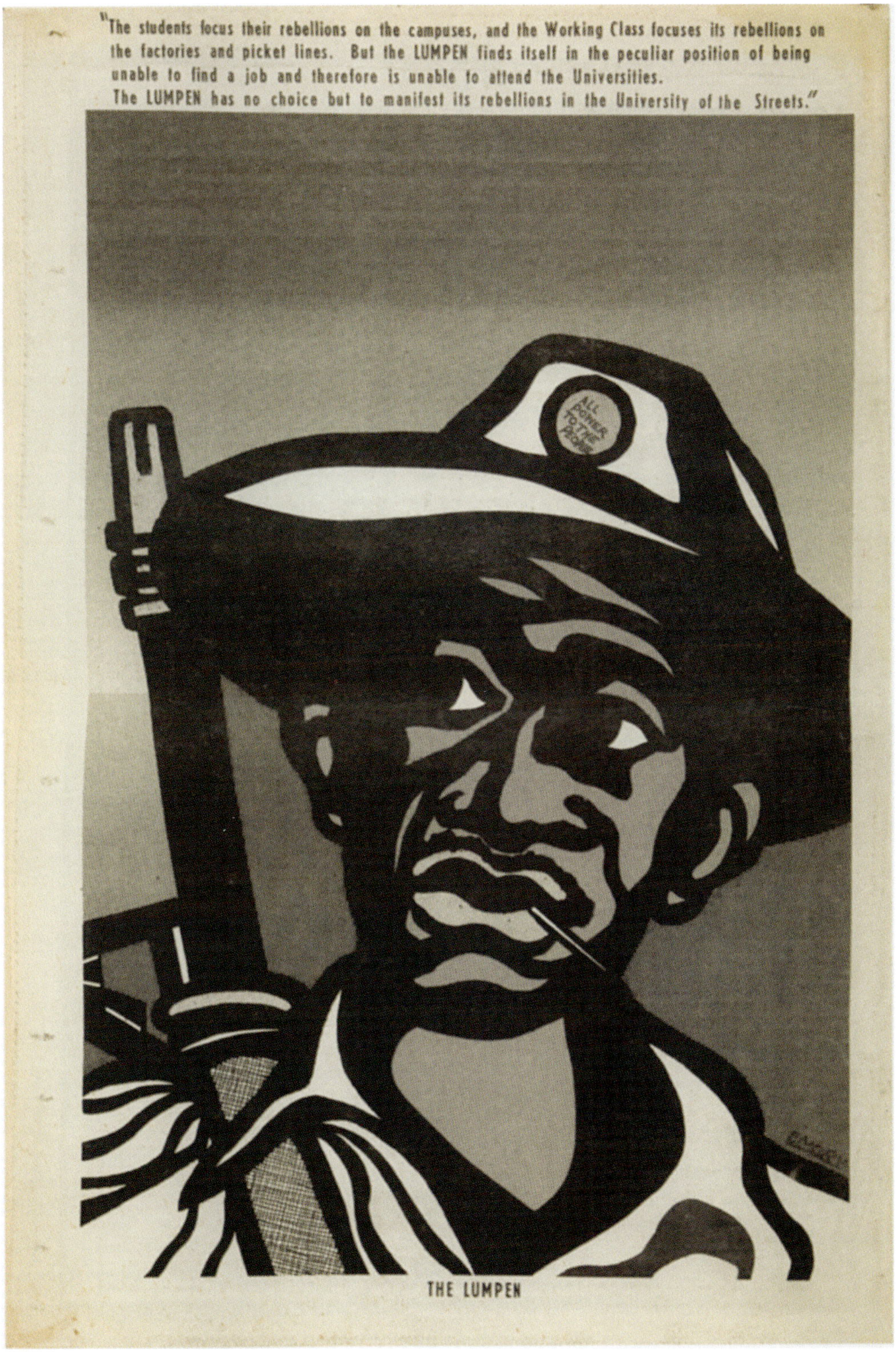


**62** Emory Douglas, "The Lumpen," back cover, *Black Panther*, San Francisco (31 May 1970)

of 1968 and 1969. To keep with Douglas's "The Lumpen" as a marker, the months leading up to its May 1970 publication embroiled Douglas in the next phase of this struggle, one that followed directly upon Bobby Seale's kangaroo trial in Chicago. In order to raise funds for his defense, Seale traveled to New Haven for a paid speech at Yale. Taking advantage of this exposure, George Sams, a Panther mole and violent provocateur in the pay of the FBI, arrived on a pretended mission to the nascent Panther chapter in that city.[20] Having organized the torture and murder of a supposed informant, Sams fled, escaping culpability but implicating Seale, who was arrested on a murder charge in New Haven, accused of ordering the execution with his codefendant Ericka Huggins (the widow of a recently assassinated Los Angeles Party leader).[21] Douglas and another senior Panther—being among the few leaders not indicted, in exile, or dead—traveled to New Haven to provide support during the trial, only to find themselves indicted and jailed in turn for merely receiving a note in the courtroom from Seale's attorney.

By this time, the spring of 1970, a large portion of the Yale student body had been mobilized on the Panthers' behalf, with Kingman Brewster, the university's president, eventually being moved to question in a public statement whether Black militants could ever receive a fair trial. As a campus strike was called, vituperative recriminations rained down on Brewster from the likes of Spiro Agnew, Nixon's thuggish vice-president, and Connecticut's Democratic governor. At the latter's request, the Attorney General sent active-duty troops to back up the state's police and National Guard.[22] Adroit collaboration between university actors and a brilliant young Panther organizer named Doug Miranda denied these politicians the incendiary conflict they desired, but then the stakes were raised immeasurably higher by Nixon's invasion of Cambodia on 29 April. Yale's strike over racial justice joined the nationwide wave of student walk-outs that would bring the greater part of American higher education to a practical halt and to at least a momentary reckoning with the reigning barbarism.

Douglas had been released as part of tension-reducing maneuvers in April and so was in a position to restart his graphic work as the national crisis reached a horrific pitch with the murders of white demonstrators at Kent State on 2 May. Douglas's designs take the measure of the moment, both in defiance and in desperation, more immediately and confidently than virtually any contemporaneous visual responses.[23] The lessons he took from the political crisis align with his convictions from the start of Black Panthers as a movement, unmollified by the largely peaceful effectiveness of the wide mobilization on Seale's behalf (indeed the Panther leader would remain incarcerated into 1972). Douglas's seasoned soldier in "The Lumpen" bides his time with an alert, sidelong glance, his Black identity and Asian guerilla's garb unified in the black arabesque of Douglas's characteristically bold pattern. A few weeks later, he produced for the paper's back page a female counterpart, as part of his campaign to bring the war home, titled "Warning to America" (fig. 63). Highlighted with an extra pass though the printer in yellow ink, his rendering of the weapon held by the woman exploits every bit of Roy Lichtenstein's brand of industrial clarity to place the means of Self-Defense (emblazoned on the yellow badge) to the fore with maximum resolution against the off-the-shelf, line-pattern background. The warrior herself manifests

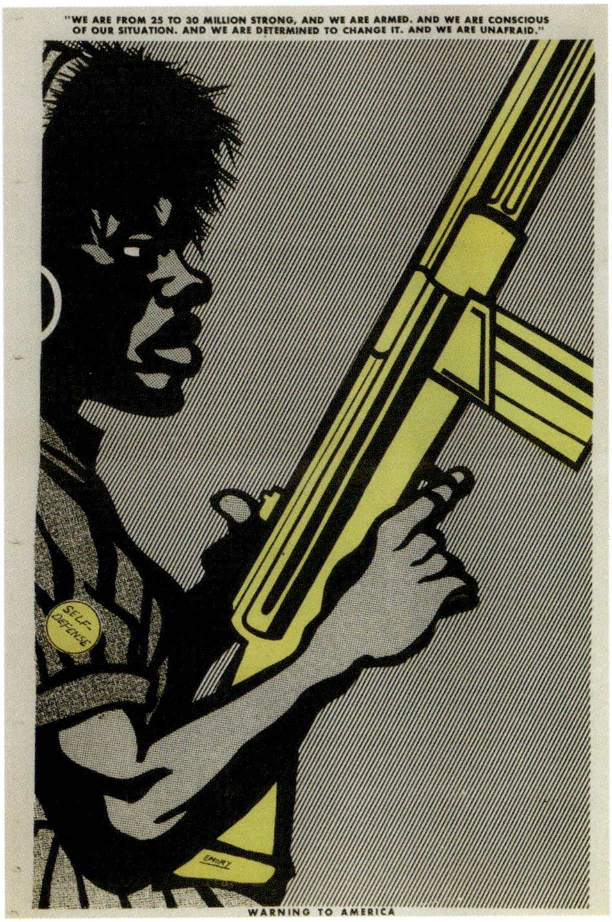


**63** Emory Douglas, "Warning to America," *Black Panther*, San Francisco (27 June 1970)

to an even greater degree Douglas's adept economy of chiaroscuro, his customarily smooth contours interrupted by spiky tendrils that individuate the silhouette, makes her figure more than a type, while playing against the inhuman regularity of the killing machine on its dominating diagonal.

■

The wave of protests that engulfed the university campuses did not let up before reaching the Chicano neighborhoods of East Los Angeles. In an evolution from the "Blowouts," the mass boycott of the Eastside high schools in 1968 in protest at inferior conditions and police harassment, the Chicano Moratorium Against the Vietnam War organized a march that took place in East Los Angeles at the end of August 1970. The violent repression that had been brought down on the student protesters two years before was now redoubled. In contrast to contemporaneous protests mounted by predominantly white, middle-class marchers else-

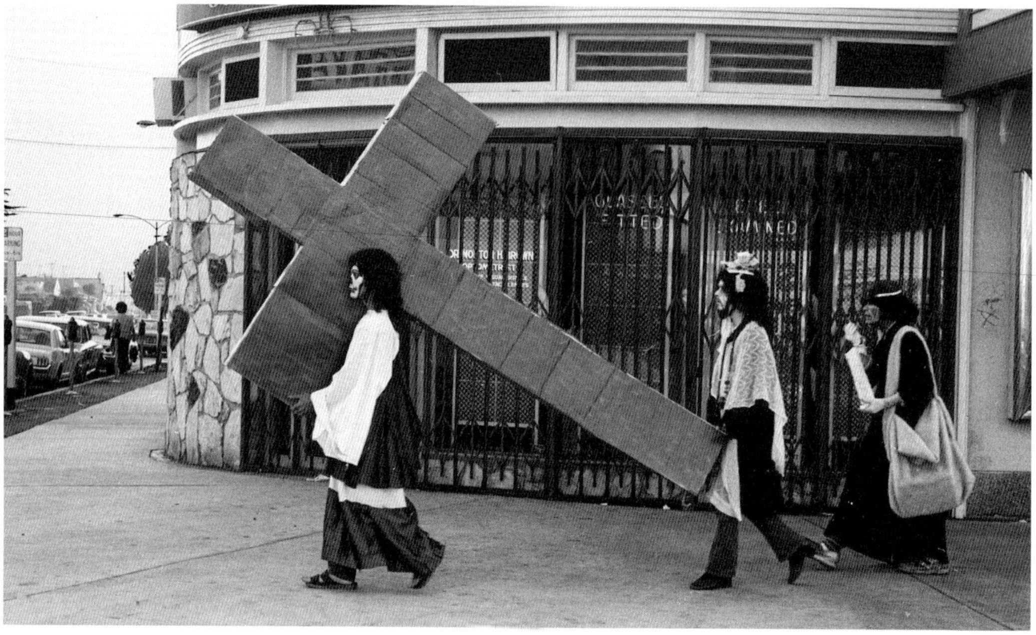

64 Asco, *Stations of the Cross*, 1971, performance, Whitter Boulevard, East Los Angeles

where in the region, their Chicano counterparts found themselves savagely set upon by the Los Angeles police and county sheriff's departments. Rubén Salazar, the most prominent Mexican American journalist in the region, was killed outright by a military-grade teargas canister fired into the bar where he and others had taken refuge from the police onslaught.

On Christmas Eve of 1971, four unheralded young artists staged in full costume a mock-religious procession enacting the Christian Stations of the Cross (fig. 64), marching along Whittier Boulevard, the main shopping and car-cruising thoroughfare of the Eastside. Their march concluded when they deposited their fifteen-foot-long cardboard crucifix, decorated with spray paint and glitter, in front of a Marine Corps recruiting office. In their wake, as one of them reported, "rumors of a bizarre religious sect in East L.A. began to surface . . . a reverberating impression of spiritual doubt and doubtful spirituality."[24]

The artists who staged this pageant, with its travesty of ornate Latino Catholicism, were Patssi Valdez, Harry Gamboa Jr., Willie Herrón III, and Glugio Nicandro (who calls himself Gronk).[25] The four had first come together as teenagers, working together on alternative publications, and all had joined in the Blowouts. The Stations of the Cross procession mourned Salazar, along with the assaulted dignity and hopes of the victimized marchers; it also channeled frustrated outrage over the disproportionate military intake of disadvantaged young Chicanos, with the consequently disproportionate number of deaths and

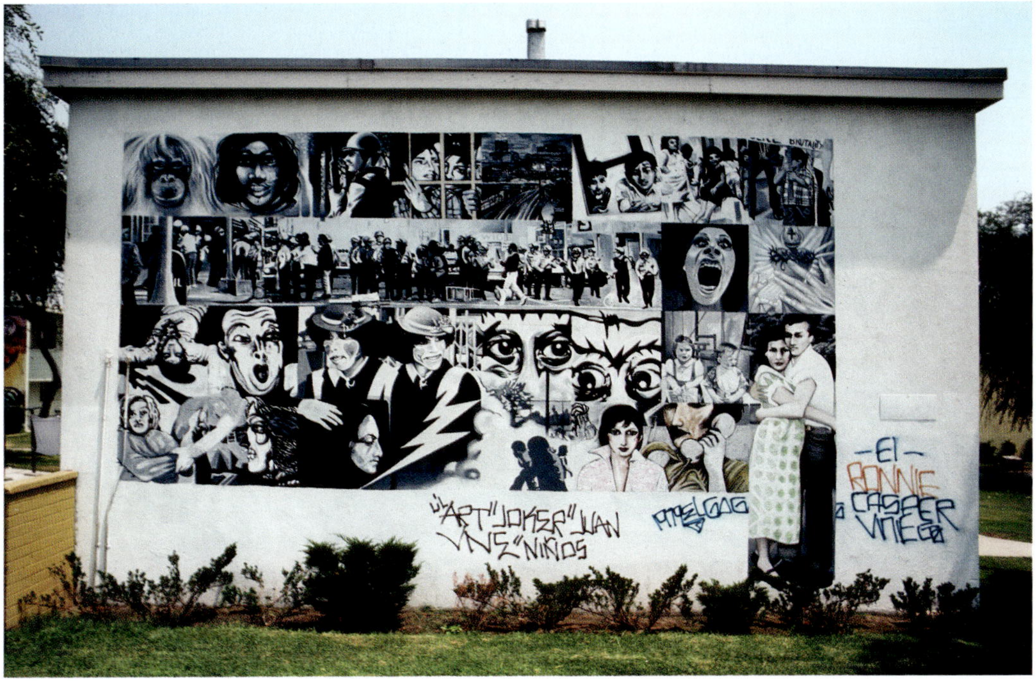


65 Willie F. Herrón and Gronk, *Moratorium: The Black and White Mural*, 1973, Estrada Courts, East Los Angeles, photograph by Harry Gamboa Jr.

injuries among them. After Nixon's elimination of the military draft and the winding down of the war, that threat receded for all ethnicities, but the threat of intimidation, arbitrary detainment, or violent injury at the hands of the police remained an everyday constant for young people in East Los Angeles, subtended by the Catholic conformism of the underlying culture and endemic danger posed by gang territoriality. But no visible, galvanizing movement, of the kind that energized Rupert García, had followed the repression of 1970. For these young Chicano artists, excluded at the same time from any compensating support from local art institutions, gaining public attention and scope for action required going outside the system. In 1973, after performing such exploits as "signing" the Los Angeles County Museum of Art (having been told by a curator that Chicanos only made folk art and gang graffiti), Gamboa, Valdez, Herrón, and Gronk formally named themselves Asco—after the Spanish phrase *me da asco*: it makes me puke.

Work of lasting physical permanence on the part of the group is rare, but their shared cinematic inclination infused the large mural painted by Herrón and Gronk (fig. 65) at the Eastside Estrada Courts housing project. The sight of freshly painted murals on outdoor surfaces in that area was by no means uncommon (eighty-two murals were commissioned for the Estrada Courts alone between 1972 and 1978). And Herrón and Gronk's contribution to the genre might have appeared at first encounter as conforming to type by its scale and militant subject matter. But the pair's first departure from the norm lay in the restriction of their palette to black and white.[26] They offhandedly claimed that the cheapness of the pigments dictated their choice, but the grid-like arrangement of motifs effectively called to mind the black-and-white grittiness of reportage on cheap televisions, alongside grainy projected images of the classic and New Wave European films that provided them with an alternative to the confining points of reference in their local surroundings. Those motifs pointed in particular to Gillo Pontecorvo's 1966 *Battle of Algiers*, which used quasi-documentary techniques to make vivid the Algerian nationalist resistance to French occupation—the anticolonialist struggle (and Irving Petlin's initial, radicalizing cause) that followed directly upon the expulsion of the French from Indochina by the forces led by Hồ Chí Minh.

*Black and White Mural* thus linked the open wounds of French atrocities to fresh, aggrieved political memory of the events surrounding the Chicano Moratorium march against the Vietnam War. Alongside Warhol-like renditions of news photographs, Herrón and Gronk included a panel depicting the slain Salazar, his backward-tilted head in the foreground as if crucified upside down, a black arabesque of blood on his chest. Adjacent to the Salazar martyrdom they placed a close-up rendering of the white-faced mime Baptiste, the character played by Jean-Louis Barrault in Marcel Carné's 1945 *Children of Paradise*, a film produced under German occupation, a condition they implicitly likened to the permanent occupation of the Los Angeles *barrio* by the Anglo forces of order. Next to the mime's stock expression of shock, Gronk placed a double portrait of himself in the comparably stylized, androgynous costume of the self-invented character he called Popcorn. Even in the more enduring medium of paint on plaster, Asco's activity comes close to the gestures by artists operating at the same time under the surveillance of the Brazilian dictatorship—coded and loaded to insiders, opaque and misdirecting to anyone else.

A few of their actions emerged into public awareness via distorted echoes, like the cult rumors following their Stations of the Cross procession or the photographic record of a 1974 performance they called *Decoy Gang War Victim* (fig. 66), during which Gronk lay as dead, surrounded by flares, at the center of an empty downtown street during the early morning hours. Gamboa succeeded in inducing several television and print outlets to feature the image as showing the actual final victim of some ultimate gang war of attrition. His immediate target was the political stereotyping—undiminished since—of young Latino males as gang members and criminals. The history of the Vietnam War may by that date have been undergoing hasty repression from American collective memory, but Asco's form of activism—like those of Hammons, García, and Douglas—had never admitted any separation between what they viewed as unconscionable aggression abroad and unjust oppression at home; nor would their own history have allowed them to forgo the implication in *Decoy Gang War Victim* of their classmates among the draftees brought home in coffins. Gamboa's stark, powerfully simplified photograph testifies to the war that never seems to end.[27]

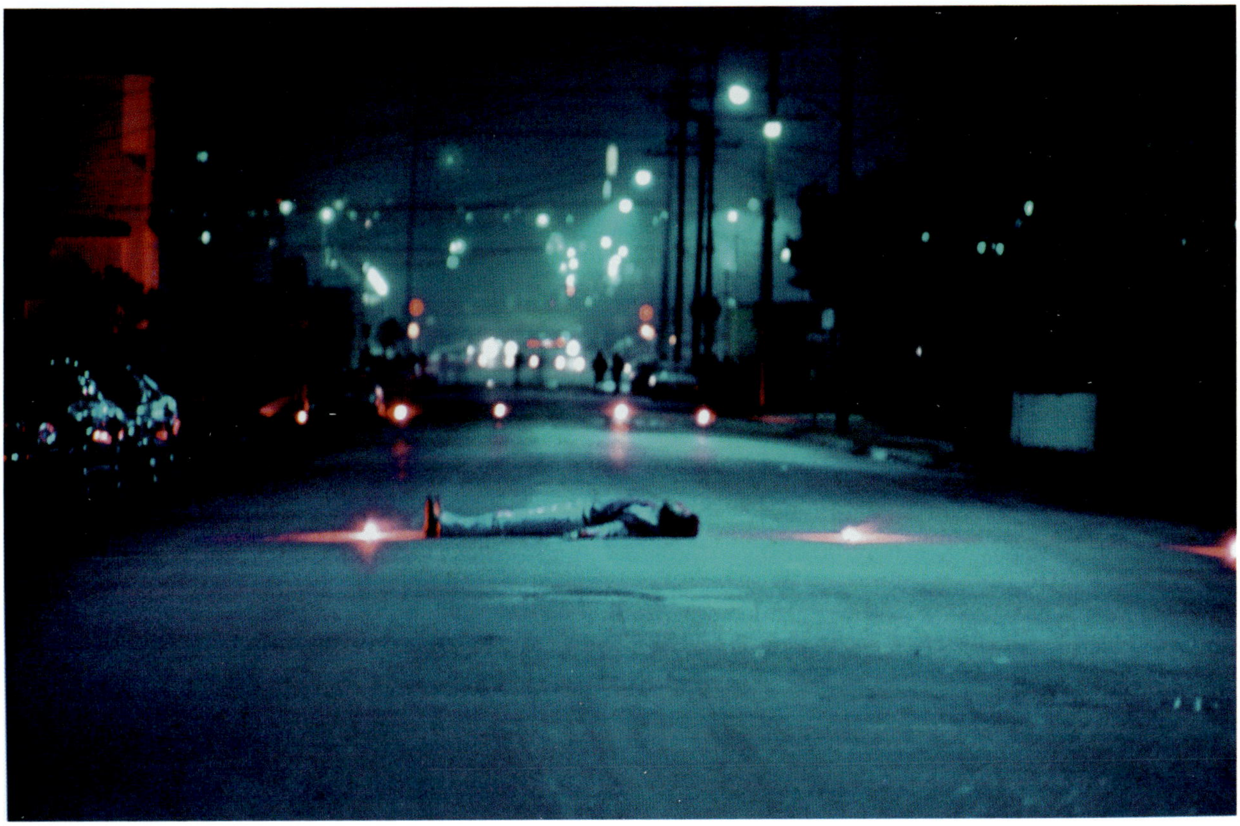

**66** Asco, *Decoy Gang War Victim*, 1974, chromogenic print, 32.1 × 48.3 cm, photograph by Harry Gamboa Jr., Smithsonian American Art Museum

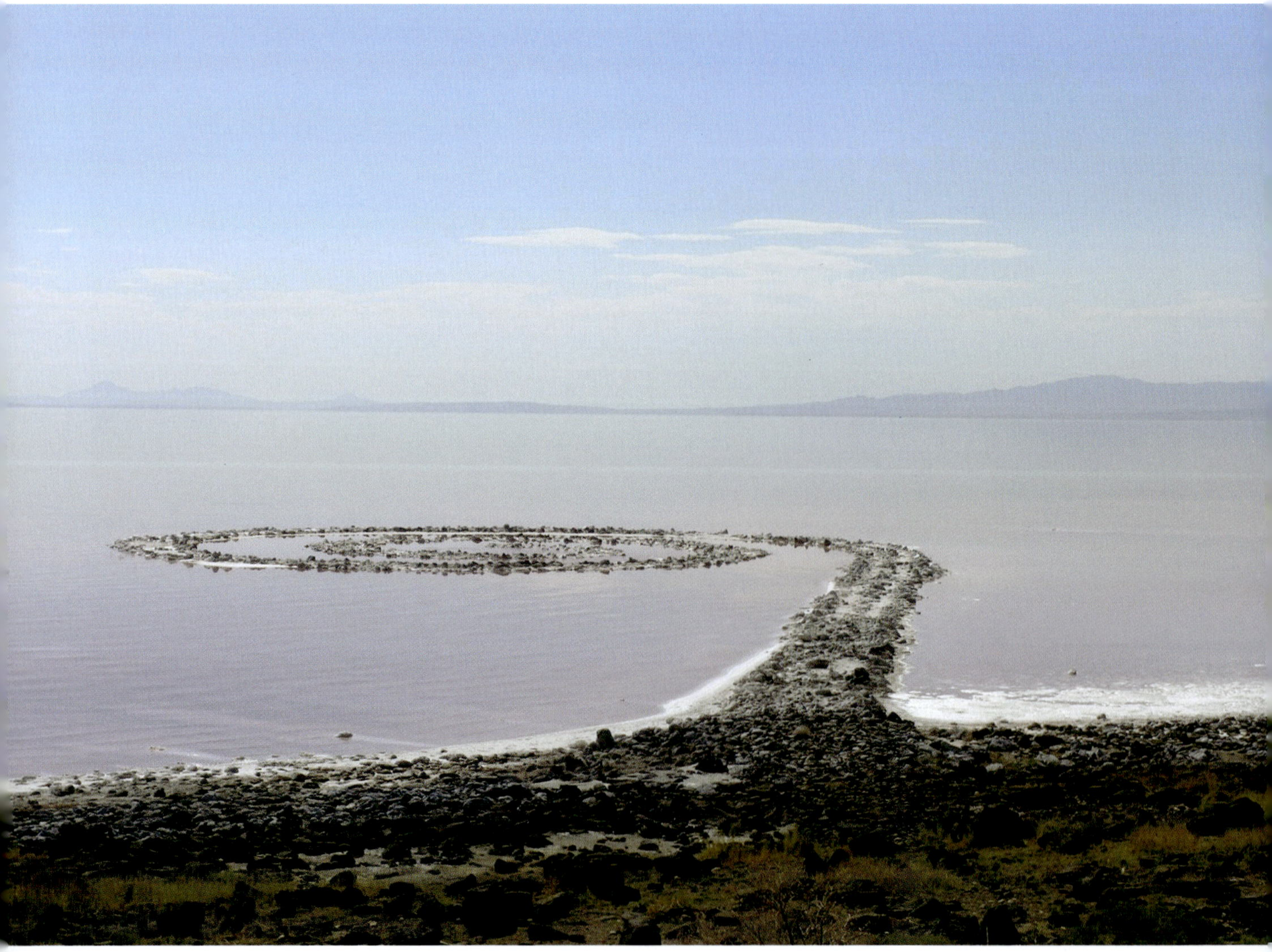

**67** Robert Smithson, *Spiral Jetty*, 1969–70, Rozel Point, Great Salt Lake, Utah

EIGHT

# TOWARD 1970: "THE EVER-DEEPENING SPIRAL OF POLITICS"

A FLIP THROUGH THE PAGES OF *ARTFORUM* IN 1965 would have yielded a split and contradictory impression as to where its main allegiance resided. In the recollection of New Yorker Mel Bochner, the upstart Los Angeles publication had undergone a palpable shift in tone over its short, three-year period of existence: "They were no longer, by that point, about younger California artists," he remembered thinking. "It was more about the 'scene.' I remember one feature, Dennis Hopper photographs, of Jasper Johns, Henry Geldzahler and Andy Warhol. They were almost like fashion magazine photos."[1] While the style of the piece and the identity of the photographer may have said Los Angeles, however, the portrait subjects recalled by Bochner say New York. Indeed, in the mind of *Artforum*'s editor, Philip Leider, the magazine's attention was no longer on the West Coast at all: as he told Amy Newman in her oral history of the publication, "around '65 I shifted the emphasis to New York very consciously, very deliberately."[2] But his intention was in no way to scatter Hollywood stardust over the Manhattan art world; he had in view an East Coast cohort of bookish young writers, whose fragile coalition he imagined as remaking *Artforum* into a byword for ambitious critical thought.

Given the variety of temperaments involved in the project—which included Barbara Rose, Michael Fried, Rosalind Krauss, and Max Kozloff—Leider expected the move to be a short-lived experiment: As he wrote to Fried early in 1966,

> from the moment I decided to shift ARTFORUM away from the hopeless task of making a West Coast art magazine toward becoming a vehicle for the group of younger people like you, Barbara, Max, la Krauss etc., I knew that the days of such a venture were limited by the volatile nature of the personalities involved, and that I could expect a year, perhaps two, during which I could hold the mixture in some kind of suspension, after which it would explode into its incompatible, irrevocably hostile elements.

One of those years, he reflected, had already expired, "and all the signs are that I will be lucky to manage the second."[3]

Lieder's prediction of volatility and interpersonal drama came to be amply borne out, as Newman's candid informants confirm, but it was, in the end, their solidarity in the face of

Leider's own need for change that propelled him away from the magazine he had done more than anyone else to define. By 1969, he felt that he had discovered on his own a compelling new body of art, one that demanded recognition in *Artforum*'s pages, but in distinctly different terms and with a different vocabulary than the cohort of '66 would or could deliver: "There was a scene happening, unexpected, unpredictable and unpredicted, but there and real," he would later recollect. "The scene was the emergence of a coherent group of very, very good artists at the core of which were [Robert] Smithson, [Richard] Serra, [Michael] Heizer, [Alan] Saret, [Keith] Sonnier. They were connected with something new in film—Michael Snow—and something new in music—Philip Glass. It was very exciting, and I couldn't get any of the writers I cared about to get interested in it."[4] Those New York-based names may not carry a countercultural ring today; indeed, they enjoy, on the whole, a shared standing as mainstream masters. Yet, as Leider testifies, their art seemed indigestibly outré to the critics whose sensibilities had been formed in the early 1960s.

Not only were the geographical boundaries of significant art exploding beyond the confines of Manhattan art spaces across the hinterlands of the continent, but there had also emerged new models of cultural journalism exemplified by Jann Wenner's *Rolling Stone*, launched in San Francisco just as *Artforum* itself had been. Since its debut in 1967, *Rolling Stone*'s stable of writers condensed the transformational social ethos of the West Coast counterculture and rock world into long-form, personalized narratives, heavy on vivid reportage, light on intellectual decorum. Leider singled out for praise Michael Lydon—Yale graduate, mainstream journalist turned hippie—whose main beat at *Rolling Stone* was immersive road dispatches from the carnivalesque tours of the newly anointed rock aristocracy. Lydon's reporting reached a summit in the massive piece he filed for the more politicized, likewise San Francisco–based *Ramparts*: "The Rolling Stones—at Play in the Apocalypse," his close-up view on the zombie march toward Altamont.[5] "I was so taken with that essay," Leider recalled, "I so wanted that element, that quality, that hip, lively quality . . ."[6]

*Artforum*'s staff writers of the day were suffused with a Mandarin aversion to popular culture, so Leider held little hope that this new model would register in their ranks, any more than would the new art that excited him. That left no one to undertake the task but himself. So, in the summer of 1970, he stepped out of his normal arbiter's role to chronicle a cross-country trip from New York to his old Berkeley home, a base from which he would launch pilgrimages to Smithson's and Heizer's grand and remote workings on the western landscape. When he returned, he wasted no time publishing his first-person account of these adventures in the September issue, under the slightly manic title "How I Spent My Summer Vacation or, Art and Politics in Nevada, Berkeley, San Francisco and Utah (Read about It in Artforum!)."[7] Leider consciously modeled his essay on "the hippy stuff I was reading in Berkeley that I was very impressed by . . . the stuff I had been reading in *Rolling Stone*."[8]

■

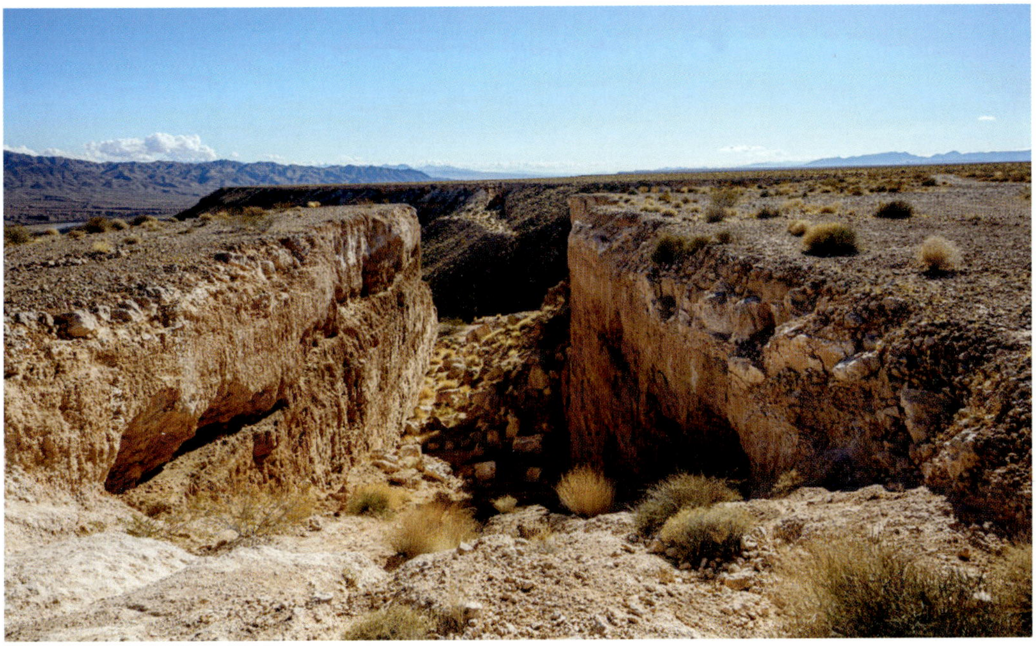

**68** Michael Heizer, *Double Negative*, 1969–70 (present state), Virgin River Mesa, Nevada, earth and air, Museum of Contemporary Art, Los Angeles

In examining the interface between self-consciously advanced art and the counterculture, one looks for help from observers with significant commitment to both sides of the equation. The Swiss curator Harald Szeeman, as detailed in the Prologue above, was definitely one such rare individual. And all the artists whose work occasioned Leider's growing self-doubt had also been taken up by Szeeman. As Lieder recounts the drive to Nevada in the company of native Californian Richard Serra, he echoes the Swiss curator's fascination with mind-altering substances, as he says of his companion, "Ideas explode in his head with the regularity of Dexedrine spansules popping." And the two of them soon tangle up the political theatrics of Abbie Hoffman (descended from Allan Kaprow's Happenings) with Michael Fried's strictures against contaminating the exclusive sphere of art's inherited conventions with "theater." But such strictures soon shrink to a vanishing speck in the rearview mirror; and the first sight of the road trip's goal, Heizer's *Double Negative* (1969–70) (fig. 68), tips them into near-psychedelic disorientation and release: "We were all yipping and yowling as if Matisse had just called us over to look at something he was thinking of calling *Joy of Life*. The sun was down; we wound up slipping and sliding inside the piece in the dark. . . . The piece was a new place in nature."

Despite this being a first report to the magazine's readership on these brand new works of land art, Leider spares no more attention to their formal details than Michael Lydon would have devoted to the chord changes in "Street Fighting Man." His essay concludes with an even more elliptical encounter with Smithson's *Spiral Jetty*, which he finds so fraught with larger implications that he neglects to speak at all about the matter and form of the monument beyond a worm's-eye observation concerning crystalline encrustations. As he doubtless walked around its coil, was he apprehending how unfixed its scale becomes? As any receptive visitor can attest, the *Spiral Jetty* (fig. 67), while an enormous accumulation of boulders by any human-scaled reckoning, appears miniaturized in relation to the expanse of even one corner of the Great Salt Lake. Yet to stand on it is to experience the circular horizon, bounded by distant ranges, incorporated into the work and vastly enlarging it. While fixed in size, the product of the simplest set of physical stipulations, the work shifts continually and dramatically from the immediate to the far distant. In that perceptual transformation, moreover, the scale of the sculpture to that borrowed landscape becomes analogous to the invisible, stepwise crystallization in the salt in relation to its own rocky mass. Smithson wrote at the completion of the work, "Growth in a crystal advances around a dislocation point, in the manner of a screw. The *Spiral Jetty* could be considered one layer within the spiraling crystal lattice . . . "[9] No brake need interrupt the movement of mind between the extremes of speck and infinitude, that is, the imagination of the divine according to Smithson's favorite philosopher, Blaise Pascal.

Such an undertaking in short was far more an exercise in metaphysics than in earthmoving pragmatics, one quietly but fiercely opposed to the disabused empirical attitude that had come to signify rigor and seriousness in advanced New York circles. Dealer John Weber reports that Smithson intended a direct riposte to the famous pronouncement by Frank Stella, offered in a joint interview with Donald Judd in 1966: "My painting is based on the fact that only what can be seen there *is* there. . . . What you see is what you see."[10] By contrast, Smithson envisioned early on a "non-anthropocentric extension into an abstract infinite sphere," but it took him the better part of decade to achieve an adequate approximation of that ideal.[11] In the context of youth culture in the late 1960s, his expanded awareness beyond immediate sensory data would readily come across as mysticism. Leider makes a note that Smithson "gets into conversations with Mexican gods," a thought in keeping with his near-psychedelic ecstasies as he descended the incline of Heizer's *Double Negative*. But that sort of high, at this hinge of the decades, was prone to flipping into dark disillusionment, as the editor's thoughts migrated from the reddened waters surrounding Smithson's *Jetty* (owing to microscopic organisms able to thrive in extreme salinity) into the vortex of escalating violence roiling the conjunction of the counterculture and the political left. As Lieder puts it toward the end of "How I Spent My Summer Vacation": "Altamont and Manson. . . . The [Berkeley] *Tribe* printed a letter from a girl named HN drumming Manson out of the hip community, and devoted its center page to Manson's answer. Tom Hayden called the Weatherman the Id of its generation, because it supported Manson (there is violence and there is Violence). The ever-deepening spiral of politics."

Dennis Hopper's countercultural testament *Easy Rider*, released in theaters the year before, had built its climax around a presumption of inevitable violence dealt to liberated youth by the agents of oppressive social conformity. The first half of the film, however, before the descending arc of the story into the choked, overgrown landscape of rural Louisiana, had struck a far more optimistic note, one in keeping with the clarity and far-reaching vistas afforded by the desert, southwest through which the two protagonists first pilot their motorcycles. The land art undertakings to which Leider makes his pilgrimage drew much of their charge from that same aesthetic exhilaration that Hopper's inspired cinematographer, László Kovács, drew from the sweeping distances and sculpted topography across Arizona and New Mexico. Harald Szeemann, as quoted in the prologue above, overtly linked the advanced art of the moment to "Mother Earth as medium, workplace, the desert as concept." And Heizer indeed deployed a 350cc motorcycle to carve circles into a dry Nevada lakebed in 1969, titling the outcome with wry descriptive precision *Circular Surface Planar Displacement*. Robert Deiro, Heizer's Italian-born pilot and all-around practical and administrative factotum, marveled at the artist's paradoxical precision of technique: "he didn't use a string or tape or any other assistance. I mean, this is freehand drawing, I don't know how he made them touch tangentially like that, and to be such perfect circles, going at speeds up to a hundred miles an hour."[12] As *Double Negative* had impressed itself on Leider, this was likewise a "new place in nature," both of them, however, effected by decidedly non-natural means, the intrusion of petroleum-powered technology into fragile, never-lifeless equilibria (an earth-moving contractor from the neighboring town of Overton, Nevada, carved out the massive cuts to the earth in *Double Negative*). In that respect, Heizer's undertakings would more have clashed with the just-emerging ecological sensibility, which would hold, by definition, that "nature" already possesses all the "places" it requires, while discerning the resilient life present in the most desolate-seeming locales.

During 1969, much of Smithson's time had been consumed in complex negotiations over a planned *Island of Broken Glass* in the Queen Charlotte Islands of British Columbia. Their initial success had extended to his receiving the island in question as a gift from Queen Elizabeth herself. But the agitation of local environmentalists over potential damage to wildlife on the guano-covered rock brought the whole enterprise to a standstill. Trucks carrying the exact sort of remaindered glass with which he intended to blanket the island had been dispatched from Los Angeles but turned back at the Canadian border in the face of the protests (and the queen ultimately took back her gift).[13] That setback sent the artist reeling toward territory largely untroubled by such advanced environmental concerns: the remote, conservative Mormon country around the north margin of Utah's Great Salt Lake. His friend and dealer Douglas Chrismas recalls receiving his first intimation of the project in the form of an out-of-the-blue telephone call.[14] Smithson was checking in from what he referred to as "Mormon country" and exulting in the crimson hue of the water at Rozel Point which stood out against the black of the surrounding basalt and the white of the salt crystals. In prose to match any adept in the mysticism of the period, he recounted being seized by a vision of the spiral in the red-dyed waters at Rozel Point: "As I looked at the site, it reverberated out to the horizon only to suggest an immobile cyclone while the flickering light made the entire landscape appear to quake. A dormant earthquake spread into the fluttering stillness, into a spinning sensation without movement. The site was a rotary that enclosed itself in an immense roundness."[15]

For all of these visionary raptures, however, Smithson was, nevertheless, acutely aware that the actual site had been considerably distressed and degraded. When first-time visitors arrive at the lakeshore, their initial sight is a derelict pier and remnants of abandoned oil rigs, with the *Spiral Jetty* lying someway further along. Smithson found these old industrial ruins entirely congenial to the siting of his sculpture, just as he did the high salinity of the water, which was equally man-made, the result of fresh water from the Bear River being choked by dams upstream, as well as the railroad causeway that crosses the lake further south and impedes circulation with less salty waters on the other side. Even the low groundcover that covers the adjacent hillside is an invasive plant.[16] In Smithson's mind, the work of land art cannot pretend to innocence in its occupation of the site, indeed it belongs to a pervasive condition of human corruption signaled by all the other ways in which the land had been degraded, one an artist would be hubristic not to embrace.

The full ramifications of Smithson's thought and practice have been decades coming to light since his premature death in 1973 and would still have been largely opaque to Leider at this early date. But the latter's mental segue from the sanguinary red of the water to the cults of violence descending on what had been movements for peace suggests he rightly intuited some struggle between human corruption and extra-human redemption encoded in the *Spiral Jetty*. He was looking for some solace or place of rest amid the turmoil, which he ends up seeking at another sort of site, one he found nearby in his old East Bay haunts. Having known the sculpture of David Lynn from coverage in *Artforum* in the early 1960s, Leider now encounters him in self-exile from fine art, building eccentrically crafted dwellings in an unincorporated encampment on the eastern slope of the Berkeley Hills, a place its residents call simply Canyon (fig. 69).[17] He finds Lynn in the process of building a four-story house that snakes up through the tree canopy, framed with discarded timber from old piers and with no regard for the building codes that dictated the cookie-cutter construction of nearby subdivisions: "The corner beams kept the original shape of the trees intact: they were not even planed," he marvels. "We didn't talk about sculpture at all," he goes on to say, but at the same time "it seemed pretty clear that as far as Lynn was concerned, every sculptural idea he had ever had was in his building." Leider describes himself as having become "more interested in the people in Canyon, California, than I was in the East Coast art world";[18] but he departs with foreboding over Canyon's future under a state regime that has just rained down lethal force on the protestors at Berkeley's People's Park.

As Leider may have been aware, Canyon had once given rise to a centrally important vehicle for experimental art in San Francisco: in 1961, the independent filmmaker Bruce Baillie began projecting his work on an army-surplus screen set up behind his house as a form of community self-entertainment; others joined in, Baillie's homegrown initiative

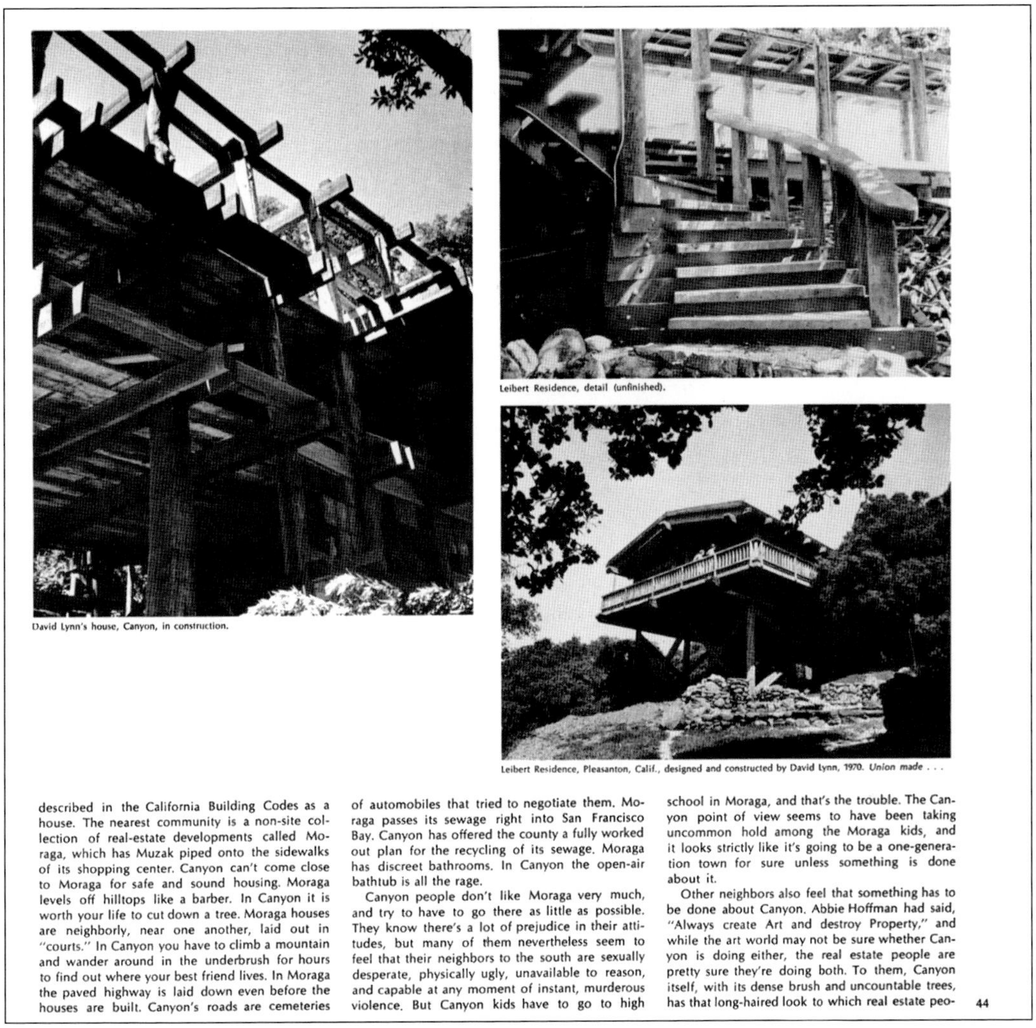

David Lynn's house, Canyon, in construction.

Leibert Residence, detail (unfinished).

Leibert Residence, Pleasanton, Calif., designed and constructed by David Lynn, 1970. *Union made . . .*

described in the California Building Codes as a house. The nearest community is a non-site collection of real-estate developments called Moraga, which has Muzak piped onto the sidewalks of its shopping center. Canyon can't come close to Moraga for safe and sound housing. Moraga levels off hilltops like a barber. In Canyon it is worth your life to cut down a tree. Moraga houses are neighborly, near one another, laid out in "courts." In Canyon you have to climb a mountain and wander around in the underbrush for hours to find out where your best friend lives. In Moraga the paved highway is laid down even before the houses are built. Canyon's roads are cemeteries of automobiles that tried to negotiate them. Moraga passes its sewage right into San Francisco Bay. Canyon has offered the county a fully worked out plan for the recycling of its sewage. Moraga has discreet bathrooms. In Canyon the open-air bathtub is all the rage.

Canyon people don't like Moraga very much, and try to have to go there as little as possible. They know there's a lot of prejudice in their attitudes, but many of them nevertheless seem to feel that their neighbors to the south are sexually desperate, physically ugly, unavailable to reason, and capable at any moment of instant, murderous violence. But Canyon kids have to go to high school in Moraga, and that's the trouble. The Canyon point of view seems to have been taking uncommon hold among the Moraga kids, and it looks strictly like it's going to be a one-generation town for sure unless something is done about it.

Other neighbors also feel that something has to be done about Canyon. Abbie Hoffman had said, "Always create Art and destroy Property," and while the art world may not be sure whether Canyon is doing either, the real estate people are pretty sure they're doing both. To them, Canyon itself, with its dense brush and uncountable trees, has that long-haired look to which real estate peo-

44

**69** Philip Leider, "How I Spent My Summer Vacation or, Art and Politics in Nevada, Berkeley, San Francisco and Utah (Read about It in Artforum!)," *Artforum* (September 1970)

before long becoming a moveable feast of screenings that migrated from venue to venue across the East Bay. By 1966, Canyon Cinema had settled into a stable life as a filmmakers' cooperative in San Francisco, exhibiting and distributing the work of Bruce Conner, for one, along with his many gifted local peers—the sole tie to its rustic birthplace fondly retained in the name.[19] Considering the self-isolating Canyon of 1970, however, it would have taken nothing away from Lynn's sense of vocation to concur with Leider that his friend "wasn't an artist any more or . . . had undergone that complete redefinition of what an artist is and does." To yoke one's practice to the quest for a harmonized, undisturbed existence, one divorced as far as possible from the corruptions and hierarchies of the straight world, risked forfeiting the contrast and contradiction that allows a work of visual art to stand out as such.

In seeking their own brands of emancipation from the hierarchies of a managed and monetized art system, both Heizer and Smithson had been sure to preserve the core recognizability on which visual art depends. Heizer did so via stark, unmistakable distinction between figure and ground, while Smithson made his contrasts interior to the work: the rubble of its fabrication, emblematic of the corruption and vanity entailed in any merely human endeavor, nonetheless reached toward unattainable resolution beyond mortal cognitive grasp.[20] A parallel exists in the sculptures of Bruce Conner, fashioned as they were from the heart of the early counterculture, where disabused exposure of violence and corruption of the flesh lent necessary weight to the elevated, extra-human apprehension conferred by psychedelic drugs (Conner, like Smithson, got into his own conversations with Mexican gods). But he had largely concluded that body of work by 1964, bitterly alienated by the proprietary arrogance with which museums had treated his work, going so far as to declare, in 1967, that he was finished with art.[21]

Conner was far from alone in this disaffection, and one senses that Leider, too, in his fascination with David Lynn, was likewise looking for the exit. But if he had been seeking, as he settled back in Berkeley, an available art of requisite substance and complexity, but still plainly marked by countercultural experience, he need only have looked west across the bay to the congested city rather than east over the hills to bucolic Canyon.

■

In that same year of 1970, the young artist Bonnie Ora Sherk, barely out of her graduate studies at San Francisco State, was casting her eyes on some of the worst disruptions and insults to the built environment around her. The bay side of the city had been massively altered by the construction of a tangle of freeways, their massive abutments brutally monumental testimony to the priority enjoyed by suburban commuters demanding unimpeded access to their offices in the city (notwithstanding the predictable congestion engendered by every freeway expansion). To the southeast, against the backdrop of Bernal Heights, some of the ugliest detritus from the road construction struck Sherk with the force of an epiphany: "I came upon this large area of garbage where water had collected. That was because there was heavy construction of the 101 Freeway Interchange and debris was all around. In the center of this particular space was a large, overstuffed armchair floating in the water with tires, a tricycle, and other objects." Her immediate response was to go home, change into an evening gown, and return to perform the work she titled *Sitting Still I*: "I waded in and sat in the chair facing the 'audience,' which was comprised of the people in the cars that were moving very slowly because of the construction of this Freeway Interchange."[22]

The adjacent neighborhood, to which her performance called momentary attention, had a history of housing Black workers recruited for wartime ship construction, then as an enclave of militant anti-war collectives. Not that her "audience" of commuters crawling along the frontage road detour would have had the slightest awareness of that significance, any more than they could have fathomed why a formally dressed young woman would be sitting in the middle of a backed-up, waste-water pond. If one were searching for a moment of synthesis between the inheritance of the Haight and the contemporaneous moment of advanced art, however, it would be difficult to find a richer one. The costume and the serendipitous, overstuffed armchair captured the dressing-up side of counterculture's youthful cohorts, alongside all the inspired repurposing of the city's stock of inherited architecture and ornament—all of which had been flaunted before the hostile, uncomprehending eyes of the straights in their cars. Sherk's lonely presence carried the recognition of that recent efflorescence already facing decrepitude and disintegration, but by no means extinct or abashed. At the same time, she grasped that one alien intervention can snap an otherwise disorganized context into order and clarity, just as she enlisted the backed-up water on the construction site to stand in for any number of distant environmental features on the order of Smithson's stagnant northern reach of the Great Salt Lake, while the chaotic context of random signage, incoherently scattered structures, and stacked unused materials also offered a fair approximation of the latter's idea of ruins in reverse.

*Sitting Still I* had not been Sherk's first exploitation of the oppressive monumentality of the freeway supports that allowed these roadways to surmount the old urban fabric. A few months before, with her collaborator Howard Levine, she had assembled the first of three *Portable Parks* atop a soaring stack of two ramps (an eyesore now demolished) as they surmounted the surface artery of Market Street near the Civic Center. Aided with funds from some adventurous local art patrons and even the state's transportation department, Sherk rolled out turf, adding potted palms, a live calf, and her own presence to complete the ensemble. While she had permission to occupy her space for the day, the crowd of journalists attracted by the novelty of the event did not; the only way to access a freeway being by motor vehicle, all were ticketed by highway patrolmen for parking in the breakdown lane, while rubbernecking by the drivers passing the ensuing melee brought the adjacent lanes to a halt.[23]

Her gesture, taken by itself, might appear a somewhat naive moment of pastoral consolation, like a child's drawing of a farm. She calls it a still life, but its apparent simplicity belies the extent to which it commandeered the entire transit fabric into its orbit, testifying to the power of the well-calculated intervention in such a site to enlarge the boundaries of the artwork by orders of magnitude, as she would shortly do with much less ceremony but greater poignancy and focus in *Sitting Still I*. One might go further and credit *Portable Park I* with apprehending on the level of art the impulse that led a David Lynn to subsume his practice into rustic solace and retreat. The San Francisco counterculture, apart perhaps from Ken Kesey's manic mountain cabin in La Honda, had been an urban phenomenon; its ways of being depended on a uniquely compact and aesthetically rewarding city, one navigable by

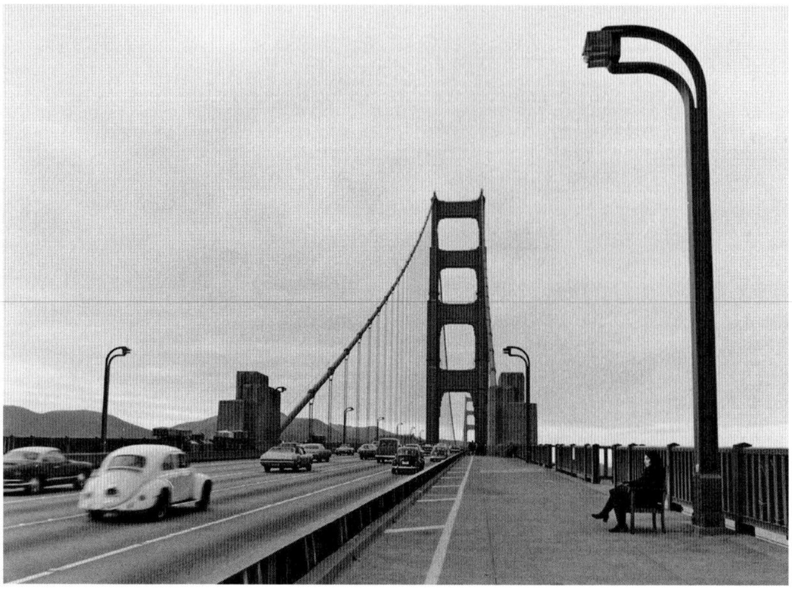

**70** Bonnie Ora Sherk, *Sitting Still II (Golden Gate Bridge)*, 1971, courtesy Library Archives, San Francisco Museum of Modern Art

the hard-up young on foot or by public transport. Freeways served and stood for alien, parasitic sprawl, to which Sherk bore witness in a subsequent *Sitting Still* at the entrance of the Golden Gate Bridge, portal to the northern suburbs (fig. 70). One anticipation of countercultural solidarity and self-consciousness had taken the form of a 1964 rally against further freeway construction, which drew some 200,000 people to Golden Gate Park. The plans in question would have eradicated a sizable portion of the park's Panhandle extension—the green lifeline for the Haight-Ashbury—while ruining the rest with racket and shadow. The folksinger Malvina Reynolds sang her newly written "Cement Octopus" for the occasion.

The structures enlisted by Sherk—even if her interventions might have disarmingly been read as benign embellishment, even beautification—remained Moloch-like idols worshipped by the many in thrall to greed and power. That baleful power lent these pieces the conflictual tension required to transform otherwise unassuming gestures into art.

■

Sherk's San Francisco contemporary Terry Fox, likewise in 1970, invested the freeway with talismanic significance. In preparation for the performance piece *Levitation*, he excavated from beneath a freeway (the same interchange construction site that Sherk had exploited for her *Sitting Still I*) the ton-and-a half of dirt on which he would lie for six hours in the Richmond Art Center, attempting the feat announced in his title: "The dirt was taken from the freeway because of the idea of explosion. When the freeway was built, the earth was

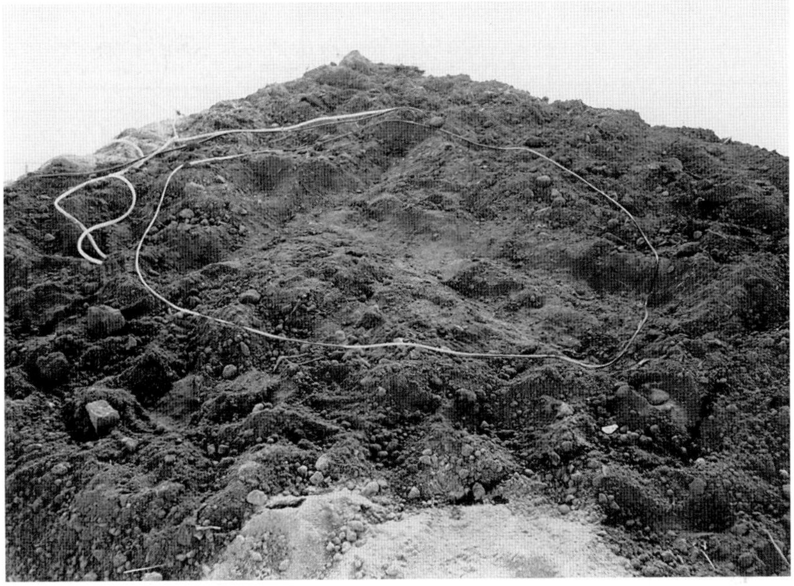

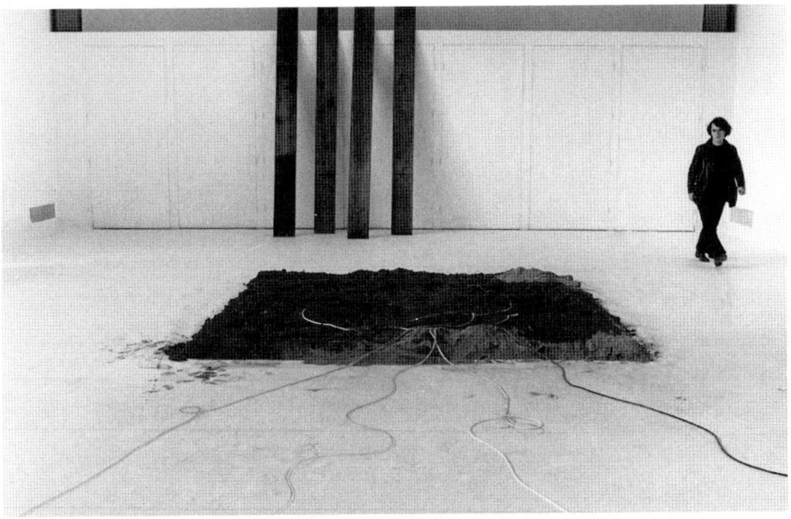

**71 and 72** Terry Fox, *Levitation*, installation at Richmond Art Center, 1970, courtesy Library Archives, San Francisco Museum of Modern Art

compressed, held down. You can conceive of it expanding when you release it rising, becoming buoyant."[24] He remained alone on this earthen bed for the duration of this performance (fig. 71), the audience milling outside the locked venue, treated only to a handout describing the artist's unseen actions. These included fasting that had taken place the previous day; drawing a circle in the earth with a tube containing his own blood, one large enough to accommodate his body with arms and legs extended in a way that approximated

Leonardo's famous emblem of "Vitruvian Man"; extending to the wall above his head four other tubes, fifty feet in length, filled with water, milk, blood, and urine, "the elemental fluids that I was expelling from my body," like a modern version of the four internal humors of ancient Greek medicine.

All of this self-lightening, by his testimony, produced the sensation he desired once he stopped mentally dwelling on the earth and focused on entering the air: "For me that changed everything, made it work, I mean, I levitated. . . . I felt as if I was somewhere else. I'd gone. I'd left my body." Session concluded, Fox departed before spectators were let into the gallery, leaving them confronted with only the apparatus and the imprint of the artist's body in the mass of earth liberated from the freeway (fig. 71): "the whole room was energized," he later exulted; "You didn't have to trip over the piece, you felt it the minute you walked in" (fig. 72).

All these remarks by Fox are drawn from a thoroughly sympathetic interview with Willoughby Sharp, at that time the doyen of the downtown Manhattan art scene, amply testifying to the largely forgotten occultism woven through much of the conceptual, performance, and process art of that moment. Sharp coined the term Earth Art, for example, not as any prosaic acknowledgment of excavated matter, but rather as an analogue to the status of Earth as one of the four ancient elements (along with Air, Fire, and Water), which mapped onto the four bodily humors and in turn the four temperaments (Melancholic, Sanguine, Choleric, and Phlegmatic). If such atavistically analogical thinking had found a place even in hip New York circles, how much stronger its hold in the epicenter of countercultural mysticism and revivals of magic.

Fox, it should be said, was no dreamy hippie. He was at home in Europe and had immersed himself in the revolts of May 1968, once driving a car loaded with cobblestones and a canister of gasoline across the German–French border as a kind of risk-laden performance piece. Neither was his performance at the Richmond Art Center detached from hard political realities. The area figured in the previous chapter as the locality where Denzil Dowell had been murdered by sheriff's deputies in 1967, bringing the young Black Panther Party into full public view for the first time. Sharp found further evidence for the power of Fox's piece in the irrationally hostile response of the authorities in this industrial outpost at the north end of San Francisco Bay for whom the Center's artist-director (more like ringleader), Tom Marioni, had been a continual thorn in the side. The local official responsible for the venue claimed the smell from Fox's earthen bed was overwhelming and a patent health hazard—in a jurisdiction best known for its spewing Chevron oil refinery, spill-prone tanker port, and seeping tank farm.[25] The Richmond health inspector, who daily presided over this petrochemical dump, declared "there's no way of determining the dirt didn't come from a sewer," and the show was closed down. If modern science engendered wonders like the Chevron refinery or the Army Street interchange, it became a plausibly appropriate question to ask, where else to turn for an antidote *but* to prescientific wisdom and out-of-body escape?

There was, however, one thoroughly scientific background to Fox's acute awareness of the body's patterns of liquid circulation. Diagnosed with Hodgkin's Disease in his teens (and not cleared until 1972), he had endured lying on a table for the same six hours, blue fluid injected into his lymph system through his feet: "You lie there and watch the Xray of your whole body in action . . ."[26] But *Levitation* never overtly dwelt on such intensely private inner experience, Fox taking care to lend it substance via more than one shared symbolic matrix. In so doing, he set off waves of public reverberation that induced the agents of straight authority to perform their tragi-comic puppet dance, unwittingly acting out their own malfeasance and bad faith in order to kill the work of art. Depth of depravity in the countervailing forces can lend the highest metaphysical flights a sturdy quotient of social realism.

Common reference to the freeway juggernaut by both Sherk and Fox, while entirely understandable from a green perspective, at the same time signaled a significant change in the nature of protest from the dominant peace campaign against the war in Vietnam—exploding that same year after Nixon's invasion of Cambodia. The image of the octopus in Malvina Reynolds's song of protest evokes a force that was everywhere and nowhere in particular. While war policy bore the hated faces of Nixon, General Westmoreland, and Henry Kissinger, the ills of traffic, pollution, over-development, and environmental destruction presented no clear targets or decisive solutions like military withdrawal. Stop one freeway and another takes its place—and another and another after that. A pervasive, sinister, and largely hidden array of forces seemed always to prevail, such that the dissent becomes a bleaker, more lonely witnessing to inhuman conditions largely immune to principled resistance.

Fox's performance anticipates this mood, which will seep into more and more art practice over the course of the 1970s. And his acute interplay between the artist's withheld presence and visible absence would find repeated counterparts in the work of artists to the south, for both parallel and divergent reasons. So far in this book, Los Angeles has largely figured as headquarters of commercial film and a local counterculture convened beneath the flashy neon of the Sunset Strip, but the same juncture of 1970 launched a cycle of performance-based art that symbolically pitted the vulnerable individual against forces immeasurably larger than the capacities of the isolated, exposed artist. These repeated dramas, resistant to resolution, nonetheless arose from the emergence of a resilient artistic community, one stimulated rather than hindered by the daunting distances over which they traveled to support and learn from one another.

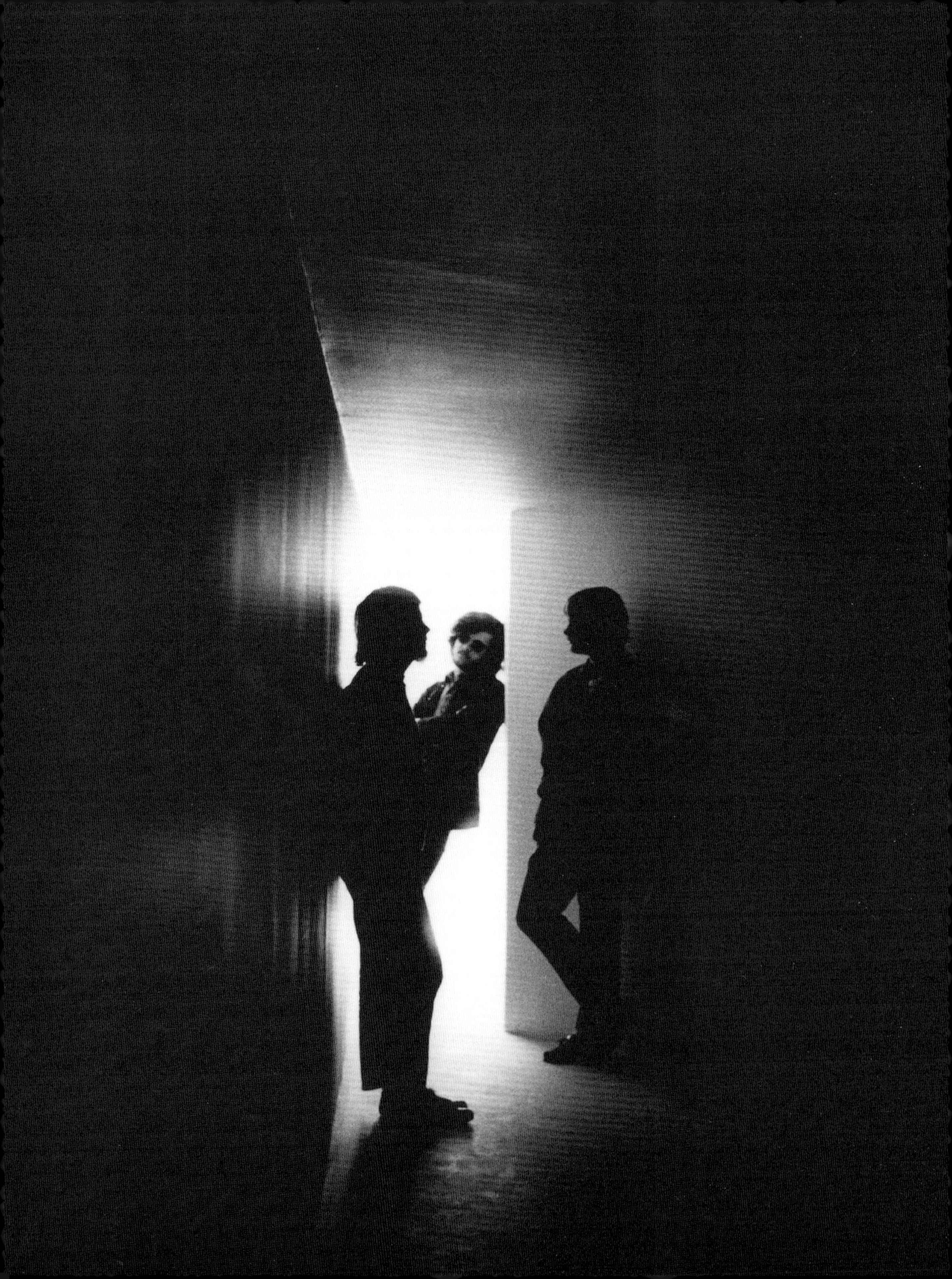

NINE

# THE ART OF DISAPPEARANCE

AN ABIDING THEME THREADING THROUGH THE BOOK THUS FAR has been rejection and excoriation of the American national security state, whether embedded in Bruce Conner's style of personal witnessing or by overt dissent, protest, and disruption on the part of his politically committed contemporaries. While artists seized upon the most visible and lethally destructive projections of American power into Indochina, the entire surrounding social and economic fabric of California remained a monument to the overweening "military-industrial complex," as described by outgoing president Dwight Eisenhower in words of warning as he left office in 1960. The war in the Pacific had resulted in gigantic naval ports in Oakland, Long Beach, and San Diego. The hospitable climate and the concentration of engineering expertise had focused the manufacture of military aircraft and electronics in the southern part of the state, where it came emblazoned with heraldic trademarks like Lockheed, Douglas, Grumman, Raytheon, Rockwell, General Dynamics, and Hughes, to name only the most prominent. The insatiable demands of the Cold War arsenal during the 1950s built up the infrastructure to a scale unimagined even at the height of the Second World War. Concurrently, the fabled sprawl of the Los Angeles region (seen also around the southern San Francisco Bay) arose out of the need to house its white professional and line-work forces in ways that answered their collective desire to leave Depression and wartime privations decisively behind for a secure, middle-class future.[1] The splendid, three-tiered system of public higher education (with no tuition fees) that distinguished California in this period absorbed massive injections of federal funds for training and research justified in Washington by the needs of defense planning.

The geographical locus where this reality most abundantly presented itself lay at the extreme southern corner of the state in the mid-tier city of San Diego, which has already figured in the discussion of Martha Rosler's anti-war works of collage as a permanent fortress of American arms. Its magnificent natural harbor provided the base for the Navy's Pacific Fleet and its recruit induction. Naval and Marine jets on training exercises continually boomed overhead. Aircraft manufacturers occupied those bayside parcels of land in the heart of the city not already commandeered for military use. As nuclear confrontation and

**73** Michael Asher, Gladys K. Montgomery Art Center,
Pomona College, Claremont, California, USA, February 13–March 8, 1970.
Showing visitors in installation

the space race with the Soviet Union gathered pace, gigantic facilities for assembling intercontinental ballistic missiles sprouted on the city's arid inland mesas. Traveling overland from the superficially cognate terrain of Orange County to the north entailed a significant passage—not unlike crossing the Deadly Desert surrounding Oz—across the vast, nearly empty expanse of the Marine Corps' Camp Pendleton, no freeway exit permitted.

Notwithstanding the mission-style beauty of Balboa Park (naturally, named for a conquistador), cultural investments in the city were comparatively modest, as no one knew better than the San Diego native John Baldessari. In 1967, this supremely self-starting artist was teaching in a freshly minted community college within a few miles of both the Pacific and the Mexican border. Already exercising his knack for enticing well-known artists into his classroom, he had drawn the painter Sam Francis down from Los Angeles to give a lecture. Before the assembled students, he asked Francis what he found interesting about the area. "Well, it's the end of the line," came the answer; "You can't get any further from the U.S. than this."[2]

Baldessari had every reason to be acutely aware of this condition. Just to approach his home in the inner suburb of National City entailed passing on the bay side a gray wall of towering, mothballed Navy hulks, the obsolete oversupply left behind after World War II. The very name National City owns up to this unapologetic utility, the only material difference with its neighboring municipality, Chula Vista, being the latter's aspirational name (Pretty View). To be an artist at all in such a setting meant stubbornly hanging on. At one point, contemplating a quest for extra-worldly reassurance, he applied to the Princeton Theological Seminary (accounts vary as to whether he was rejected or declined their acceptance). The comparative security of his community-college post had come after supporting a young family on teaching jobs that came to hand in high schools, college extension programs, and one summer stint at a rural camp working with delinquent teenagers. Through all this, he dutifully performed the rituals of countless artists from the pedagogical and semiprofessional ranks: carefully sending off the slides of his paintings to local and regional juried shows mounted at community centers and county fairgrounds, waiting and hoping for a little exposure, a chance to make a mark.

About the time of the Francis visit, however, Baldessari turned his back on the pleasingly expressive idiom he had developed in favor of an approach that stripped incident on the canvas surface to components intentionally, in his words, even "less artful than Rauschenberg and Warhol." Having printed willfully naive photographs on standard-sized canvases, he employed a local sign painter to inscribe drolly deadpan captions underneath (fig. 74): "This is a photograph, here's a text. That's it. And I thought, because they're done on canvas, they might be equated with art."[3] That these works have, of course, attained far more than provisional stature as art—indeed setting the agenda for a generation of artists aiming to defeat solipsistic subjectivity—has obscured the portrait they provide of typical dormitory towns, the frame and stucco sheds and cookie-cutter houses, built in the lee of the new American arsenal.

Coincidentally with his aesthetic breakthrough, Baldessari's appeal and gift as a teacher was resonating further within the small world of San Diego, which was beginning to change

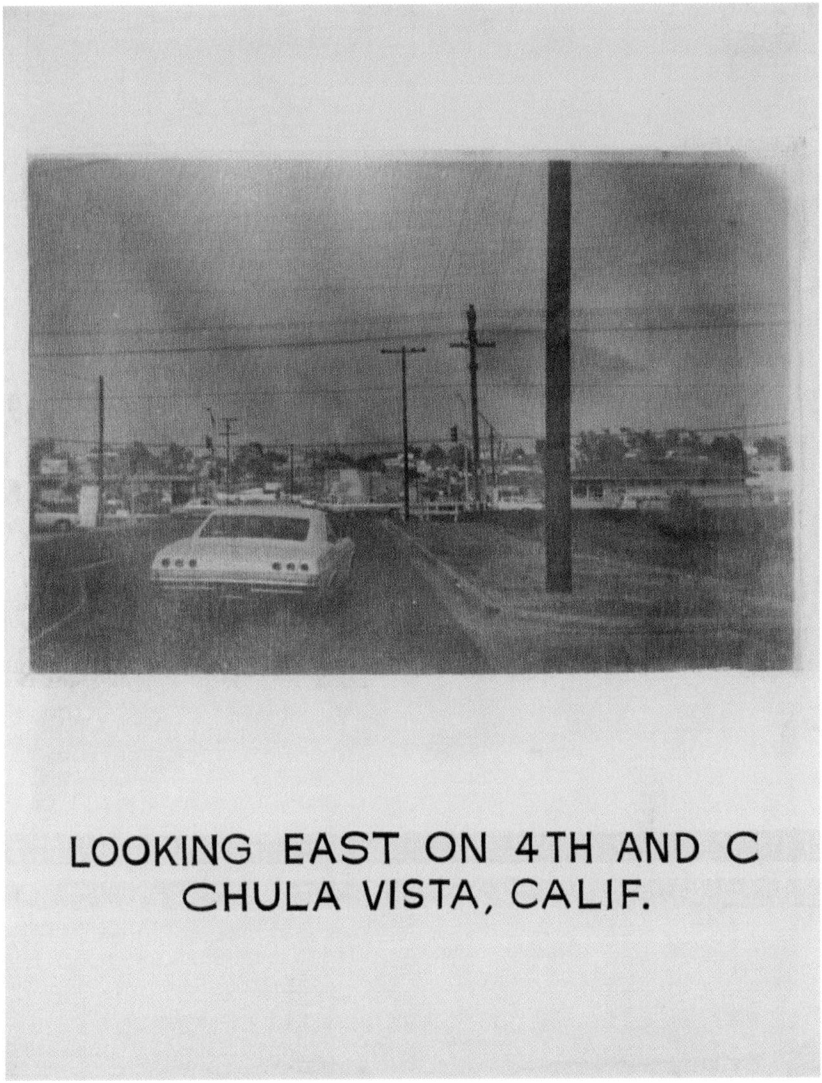


74 John Baldessari, *Looking East on 4th and C, Chula Vista, Calif.*, 1966–68, acrylic and photo-emulsion on canvas, 149.9 × 114.3 cm, Collection San Francisco Museum of Modern Art, Accessions Committee Fund: gift of Evelyn and Walter Haas, Jr., Mr. and Mrs. Donald Fisher, Modern Art Council, and Norah and Norman C. Stone

in ways that dramatically worked to his advantage. A job with the adult extension of the new University of California campus drew the attention of the acerbic New York painter Paul Brach, who had been enlisted to chair the fledgling art department. Like its equally fresh sister campus at Irvine in southern Orange County, the principal mission of UCSD lay in the technical and scientific disciplines, but an expansive view of higher education still prevailed under the Democratic governorship of Edmund G. Brown, such that the humanities and the arts were developed to commensurable scale. The moment of this project in the latter part of the 1960s meant that arts subjects would be porous to countercultural elements. Most notably, the German neo-Marxist Herbert Marcuse was hired to teach philosophy (to the unrelenting outrage of powerful local right-wingers), which drew radically oriented students

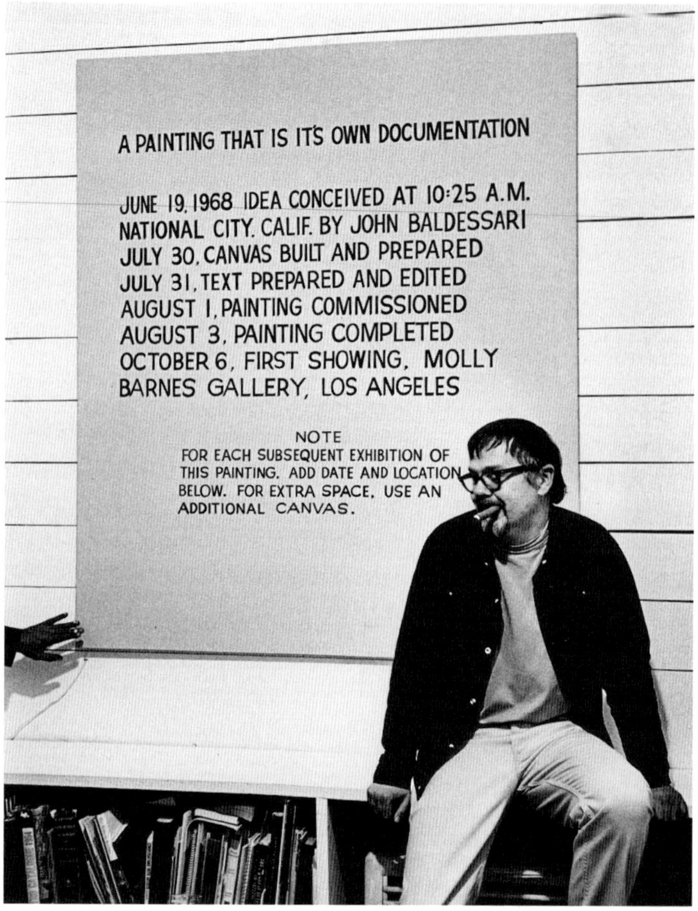


**75** John Baldessari at the opening of his exhibition at the Molly Barnes Gallery in Los Angeles, 1968

like Angela Davis to study with him. Out of a democratic and politic desire to enlist a local artist in his program, Brach hired Baldessari to the regular faculty. That major validation, a position in a major university, brought with it the friendship of the genius poet-critic David Antin, like Brach imported, along with the leading feminist artist Eleanor Antin, to lend East Coast cachet to the new undertaking.[4] Their imprimatur helped Baldessari secure his first Los Angeles show at the Molly Barnes Gallery in 1968 (fig. 75).

By coincidence, the conceptual artist Joseph Kosuth was showing a suite of his word-definition panels at another gallery just down the art strip along La Cienega Boulevard. As Baldessari had begun to jettison images altogether, Kosuth would have had occasion to note parallels between Baldessari's National City canvases and the self-descriptive text paintings by his friends in the Art & Language group in the UK. A good deal of wit is present in the

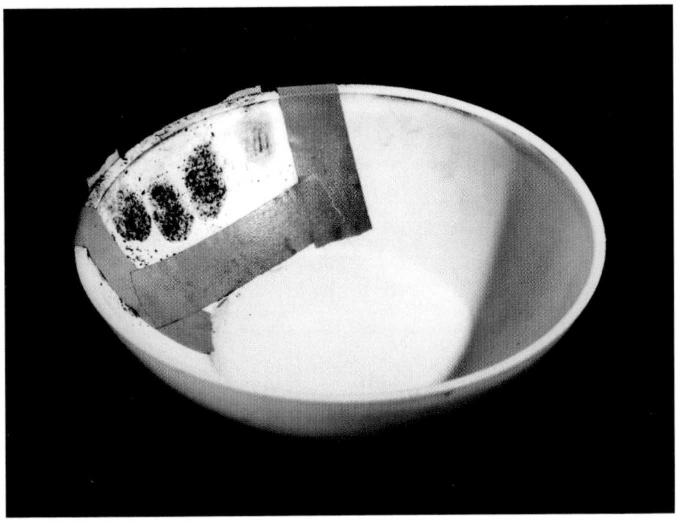

**76** John Baldessari, *Cremation Project* (detail: bowl dusted for fingerprints), 1970, Benton Museum of Art at Pomona College

latter, but its charm came surrounded by heavyweight citations of analytical philosophy and a good deal of the self-serious posturing to which Baldessari was temperamentally and morally allergic. In an essay published the next year (titled "Art after Philosophy"), Kosuth dismissed the Californian's efforts as no more than "cartoons" of conceptual art. Showing for the first time on a main stage at age thirty-seven, he must, indeed, have seemed a dismissible outsider. But Baldessari was long immune to being underestimated: as Brach had earlier marveled, "John was this low-key, bemused man, in a two-bit junior college in San Diego, acting as if he was the absolute center of the international art world."[5]

All the paintings he retained from his early yearning and searching mode went into the fire, immolated in the ritual *Cremation Project*, duly certified in July 1970 by the county crematorium of San Diego. But where might such a work be put on view and how? He took the ashes in a bowl (fig. 76) to Helene Winer, director of the small art gallery at Pomona College, its New England-style campus located at the far eastern fringe of Los Angeles County: "At the time I was into police photography and when [Helene Winer] came to the door I gave her a bowl, which she grabbed. I dusted it for prints and said, here, show this, which she did. I had burned all my paintings and had the ashes. I gave them to her and said, Scatter them in the corner; after the first person walks in, rope off the area."

Baldessari had, in what was a momentous year for him, scored his first metropolitan gallery show and gained a teaching position at the California Institute of the Arts, courtesy once again of Brach, who had moved there as founding Dean of the School of Art. CalArts would of course become, thanks in many respects to Baldessari, a prodigious forcing house of international art talent. But at this juncture it was an idea yet without a home, its still-unfinished building in a remote exurban location to the north of Los Angeles. Its Disney patrons had facilitated the creation of its studio-art program by acquiring the Chouinard

School of Art in the central part of the city. Despite its precarious finances, Chouinard had reliably attracted a wealth of talent, Ed Ruscha then being only the best known of its recent products. A younger cohort of graduates or advanced students—among them, Allen Ruppersberg, Jack Goldstein, and Japanese transplant Hirokazu Kosaka—were poised to begin making significant marks of their own. As the old Chouinard was hollowed out and CalArts still lay over the horizon, eyes turned to the unlikely outpost of Pomona College, clustered to the east with four other colleges in the likewise exurban town of Claremont.

■

On the social spectrum, the preppie environs of Claremont—still semi-rural with its lemon groves, quarries, and boulder-strewn riverbeds that stretched up to the arid foothills of Mount Baldy peak looming in the distance—lay at an enormous distance from National City, but would have appeared just as unlikely an incubator of major art. It is, nevertheless, a credible proposition to assert that the art made and shown at the Pomona College art gallery between 1969 and 1972 was as important as any being made and shown anywhere else. How and why would such a place attract artists of this caliber, giving them, for that brief historical moment, an exceptionally sympathetic platform and showcase, which ultimately inflected the terms of serious art making across a far wider terrain?

One approach to answering that question would be to concede the improbability of this phenomenon by citing a series of chance contingencies at its inception. The two best-known Pomona alumni to figure in this conjunction, James Turrell and Chris Burden, arrived at the college four years apart and from such disparate backgrounds and directions that no positive correlation could be adduced from the fact of their contiguous Claremont careers (the former's remarkable pre- and post-college adventures having been recounted above). The presence at the Claremont Graduate School of Bas Jan Ader, their peer in the esteem of posterity, can be explained by his friend from adolescence, the ceramicist Dennis Parks, having preceded him there. Mowry Baden, the guiding force on the Pomona studio faculty, would not have been a likely faculty recruit had he not attended the college himself. The gallery director, Hal Glicksman, had absorbed his vocation as an exhibition preparator at the Pasadena Art Museum, albeit under the great Walter Hopps, but had never previously served even as a curator.

From these randomly assembled elements, however, a remarkably coherent collective project emerged, latent in the approach to sculpture that Baden brought with him on joining the faculty in 1967.[6] A gallery visitor in October of the next year, encountering Baden's sculpture titled *Auger* (fig. 77), might at first have been reminded of an over-ambitious exercise by one of the college's ceramicists. Closer inspection, however, would have revealed that its manufacture and material, hollow fiberglass-resin composite, lay at the opposite end of the weight and density continuum. Baden had engineered the shape of *Auger* by carving into a block of polyurethane foam from the inside, blindly feeling his way as he entered its volume:

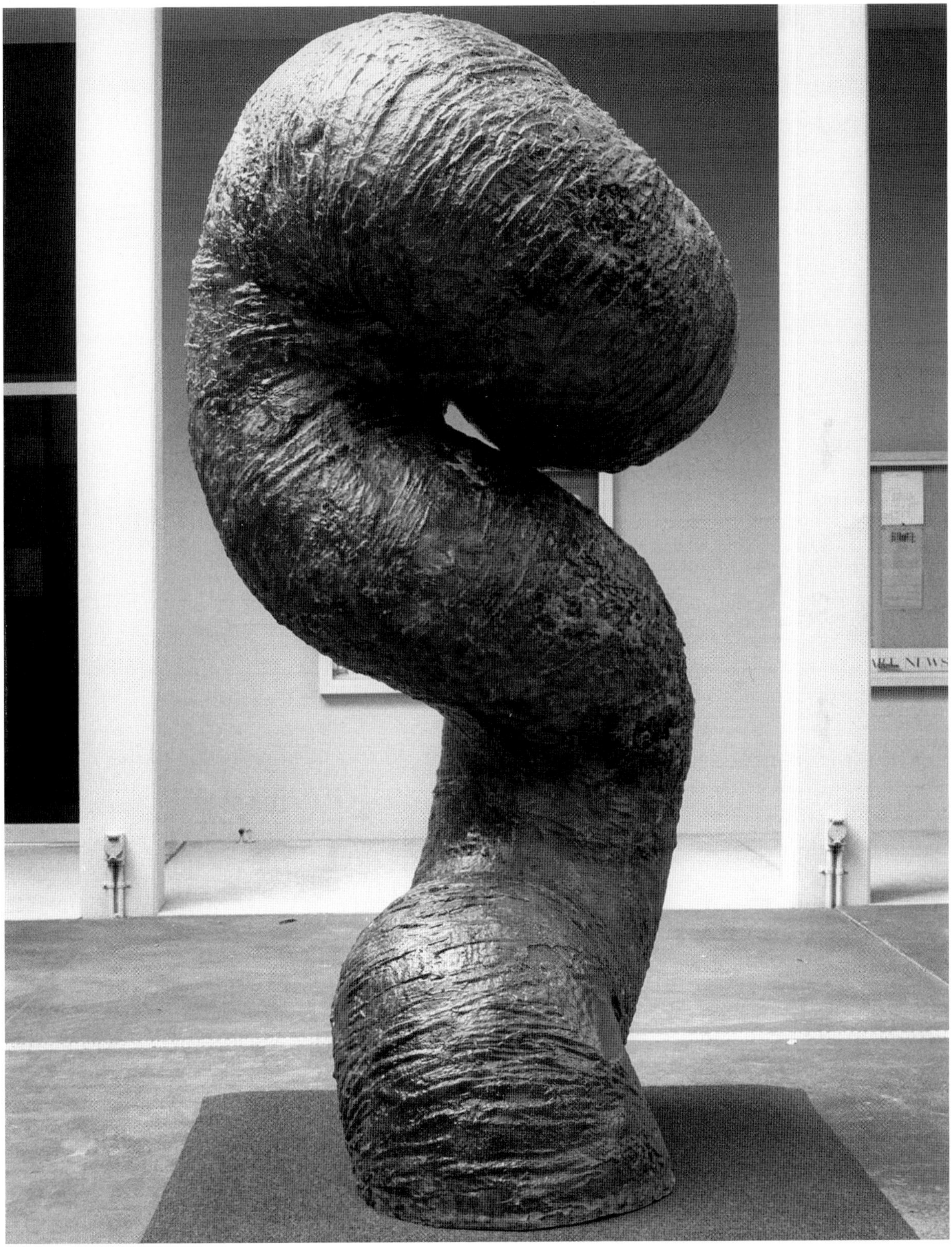

77 Mowry Baden, *Auger*, 1967, fibered polyester, 2.44 m high, collection of Felicia Kuen

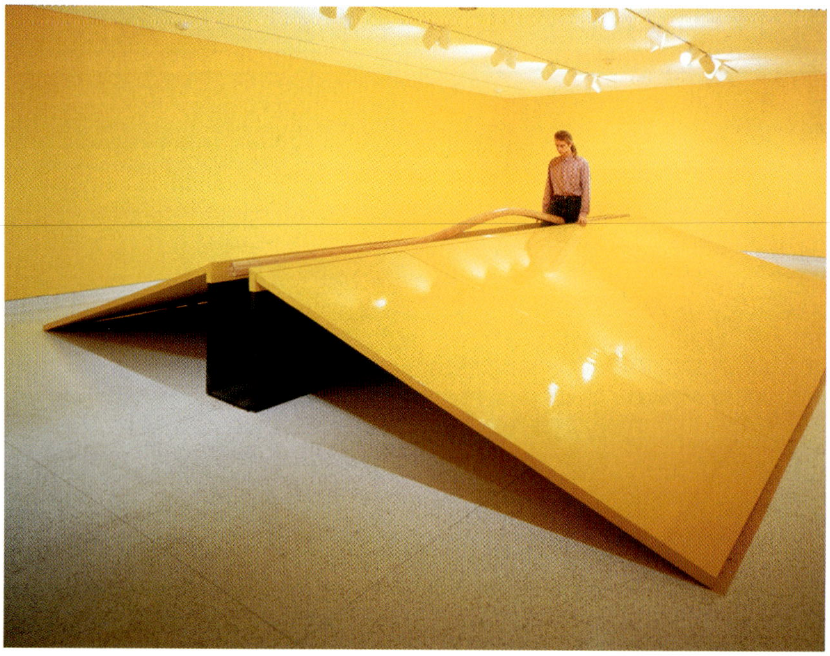

**78** Mowry Baden, *I Walk the Line*, 1967, wood, steel, carpet, 6.09 × 5.18 × 0.8 m, Museum of Contemporary Art San Diego

"I didn't know what it would look like," he told a student reporter at the time, "and I didn't much care. I was more interested in the experience of generating my own physical space."[7] From the resulting cavity, he cast *Auger* as its negative remainder in the street materials of surfboard manufacture. Baden's procedure thus removed vision from its position of sensory mastery, rendering the formal outcome of the exercise a secondary and somewhat pathetic residue of the main event, which was the blind act of tunneling itself. As he told the critic Jack Burnham, "Boring my way through . . . urethane foam may not have been the most reflective way to confront my body, but it certainly removed all the usual stand-off-and-look-at-it attitudes, which to me are irrelevant."[8]

*Auger* took its place in a sequence of sculptures engineered by Baden to diminish the salience of contemplative vision. Cleanly fabricated pieces of apparatus made in a period of intense activity between 1967 and 1968—*Phantom Limb, Stop Gap,* and the deft Johnny Cash name check of *I Walk the Line* (fig. 78)—put the "viewer's" body through various paces that rendered any external witnessing of the sculpture more or less beside the point. The pieces communicate only by the pressures they place on the sensitive parts of the body that come into contact with their surfaces, such that sculpture is possibly the wrong word for them; the space they define is in the body of anyone who submits to their built-in regimen. But there were two quite distinct aspects to this transformation of viewer into living art object. As Baden made plain, the dimensions of each piece were configured to the dimensions of his own body: "I am the laboratory," as he put it, "and, by extension, the art."[9] So anyone else traversing the pieces became forcibly aware of the greater or lesser resistance that by implication impose the shape of the creator on his or her awareness. The presence of the artist could thus be made as forcibly, perhaps even more sensorially present in his absence than if he were acting out some performance before the comparatively jaded sense of vision alone.

■

One basic permutation from Baden's example would have been somehow to combine exposure of the participating body with the concealment of *Auger*. In the spring of 1969, Chris Burden could be said to have accomplished that feat with a senior project constructed on an athletic practice field east of that rustic part of the Pomona campus referred to as the Wash (fig. 79). Suspending black plastic sheets from two parallel metal frames two hundred feet in length and eleven feet high, their posts set into the ground with concrete, he created what might have seemed like an enlarged, open-air equivalent to one

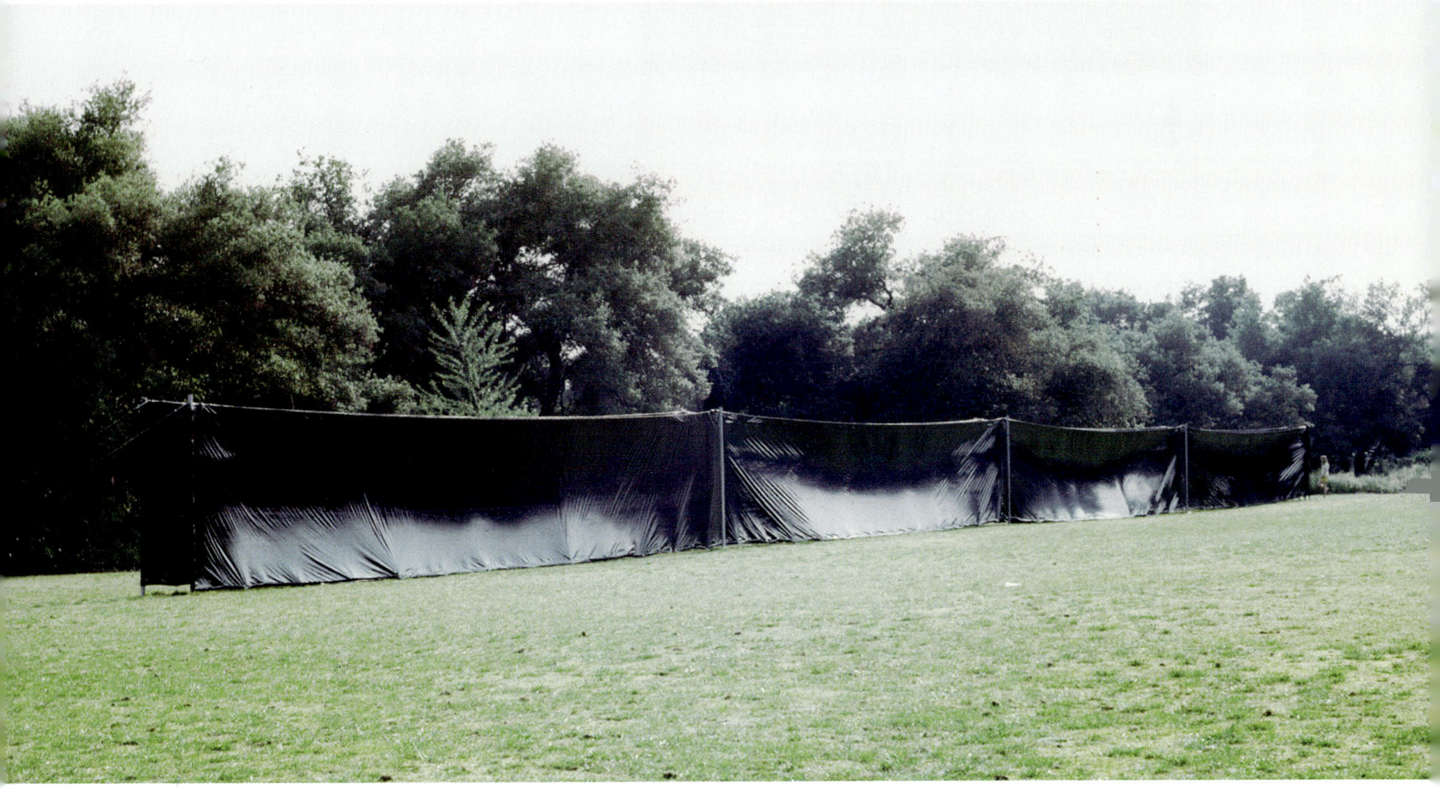

**79** Chris Burden, *Untitled*, 1969,
polyethylene sheeting, pipe, galvanized wire, 61 × 3.4 × 0.9 m,
installation at Pomona College, Spring 1969 (destroyed)

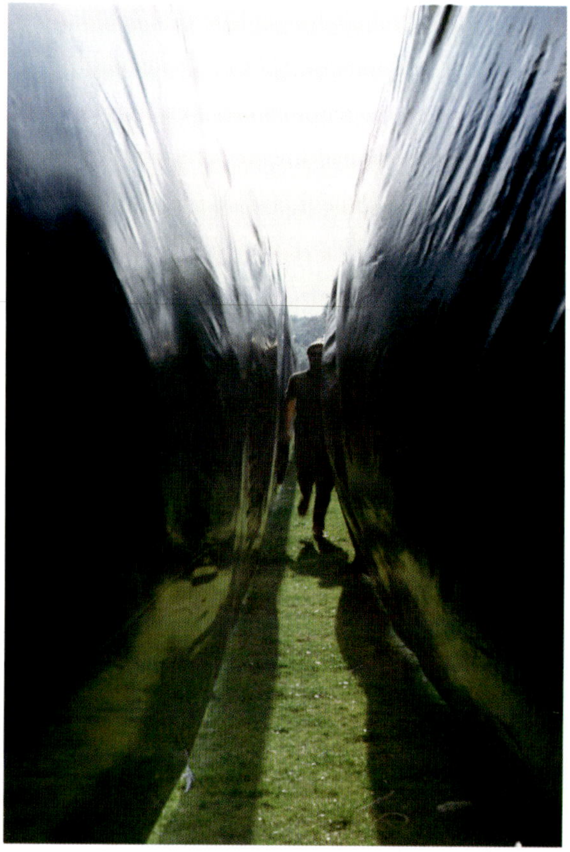

**80** Chris Burden, *Untitled*, 1969 (detail)

of Bruce Nauman's stud-and-plywood corridors. The animated effect of Burden's piece, however, diverged significantly from the experience induced by Nauman's rigid enclosures. Once a participant (*viewer* again does not seem the right word) plunged into the narrow passage between the frames, the Venturi effect of changing air pressure induced by the body's own movement caused the suspended plastic sheets to close around it, thereby shutting out the view both in front and behind (fig. 80). As Burden remembered it,

> I thought of it as a corridor, but then things started happening that I didn't plan on. . . . It was such a big structure that the wind would hit one side of it and blow the plastic in, and this created some sort of vacuum that would suck in the plastic on the other side. So the whole thing was always pressed together. You couldn't see down it except on rare occasions. If you walked down it, it would engulf you, but if you started running, your body would make an air pocket that would push it open in front of you. It was like magic.[10]

From the outside, the concealed bodies inside the structure appeared like elongated peas in an undulating pod. Racing from one end to the other quickly became a favorite pastime for kids from the adjacent Claremont *barrio*, the sculpture channeling the hippie ethos of play and induced exhilaration into its expanded meanings.

■

It could be argued that Burden had been an early adopter of that ethos before it even had a name or a social identity, a discovery that led him to enroll at Pomona in the first place. Several years older than almost all the members of his college class (of which the author was one), he came from Cambridge, Massachusetts, and had lived in France and Italy while growing up. A summer job in San Diego while still in high school had naturally led to his spending time on the beach at idyllic La Jolla Shores (far from Baldessari's down-at-heel National City). It was not the surf, however, that captured him, but a group of motorcyclists who congregated in the parking lot, an encounter that planted the idea both of returning to California for his education and taking up, alongside his ambitions to become an architect, motorcycle riding on the small, fast British models of the day. Burden brought both attachments with him to Claremont, the architectural vocation persisting through his first two years, with the rigors of its attendant courses in physics and mathematics. But another summer internship, this time in a large architectural firm back in Cambridge, left him disillusioned by the hierarchical nature of the profession and discouraged by the realization that it would take years to move up the ladder toward original design.

Burden's attachment to daredevil motorcycle riding—launching himself into the air over the dips on the old Baseline Road through the lemon groves—could also be said to have lent another dimension to his own imagination of bodies in motion, while tinkering with the mechanically cranky British bikes of that era would also have made him mindful of the Venturi effect entailed in the operation of their carburetors. His famous later involvement with motor vehicles in his sculpture could also be said to have existed as a latent potential at this stage, but that would wait on his extended elaboration of the possibilities offered by the human body physically adjoined, Baden-like, to the work of sculpture. While he found himself essentially living inside his black-plastic corridor piece as a precaution against vandalism, he was at the same time bearing witness to the necessary presence of bodies—starting with his own—in the activation of the sculpture, which could be said to have come into being only when entered by active human beings.[11]

The autumn after mounting this senior sculpture project, he moved, as Turrell had done four years before, to the fledgling MFA program at the University of California's new campus at Irvine, its Orange County location a short drive from the Pomona Valley. As was the case with the new UC San Diego campus to the south, the importance that California culture laid on self-actualization, the creative use of leisure time, meant that art played an expected part in the curriculum of the state's massive and then well-funded system of higher education. The timing again meant that the early cohorts of students had begun to absorb the novel sensibilities incubated within the counterculture, and much the same can be said of the rapidly recruited faculty for the visual arts, who favored a free-form, radically egalitarian ethos.[12] "It was," in Burden's words, "very small. They didn't provide you with really any facilities; you had to get your own studio, your own tools . . . The first thing they told you when the

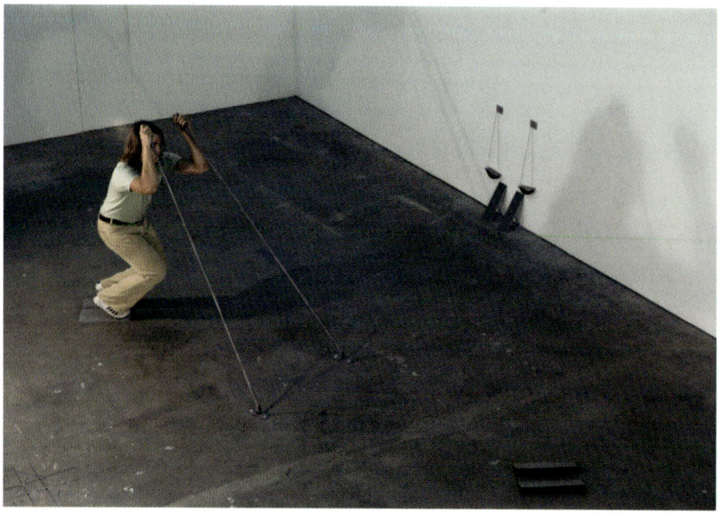

**81** Chris Burden, untitled apparatus sculpture no. 9, 1967, dimensions variable

group of 13 met was that acceptance to the MFA program was tantamount to an MFA degree. So you could literally go and stare at the surf for two years and you would walk away with an MFA, which is still kind of a radical notion."[13] In the absence of facilities, there was an impressive, changing roster of teachers: Burden remembered in particular the Los Angeles stalwarts Robert Irwin and Craig Kauffman, along with the visiting Robert Morris, a New York pioneer of static Minimalism in sculpture, who had lately moved to what he called "anti-form," room-filling installations of scattered, heterogeneous material.

Inspiring though these mentors may have been, Burden chose to continue working out the implications of what he had started at Pomona. He did so, however, with no thought to continuing in the vein of paradoxical monumentality: "These pieces were about physical activity, about how they manipulated my body," he recalled thinking about the Pomona work; "When I realized that, they stopped being sculptures and there was no reason to make them that big."[14] Open-ended dynamism reversed itself in the direction of stasis, while the material components of the work went from gargantuan to the scale of the human hand. Each of his untitled pieces from this phase entailed one or two participants achieving a precarious balance that was, by definition, extremely short-lived (fig. 81). In one, you were to sprawl on an aluminum sheet with hand and foot holds at its corners; then, rocking over a short, vertical post set into the floor, try to keep the sheet suspended over that pivot point. Another demanded that you suspend yourself facedown from the ceiling with feet and hands braced in a contraption of wire cables. A third required two people to stand on a low, horizontal bar suspended above the floor, then to hold themselves in place by grasping two identical bars connected by a pair of flexible cables and leaning away from one another—a state practical for at most a few minutes, during which brief time every muscular twitch would be transmitted to one's partner.

Burden's refined machine aesthetic was evident in the immaculate manufacture of these enabling bits of apparatus, but without human subjects they remain inert and pre-artistic, not rising to the level of sculpture in themselves. Via action not stasis, in a startling reinvention of the figurative statue, the human subject becomes the work of sculpture, the metal parts relegated to the accessory status of pedestals—but only as long as the precarious

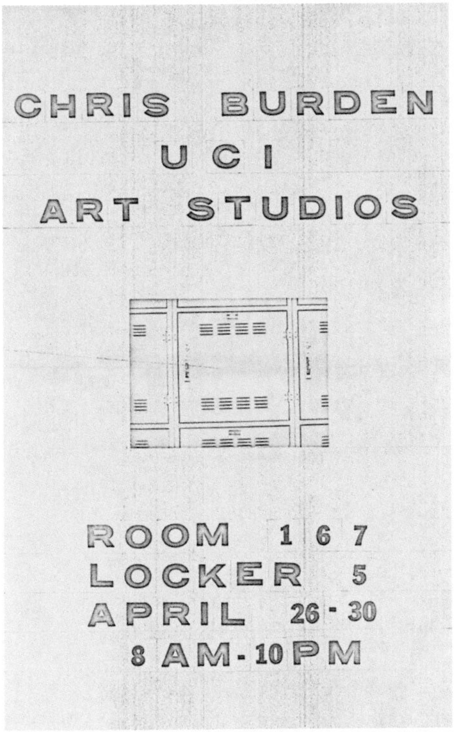


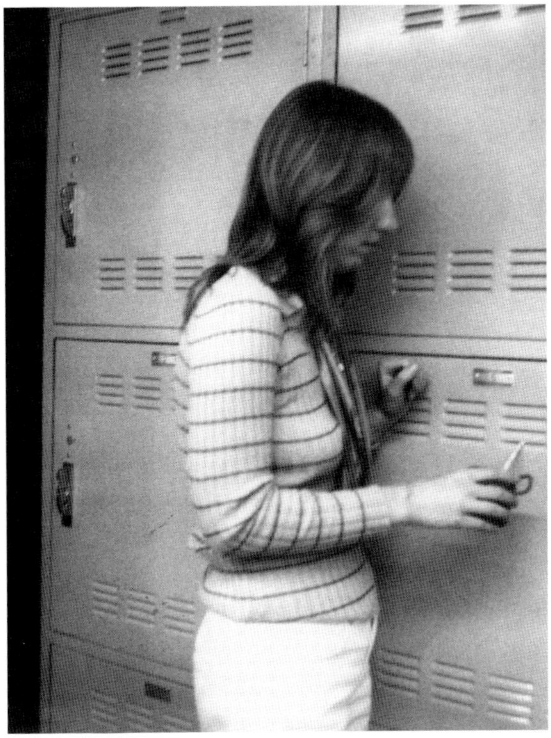

**82 (ABOVE LEFT)** Chris Burden, announcement for *Five Day Locker Piece*, 1971, Xerox, 35.6 × 21.6 cm

**83** Barbara Burden feeding Chris Burden juice through the louvers of the locker, 1971

state of equilibrium can be maintained. The "viewer," at the cost of awkward and vulnerable self-exposure, acquires personal responsibility for these pieces existing at all. In their photographic documentation, Burden assumes the place of the generic viewer-activator (in the double work, acting it out with his then spouse, Barbara). When time came for his master's-degree project in the spring of 1971, he made that stand-in role into the defining condition of the work, but at the expense of his being visible at all. For *Five Day Locker Piece* (fig. 82), he squeezed into a student's storage locker, two feet square on its face and three deep. The locker was positioned midway up a three-high bank of such receptacles installed along a corridor in the art department. The locker above served for water; the one below for elimination. He could access nutrition via a straw pushed through the standard downward facing vents in the door, which allowed air circulation but no visual contact between artist and spectators (fig. 83).[15]

Though Burden could be said to have placed his body within just another, if more extreme, physical-mechanical constraint, an unintended excess of meaning arose among the growing parade of visitors drawn to the bank of lockers during the days of his occupancy, some resorting to elaborate and bizarre confessions in their anxiety to breach the barrier and elicit a response from the resolutely silent Burden. In this early case, his acting out an inwardness and individual isolation to a self-punishing degree turned the work into the focus of spontaneous gatherings and social interactivity. As he recalls:

> It was an experiment. I wanted to see what would happen. I thought this piece was going to be an isolation thing, but it turned into this strange sort of public confessional where people were coming all the time to talk to me. At first, just my friends and the other grad students knew about it. Then it started building up, rumors were spreading. The university's a pretty big place and people who weren't interested in art, specifically, came over just to see this guy locked in a locker. I think that the further away you were from this, the more strange it seemed, and I noticed that when people actually came to talk with me, they were reassured in a way . . .[16]

It might seem a minimal requirement for a work of visual art that it gives you something to see, but *Five Day Locker* did not alter its sterile institutional corridor in any way; it appeared exactly as it would have done whether or not Burden was wedged into one of its student lockers. The appearance of the setting was, nonetheless, transformed, dramatically so, by the presence of visitors who had nothing novel to contemplate except one another. Spectatorship had been turned on its head to become the object of visual spectacle, with an admixture of unpredictability and the prospect of dangers other than the effects of physical duress. "The Dean of Fine Arts found out about it," said Burden, "and he was real panicky. There was a debate about whether or not they should try to pry me out with crowbars. And there was nothing I could do. Just toward the end I got panicky myself. I started getting that weird feeling that a REAL crazy was going to come and do something to me. There were periods of time when I was alone and I knew my vulnerability might inspire someone to do something crazy. But that was only toward the end . . ." It would be reasonable to infer in Burden's anxieties in 1971 the realization that countercultural spontaneity in social experiments had yielded its significant share of violent dysfunction, which his famous performance pieces that followed, entailing risk of violent injury to his own body, would take as their baseline assumption.

■

As Burden followed his unique performance trajectory away from the body-implicating sculpture initially fostered by Mowry Baden at Pomona, those precedents vividly played themselves out on their home ground. The fact that the new Pomona gallery director, Hal Glicksman, had acquired his curatorial acumen while working as an exhibition preparator

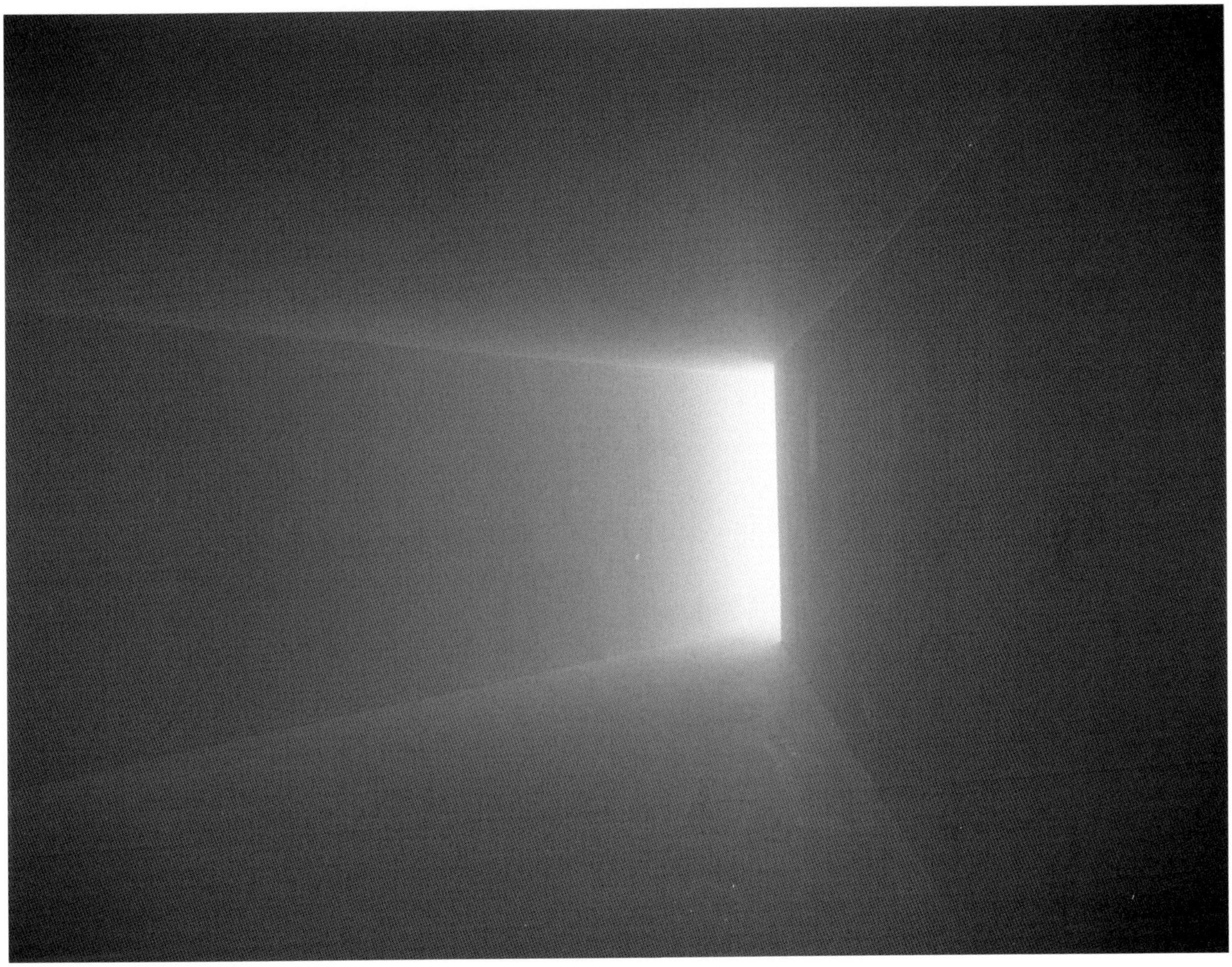

84 Michael Asher, Gladys K. Montgomery Art Center, Pomona College, Claremont, California, USA, February 13–March 8, 1970.
Photo taken from back wall of large triangular area, viewing toward passageway into small triangular area

meant that he was particularly attuned to large, built structures and transformations of the gallery space, and he commissioned sympathetic artists to take over the gallery entirely in a series of comprehensive installations at a time when the idea of site-specific sculpture was still in its infancy. In February 1970, he staged what was perhaps the most uncompromising of these endeavors to the design of Michael Asher, then a nearly unknown, young Los Angeles artist with few realized works to his name. Asher's plan was to create a parasitic interior architecture that would nest inside and entirely conceal the two offset rectangles that constituted the entire exhibition and office space of the gallery. He drew the outline of the new space as two opposed right triangles meeting to form an hourglass shape, the narrow throat of which lay within the old opening between the two galleries (fig. 84).

Asher's initial plan was that the inserted volume would have two openings, one end giving onto the street, the other to an inner courtyard. But that arrangement generated such a strong and continuous flow of air through the space that the inner one had to be plastered over, which changed the experience of the visitor from traversing a Burden-like corridor, rushed through by a wind-tunnel effect, to penetrating a hushed cavern with an implicit invitation to linger and savor the subtlety of sensation that the artist wanted to foster.[17] The pristinely white space, only six-and-a-half feet high, received no illumination apart from whatever light fell through the front opening, the doors of which were removed so as to permit round-the-clock access to the space. As the fame of the piece has grown with Asher's subsequent reputation, it has come to be aligned—on account of its nullification of the normal display, security, and administrative functions of a small educational gallery—with a "critique" of art institutions.[18] But few if any who confidently interpret the piece along these lines had any direct experience of it. And few such concerns appeared to be on the minds of the principals and observers at the time of its construction; they dwelled instead on effects of ambient sound (as from the frequent passing freight trains) and the changing light as perceived from within the space through the day and night[19] Rather than some complicated series of intellectual operations predicated on an underlying attitude of suspicion, the piece encouraged a subdued sensory receptiveness to evanescent sensation, along with spontaneous communal interaction—both effects entirely in keeping the countercultural preoccupations of the moment. Asher's partners in the project recall with amusement the intensity of his preoccupation with the wafting air currents inside the enclosure; to this end, he asked Glicksman to obtain a pistol-like device used by architects and HVAC engineers called a T.T. Smoker, its name standing, as the curator explains: "for titanium tetrachloride, which is a chemical that forms smoke when it meets air. Since the smoke is not hot, it doesn't rise. The smoke just sits there and lasts for a long time." Firing off repeated puffs of the cold smoke and tracking their paths, "Michael used it to see where the air movements were."[20] In a surviving note to Glicksman on Pomona memo paper, he may or may not have been referring to the smoker when he asked him for a "low range air velometer to read ambient air."[21]

As a gallery is a container for art, moreover, Asher turned any visitor inside the container into an element of its sculptural volume (fig. 73), much as Baden imagined his devices subjecting their users to redescription as art. There was no possible way to experience the piece, still less to "see" it, without simultaneously *being* the piece—you were not in it, but of it, overtaken by an art condition without temporal boundaries. But that condition did not leave the visitor bereft of something to see. As he or she turned back toward the single entrance and exit and looked through its fixed, box-like enclosure, there was a *picture*: an idyllic landscape in a frame, a well-watered greensward in the desert, studded with palms and eucalyptus (fig. 85). This landscape, for all of these generic attributes, was no work of artful fiction but as impeccably real and anti-illusionistic as the structure of the sculpture itself.

■

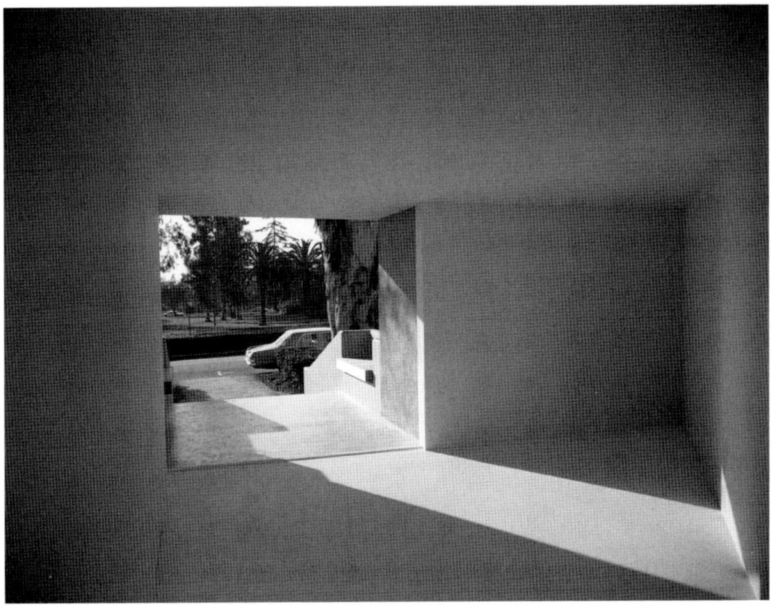

85 Michael Asher, Gladys K. Montgomery Art Center, Pomona College, Claremont, California, USA, February 13–March 8, 1970. Viewing out of gallery toward street from small triangular area. Photo taken with daylight

Asher was not alone among Los Angeles artists in seeking to orchestrate sensations by strictly non-fictional means. The non-public art events then being orchestrated by James Turrell at the Mendota Hotel in Santa Monica, the controlled release of ambient light into his bare, darkened studio, obeyed a parallel protocol. The simultaneous eclipse of Turrell as a visible persona within the art world only redoubled the prestige of these experiments. The downtown Manhattan art entrepreneur Willoughby Sharp, a key underground opinion maker, wrote that "Turrell's refusal to show after invitations from Nick Wilder and Leo Castelli, and vague reports of works with natural light constructed in the walls of his studio have made him a heroic figure for a younger generation of Los Angeles artists."[22] For an artist whose very medium was visibility, it was his invisibility in the normal venues of art, a controlled vanishing—much as Bruce Conner was attempting during the same years in San Francisco—that helped cement his charismatic reputation.

Not even the Museum of Modern Art could tempt him away from his retreat with an offer of an exclusive space (to be assumed instead by Asher), but Baden was able to overcome Turrell's resistance to re-entering the institutional realm by hiring him back to his old campus as a teacher (discretion about his imprisonment for abetting draft evasion forestalled the complications of a criminal record with college authorities). This undertaking has since become invisible twice over. While his Mendota seclusion was widely noticed and remarked upon, his second round in Claremont remained outwardly unnoticed for decades, effectively erased from the record as Turrell's fame grew—with the paradox that he was as visible and socially engaged as he could possibly have been within the orbit of Pomona College and its sister institutions. While this new responsibility conformed to the Quaker ethic of service, it was not by itself unusual in a region where teaching by the most prominent artists, such as those attracted to CalArts and the Irvine program, was unexceptional. Turrell, however, put his commutes back to Claremont in the service of a further self-humbling, as he chose to recommence his studies toward the master's degree in fine art, abandoned at Irvine after his sentencing in 1966, now resumed under the auspices of the Claremont Graduate School.

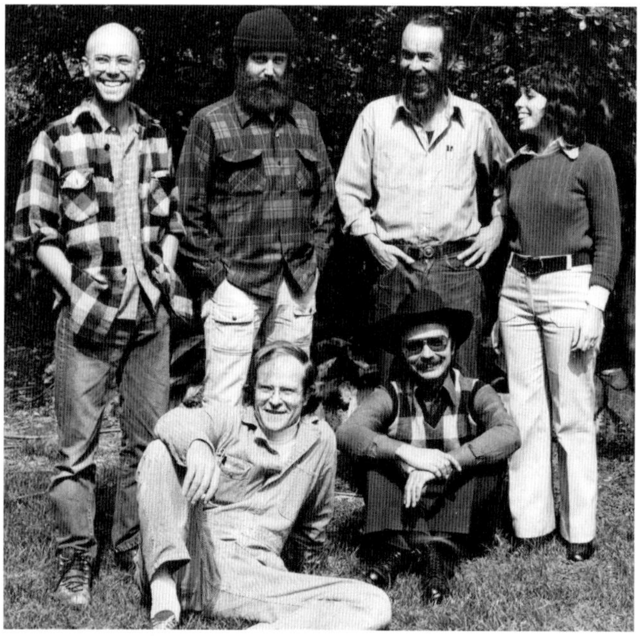

**86** Pomona College art faculty, 1972: back row, Hap Tivey, James Turrell, Gus Blaisdell; front row, Mowry Baden and Guy Williams, Marcy Goodwin far right. Photograph by Lewis Baltz

Because graduate programs in Claremont were taught via a consortium of faculty from the several affiliated colleges in the town, Turrell found himself at one moment a teacher of some authority and, at another, the ostensible pupil of his teaching colleagues. A photograph of the Pomona studio faculty shows him standing second from left, his identity almost buried under a dark, full beard, watch cap pulled low over his forehead, Pendleton shirt buttoned to the neck (fig. 86). In 1971, student assistance was instrumental in a piece he staged, presumably as a contribution to his master's portfolio, with red highway flares, set behind the colonnade of Pomona's massive, classical/art-deco Bridges Auditorium (fig. 87). In Turrell's own description: "I did this one piece called *Burning Bridges* . . . I had these sandboxes and put flares in them and reflectors, and put them behind the columns of Big Bridges, the theater building. When the flares were set off, it just looked fantastic because it put the light right into the space . . . behind the columns . . . "[23]

Everything about this exercise, which does not today figure in the permanent catalogue of his work, was social and ephemeral. The explosion of the simultaneously detonated flares was instantaneous, their ambient light transforming the portico interior as they slowly burned down. His rapport with his students supplied the spirit and organization required to pull it off, while the impact of the piece depended on surprise sufficient to call out the town fire department. “Of course,” as Turrell recalled, “somebody reported that Bridges was on fire. They actually had the fire trucks come out. And I moved the crew to go to these different places, right after they got it going, I was happy so I'd go to the next place and prepare that . . . have it ready. Roland Reiss [the graduate art chair] had to explain that this is an art piece, which was interesting for everyone at that moment.”[24]

There were more such controlled flare detonations, one that same night, others that filled concrete service tunnels under campus buildings with reflected light and smoke. The off-the-shelf devices of highway flares returned him to the gas experiments with which he had begun his art career at Irvine, but without the tricky business of managing steady illumination from incendiary material. The contrast with his cool light projections and isolating

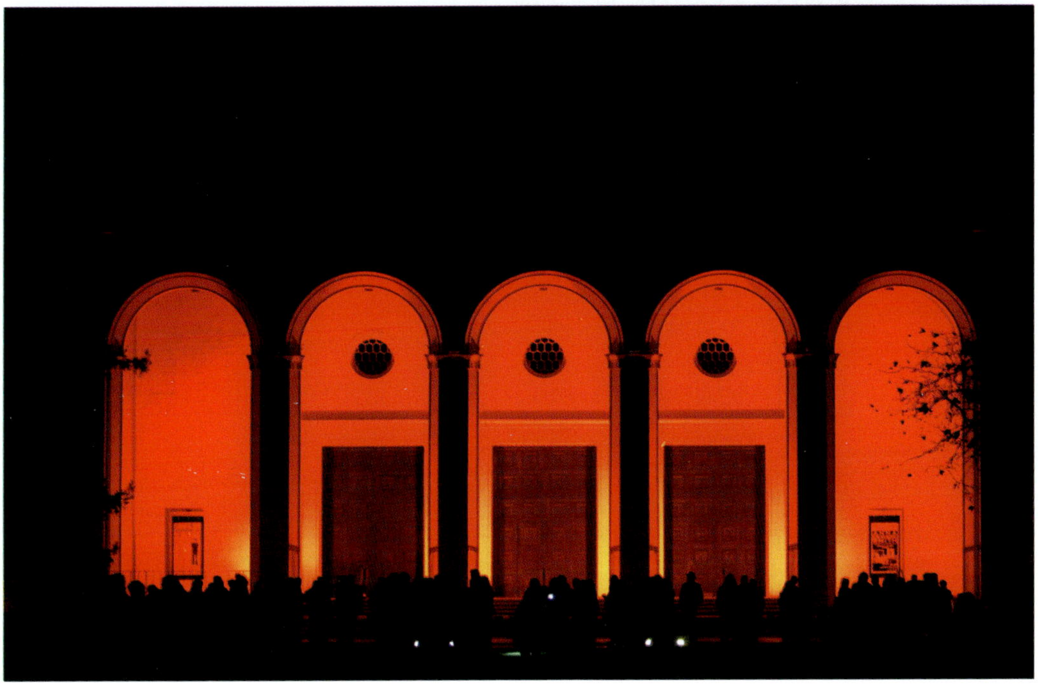

**87** James Turrell et al, *Burning Bridges*, 1971 (re-creation 2012), performance, Pomona College, Claremont, California

environments sets up something of an Apollonian/ Dionysian dichotomy, one that culminated in Turrell's contribution in 1972 to an elaborately staged, cheerfully neo-pagan, nocturnal pageant orchestrated by his English-department colleague, the medieval scholar and poet Richard Barnes. *The Death of Buster Quinine: A Sacramental Farce and Fire Opera* began with a procession of several hundred participants accompanying the grotesque, towering effigy of the titular character into the deep, steep-sided arena provided by an area of abandoned

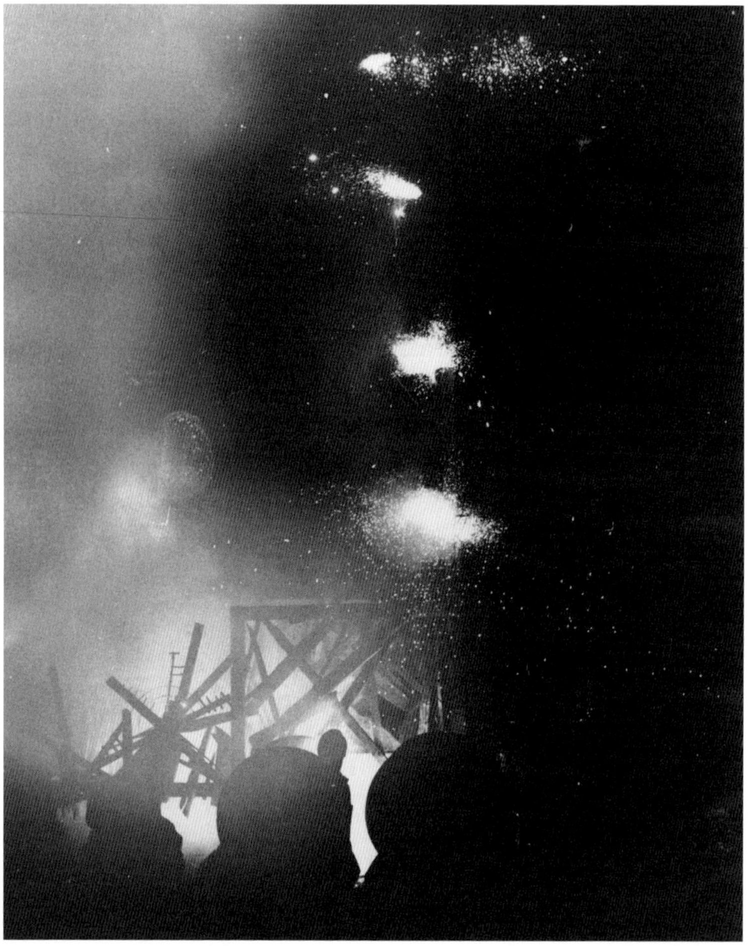

**88** Richard (Dick) Barnes, *The Death of Buster Quinine*, October 1972, performance, Pomona College, Claremont, California

quarries in the semi-desert terrain adjacent to the Claremont town line. Spectators began to be confused with performers, as all descended into the deep crater carrying lighted sparklers, the night sky as a canopy overhead (fig. 88).

Their path took the throng under a stone arch carved beneath a highway, which Turrell and his students lined with yet another array of aluminum-reflected flares. As described by the artist Hap Tivey, who assisted Turrell, "[The fire arch] focused all of the sound of the flares directly on the people walking through it . . . You walked through a shimmering red fire and heard the amplified sound of all those flares hissing."[25] That accomplished, Turrell and company shifted to managing two large, blue-tinted beacon lights. One of these he eventually trained steadily on the moon, as the holy fool Buster expired by a rocket to the heart that set off an explosion of fireworks planted inside the body of the gargantuan puppet. Barnes, Turrell, and all of their enthusiastic collaborators plainly believed that there was mileage yet in the counterculture's penchant for phantasmagorical extravaganzas and cosmic light projections, as well as the idea of art as a celebratory communal exercise.

The uncanny setting for the event, along with the ritual destruction of Buster like a sacrificial bad object, nonetheless carried more ominous overtones, just as the full implications of *Burning Bridges* far exceeded Turrell's lighthearted reminiscence about light effects and a misunderstanding with the Claremont Fire Department. Distress flares are just that, signals of danger and peril; red is the color of conflagration; smoke detonated in tunnels is the stuff of warfare. In the light of the performance, it was possible to imagine the idyllic college campus as overtaken by the distant violence carried on in the name of the sheltered American way of life, shielded by the vast armory into which California had been transformed. Even as the war in Indochina receded, artists who had come of age in its shadow did not easily cast off the foreboding and dread that its distant thunder had engendered.

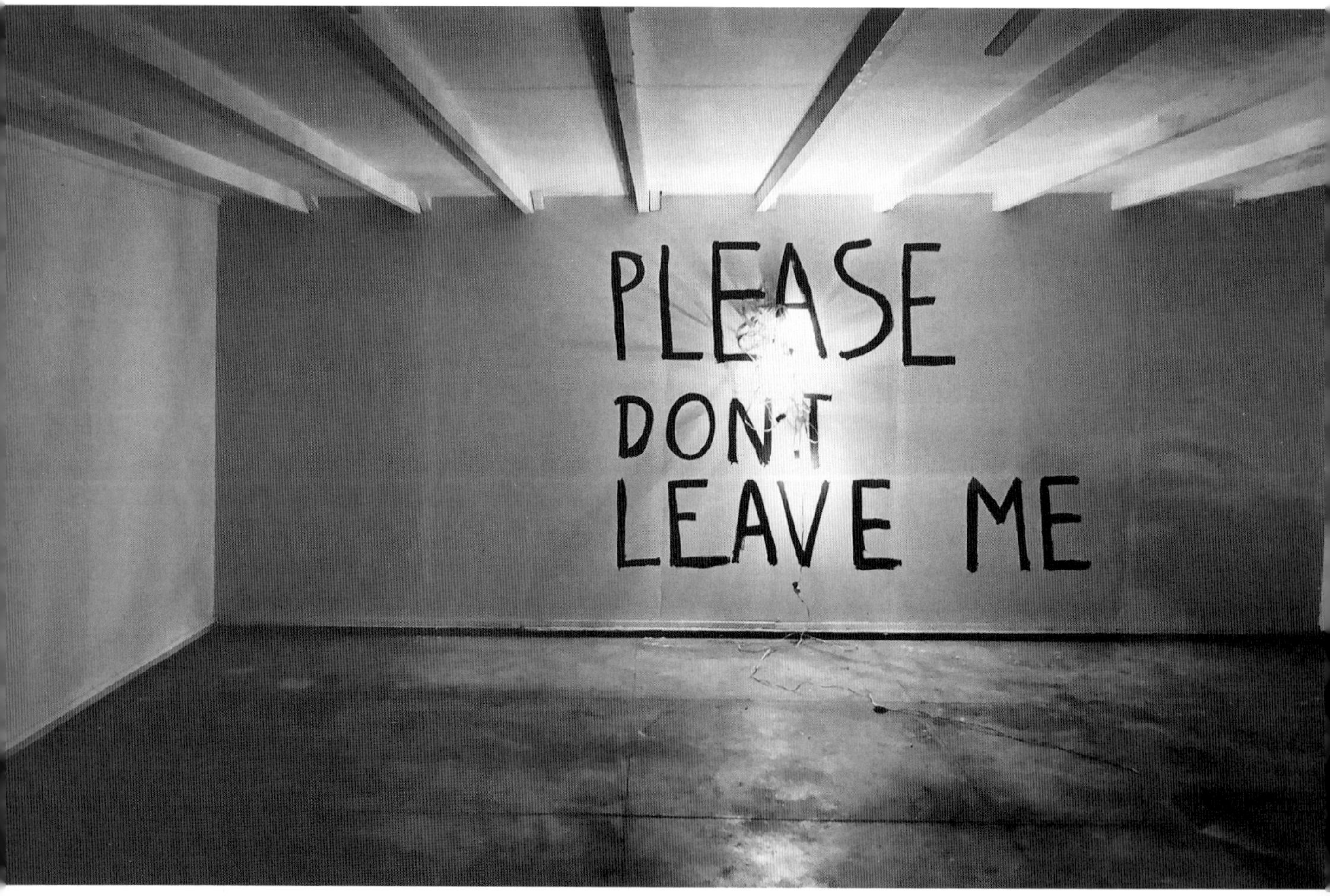


**89** Bas Jan Ader, *Please Don't Leave Me*, 1969, installation, Mount San Antonio College, Walnut, California

TEN

# *NOIR* VORTEX

THE CRUCIBLE THAT HAD BEEN IMMACULATE HEART COLLEGE in central Los Angeles, the home of Sister Corita Kent, has figured importantly in the pages above on account of Kent's forthright anti-war graphics and national celebrity. That institution's charitable spirit of welcome had further enriched the local art community by launching the California career of the young expatriate Bas Jan Ader. A disaffected and semi-successful student in his native Netherlands, Ader had emigrated to the United States in 1963 by crewing on a yacht en route from Morocco to Los Angeles, helmed by a film-studio artist who had worked at MGM (after a mishap late in the accident-plagued voyage, Ader arrived on American soil in San Diego courtesy of a Coast Guard rescue). Seeking out his school friend Ger Van Elk, who was enrolled at Immaculate Heart, Ader was taken up by Corita's superior, Magdalene Mary, who found him a job on campus. That led to his enrolling at the nearby, public Otis Art Institute, where his native charisma along with his gifts as a figurative draftsman and graphic storyteller smoothed the way to his degree.

Another old friend, whom he had met during a high-school exchange year outside Washington, the formidable ceramicist Dennis Parks, was pursuing an MFA degree at the Claremont Graduate School. Ader followed him in 1965, pursuing both studio-art and philosophy degrees at the same institution, thus putting him within the Claremont crucible that has already appeared so prominently in these pages. This capsule biography suggests a certain tendency to drift on the basis of fortuitous personal relationships. These included, most centrally, his marriage to fellow artist Mary Sue Andersen, the daughter of the dean of Otis. The more professionally advanced of the pair, Andersen had been appointed to a teaching post in San Bernardino, an exurb even further east but convenient enough from Claremont. So the couple settled in a picturesque, slightly ramshackle, prewar bungalow to the south of the college campuses, where Ader had time to ponder his direction as an artist.[1]

His thoughts in the main took him in the direction of his own disappearance. Like his spouse, he had begun teaching at a local community college, where, in 1969, he installed *Please Don't Leave Me* in his studio (fig. 89), the spot-lit words scrawled on the wall in crude capitals giving voice to the absent artist subject protesting his abandonment by the perceiving spectator. Performance pieces in which male bodies undergo occlusion and abjection can entail a kind of regression, an infantile state in which others become responsible

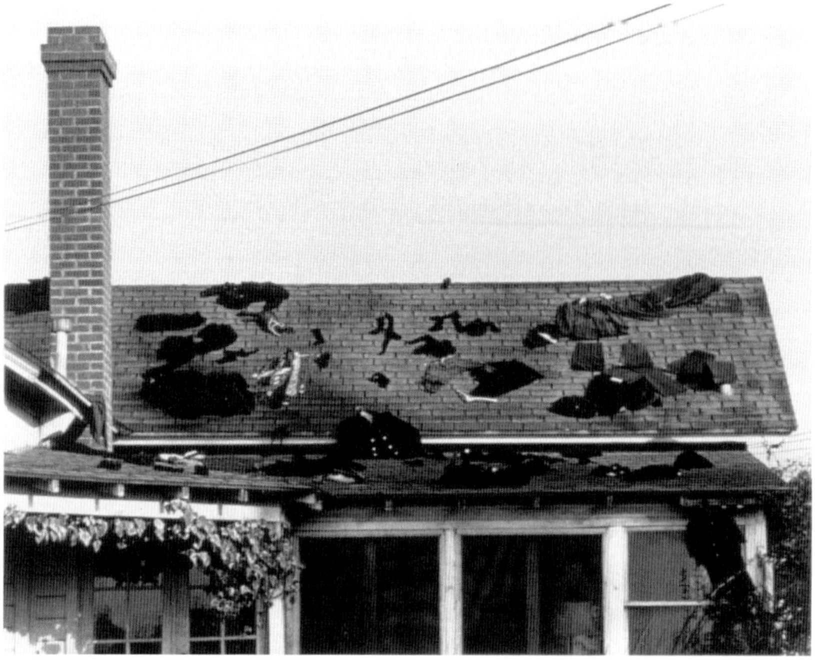

**90** Bas Jan Ader, *All My Clothes*, 1970, gelatin silver print, 28 × 35.5 cm, Meliksetian | Briggs, Los Angeles

for your care, as with Barbara Burden's seeing to her husband's nourishment during Chris Burden's 1971 *Five Day Locker Piece* (fig. 83). Ader's laconic plea anticipates this insight, its note of distress echoing in the staged photograph *All My Clothes* (fig. 90) of 1970, a work that enlisted the architectural personality of the bungalow he shared with his own artist-spouse as support for the inventory promised by the title, which appears at first to be an ironically deadpan physical translation of a verbal phrase akin to certain works by Bruce Nauman. But a sinister intimation of remains and dismemberment also attends the piece. The owner of the clothes must be hiding away naked or no longer living and past all need of clothing. What one sees could be the clues.

Intimations of violence and despoliation would come to Ader as part of a terrible family inheritance. He never really knew his devout pastor father, whom the Nazi occupiers of the Netherlands executed by firing squad in 1944 for having aided the escape of several hundred Jews from deportation. The Ader family household had been ransacked, their intimate belongings strewn into the street.[2] At the same time, the disposal of the items in *All My Clothes* carries a certain antic quality reminiscent of perilous stunts by the silent-film comedian Buster Keaton, those heyday of the 1920s is also the period of the house. Both peril and comedy converged in the brief, filmed performance of the same year *Fall 1*, in which Ader tumbles from the chair perched on the peak of the roof of his bungalow, disappearing from view into the overgrown shrubbery beneath the porch.

As well known as these works have since become, at least to close followers of recent art history, they were barely visible to anyone outside of Ader's intimate circle during the years in which they were made. The artist Hirokazu Kosaka, who was working in Los Angeles in the 1970s, described the neglect that all of them perceived at that moment: "Art in L.A. was about making objects that were beautiful and that you put in the wall. Decoration. All of a sudden there was space, a small space, for a different kind of work that dealt with more important issues. There were a small number of people doing this new kind of work: Bas Jan Ader, John Baldessari, Chris Burden, Jack Goldstein, Bill Leavitt, Bruce Nauman, Al Ruppersberg, Wolfgang Stoerchle, Bill Wegman. . . . There were maybe a dozen people, you could count them on your fingers, and we were outcasts, complete outcasts . . . separated from the Venice artists . . . not known by anyone."[3]

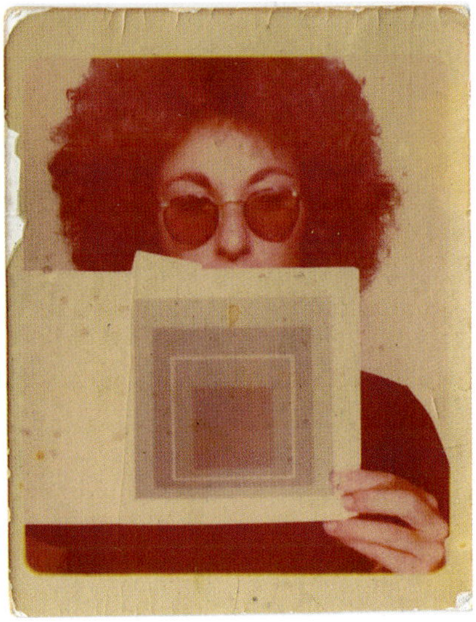

91 Helene Winer, photobooth self-portrait, c. 1969, Benton Museum of Art at Pomona College and Helene Winer

Not known by anyone—until Helene Winer (fig. 91) arrived as gallery director at Pomona in autumn 1970, after which this roster, including Kosaka himself, became the ready-made core of her exhibition program. Glimpsed briefly in the previous chapter as she accepted the ashes of John Baldessari's burned paintings, Winer had just previously spent a crucial few years working at the Whitechapel Gallery in London, which had in the previous decade played a key role in selecting and clarifying advanced American art for a British audience. While there, she had enjoyed a close-up view of Harald Szeemann's *Live In Your Head: When Attitudes Become Form* (the focus of the Prologue, above) at the last stop of the show in 1970 at London's Institute of Contemporary Art. To her surprise, the best art she encountered in Los Angeles proved to be of a piece with Szeeman's roster, and no one else was paying attention to it. "At the time I couldn't have told you what it was," she has reminisced, "but I always recognized it when I saw it."[4] Her out-of-the-ordinary acumen and intelligence as a curator shaped this inchoate group sensibility into a coherent cycle of exhibitions and events enshrining, as Goldstein put it, "a whole new attitude about what art could be, not expression but investigation."[5]

One could say that the group remained outcast in a more literal sense, that is, cast out from a deteriorating urban core to a new and far more receptive location on the geographical periphery of the metropolis. At this time, the intellectually sympathetic environment of Claremont offered perhaps the only venue where art making could engage formal learning without apology. Ader's preoccupation in these years with Ludwig Wittgenstein's *Philosophical Investigations* exasperated some acquaintances; Turrell's scientific and mathematical training, carried more lightly, under-girded all of his investigations of light and space; Baden (now departed for the University of Victoria) had thought simultaneously like a physiologist, psychologist, and engineer. And a new standard for such endeavors had been set by Burden's *Five Day Locker* performance, a Pomona piece by proxy. That self-imposed ordeal of confinement diverted standard avant-garde devices of the ready-made and Minimalist container into the most thoroughgoing concealment of the artist to date, acted out, what was more, over that unbroken, round-the-clock continuity of time that Asher's gallery installation had made manifest the year before. The interplay between the artist's presence and absence, between self-possession and loss of control, emerged as a shared preoccupation binding together this network of Claremont-oriented peers. Concealment or disappearance were the necessary complements to exposure and manipulation of the body over time as a primary medium of art, the means by which bodily presence would escape the pre-articulate condition of just being there and so enter into the realm of signification.

A series of performances that Winer organized in 1972 included a contribution by Kosaka that drove these implications to the fore (fig. 92). Lying on the floor of the Pomona gallery, he encased himself in an electric blanket turned up high, over the top of which was shoveled a thick covering of earth, such that the shape of his body and his individual features were lost to view. The performance consisted of his enduring the weight and oven-like heat for its duration, while a subdued audience hung back against the walls of the space uncertain as to whether humanitarian intervention was required. The artist's actions and materials bear an analogy to Terry Fox's *Levitation*, executed in the Bay Area the year before and discussed above in Chapter 8. But Fox's secrecy, aerial conceit, and mental escape from debilitating constraints (his illness, the pollution of the site) found themselves reversed in Kosaka's submission to weight, gravity, and near-suffocation, endured in front of witnesses implicated in a way that made them integral to the performance rather than excluded, as they had been with Fox's piece, so as not to compromise the hallucinatory inward focus of the artist as performer. If Kosaka experienced hallucinations, they were doubtless unpleasant.

One spectator visible in the accompanying photograph of the sweltering Kosaka, slouching against the wall with legs extended, is his close friend from his time at the Chouinard School of Art, Allen Ruppersberg, an actual exhibitor in Szeemann's *Live in Your Head*, whom Winer had likewise astutely enlisted into her program. The harder the artist became to see, the harder his peers would work to bear witness. Other photographs of the Kosaka performance document John Baldessari's presence among the observers along the wall: "In my VW bus," he recalled of his first years teaching at CalArts, "I would take students out to see Helene Winer's shows at Pomona College. . . . She would show work no one else was interested in. For every one of her shows, I would load up students and take them out to Claremont."[6] Matt Mullican, then among the magic circle of Baldessari's CalArts students, likewise remembers both the need to keep up with the Pomona scene and the effort it took to get there: "We went out to Claremont a bunch of times; it was a long trip."[7]

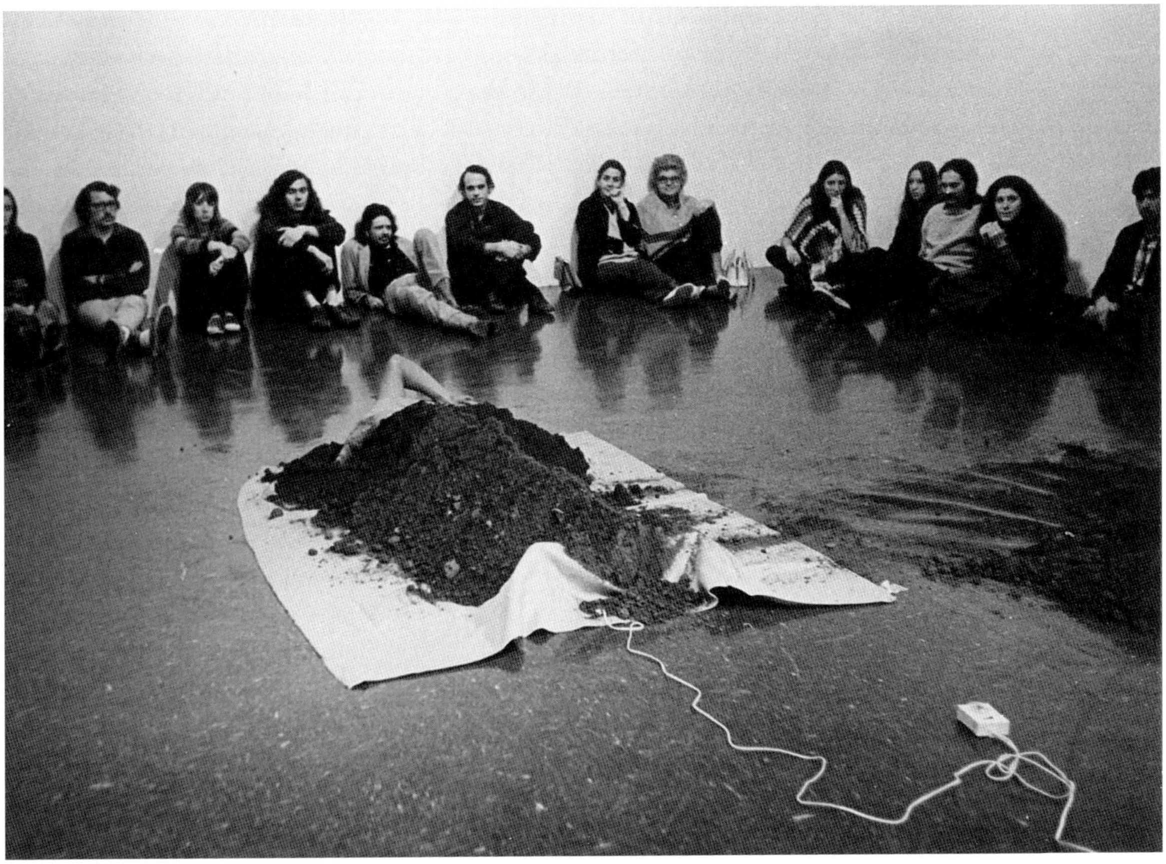

**92** Hirokazu Kosaka, *Untitled*, 1972, performance documentation, Benton Museum of Art at Pomona College (Allen Ruppersberg is slouched against the wall to the left of William Leavitt, Barbara Burden two places further along)

As CalArts got up and running, traffic in these extreme actions went the other way: in 1971, a small, self-selected group of witnesses stood on a hillside adjacent to the still unfinished CalArts campus on the occasion of the MFA graduation performance by Jack Goldstein. Already an advanced student at Chouinard, Goldstein had found little affirmation from Baldessari for a cycle of sculptures composed of stacked sheets of unsecured wood conceived in a distant dialogue with Richard Serra and Carl Andre.[8] In an abrupt shift of direction, the young artist concluded his formal art training by subjecting himself to perhaps the most perilous act of Houdini-like self-immolation over an entire night on a hill above Interstate 5 in Valencia. Baldessari himself offers this recollection: "The work of Jack's that sticks in my mind is when he buried himself underground and got his air from plastic tubes;

it was one of the most risky pieces I have ever seen. It took place at CalArts and Wolfgang Stoerchle was there; it was in the evening. The sun was setting, and Jack had a stethoscope, which measured his heartbeat from about twenty feet away. It was connected to where he was buried and where he was symbolically dead. What a terror being buried like that must have induced. Jack said that he was trying to give up something organic to make a symbolic statement."[9]

Well might it have stuck in the mind of a mentor. And well might he have discerned a symbolic intent whereby the presence and absence of the artist finds itself reduced to the simplest on-off binary, converting, in Goldstein's words, "subjectivity to anonymous objective impulse."[10] In some sense, that performance (it may be corny to say so) inaugurated a certain rebirth to his mature trajectory as an artist, as he himself acknowledged: "I tried to disappear by hiring actors and by hiring others to manufacture my paintings. The movies and performances became symbolic of my disappearances, just as in my final show at CalArts I was buried. All anyone saw was the blinking light, which was symbolic of my heartbeat."[11]

Perhaps the most storied capture of ultimate disappearance as a theme in art arrived when Chris Burden arranged to have a rifle bullet graze his upper arm in the performance piece *Shoot* of November 1971. The enduring fame of the work rests to be sure on other provocations, on chains of association converging toward the violence of the Vietnam War—threat or reality for every American male of Burden's age cohort. *Shoot* also channeled and condensed the cultivation of physical risk-taking widely distributed among the masculine subcultures of Southern California—a conspicuous local ethos ultimately traceable to the returning veterans of the Korean War and the Second World War, resourceful and resistant to confinement, who swelled the regional population at the conclusion of those conflicts (Burden's personal connection being his recreational limit-pushing on light, British motorcycles). The illegality of the action in *Shoot* connects itself to the regular brushes with the law courted by Hell's Angels, hell-raising surf clubs, and Dead-Man's-Curve street racers. The undying historical vividness arising from such unbidden connotations generates the paradox at the core of the piece: the bullet's instantaneous impact seems to encompass of world of mayhem and adventure, but no more than a handful of invited spectators actually saw it performed. Its principal documentation remains a scar on the private person of the artist, with photographs and video documents intentionally left meager and indistinct. The setting was quasi-academic: a small and bare whitewashed box in a light-industrial park, organized by students at the nearby Irvine campus of the University of California and dubbed simply F-Space after its alphabetical designation in the floor plan of the complex.

The setting in which *Shoot* was sequestered thus bore all the traits of the impersonal, formal order espoused by contemporaneous Conceptual artists in their charts, grids, and typewritten inventories, but Burden and his friends found a three-dimensional equivalent ready-made in the exurban development where *Shoot* was performed. The first stage of the entire Irvine complex—university branch, housing, office blocks, light industry—had only just emerged from hilly, undeveloped ranchland an hour's drive south of Los Angeles (fig. 93). Curving residential streets attempted the picturesque, while the working thorough-

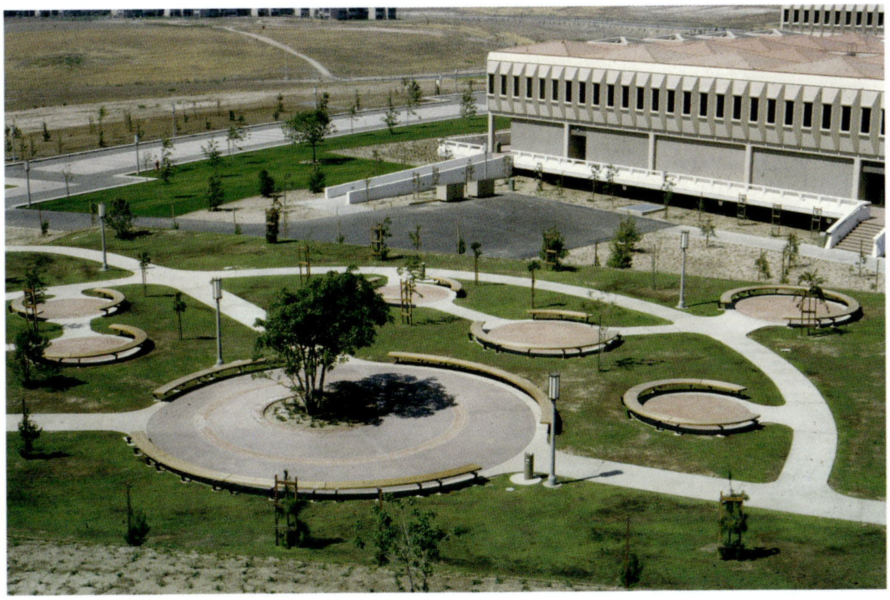

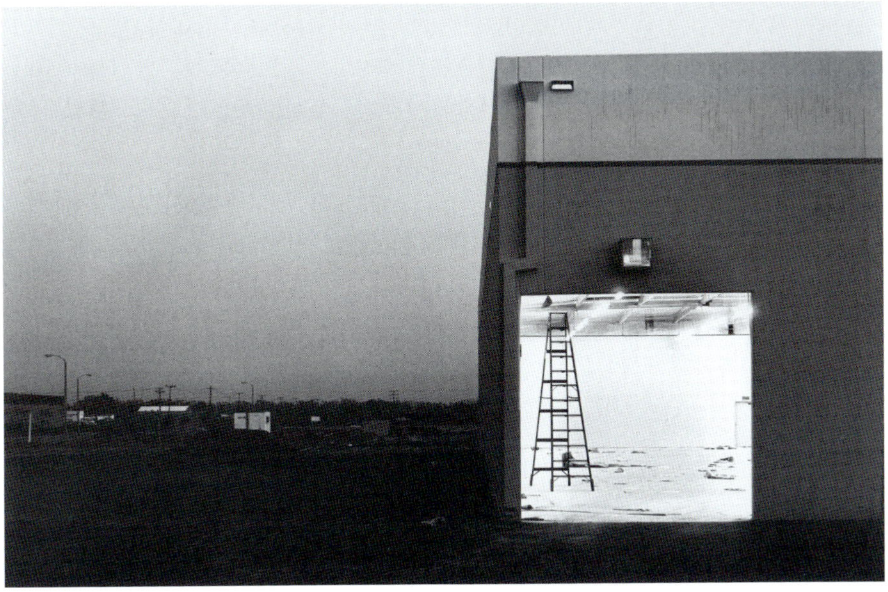

**93 (TOP)** Aerial view of the Fine Arts Building at the University of California, Irvine, late 1960s, University Communications Photographs (AS-061), University of California, Irvine Libraries. Special Collections and Archives

**94** Lewis Baltz, *West Wall, R-ohm Corporation, 16931 Milliken, Irvine*, from “The New Industrial Parks near Irvine, California,” 1974, gelatin silver print, 15.2 × 22.9 cm, Collection San Francisco Museum of Modern Art fares followed the modernist grid, just as did the tipped-up, cast-concrete slabs that surrounded generic enclosures like the one that comprised F-Space. And so their elevations appear in the frontally presented and formally exacting photographic documents that the Claremont graduate student and instructor Lewis Baltz was making of the same prefabricated, multipurpose structures in his landmark series, "The New Industrial Parks near Irvine, California" (fig. 94).

In more recent times, Irvine became the epicenter of the high-risk mortgage packaging that brought down the global economy in 2008. During the early 1970s, it provided a band of art outsiders with a *de novo* manifestation of late twentieth-century economic order and efficiency unconstrained by a preexisting historical fabric: thus, a perverse but telling mirror held up to the grid, series, and ready-made as widely accepted hallmarks of advanced artistic probity. The function of such a setting in regard to *Shoot* was to frame and isolate the action into a space where the variables of art could hold their own for a moment against the ungovernable associations that the explosive nature of the performance otherwise engendered. Rather than the frame of art revealing the body, it was the body that revealed the frame of art.

Less than two weeks prior to *Shoot*, Burden had traveled to the Midwest to stage *You'll Never See My Face in Kansas City*. In its gallery manifestation, he was seated behind a barrier that prevented visitors from seeing his neck and head; during the three days he spent in the city, he wore a ski mask at all times lest his features inadvertently come to light. To efface one's identity in plain sight carried distinct overtones of criminality, which he would overtly court at F-Space shortly afterward. One month later, Burden played the fugitive in the plainest and most literal way: for the three days leading up the Christmas Eve 1971, without prior announcement, he just disappeared. "Actually," he relates, "All I did was check into a motel." By his testimony, however, *Disappearance* entered his own consciousness in ways that transcended the seeming banality of his action: "It was a funny thing: I didn't feel I could do anything during those three days. I didn't read, or eat or even watch television. How could I, when I'd disappeared?"[12]

The arbitrary duration of *Disappearance* might seem comparatively slack, but the work added two layers of secrecy to Burden's simply absenting himself from normal contact with the world. His fasting in secret introduced a time exigency, but a clandestine and unknowable one for external observers, since there were no spectators—all of which compounded his initial secrecy with regard to even the existence of the piece. The term *experimental art* is a commonplace, but Burden knew enough to accept the unexpected outcomes of a performance as the valid extension of his own initial thought. The fact that *Disappearance* was comparatively little noticed then or recalled since seems an affirmation of its cogency (raising the philosophical question in the vein of Bishop Berkeley: is it a performance if nobody comes, including the artist?). It distilled the lessons of 1971 into something like a pure confrontation with the self—not identified exclusively with the body—becoming the subject of art. Burden found himself facing less his physical alienation from all customary contacts than a splitting of the self, a decisive interruption in his assumed scope of personal agency once he had followed through on his initial decision.

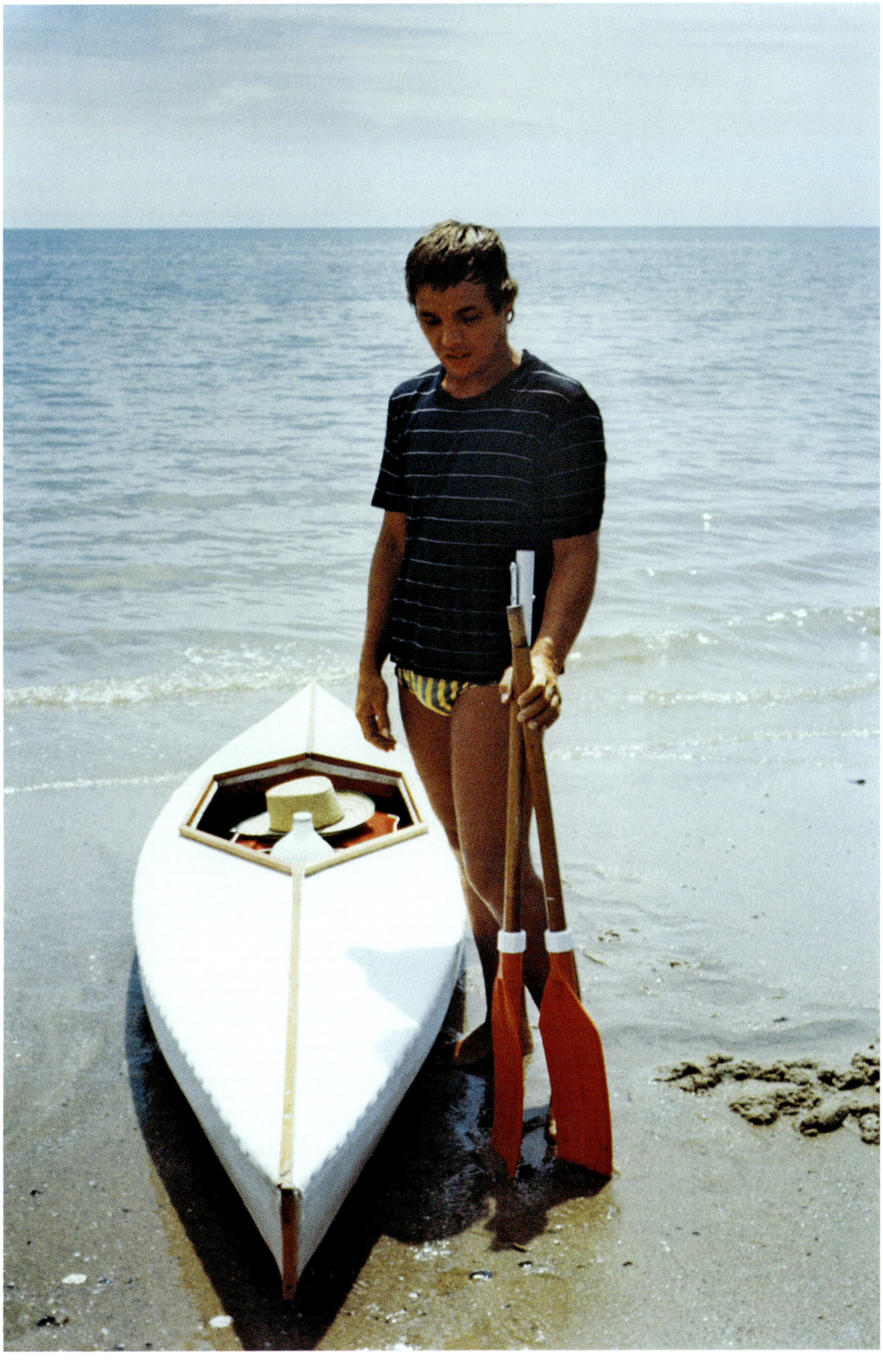

**95** Chris Burden, *B.C. Mexico*, 1973, performance documentation

In *B.C. Mexico* (fig. 95) Burden set out in May 1973 from the fishing resort of San Felipe on the Sea of Cortez, paddling a kayak "with some water" to a remote beach where he subsisted unobserved for eleven days in daytime temperatures approaching 120 degrees Fahrenheit. That lonely quest embellishes the purity of the original *Disappearance* with what amounts to a Crusoe-like literary analogy. Throughout Burden's absence in Baja California, a placard noting this absence rested in the Orange County gallery Newspace, to which he returned to read from the diary he had kept during his sojourn and to document his embarkation in a short film. While the diary might be a persuasive document, it cannot be independently verified; the possibility of its being fiction—like the first-person account Defoe provides in *Robinson Crusoe*—cannot be ruled out. The film, by contrast, provides at least one clear form of verification: it establishes that the person who set out on the journey is the same as the one recounting it in the gallery and not an imposter.

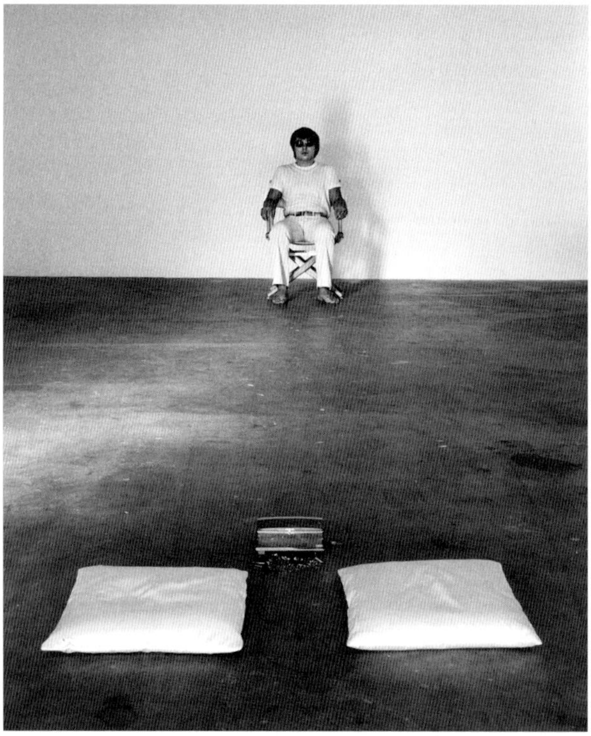

96 Chris, Burden, *Jaizu*, performance documentation, 1972, Newport Harbor Art Museum, Newport Beach, California

That demonstration might seem trivial, but it raises the stakes in this cycle of work beyond its already trenchant investigation of key, defining terms in performance art. The persistence of a self over the lifespan of an individual human animal has remained a persistent philosophical problem, one for which no convincing logical solution has been found: what permits us to assume, on the basis of intermittent exposures to the physical substance of a person, that there is a continuous "self" connecting them? "When we take the trouble to look," the philosopher Mark Johnston observes, "We do not find much evidence that in tracking objects and persons through time we are actually deploying knowledge of *sufficient* conditions for cross-time identity."[13]

From the start, Burden's signature performances either undersupplied our expectations of another person's availability or oversupplied them in ways that proved equally confounding. The absence-in-presence of *You'll Never See My Face in Kansas City* recurred the following year with even greater economy in *Jaizu* (fig. 96) where Burden stationed himself in a seated position confronting the gallery door, which was opened only to allow individual visitors to enter and leave. His dark glasses having been rendered opaque with undetectable black paint on the inside, witnesses were denied the physical cues that accompany even passive recognition—the artist's manifest presence thereby draining away to approximate the impassivity of an inanimate art object. "Many people tried to talk to me," Burden related; "One assaulted me and one left sobbing hysterically."[14] Alongside the works adduced above by male artists, Barbara T. Smith, another Pomona alumnus, performd the audacious *Feed Me* in 1973 at Tom Marioni's Museum of Conceptual Art in San Francisco. This entailed each visitor, enjoined to act freely on that instruction, entering a closed chamber with the naked artist; what occurred on each encounter was invisible to all but the two participants—a jarring, to say the least, condensation of the public and the clandestine, one she intended in particular to turn the tables on sexually exploitative males in disarming hippie trappings.[15]

■

There was the scent of the decayed counterculture about both *Jaizu* and *Feed Me*: in one, corruption of the once-sacramental attitude toward drugs and the passive-aggressive guru whose imperturbable silence goads the disciple to some self-generated spark of enlightenment; in the other, the promises of the gift economy and free sex reduced to unsavory transactions. Their implied cruelty and corruption evoke the substratum of criminality ascribed to Los Angeles in the long tradition of *noir* literature, which so often takes Southern California for its setting: Raymond Chandler, James M. Cain, and Ross McDonald provided a reading public, whether local or far-flung, with its most vivid pictures of an elusive metropolis mined with hidden malfeasance. Criminals and victims alike vanish from sight, leaving their discovery to the detective, a fictional figure embraced in this period as an alter ego by more than one Los Angeles artist. As the elation and optimism of the counterculture receded, *noir* provided the ensuing disappointments with a rich analogue of its own, not to mention a logical next episode in the repeated saga of the disappearing artist: a way back into the light.

Among the first of this cohort to make explicit the identification with the sleuthing and plotting of the detective story was another graduate of the Irvine art program, an artist who had taken the name Alexis Smith. Born Patricia Anne Smith, she had adopted Alex as a substitute while still a teenager, then adopted the variant "Alexis Smith" in congruence with the prestige actress of the same name, whose film career had flourished in the black-and-white 1940s. This new Smith brought with her an unusual upbringing, one partly spent living on the grounds of a California state mental hospital, where her psychiatrist father had been a clinician and administrator. After beginning at Irvine with vague thoughts of studying French, some chance encounters led her to the fledging studio art department, as free and open for its undergraduate majors (as Michael Asher had been) as it was for its willfully unorthodox graduate students like Turrell and Burden.

The fact that she had not practiced art before proved no drawback to her participating fully in the life of the program, which manifested an egalitarianism consistent with the countercultural moment of its formation. Smith was soon on a first-name basis with Robert Irwin, already the elder statesman of advanced Los Angeles art, and with Vija Celmins, the

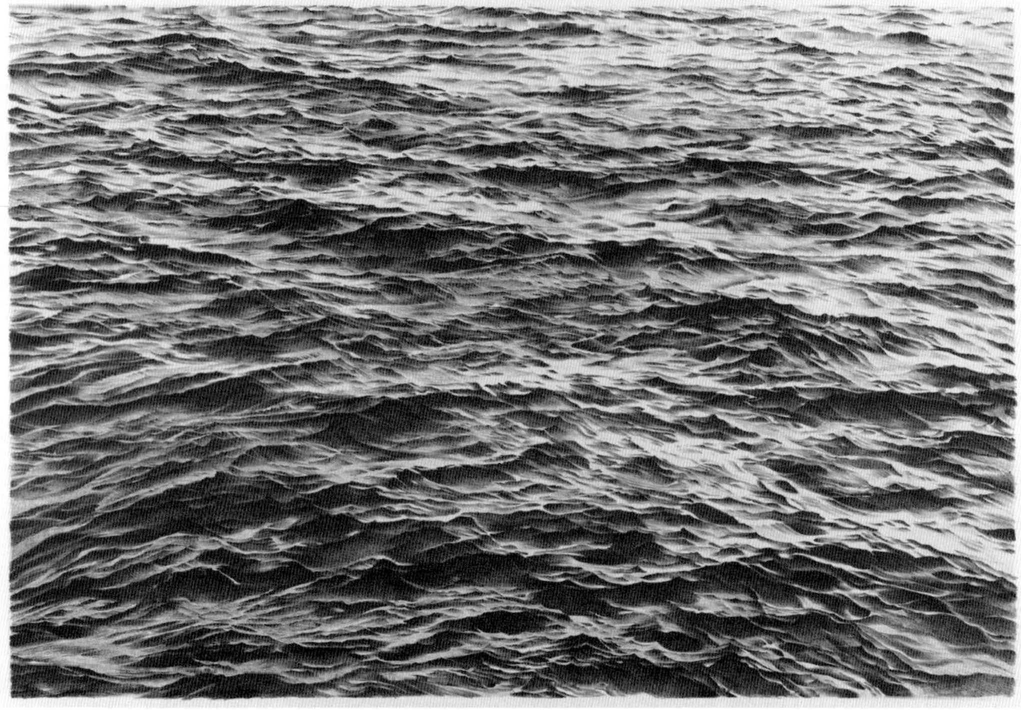

**97** Vija Celmins, *Untitled (Ocean)*, 1970,
lithograph, 51.4 × 74.3 cm,
Collection San Francisco Museum of Modern Art

integrity of whose smaller-scale, carefully wrought paintings and drawings had forced an opening through the wall of male privilege. She shared with Ader direct experience with the violence of war in Europe. As a childhood refugee from wartime Latvia, Celmins had been settled with her family in Indianapolis. Like so many others, she forsook the Midwest to study art in Los Angeles; but, instead of Chouinard, she chose UCLA, so was isolated on the far Westside, away from the cluster of young male artists who have dominated these pages. Always painstaking in her naturalistic depiction of common objects, she gained a securely prestigious place in the hierarchy of Los Angeles art by the close of the 1960s on the strength of her meticulously rendered, modestly scaled graphite and lithograph renderings of the choppy surface of the Pacific as photographed from the end of the Venice Beach fishing pier (fig. 97). The corner-to-corner evenness of incident across these sheets jibed with the emphasis on impersonal, undramatic objectivity in much of the admired art at that moment, both in the rough, humdrum materials favored by process-sculptors emerging in the wake of Minimalism and in the plainspokenness of Conceptualist documents. Each expanse of windblown water seemed to partake of the same continuum of what was merely, inhumanly there.

Yet the fascination exerted by the drawings signaled something unaccounted for in any of those formulae. All of them seemed to be of the same thing, yet each was, at any significant level of detail, entirely different from every one of the others. Any form of liquid turbulence, a category to which Celmins's light ocean chop belongs, occupies a position apart from the normal capacities of scientific description, as it cannot be translated into mathematical equations. In order to overcome that deficiency in the physical sciences, the entire field of complexity theory has arisen since she took up the motif. Though that might seem a remote and esoteric concern to a lay person, its corollary in ordinary visual apprehension is consistency without regularity, such that even the most closely adjacent passages in her drawings will bear no logical or predictive relationship to one another. In their meticulous rendering, that condition rules out any shortcuts or predigested device she might bring to the task.

The extraordinary acuity of attention and enforced concentration that her works demanded bear comparison with the ink drawings by Bruce Conner examined above in Chapter 4. In both their cases, internalized mental schemata, central to Ernst Gombrich's account of visual representation in his widely influential *Art and Illusion* of 1960, find themselves disabled;[16] in their place, the artist must find another slowed, meditative psychological state if the work is to sustain its "mindless but mindful building," as Celmins put it.[17] In physical terms, that discipline entailed maintaining a faultlessly sustained lightness of pressure in building up her lustrous dark passages— in her words, "a touch that you could hardly tell was a touch"—so as to prevent the grain of the paper from being crushed and thereby ruined by reflective sheen.[18] Conner faced the cognate demand that his fine, meandering marks stay separated and distinct at the most minutely feasible scale, thereby avoiding any fall into knots of confusion. Via both of their paths, the drawing became a field in which emergent effects on the order of complex natural processes, like the flow of water, might manifest themselves via the artist's surrender to an unrelenting, extra-personal discipline.

Viewers' minds disposed to seek relief from the ego's imperious demands for mastery over cognition could well find sustenance in the work of either artist, Conner being the overt adept of art in the service of expanded consciousness but Celmins, too, finding herself in analogous territory: "I've always been interested in very impossible images . . . things disappearing in a breath. Things like the sky, which doesn't even exist."[19] And such intimations would have been entirely in keeping with the Irvine ethos of the moment. What Alexis Smith absorbed from Celmins as a mentor demonstrates that the latter's formidable technical skills enabled but did not impose an approach to art. Here the novice pupil adopted the paper substrate but with embellishments of typed lettering and discreet appliqué in ways that echoed by alternative means Celmins's powers of understatement in the face of more assertive statements coming from the other side of the gender divide—in the process finding means to steal a march on the same thematic terrain.

Staged episodes of disappearance like those of Chris Burden entailed the enactment of conventional plotting in fiction: proceeding from a stipulated set of circumstances, the vanishing of the protagonist constitutes an enigma, a puzzle that leaves the viewer in a

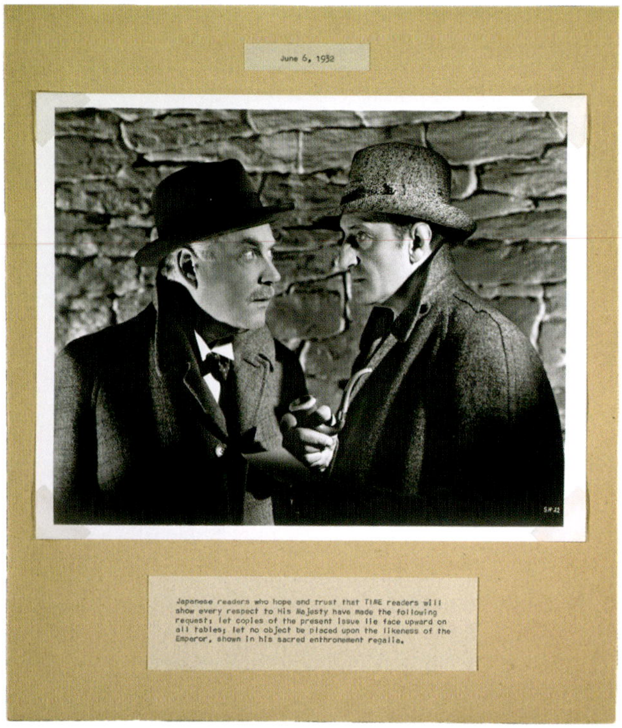


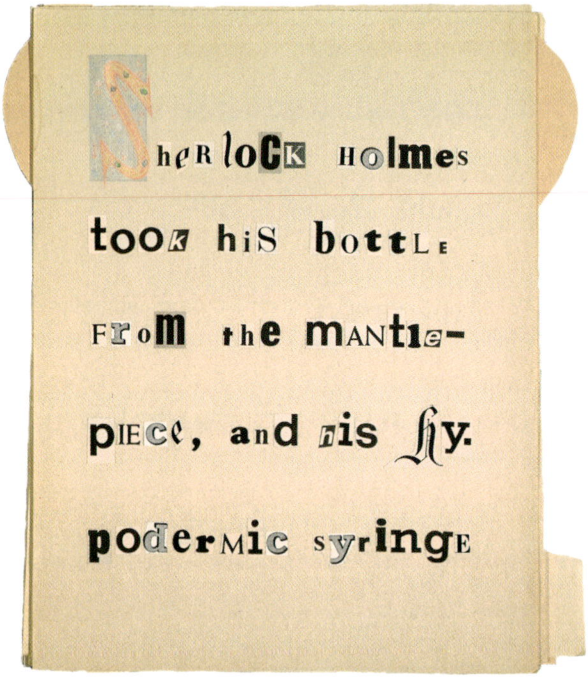


98 **(ABOVE LEFT AND RIGHT)** Alexis Smith, untitled artist's book on the theme of Sherlock Holmes, 1971, two pages of thirteen, Getty Research Library, Los Angeles

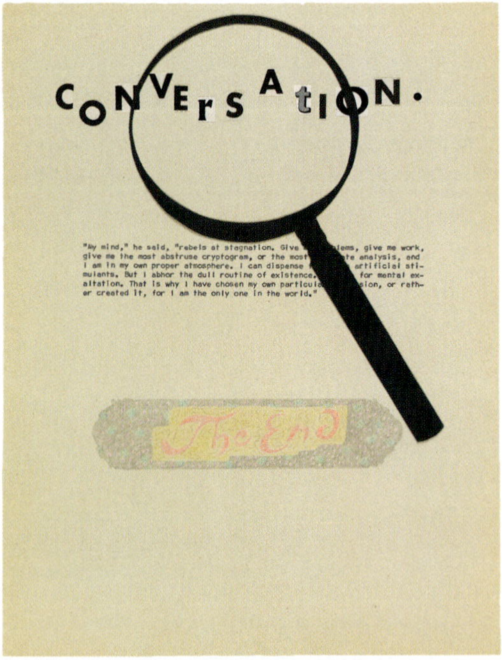


99 Alexis Smith, untitled artist's book on the theme of Sherlock Holmes, 1971, final page of thirteen, Getty Research Library, Los Angeles

state of suspension until a revelation or resolution closes the duration of the piece. Smith, for her part, likewise embraced temporal unfolding but returned its succession of moments to the imprinted page: sequences of sheets either bound together or distributed in lines across a wall. In one early effort of 1971, a book with unbound pages devoted to the archetypal detective (figs. 98, 99), Smith rendered the opening twelve words of Arthur Conan Doyle's *Sign of the Four*—"Sherlock Holmes took his bottle from the mantlepiece, and his hypodermic syringe"—in the cut-out letters of a stereotypical ransom note or poison-pen threat. She cuts off the passage before the shocking description of Holmes as "he thrust the sharp point home, pressed down the tiny piston, and sank back into the velvet-lined armchair with a long sigh of satisfaction." But that action finds a description on an inner page spelled out by myriad pinpricks, analogous to the needle tracks along the character's arm described in the text, while the final page (above the words "The End" in hand-written cursive script) features typewritten script quoting Holmes's abhorrence of "the dull routine of existence," his need for "artificial stimulants" when no satisfying puzzle intervened to occupy his thoughts.[20]

So to single out the injury to the character's skin translates the intimations of violence that threaded through so much of Los Angeles performance art, while a psychoactive substance touches the defining presence of drugs in the counterculture, within which all of these artists were formed, along with the altered mental states with which Smith had been familiar since childhood. Her opening illustration, opposite the ransom-note typography, is a black-and-white still taken from a 1932 Hollywood film version of Holmes and Dr. Watson that transposed the fictional mis-en-scène from Edwardian London to the image factories of Los Angeles. By the close of the decade, Smith would proceed to the first-person voice of detective Philip Marlowe (famously portrayed by Humphrey Bogart in Howard Hawks's 1946 *noir* classic *The Big Sleep*), the ornate and simile-laden narration crafted by the London-educated Raymond Chandler. In Chandler's tales, Los Angeles functions as a character as much as a setting. "Hollywood is a fantasy place that has a real locale," says Smith, "Here, L.A., where I live. It's also a place of the imagination."[21]

During the 1970s, the imaginative exploration and re-inscription of the city became a shared preoccupation on the part of a number of artists with whom Smith felt an affinity. She naturally cites the example of Ed Ruscha, whose books, such as *Some Los Angeles Apartments* (1965) and *34 Parking Lots* (1967), preceded her variations on the format and placed the older artist squarely within their perpetual conversation about Los Angeles as a physical and historical phenomenon. Smith's sympathetic contemporary the Ohio-born Allen Ruppersberg felt a similarly deep preoccupation with the city, which likewise led to Ruscha and somehow ineluctably to the medium of the book. As Ruppersberg says of the Oklahoma migrant: "He came with the same curiosity from a small place to this wonderland, so I think there are comparisons between what Ed did in his books and my work: it's the effect of Los Angeles."[22] Those counterpart books—*23 Pieces* of 1969 and *24 Pieces* from the year after (fig. 100)—display an analogously unadorned plainness of aspect, but there the similarities

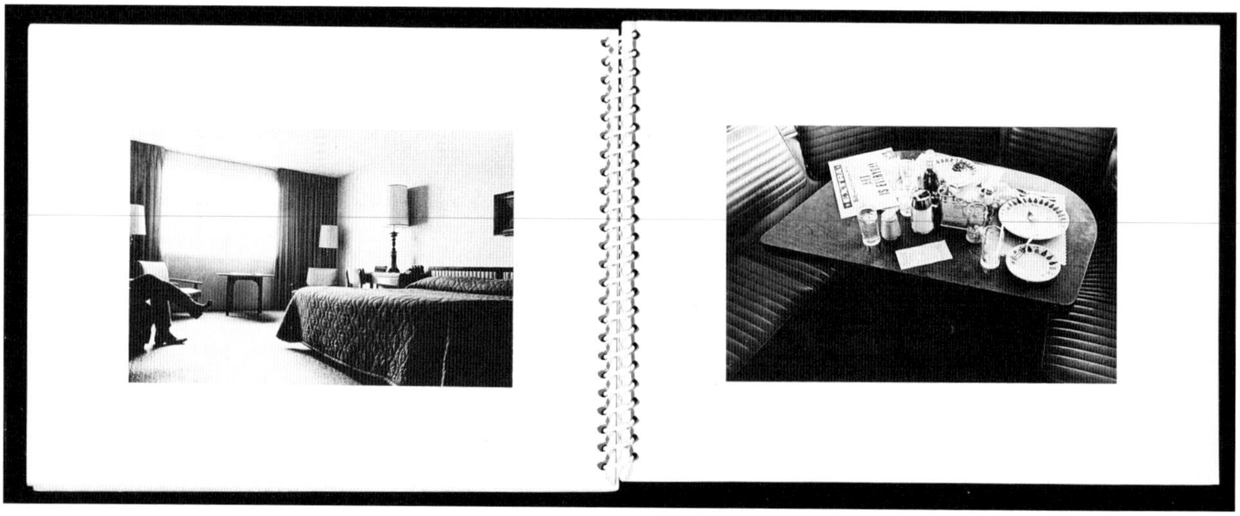

**100** Allen Ruppersberg, *24 Pieces*, 1970, spiral-bound offset lithograph, self-published book, 15.9 × 21 cm, collection of the author

stop: where Ruscha renders the storied aura of the city in the form of deliberately impersonal inventories, Ruppersberg offers a repertoire of unlabeled spaces that come seeded with small anomalies, visual disturbances suggestive of enigmatic events. The locations themselves, many of them old-fashioned hotel rooms, corridors, and lobbies, suggest the habitat of the *noir* detective, alert to any unexpected sign or occurrence. The codes of detective fiction were strong enough to seize the most subtle features of these scenes and invest them with literary meaning—as Ruppersberg well realized and exploited.

Seemingly across the board, younger artists in Los Angeles were embracing scenarios of criminals, fugitives, and their pursuers, as if the draft dodging, civil disobedience, sexual freedom, drug taking (and peddling) that seemed insouciant aspects of the countercultural life now made them the criminals they had always been in the eyes of the straight world. It was no small thing that Charles Manson and his "Family" had put a homicidal face on idea of a free-loving hippie commune, nor that they had laid claim to the Spahn Movie Ranch, a Western set for hire in the city's hinterlands. When Wyatt and Billy met their demise at the end of Dennis Hopper's 1969 *Easy Rider*, martyrs to the cause of countercultural emancipation, the script by Hopper and Terry Southern recapitulated the ending of Arthur Penn's *Bonnie and Clyde*, released two years before. Its sympathetic outlaw couple, impersonated by the ultra-glamorous pair of Warren Beatty and Faye Dunaway, transposed to the Depression era a fully contemporary sense of the tragic futility concomitant with living beyond the law.

The writer Robert Towne (an earlier Pomona graduate) had contributed crucial revisions to the script for *Bonnie and Clyde*. He and Jack Nicholson, the secondary martyr to freedom

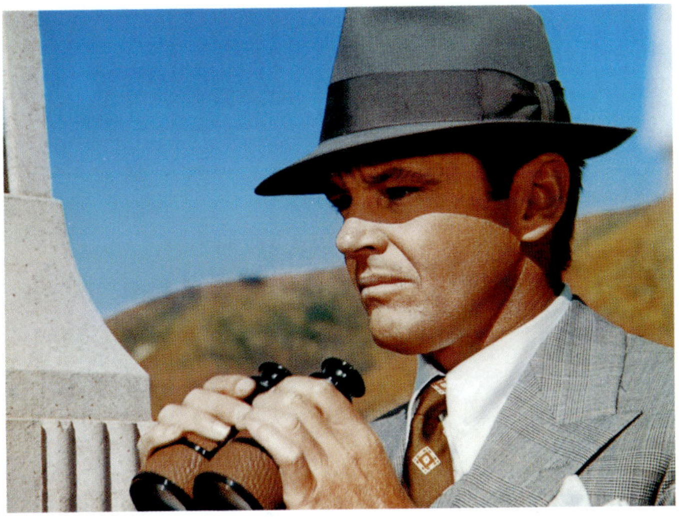

**101** Jack Nicholson as Jake Gittes, *Chinatown*, 1974, dir. Roman Polanski, Paramount Pictures publicity still

in *Easy Rider*, had been friends and collaborators for more than a decade when Towne found himself preoccupied in 1971, much like Smith and Ruppersberg, with the city of Los Angeles as conjured by Chandler:

> I began to work on "Chinatown" and began by searching for the story in the streets. I would take to driving around the city at night, through Silverlake, Echo Park, down Temple, where the streetlamps were low and yellow and nippled and the palm trees were high with scrawny fronds like broken pinwheels, and now and then on top of one of the precipitous and sandy hillsides of corner lots high concrete retaining walls cracked and droopy ice plant could never quite hold the earth and clapboard in place and you could still see an oil derrick looking like a rusty praying mantis, trying to suck the last few barrels out of the dying crab grass in the backyard.[23]

Towne haltingly found his story, building it around the lead performance of his old friend Nicholson. As *Chinatown* moved toward its theatrical release in 1974, the actor achieved a consummate re-imagination of the *noir* detective in the character of Jake Gittes (fig. 101), while Faye Dunaway brought forward her doomed 1930s charisma from *Bonnie and Clyde*. Roman Polanski, who had lost his pregnant wife to the Manson killers in the most violent possible fashion, famously came on to direct.

Towne had found the core of his plot in the ruthless subterfuges entailed in bringing water from the Owens Valley below the eastern slope of the Sierras to support the growth of Los Angeles (an artificial drought contrived by land speculators, ensuring both cheap agricultural land and the acquiescence of a panicked public),. He personified the crime in the character of the property developer Noah Cross, whose bottomless depravity (monstrously embodied by John Huston in the role) reveals itself in a Shakespearean tragic climax engendered by Cross's past incest with his daughter, the Dunaway character. As Towne assessed his creation,

> The truly murderous act in the movie was laying waste to land and to fragile communities as though they were an incidental part of Noah Cross' grand vision—a vision about as grand and expansive as cancer. It was rape worse than Cross could visit on his own daughter—hurting the land he inevitably hurt all children, affected where they'd live and what they'd see and even what they breathe. When a crime can no longer contain or content itself with the past and insists on visiting the future it's no longer a crime—it becomes a sin, and very difficult to punish.

The outrage that drove his scenario parallels that mutation of countercultural protest examined above in the work of San Francisco artists Bonnie Ora Sherk and Terry Fox, the ways in which they set their acts of implicit witness against the devouring Moloch of the freeway system and the refineries that fueled the choking traffic it carried. But it was Los Angeles that offered the richer literary tradition of lone, Quixotic knights, from Marlowe to Gittes, snatching small victories at best from hidden, indefeasible powers always in the shadows (hence *noir*). Would it be overreading to regard even Vija Celmins's broodingly dark ocean surface at the end of the Venice Beach pier as having swallowed evidence of manifold crimes?

■

It might be something of a jarring leap to come down from Towne's portentous sermon to Ruppersberg's genial installation work *Al's Café*, but that 1969 project anticipated the screenwriter's recourse to the *noir* mythos of crime, betrayal, and illicit desire. As Ruppersberg recollected about this period, "most of our conversations took place within the context of talking about L.A."[24] And the Los Angeles under discussion tended to resemble Towne's collapse of the present into the city of both Chandler's imagination and his own 1940s childhood. The city that so fascinated Rupperberg lacked one amenity important for artists. "New York," he thought at the time, "had always had meeting places . . . all the bars and events where people met and talked." To redress the disparity to

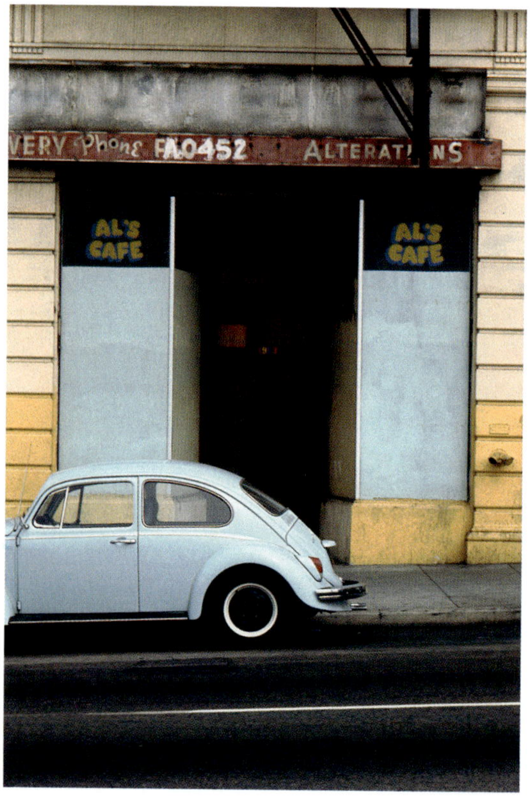


**102** Allen Ruppersberg, street view and facade of *Al's Café* at 1913 West 6th Street, Los Angeles, 1969

some small degree he installed *Al's Café* (fig. 102) in an abandoned cleaners' premises close to the old site of the Chouinard Art School. Despite its inner-city location, the novelty and flair of the gesture attracted crowds that began to overwhelm his capacity to manage the enterprise, but more than achieved his aim "to try and create a place to connect for others and myself." But he has nonetheless been quick to add that his "impetus was to first make a work of art, and secondly to provide a common place for the community," which was to say that he insisted on its status as representation.[25] Though opening the premises only on Thursday evenings, he endeavored to impart an air of age and permanence to them, as if, said his friend the artist Allan McCollum, "nurtured for forty years by a caring café-owner."

To that end, he fashioned the premises along the lines of a roadside café like the one central to *The Postman Always Rings Twice*, a premier example of Hollywood *film noir* adapted in 1946 from the hardboiled novel by James M. Cain and featuring Lana Turner with John Garfield as the murderously adulterous lovers who meet inside the establishment. He acquired the requisite checkered tablecloths and festooned the walls with giveaway calendars, felt pennant souvenirs, and autographed photos of celebrities.[26] In keeping with that prototype and numerous such films made in the boulder-strewn environs of Bishop

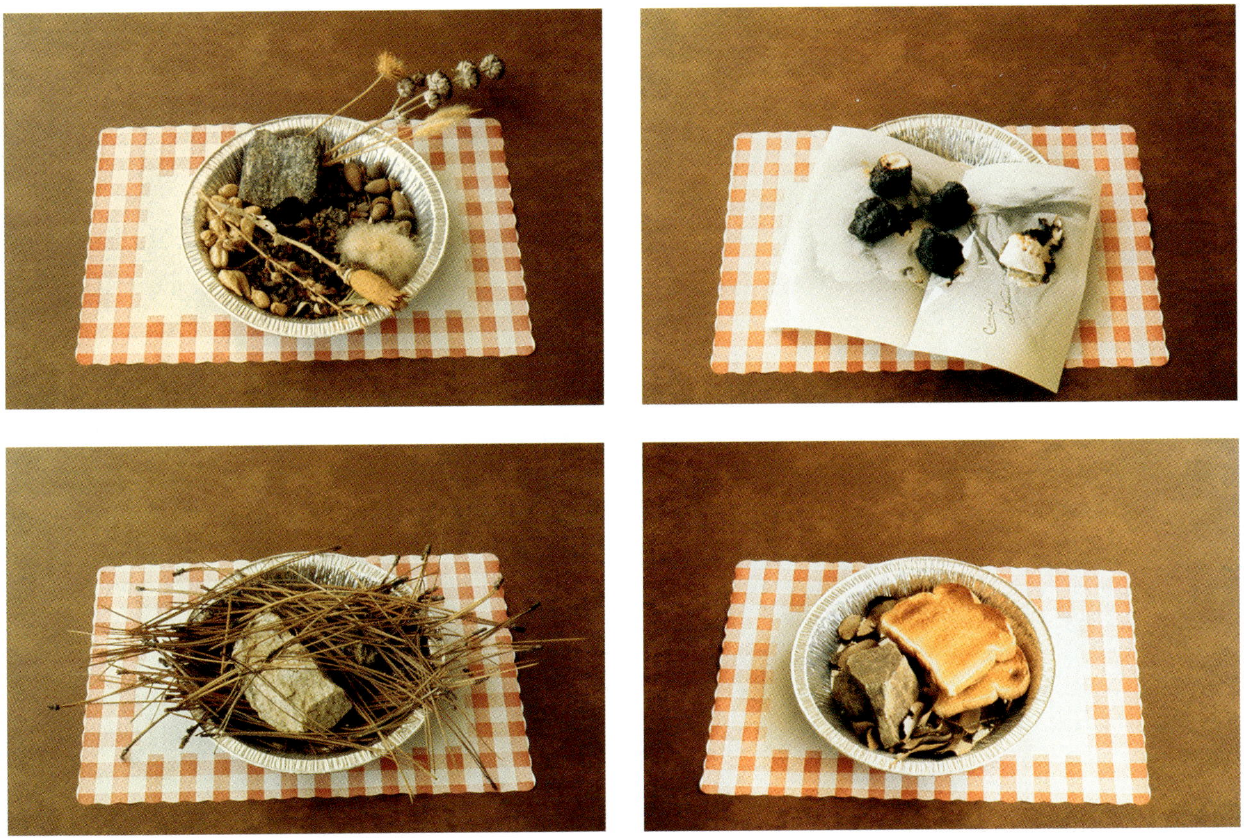

**103** Allen Ruppersberg, meals from *Al's Café* ("Patti Melt," "Toast Rocks," "Pine Needles," and "Acorns"), 1969, mixed media, aluminum pie tins, paper placemats

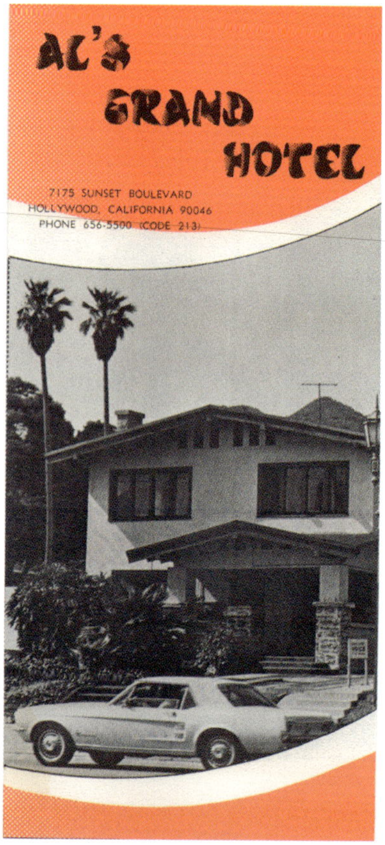


**104** Allen Ruppersberg, *Al's Grand Hotel*, brochure, 1971, offset lithograph on paper, collection of the author

and Lone Pine on the eastern slope of the Sierra Nevada, he imparted a rural California-highway feel to a good number of the items on the menu (fig. 103): "rock varieties smothered in pine needles" or "burned pine needles a la Johnny Cash served with live fern." These "dishes," which Ruppersberg busily assembled behind the counter, carried a requisite show-business feel. Cash, for example, was then living in the Tehachapi foothills near the planned site of CalArts. Patrons could also savor the "Patti Melt," its ingredients being a photograph of the bland pop singer Patti Page "covered with toasted marshmallows," which proved so popular that Ruppersberg was forced to substitute shots of other celebrity Patties. But all that seeming drollery carried other kinds of significance. The gritty natural materials corresponded to the sites of land art (as well as to the imported matter of Robert Smithson's "non-sites"); "Al's burger—sky, land, and water" evoked the expansively utopian ambition of the land art by Smithson and Michael Heizer while "Al's super burger" added "a photo," a token of photographic documentation as guarantee of the art's reality.[27]

*Al's Café* thus suspended itself between centripetal and centrifugal movements: it centralized a spread-out but local geographic network, while figuring the vast western terrain over which the land artists had dispersed themselves, calling on both concrete materials and cinematic cognates as means to this end. But that left as a remainder the most conspicuous feature of the piece, which was "Al" himself, both in the title and as a constant host and short-order cook present behind the counter. Via consummate Socratic irony (the philosopher continually poses as the least wise), Ruppersberg kept up the modest surrogate identity as greasy-spoon proprietor while keeping his name as artistic creator front and center. Later, for a few months in 1971, he raised the ante by setting himself up as the visible owner and manager of *Al's Grand Hotel* (fig. 104) a functioning Hollywood hostelry with themed rooms of equivalently eccentric inventiveness as the dishes in his café. The generic Craftsman architecture evokes the period setting of early California crime fiction, while the title plainly makes reference to the prestige all-star vehicle from MGM, *Grand Hotel*, of 1932. The interior further called to mind picturesque road-trip cognates like the regionally renowned Madonna Inn in coastal San Luis Obispo, with its scores of whimsically themed rooms. Ruppersberg's massive, life-sized crucifix in the

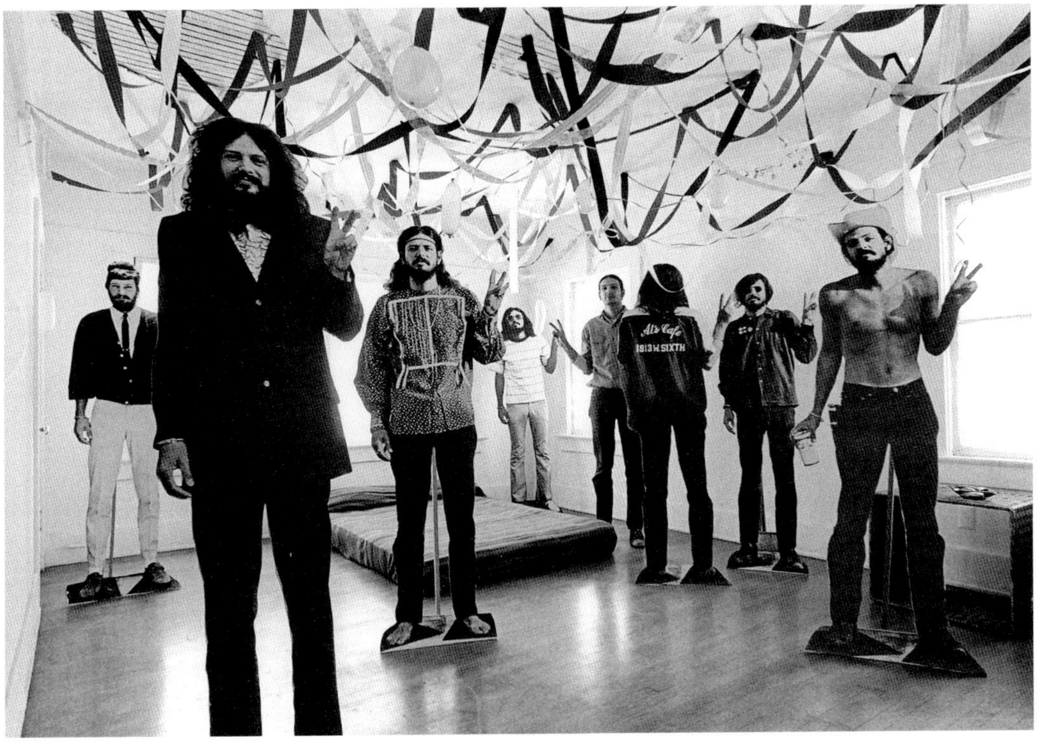


**105** Allen Ruppersberg, the "Al Room," *Al's Grand Hotel*, 1971, life-sized photographic cut-outs

"Jesus Room," for example, cast the occupant in a biblical epic like *Quo Vadis* or *The Greatest Story Ever Told* (while also resembling crash-landed sculpture by Mark Di Suvero). The "Al Room" (fig. 105) enjoined visitors to sleep surrounded by no fewer than eight life-sized cut-outs of the artist flashing the hippie-dippie peace sign, each sporting a different stereotypical outfit and hair style.

That intentional hypertrophy of self-branding, however, required for relief its diametric opposite, that is, the artist's re-disappearance. The following year saw the exhibition, first at Pomona and then in Amsterdam, of *Where's Al?*, Ruppersberg's consummate comedy on the theme of the elusive artist: 160 casual instamatic photographs of a beachside holiday reunion among friends, interspersed with bits of laconically pitch-perfect dialogue typed on 110 index cards like these:

```
he: Why didn't Al come?
he: Too busy maybe. He's been working a lot.
he: Yeah, could be.
he: Was Al coming by himself?
```

> she: Usually does.
> he: Somebody ought to check.
> he: Hotels and bars. I'm surprised Al missed this.
> he: Me too.

The presentation of the work—index card and drugstore prints tacked to the gallery walls—approximates a community bulletin board where notices of lost pets are a staple item: a disarming association that carries a delayed recognition that, for all the inane patter concerning Al's whereabouts, some serious mishap or even the death of the subject is never ruled out. "Maybe he got in an accident?" muses one partyer, though without any expected urgency of response. The most telling exchange might be the one that puts the entire "search" under the rubric of its literary godfather:

> he: Where's Al?
> she: Maybe he stayed home to read
> he: What's he been reading?
> she: Raymond Chandler

A parallel work of the same year conversely restored an identity to "Allen Ruppersberg," as himself the author of a novel purporting to lift the lid on the city's hidden crimes: *Greetings from L.A.* Its back-cover blurb promised a tale "Infused with the urgency of lotusland, informed by the dream city's quotidian loss," possibly "the most lucid and powerful examination yet of the tawdry, tarnished truth of Tinseltown." These *noir* clichés came credited to a local newspaper reviewer, his lengthy (and suspiciously Ruppersbergian) encomium the main connected prose offered by the volume, its inner pages being mostly blank. Elsewhere in the cover text, the revelatory promise of the novel seems somewhat compromised by "peculiar sentence structure and erratic spelling conveying the spoken word and sudden shifts of syntax which should put off but don't," reassurance that the anti-facility of genuine art will be equally present. Merging the two, in the absence of much help from inside the book itself, becomes the reader's intriguing task as the imaginary coauthor.

■

For Ruppersberg to be exhibiting in Amsterdam exemplified a centrifugal momentum within this circle of artists; indeed, it helped inaugurate the enduring historical pattern whereby Los Angeles artists frequently leapfrog New York in order to achieve their first wider recognition in Europe. Bas Jan Ader personally embodied this long-distance connection, as he began actively transferring his performance practice back to his native country. The filmed *Fall 1* of 1970 saw him tumble from the roof of the same Claremont bungalow featured in the sculptural event *All My Clothes* (fig. 90); in *Fall 2*, enacted the same year, he tumbled from a moving bicycle into an Amsterdam canal. Perhaps, as an outsider, analogously to Raymond Chandler's foreign formation, Ader was able to give the neo-*noir* artist's aesthetic what was

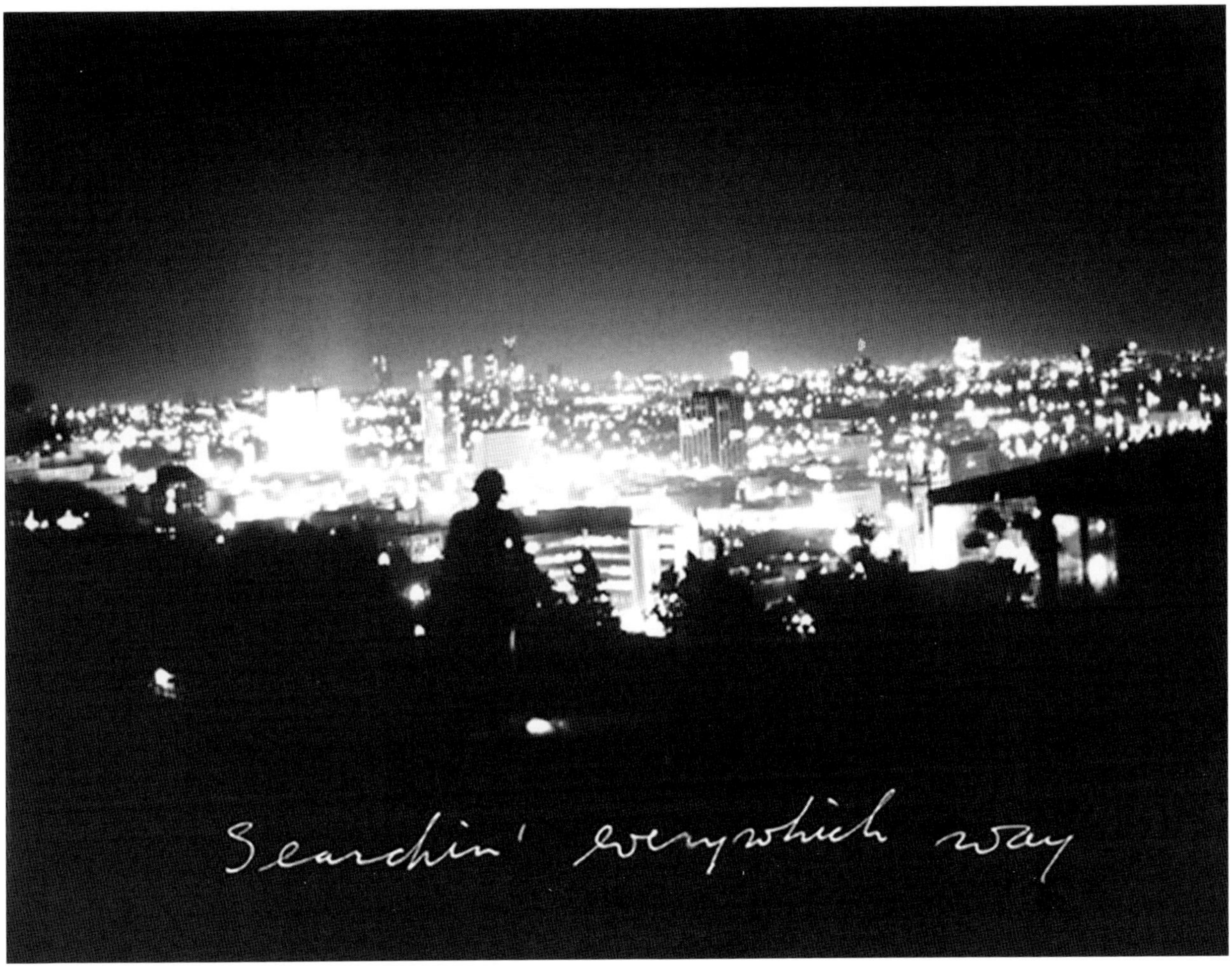


**106** Bas Jan Ader, *In Search of the Miraculous (One Night in Los Angeles)*, 1973 (detail)

perhaps its consummate expression in his 1973 cycle of photographic prints, *In Search of the Miraculous (One Night in Los Angeles)* (figs. 106–9).

The work shares something of the cinematic vision overlaid by quoted inscription that Alexis Smith had inaugurated a few years before. The artist's own dark silhouette—always viewed from behind and invariably on the verge of disappearing from view—appears and reappears across eighteen identically sized black-and-white prints, the evocative images photographed by his wife, the artist Mary Sue Andersen.[28] Only in the first (fig. 108), where, in the middle distance, he walks perilously along the break-down lane of the Santa Monica freeway, is he seen in daylight; at the end of the cycle, dawn is just beginning to break (fig. 109), while in all the intervening sixteen scenes, crepuscular darkness reigns (fig. 106), night-scapes set off by some saturated artificial illumination—one of which is the frail flashlight he carries. Scale and setting vary from photograph to photograph, like the stations of a

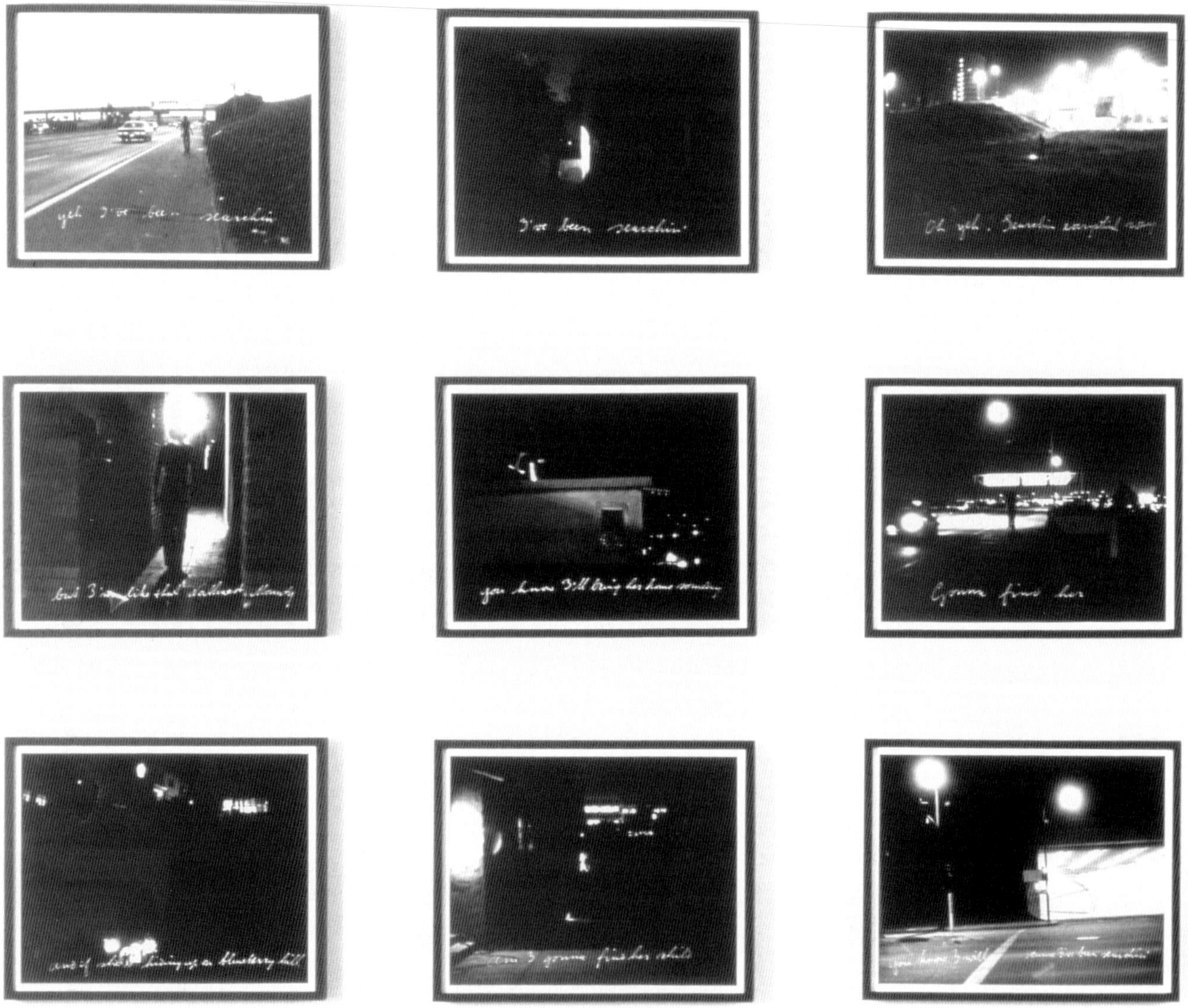

**107** Bas Jan Ader, *In Search of the Miraculous (One Night in Los Angeles)*, 1973, 18 silver gelatin prints with handwritten text in white ink, 10.3 × 25.4 cm (8 × 10 in), courtesy Meliksetian | Briggs, Los Angeles

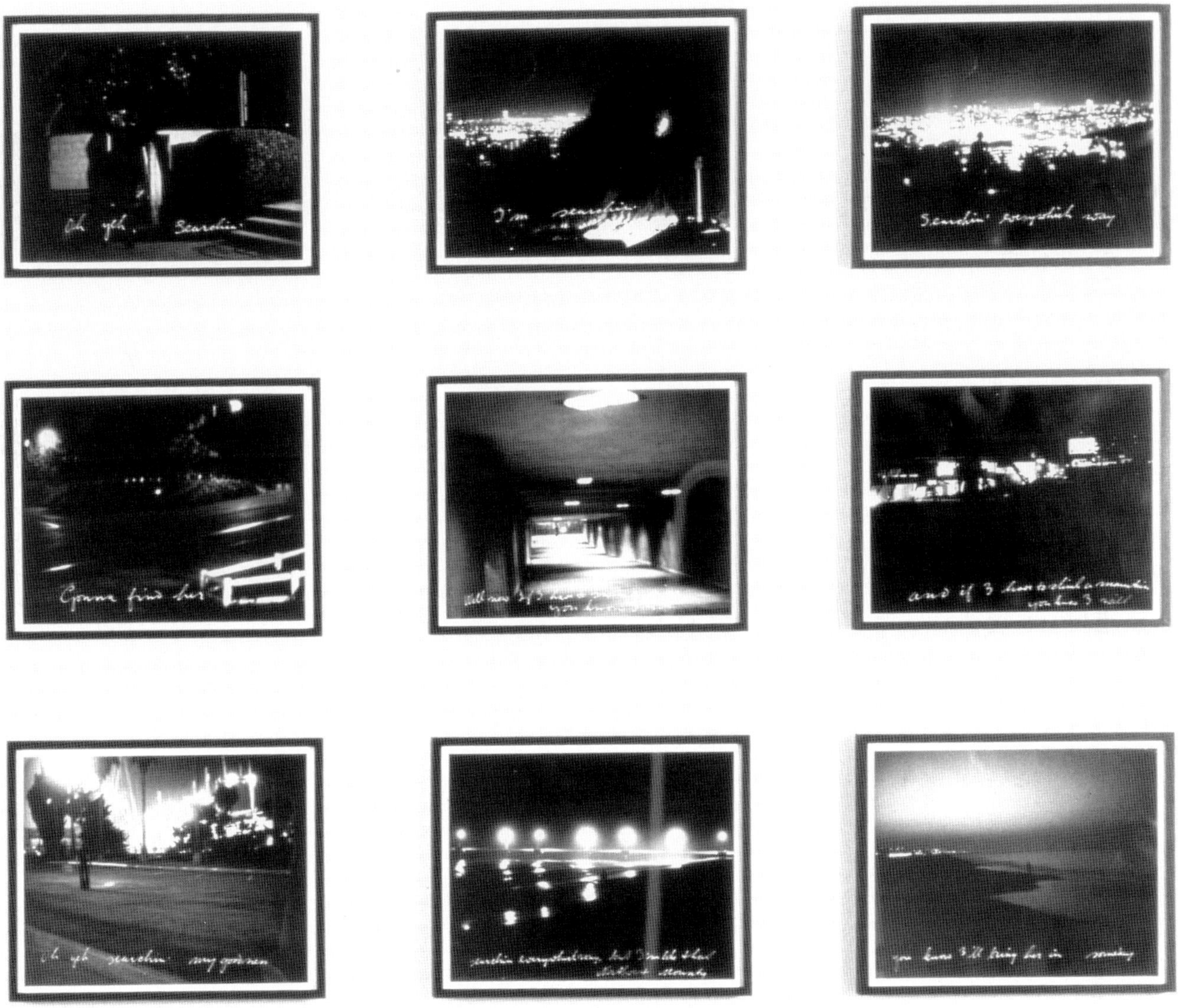
Oh yeh, Searchin'
I'm searchin'
Searchin' everywhich way
Gonna find her

medieval quest narrative or a suite of arch-Romantic landscapes by Caspar David Friedrich, the protagonist at turns framed in dark alleys, submerged in tunnels, dwarfed by looming cliffs, wandering deserted docks, emerging onto a summit from which the world appears laid at his feet, and finally confronting the vastness of the sea.

For that reason and more, it is difficult not to regard Ader's shadowy silhouette in *In Search of the Miraculous (One Night in Los Angeles)* in light of Walter Benjamin's famous query from his "Little History of Photography": "is not every square inch of our cities the scene of a crime? Every passer-by a culprit?"[29] Such was the guiding assumption of the detective fiction set in Southern California, from which the worldview of *film noir* emerged in the 1940s. Ader's piece overtly calls upon the motifs and crepuscular cinematography that typified the genre, but that modern point of reference does little to leaven the portentous intimation of a medievalizing spiritual quest (as in Chandler's chivalric "Down these mean streets a man must go who is not himself mean, who is neither tarnished nor afraid"[30]). Ader rights the balance of the work by an act of inscription at the base of each print: rendered with white ink in an elegantly confident hand are lyrics from "Searchin'," the 1957 hit by the Coasters, masterminded in Los Angeles by the white hipster writers and producers Jerry Leiber and Mike Stoller.

As rendered across the photographic grid, the first eight fragments follow the lead voice:

> yeh I've been searchin'
> I've been searchin'
> Oh yeh. Searchin' everywhich way
> Oh yeh. Searchin'
> I'm searchin'
> Searchin' everywhich way
> but I'm like that Northwest Mounty
> you know I'll bring her home someday

Then the background chorus comes to the fore over two images:

> Gonna find her
> Gonna find her

Then the lead voice returns for the final eight:

> Well now If I have to swim a river /you know I will
> and if I have to climb a mountain/you know I will
> and if she's hiding up on blueberry hill
> am I gonna find her child
> you know I will 'cause I've been searchin'
> oh yeh searchin' my goodness
> searchin' everywhich way, but I'm like that Northwest Mounty
> you know I'll bring her in someday

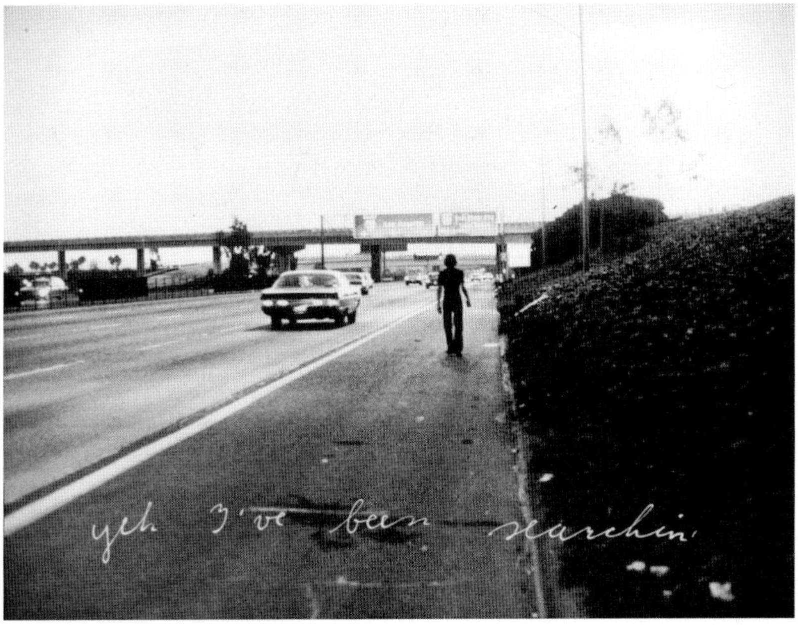


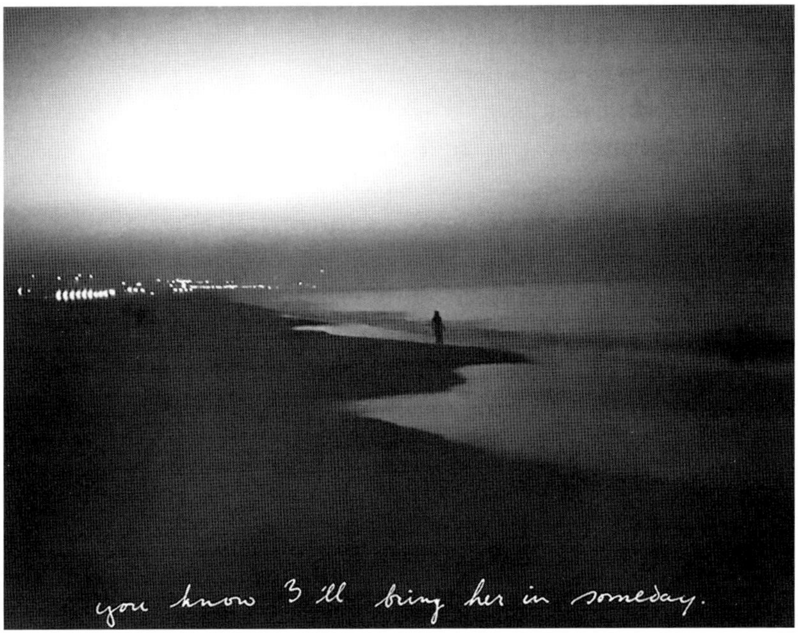


**108 (TOP)** Bas Jan Ader, *In Search of the Miraculous (One Night in Los Angeles)*, 1973 (detail)

**109** Bas Jan Ader, *In Search of the Miraculous (One Night in Los Angeles)*, 1973 (detail)

Among the doo-wop-style vocal groups, the Coasters were the great comedians and were so cultivated by Leiber and Stoller as their vehicle for incorporating humorous references to movies, radio, and television (in contrast to the romantic yearning of the songs they recorded with the Drifters). Ader takes the song from the top and gets as far as the beginning of the second verse where, for those who know the rest of the record, there appears a roster mixing Dashiell Hammett's Sam Spade from the artistic heights of *noir* with a scrum of TV and B-movie gumshoes, the serio-comic underside of the hardboiled style:

> Well, Sherlock Holmes
> Sam Spade got nothin', child, on me
> Sergeant Friday, Charlie Chan
> And Boston Blackie
> No matter where she's a hiding
> She's gonna hear me a comin'
> Gonna walk right down that street
> Like Bulldog Drummond
> 'Cause I've been searchin' . . .

Ader generously identifies with the detective genre across its entire spectrum, confident enough in his own art not to lean on the best or condescend to the mediocre. His great act of judgment and selection lay in the choice of the Coasters' music—and in the manner of its inscription. Rendered on the printed page, the sequence loses the ease and charm of the artist's handwriting, which channels some echo of the unheard music in which the repeated phrases find their compelling and affecting rhythmic sense. Any romantic quest requires its poetry, and Ader finds his in this deft appropriation of truly popular song.

Two years later, the culminating component of Ader's *In Search of the Miraculous* would transform this fictional quest into an arduous, real-world test of courage and purpose. Having originally come ashore to California in 1962 at the age of twenty, after a hazardous voyage from North Africa on a sailing yacht, he vowed in 1975 to reverse the process, which would culminate at the same Amsterdam gallery, Art + Project, at which Ruppersberg had shown *Where's Al?* two years before. Announcing the final phase with an installation at the Claire Copley Gallery that featured an earnest amateur choir from UC Irvine singing sea chanteys around an upright piano, he launched himself, in a literal seafaring way, toward its conclusion a few months later, setting sail alone from Chatham, Cape Cod, and bound for Cornwall in the shortest (twelve and one half feet) sailboat ever to attempt a solo trans-Atlantic voyage (fig. 110). Entirely confident in his ability to complete the voyage, he was undone achingly near his goal, the only evidence, his holed boat found adrift by Gallician fishermen. The artist had unwillingly and poignantly made his disappearance final and complete.[31]

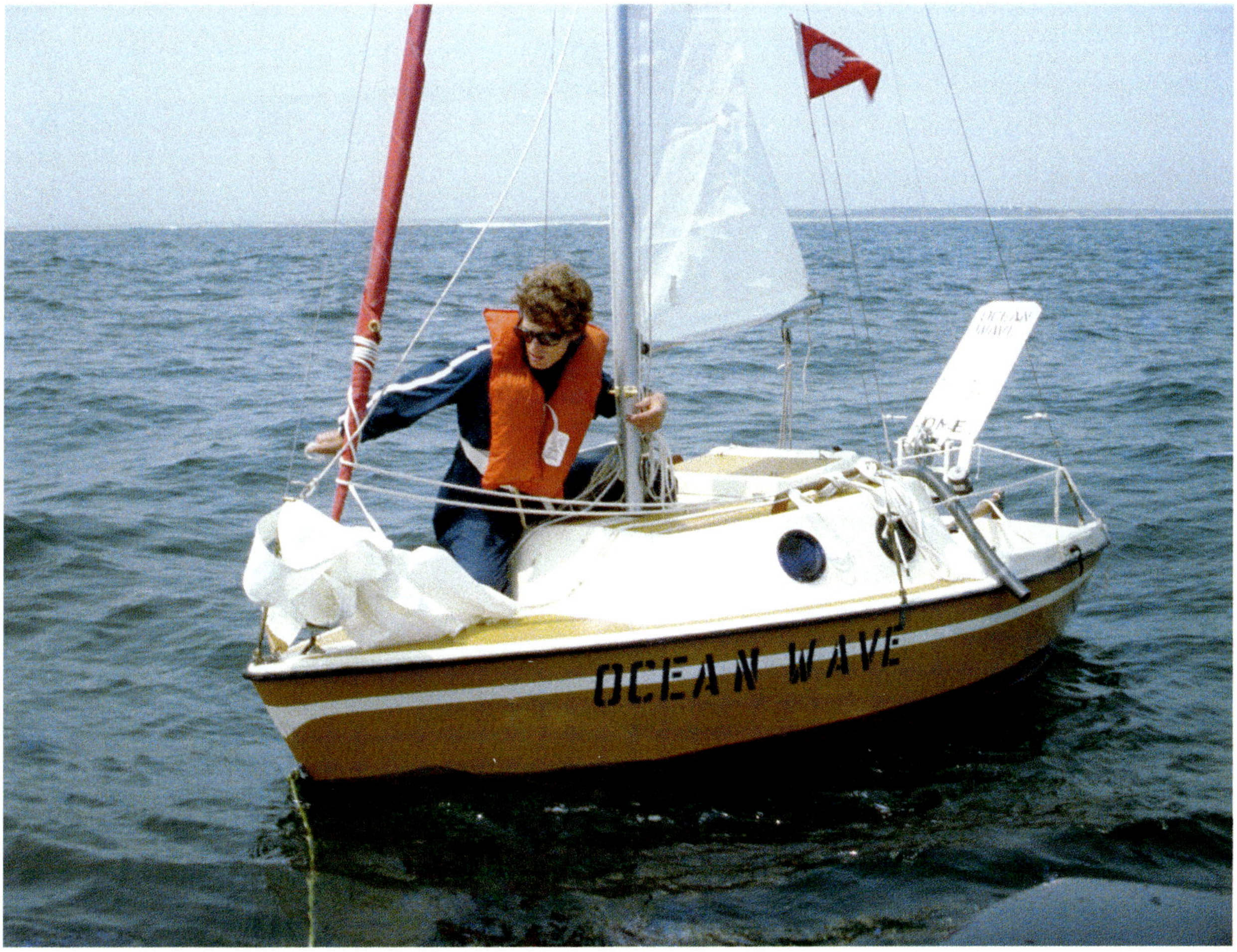


**110** Bas Jan Ader aboard the *Ocean Wave*, July 1975, courtesy Meliksetian | Briggs, Los Angeles

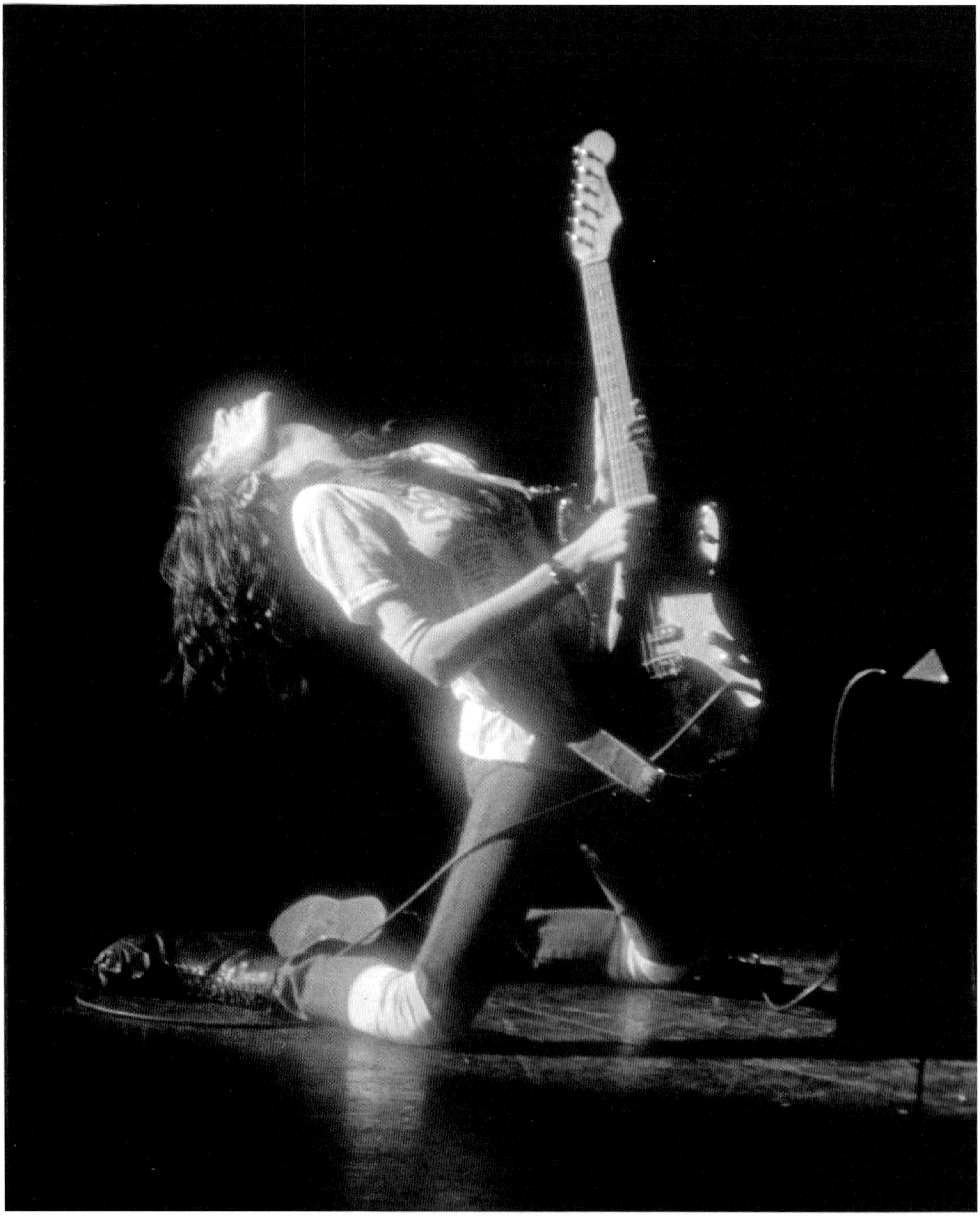

**111** Jenny Lens, *Patti Smith*, 1976,
gelatin silver print

ELEVEN

# SECRET CEREMONIES

DURING THE YEAR OR SO BEFORE HIS DEATH, Bas Jan Ader would regularly join James Turrell on the latter's plane, flying down to the Orange County campus of UC Irvine, where both were teaching. The fact that Turrell had left his productive position at Pomona College (described above, in Chapter 9) arose from an act of moral witnessing consistent with the anti-war convictions that had landed him in prison during his time as an Irvine graduate student. Accumulated tensions between the exhibition and studio-art programs on one side, and the college's conservative institutional ethos on the other had blown up in 1973, having been exacerbated by a series of provocations by performance artists in the spring of 1972. These had been programed by the gallery's director, Helene Winer (including the one by Hiro Kosaka adduced above (fig. 92), another by Chris Burden, and a third by Wolfgang Stoerchle, which entailed the artist's nudity and controlled urination). Second-hand outrage by an angry alumnus induced the president summarily to dismiss Winer. In her support, Turrell led the entire art department, including Lewis Baltz, David Gray, Michael Brewster, and Guy Williams, to resign as a body—entailing considerable personal sacrifice for several of them. And thus, the brief moment of Claremont's artistic ascendance in the region came to an abrupt close.

The events at Pomona propelled Winer to conspicuous later success in New York and soon launched Turrell into the skies over Arizona on his quest for a remote volcanic site. But the death of the Claremont experiment left the tenuous artistic network of Southern California considerably depleted. Ader's disappearance and presumed death two years later struck a debilitating blow to the affective heart of that community, the dissolution of which continued apace. During the mid-1970s, for his own pedagogical reasons, John Baldessari was urging students from his first cohort at CalArts to test themselves in New York on graduation. That policy launched significant national careers for Jack Goldstein, David Salle, Matt Mullican, and James Welling, but deprived Los Angeles of their presence. Allen Ruppersberg would shortly give up and relocate at least partially to New York. Hiro Kosaka undertook a Buddhist pilgrimage in Japan and, on his return to Los Angeles, retreated to the Koyasan Temple in Little Tokyo to focus his energy on scholarly studies. Though Baldessari remained at his post, the exhibitions of his art took him far afield to Europe and eventually to East

Coast exposure, and the same could be said for Burden. In sum, the concentrated critical mass of talent and enterprise that distinguished the early years of the decade had irretrievably dispersed.

It would be an obvious mistake, however, to equate the richness of art in 1970s Los Angeles with those figures alone. There were emergent artists more than ready and willing to step forward, though structural inequities remained in their paths. For young Chicano artists, opportunity for recognition and scope for action were much more restricted than they had ever been for any of Kosaka's designated "outcasts," with a concomitant need for even greater solidarity. The most successful and representative such group has already appeared in these pages by virtue of their collective opposition to the war in Vietnam and the casualties disproportionately suffered by their peers sent to Southeast Asia. But their artistic aspirations were by no means restricted to overt political protest. As discussed in that earlier chapter, Patssi Valdez, Harry Gamboa Jr., Willie Herrón III, and Glugio Nicandro (known as Gronk), had first come together as teenagers, working together on alternative high-school publications, and all had joined in the "Blowouts," the Chicano mass boycott of the Eastside high schools in 1968 that had brought police violence down on the students at a level anticipating the ferocious repression in 1970 of the Chicano Moratorium Against the Vietnam War. Both events recalled the Anglo moral panics of the 1940s: the arbitrary arrests and convictions following the so-called Sleepy Lagoon Murder, culminating in the Zoot Suit Riots of 1943, when the police and their surrogates among off-duty servicemen gave violent vent to their naked prejudice against stylistically flamboyant *pachucos*. Assuming the collective name Asco (after the Spanish phrase *me da asco*: it makes me puke), the four friends similarly placed great emphasis on distinctive personal style and flamboyant gestures.

Exclusion from the established career channels for young artists pushed Asco into a consciously elusive, shape-shifting array of activities, one that brought out Gamboa's gifts as a writer and recording photographer, Valdez's improvised appropriation of film glamour in both acting and fashion design, Herrón's art training, showmanship, and major musical ability, and Gronk's protean self-invention along nearly every vector of gender identity and artistic medium. Their unannounced, costumed performances that had begun with *Stations of the Cross* in 1970 (fig. 64), took on more glamorous flair during the mid-1970s under the rubric No Movies, a category that gestured to the proximity of the film industry to East Los Angeles but their effective exclusion from virtually any established avenue of expression. Their 1977 No Movie titled project *A La Mode* (fig. 112) places the retro glam of Valdez's self-fashioning front and center, her eclectic costume and make-up gravitating toward the 1940s and the look of a *noir* temptress. With Gronk and Gamboa on either side, Valdez haughtily seats herself, for all of her airs, on what looks like a bare-bones café table, stocked with the most generic dispensers of napkins, sugar, and salt. As Rupperberg's *Al's Café* had found reason to harken back to the road-house settings of the murder-seduction dramas of postwar years, so Asco found the *noir* look and its manifold associations with local history suited their own purposes a few years later—just as the New Hollywood simultaneously discovered with the neo-*noir* of *Chinatown*.

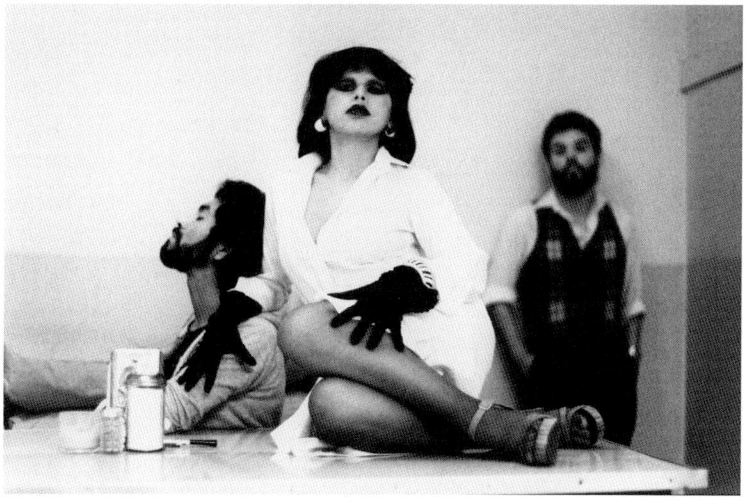

**112** Asco, *A La Mode*, 1976,
40.6 × 50.8 cm, photograph by Harry Gamboa, Jr.

Gronk complained in print that the group's movie-inflected performances and documents would receive respectful attention if ascribed to a Chris Burden or an Alexis Smith, calling out local critics as agents of this double standard.[1] Peter Plagens, an artist and local critical luminary, responded in a letter to the editor that dismissed Gronk's work as "that all too common succotash of Andy Warhol camp, fragmented Bertolt Brecht, and Sunset Strip runaway self-consciousness," with no valid claim to be "ahead of those who stay in the studio and make art objects."[2] By 1980, when this exchange took place, Plagens's "Sunset Strip runaway" epithet signals the emergence of another demonic presence to challenge the object makers. But Asco would have regarded these attempted insults more as a positive program. Their way with theatrical make-up and cross-dressing had always owed a debt to the glitter and glam of David Bowie and the English pop-music world of the 1970s. When the folkloric muralists of the older Chicano artist collective, Los Four (Frank Romero, Carlos Almaraz, Robert "Beto" de la Rocha, and the founder, Gilbert Luján) were accorded an exhibition at the Los Angeles County Museum early in 1974, Asco responded to this breakthrough recognition of Chicano art by crashing the opening in costume. As described by Herrón, "We had all these different layers of like feathers and we painted our faces. Gronk was like wearing like leopard, like a leopard shirt. We all wore platforms. I think Gronk had a pair of satin bell bottom pants. It was just our regular flamboyant."[3]

The local Bowie cult had already taken root by 1972, centered just east of the Strip around a club called Rodney Bingenheimer's English Disco. With the ebbing and relative domestication of the first wave of extreme performance in Los Angeles art, similar impulses migrated to a venue like Rodney's for its cultivation of extravagant artifice and social deviance. A close associate of Gronk, Jerry Dreva, led a drag-performing and gate-crashing group

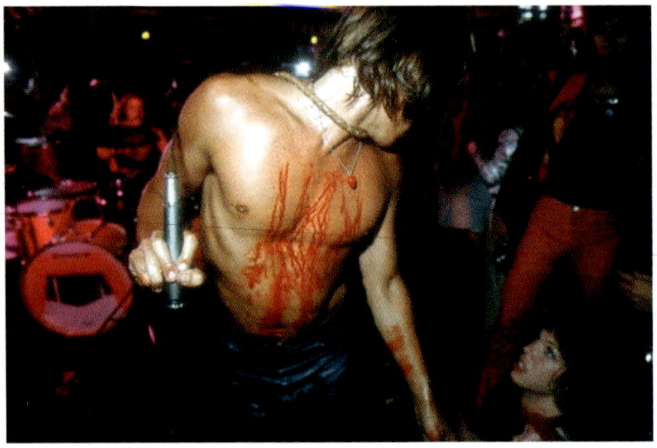

**113** Iggy Pop performing "Murder of the Virgin," 11 August 1974, at Rodney Bingenheimer's English Disco, Hollywood

called Les Petites Bons-Bons [sic] and had personally played an important part in acclimatizing Bowie to Los Angeles.[4] In August 1974, Iggy Pop, the Detroit front man for the recently disbanded Psychedelic Stooges, put on a concert at Rodney's under the title "Murder of the Virgin," which he styled as a performance work. Ritually whipped by his old guitarist while a rudimentary pickup band kept up a droning riff in the background, Iggy ended the piece by lacerating his own chest with a knife to the point that security guards stopped the show and dumped him on the pavement outside the club (fig. 113).[5]

Whatever the merits of this particular exercise, which came at perhaps the lowest physical and psychological ebb in the singer's career, it points to an expanded fluidity of what might count as an art space and art event, a phenomenon made possible in part by the precedents provided by Chris Burden, Bas Jan Ader, and Jack Goldstein, along with an enlarged sense of who might make up the audience for radically heightened actions. It is hardly surprising that Iggy should have been the focus for such a breakdown of the wall between the designated art world and "the runaway self-consciousness" of Hollywood and the Sunset Strip. Indeed, he hardly needed the honorific label of performance art, in that his stage act, from the founding of the Stooges in 1968, had thrown his habitually half-naked body into a kinetic visibility and physical jeopardy beyond the norm for any other rock singer; what was more, he closed the yawning gulf that had opened between god-like celebrity performers and an audience of passive consumers, peering at their idols across the expanses of vast stadiums. As Iggy incessantly broke through the fourth wall at the front of the stage, the Stooges' music reveled in its do-it-yourself (but inspired) indifference to conventional expectations of virtuosity.

It would have been difficult for any remotely attentive observer of the culture to go down the path of extreme performance without some awareness of Iggy Pop. The first Stooges album came with a certain artistic imprimatur in the shape of producer John Cale, once a La Monte Young collaborator and then bassist/violist in the house band of Andy Warhol's Factory, the Velvet Underground. In visual terms, Iggy's zero-body-fat torso became something of a kinetic sculpture in itself. When the Warhol-besotted David Bowie picked up on Iggy in the early 1970s, assuming the roles of record producer and career counselor, his new charge soon added the androgyny cues of eyeliner and peroxide blonde hair to his sinuous physique. One of the DJs at Rodney's recalled nights when Iggy would appear "wearing this dress and he kept pulling it up and he wasn't wearing anything under it and he was scaring the customers."[6] That was when he was not hurling a water cooler bottle to the floor and diving into the broken glass.

By the time Iggy returned to Los Angeles in 1977, his triumphant, Bowie-produced *The Idiot* in record stores, the echoes of English punk had transformed his old glitter scene on the Strip. The overlay of English cachet and the hard-edged aggression pioneered by the Sex Pistols had made the music scene even more attractive to art-school students and recent graduates for whom the local gallery infrastructure was still not providing anything like a satisfactory outlet. At the beginning of 1977, a group of CalArts students embraced the idea of forming a band as performance vehicle; the result was the Weirdos, the first musically viable group in Los Angeles to offer a credible alternative to English punk. The art-crowd component of the new punk scene, along with its penchant for competitive dressing-up, made visual presentation as important as the music.[7] The Weirdos calculated that their best stylistic option was to run counter to the austerity-chic pioneered by Vivienne Westwood and the Sex Pistols. Their singer, John Denney, related, "We adorned ourselves with happy faces, peace signs, plastic flowers and assorted doo-dads—accessories that were decidedly un-punk."[8] A photograph of the band onstage (fig. 114) in the summer of that year, taken by Jenny Lens, who had likewise studied at CalArts, conveys the effect of a contemporaneous painting from the Pattern and Decoration school having come to riotously mutant life.

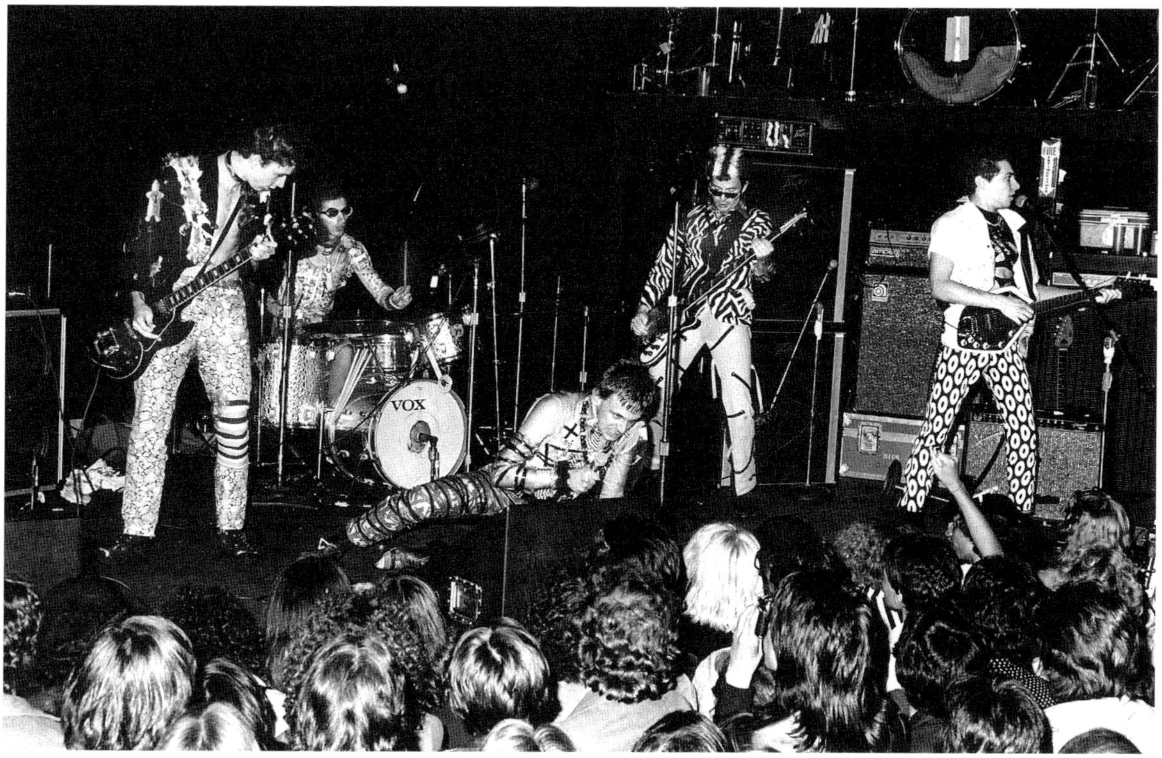


**114** Jenny Lens, *The Weirdos at the Whisky*, Summer 1977, gelatin silver print

It was not only via their Pop-inflected stage dress that the Weirdos made a decisive impression. Their sound and musical affinities set an example around which a scene could coalesce—one key aspect of which lay in an artist's openness to chance experiment. Before they had even found a drummer, the three principals were pressed by a visiting band from San Francisco to be their opening act. Throwing caution to the winds, they went on stage as just two guitars and a bass, finding a sound in the process that transmuted the borrowed breakneck tempi of the Ramones and the Sex Pistols into something more sinuous, the fluid baseline by Cliff Roman taking over from a drummer's timekeeping: "the Weirdos were something phenomenally new," said one fellow musician; "It felt different. It looked different. It smelled different. Your body moved to it differently. Even without a drummer, I couldn't stand still when they were playing."[9] With some suitably *noir*-ish song titles like "Hitman" and "Life of Crime," the band set a tone and established an early ascendancy, which they exploited on behalf of aspiring peers. When, in April 1977, they invited a Westside grouping called the Germs to open for them, they were fully aware that its members at that point possessed next to no musical competence whatsoever. Five minutes of shambolic performance was all that even an indulgent audience could endure, but the Weirdos' imprimatur authorized an approach familiar in avant-garde art but rare in popular music: innovation by deliberate impoverishment of means—even down to a Dadaist nullity. The young Eastside Chicana Alicia Armendarez, soon to become punk-band leader Alice Bag, recalled, "When I saw the Germs, I was surprised, and outraged and excited all at once. I didn't think much of what they were doing, but I thought, 'Wow, if they can do that, surely I can do something better.'"[10]

The Germs stood for a relaxation of the customary division of labor in pop-music world, whereby, for a time, musicians, wannabe musicians, writers, photocopy self-publishers, photographers, and style leaders all operated in rough parity with one another. And barriers to entry were low. For Jenny Lens, her emergence as a leading photographer of the nascent punk community in Los Angeles owed relatively little to her extensive art training. In her affecting memoir, she mentions only in passing the legacy of her time at CalArts.[11] In one photograph of her "little rented cottage in the valley," a poster for the exhibition *Anonymous Was a Woman* is visible on the wall, testifying to contact with the breakthrough Feminist Art Program at that institution led by Judy Chicago and Miriam Shapiro. Lens also joined the collective responsible for fabricating Chicago's elaborated, multimedia installation, *The Dinner Party*, starting in 1974, while pursuing her original career goal of teaching art at the college level. "My background was in art," she attested, "not in photography. I rarely ever read a rock magazine."[12] But that conventional artist's identity could not survive her first exposure to Patti Smith's music and persona when the New York poet-performer toured Southern California in 1976.

After seeing a sparsely attended—but for Lens transcendent—performance in a club on the Strip, she followed Smith to a concert in San Diego. Lacking any credentials but already close enough to accompany Smith's brother into the venue, she used his credentials to smuggle her photographic equipment past the vigilant bouncers.[13] From forty rolls of film emerged a series recording Smith clutching her Fender guitar in a seeming aura of inner luminescence, then falling to her knees and arching backward in moves patented by the late Jimi Hendrix (fig. 111). As if to disavow that taint of celebrity idolatry, Lens ascribes the aureole effect to her rudimentary skills in developing. Nonetheless, in light of Smith's singularity as a woman in the rock spotlight, along with the illumination Lens and many young women felt that she transmitted, the effect could, instead, be regarded as taking back the ground of the inspired artist from a legion of strutting male poseurs.

The greater part of Lens's photographic legacy from the flowering and decline of Los Angeles punk consists of a group of portraits taken backstage at various venues or at parties and promotional events. Mostly in fast exposure black and white, they convey the after-hours, nearly impoverished solidarity that bonded the participants in a still obscure, niche mode of existence (fig. 115). There is an apt comparison to be made between Lens's visual record of these relationships and the contemporaneous work from the opposite coast by Nan Goldin, as she began her commensurable path of self-understanding—career is not quite the correct word in either of their cases—via intimate photography within an accepting if tensely configured social circle of the abused, rejected, and misunderstood.

In Lens's case, her close circle included significant public performers, the preeminent case in point being the band around which the Los Angeles punk scene coalesced: the Screamers (fig. 116). Led by Tommy Gear and Tomata du Plenty, former drag performers and countercultural cabaret artistes, the three- or sometimes four-piece group put their initially defining imprint on a home-grown punk aesthetic via their own subtractive musical aesthetic, as they did without guitars, while singer Tomata rarely attempted much more than a monotone yell. Issuing next to no recordings, the Screamers depended more on the projection of their visual image, tended to by a stylist and promulgated by photographers like Lens across a range of semi-underground magazines and fan publications.

Tomata du Plenty had for a time had been a member of the gender-bending Cockettes revue in San Francisco, and his newest project help knit together the punk eruptions in both locales. Through the intermediary of the Target Video operation in San Francisco, the Screamers were also among the first musicians to take advantage of video as an emergent art medium. Under the direction of the artist Joe Rees, Target undertook to document local performances across the whole alternative music scene in California. The Screamers availed themselves of Target's studio production facilities to make a series of self-contained video pieces, each devoted to a single song—this coming well before the flowering of the commercial music video as a promotional medium.

In the absence of any vinyl recordings, these taped performances of 1978 remain the best document of both their music and style of performance, couched in a nascent art medium, the authorship of which falls halfway between the performers and the videographer. In lieu of an actual video, one could do worse than the evocative verbal transcription by the veteran punk chronicler Jon Savage of "122 Hours of Fear," a Gear composition on the grim theme of airline hostage taking:

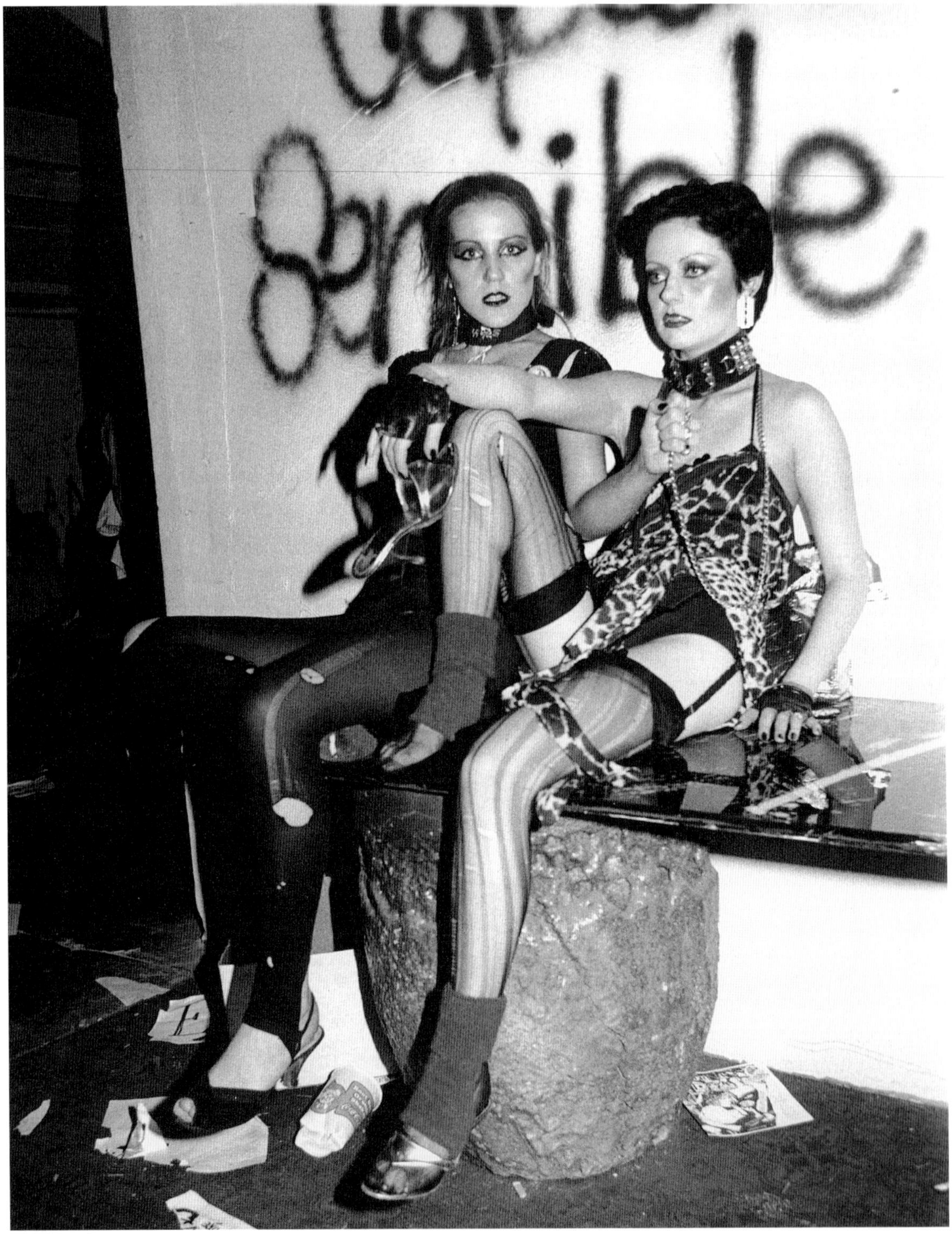


**115** Jenny Lens, *Shannon Wilhelm and Allison Buckles*, 1977, gelatin silver print

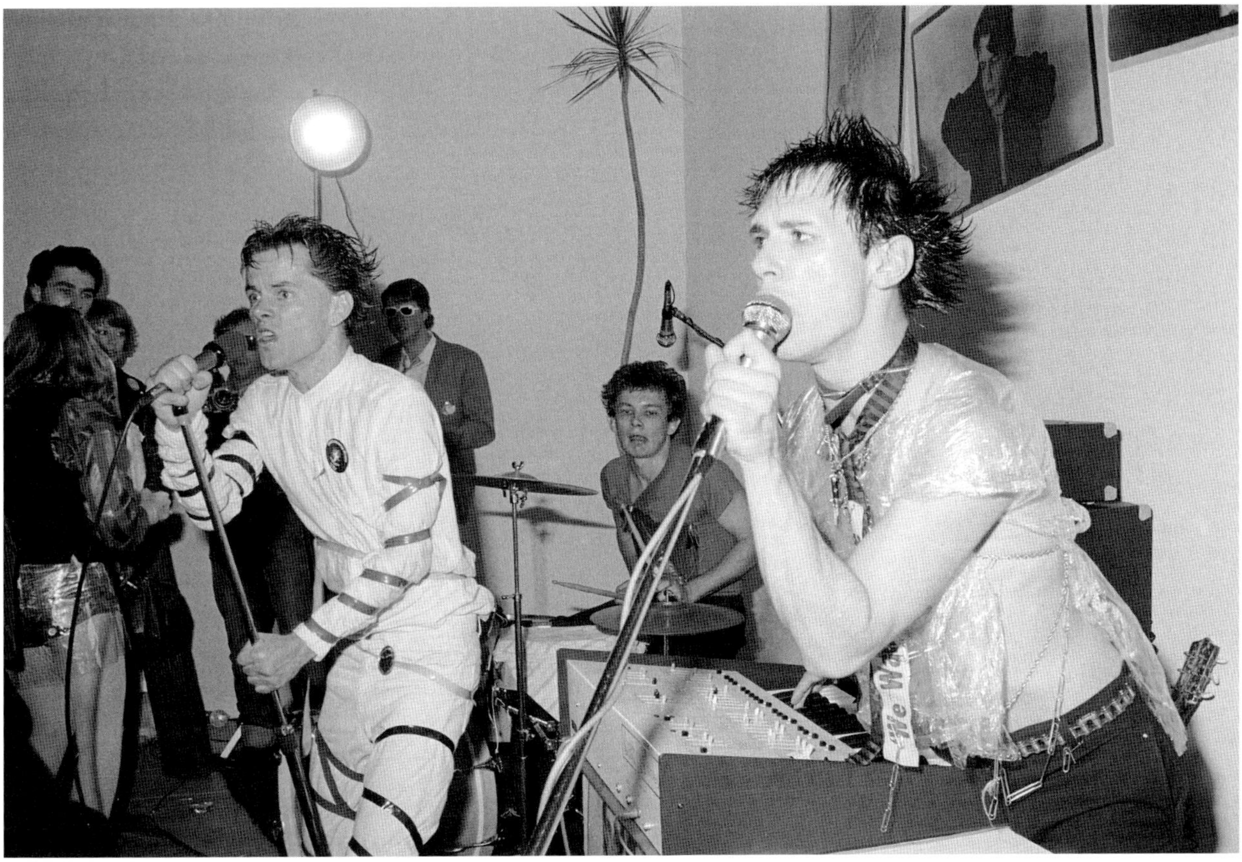

**116** Jenny Lens, *The Screamers*, 1977, gelatin silver print

The clip begins with a frontal shot of a helicopter: the sound of its take-off bleeds into descending synthesiser notes. A caption comes up: "Screamers." The second image to be seen is out of focus, a pink/brown blur against a sea green background. The ominous notes continue, with an abrasive synthesiser counter melody. Live drums come in, upping the tempo to manic punk. The Screamers' singer, Tomata du Plenty, takes you right into the chilling scenario. His background in performance art gives him total control: his sculpted, swept-up 50s psycho hustler face keeps firmly within the camera position, lapsing from anger into stillness in the space of seconds. He is simultaneously within and outside the song: this is not arch, but conversely even more involving. . . . at the end the camera returns to the singer, who stares at the lens with a gaze that runs the gamut from gurning speed psychosis to a certain, pained vulnerability.[14]

■

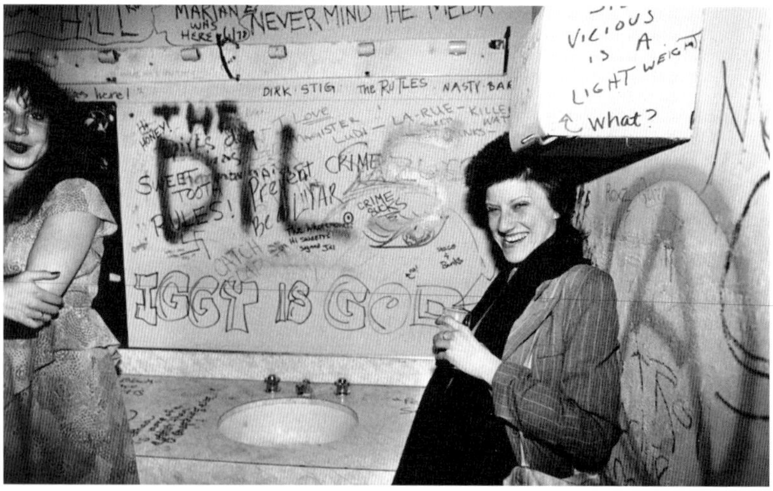


**117** Bruce Conner, WOMEN'S ROOM AT THE MABUHAY GARDENS from MABUHAY GARDENS PUNK PHOTOS, 1978, gelatin silver print, 35.6 × 27.9 cm, Nasher Museum of Art at Duke University

With Rees behind the camera, these exercises adhere more closely to the templates provided by artists like William Wegman or Bruce Conner. So it was altogether fitting that Conner's name should re-emerge here, as he returned fully into public life at the call of the San Francisco punk phenomenon, for the first time since his campaign for County Supervisor nearly a decade before. Off nights at a Filipino show bar called the Mabuhay Gardens in North Beach might have appeared a poor approximation of the old Avalon Ballroom, but Conner, now forty-five, felt the Avalon spirit revived there and became a welcome regular. His images offer some side glances at the trashed, disheveled premises—such as a look inside the women's toilet with its large wall inscription: "Iggy Is God" (fig. 117).[15] One regular, Richard Alden Peterson, testified to that spirit—mind expansion included: "At one acid-enhanced show, Sally of the Mutants ripped open Bruce's down jacket while dancing next to him, filling the air with feathers. Both were captivated by the 'sparkling' feathers backlit by the bright stage lights. Skull-and-cross-bones blotter acid, a Psychedelic era influence, was part of the scene . . ."[16]

The venue operated in a symbiotic bond with the magazine *Search and Destroy* (named for an Iggy and the Stooges song on their 1973 album *Raw Power*), edited by V. Vale, who recruited a more than willing Conner to serve as its effective staff photographer. Vale took advantage of his day job at Lawrence Ferlinghetti's City Lights bookstore to orchestrate the network behind his publication, which included seed money obtained from both Ferlinghetti and Allen Ginsberg, whose link to the shop went back a quarter century to the publication of *Howl and Other Poems*. In the actual production of *Search and Destroy*, Conner provided the living link to that Beat moment of free-spirit consolidation in the city which Vale believed had been reincarnated by the punk community.

Peterson, a fellow gig photographer, went on to describe Conner's new lease on life: "Bruce was a hard-core front-line Punk who totally immersed himself in the scene, and would be the first to jump on stage to throw the singer off. The pre-mosh-pit 1980s dance was the Pogo, and Bruce would often be seen dancing convulsively in front of the stage while balancing his camera. He was a front-line person and once broke some ribs in the process."[17] But his Rolleiflex on the whole concentrated on the performers. As he told Greil Marcus, "I had always liked the idea of action photos. . . . Like—sport events. Basketball. They're floating in the air, part of this suspended sphere, and they've got these beatific looks on their faces, they're in anguish. Or combat photography. I always thought, gosh, combat photography. Maybe I could work on that."[18]

The epitome of his approach might be ROZZ MAKES A GIANT STEP FOR MANKIND: NEGATIVE TREND, JANUARY 23, 1978 (fig. 119), which captures the punk front man launching the band's performance with a coup matching Iggy at his finest: in Conner's words, Rozz (Rebenak) "started the whole show by running from the back of the stage, jumping off the stage, landing on the tables, grabbing drinks off the tables and tossing them on the floor."[19] No wonder that Mab habitués liked to think of Rebenak as their own Iggy, while Conner regarded Negative Trend as living like the old poets of the 1950s on an extreme edge, offstage as well as on: "They're rare people, I mean like . . . I always liked Negative Trend so much because they really were fuckin' living off of food stamps; they had a dollar and a quarter in their pocket and they're still that way and they're still going on . . ."[20]

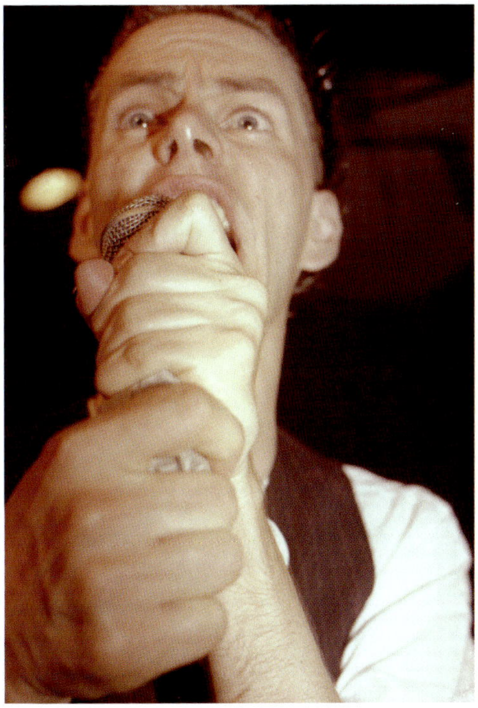

118 Bruce Conner, TAMATA DU PLENTY, THE SCREAMERS, MAY 14, 1978, pigmented inkjet print by Magnolia Editions, Oakland, California, Anglim Gilbert Gallery

Occasionally Conner captures arresting physical exertions among the spectators down in front, but he directed his greatest concentration to the stage, lead singers and guitarists receiving pride of place, but without the usual fan's subordination.[21] In the May 1978 close-up of Tomata du Plenty, the lead singer of the Screamers, up from Los Angeles, is denied his signature spiky-haired profile, filling the frame instead with his lost-looking expression and large, foreshortened hands that seem to force-feed the microphone into his mouth (fig. 118). It was probably fortunate, given Conner's visceral revulsion toward police violence and his increasingly fragile health, that he was able to sample California punk from his perch in San

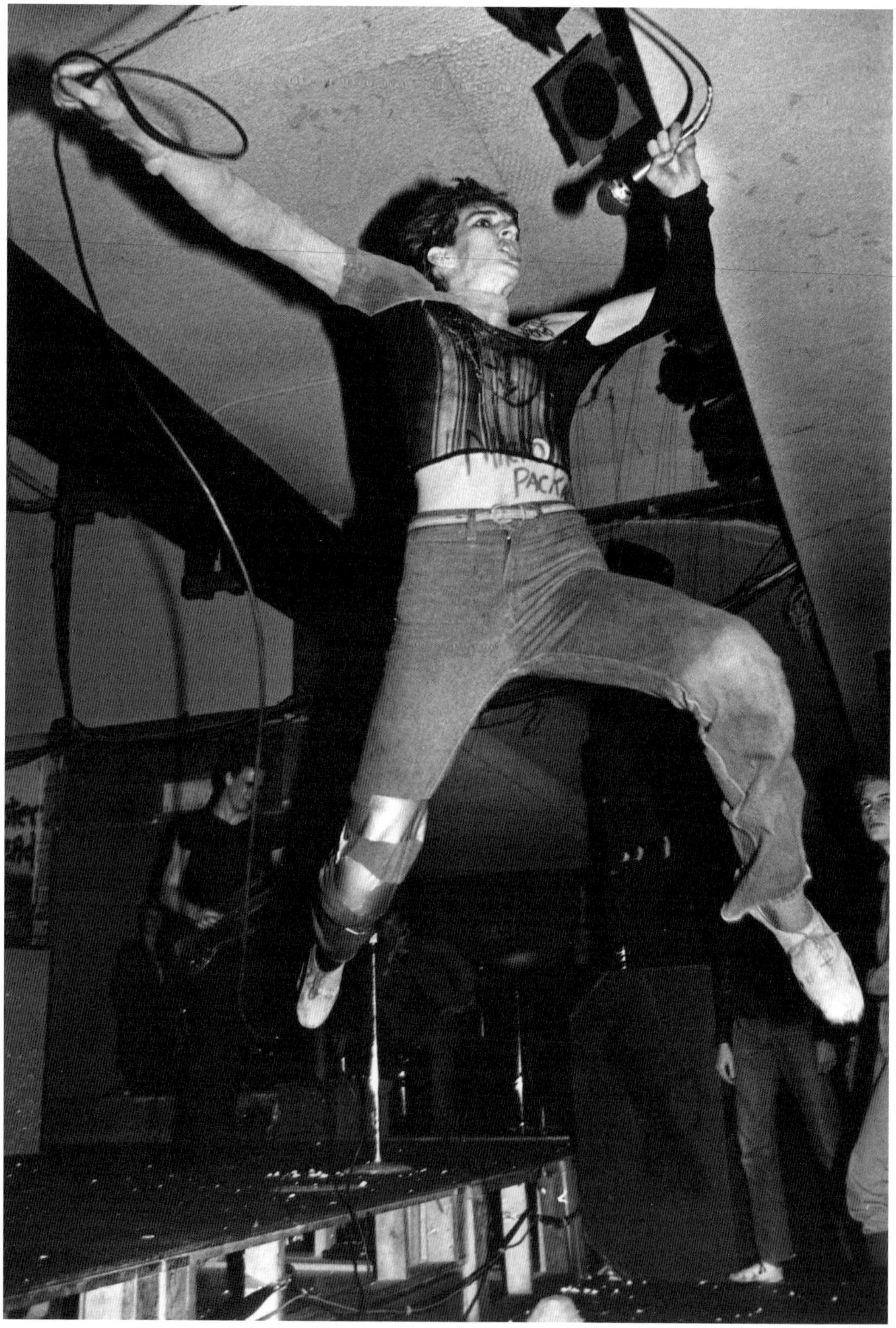


**119** Bruce Conner, ROZZ MAKES A GIANT STEP FOR MANKIND: NEGATIVE TREND from MABUHAY GARDENS PUNK PHOTOS, 1978, gelatin silver print, 35.6 × 27.9 cm, Nasher Museum of Art at Duke University

Francisco and not in the Screamers' home base. Los Angeles being Los Angeles, the implacable forces of order were gradually taking notice of what appeared to them as a widening circle of deviants in strange clothes walking the streets and gathering for events of incomprehensible racket and spillover drunkenness, indecency, vandalism, and drug use. Most of all, punk constituted an intolerable breach in the containment of disorder that the police forces regarded as their overriding mission.

■

After years of the usual harassment of Hollywood venues over building-code violations, the dam broke on Saint Patrick's Day 1979. A group of bands, none of them among the most extreme, had booked the Elks Lodge Hall, a grandly ornate relic of past prosperity in MacArthur Park, near downtown. The show had hardly gotten underway before massed police in riot gear invaded the hall, chasing, clubbing, and arresting at will, visiting on the punk audience the same arbitrary brutality that they had brought down on the Chicano Moratorium marchers in 1970.[22] "After Elks Lodge," wrote punk veterans Craig Lee and Shreader, "the police became a genuine menace and started appearing at shows with increasing regularity."[23]

This pattern continued apace into the new decade on a scale enlarged by a flood of new entrants into the punk arena from the suburban hinterlands of the city, particularly those to the south of the urban core, from the beach neighborhoods of Hermosa, Redondo and Torrance across the harbor area to the tightly packed towns of northern Orange County. Short hair, jeans, tee shirt, and sneakers of the ordinary student or manual worker: style cues far from the extravagant markers of Hollywood punk. Yet the stimulus for young suburbanites to enter the fray had come from their example. This new and growing presence at the Whisky or the Starwood nightclubs, tracking bands incubated in suburban territory, manifested a shift in affect and patterns of behavior that required a name of its own: it came to be called Hardcore. The gifted writer Kristine McKenna, both participant and observer, ruefully reflected on this moment: "Women were the first to leave—there was no place for them in the world of hardcore punk; gays and sensitive artist types went next . . . The entire scene became about one thing, aggression."[24] And it became difficult, as McKenna attests, for any female or gay glam-rock veteran to find a place for themselves in the stylistically unadorned, outwardly straight (leaving aside the sweaty attractions of the mosh pit), and athletically uninhibited world surrounding Hardcore music.

The one band that set the standard and blazed the trail for the others was the consuming project of Greg Ginn, a disaffected young engineer and UCLA economics graduate from the inland corner of Hermosa Beach, who embodied in his person and psyche much of the conflict arising from the stalled California prosperity machine in the stagflation years of the 1970s. His father, Regis, had been a navigator on bombers that flew missions over Europe during World War II, then settled, alongside innumerable war veterans, with his Estonian

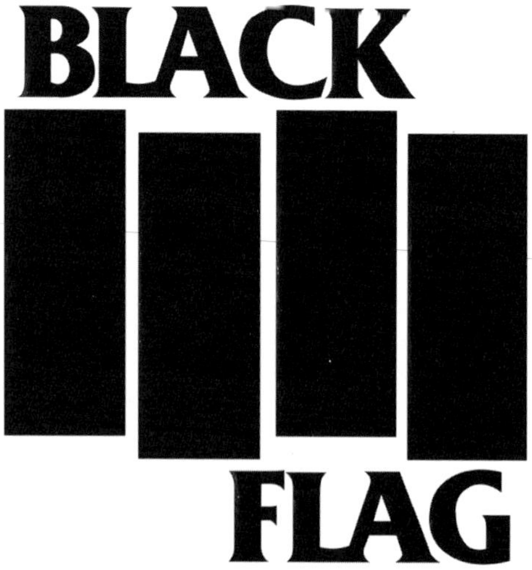


**120** Raymond Pettibon, Black Flag logo design, 1979

war bride in Southern California. Though his military experience could easily have led him into the aerospace industry, he ended up teaching literature, first in high school and later at Harbor Community College. He also wrote his own espionage and *noir* detective thrillers, which he illustrated himself. Greg, by contrast, picked up and pursued his father's abandoned technical expertise while still a teenager, mastering the technology and culture of amateur short-wave radio, publishing his own hobbyist fanzine, and starting a mail-order business for radio components, some of his own invention, under the name Solid State Tuners (SST).[25]

His study of economics and finance at UCLA would then have fit neatly into the resume of young entrepreneur who had already generated one successfully self-sustaining concern. But a belated discovery of rock music and the guitar led him—after an impressionable detour following the Grateful Dead—to the recordings of the Stooges and the MC5, Iggy's high-intensity Detroit mentors (to be explored further in the following chapter), which gave Ginn his template in terms of both music and attitude. Practicing the songs he wrote over incessant twelve-to-sixteen-hour days, he managed to find fledgling neighborhood musicians willing to keep up with him and so formed his band in 1976. His younger brother, Raymond, played bass for a time, before ceding to a more committed player, but he gave his brother's project something far more important: first a name, Black Flag, confounding historical anarchism with noxious insecticide, and, second, the four uneven vertical bars (fig. 120) that constituted one of the most powerful logos in music history, powerful, that is, in the sense of attracting and moving millions with no machinery of advertising and promotion behind it. The Black Flag bars possess a powerfully abstract economy that signals a penetrating awareness of non-objective form in the history of twentieth-century art and design. What was more, Raymond's band logo could be unmistakably reproduced, minus the geometric precision, by four simple strokes on any available surface with an aerosol can of black paint.[26]

Raymond had graduated with his own UCLA economics degree in 1977. On returning to the rambling and ramshackle family household, he paralleled his brother's diversion into a self-taught artistic vocation, Raymond's being visual art. Taking Pettibon as his artist's name, he had begun in his own driven, unrelenting way to churn out figurative vignettes with textual counterpoint in pen and ink. In so doing, alongside other preoccupations, he became the visual bard of the counter-counterculture embodied in Hardcore. During the mid-1970s transition from Bowie-style Glam to Hollywood Punk, there had persisted in the costume of both performers and fans a love of exaggerated outlines and resplendent colors with

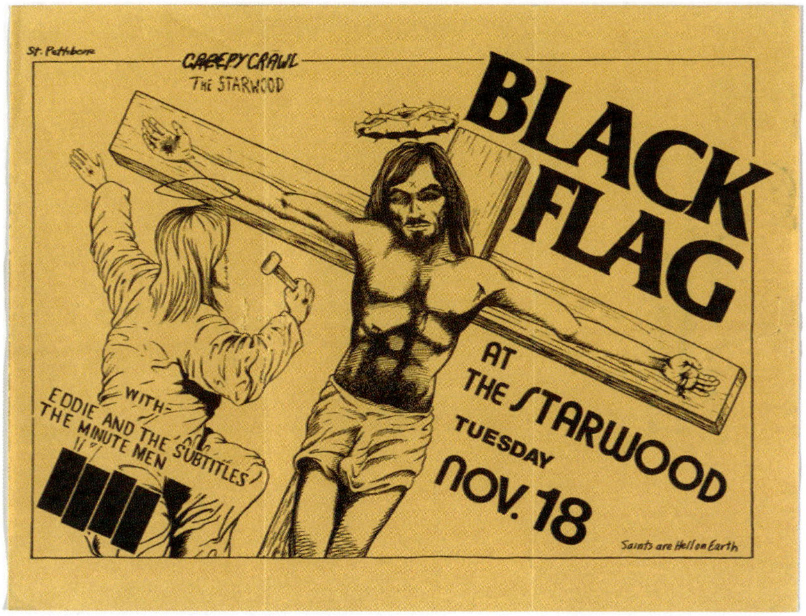


**121** Raymond Pettibon, poster for a show with Black Flag at the Starwood, 1980, offset lithograph, 21.6 × 28 cm, The Museum of Modern Art, New York

roots in the countercultural styles of the late 1960s; Asco gave their inspired Eastside spin to this dress-up tendency. But the pared-down, jock style of Hardcore severed that continuity (at least, if one leaves aside a peculiar passing fad around 1980 for male fans to wear tartan skirts over their jeans). Pettibon made that rejection more than tacit, generating a grim, disabused body of work exceptionally focused on the counterculture as a subject, overtly antipathetic to but also diagnostic of its widespread demonization as part and parcel of Reaganism's triumph.

Thus, the imagery and narrative of Charles Manson's "family" became the dominant thematic thread of this early phase in Pettibon's career, as he annexed the aspirations of the counterculture to those sordid crime dramas of the *noir* tradition so beloved by certain of his artist predecessors. By itself, that would be no great revelation, as the Manson murders, along with the Hell's Angels' murdering a Black spectator at the Rolling Stones free concert at Altamont, had long been cast for the general culture as a welcome end to the irritating idealism of the 1960s. But Pettibon's incessant use of Manson images acknowledged that cliché while refusing the complacent conclusions drawn from it; rather, he turns it inside out to expose the perverse pleasure aroused by the story in conventional minds disposed to their own murderous antipathy toward any serious moral challenge from outsiders like himself.

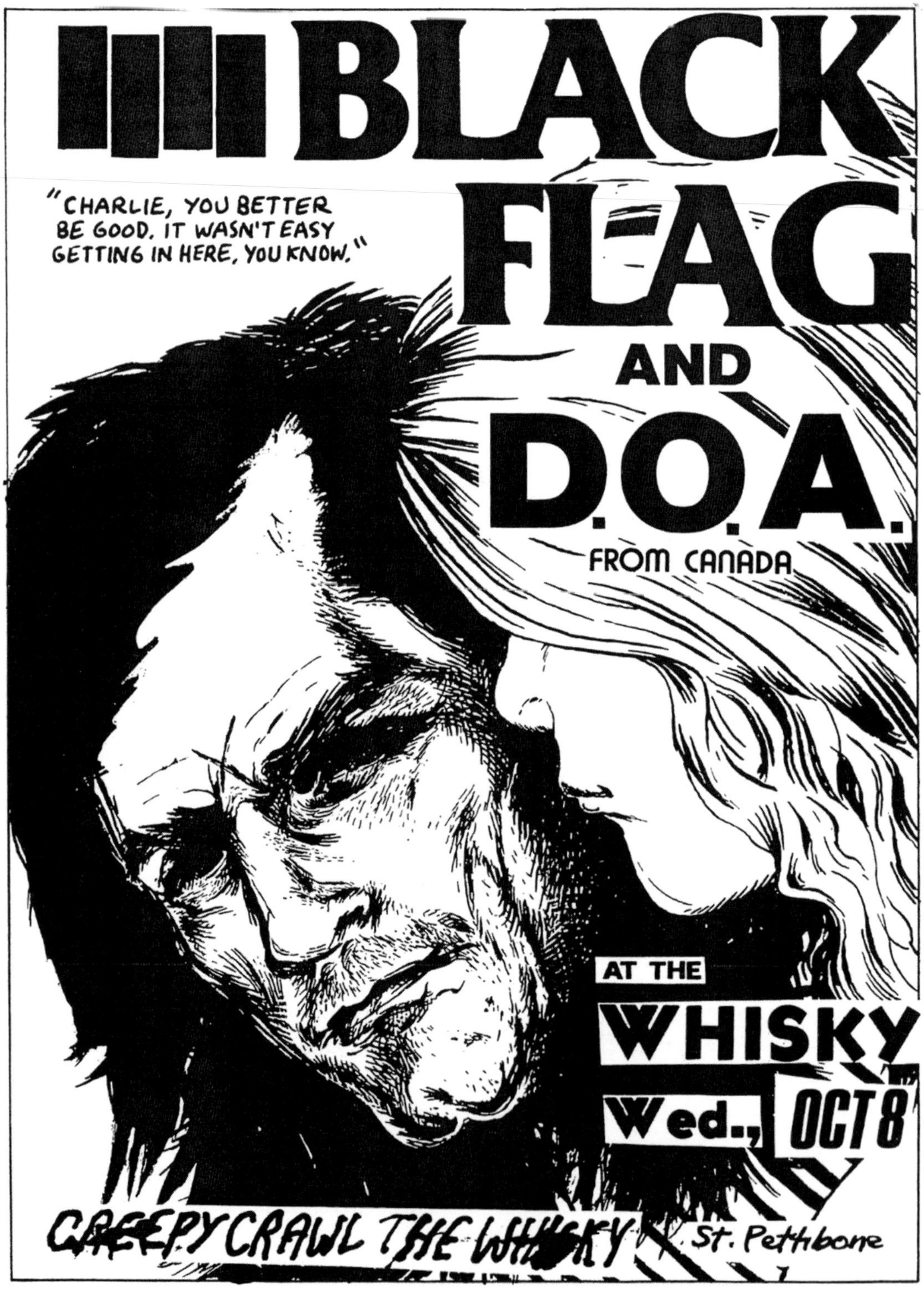


**122** Raymond Pettibon, flyer produced for a show with Black Flag and D.O.A. on 8 October 1980 at the Whisky [A Go-Go] in Los Angeles, offset lithograph, 21.6 × 28 cm, The Museum of Modern Art, New York

When Black Flag undertook a national tour in 1980, beginning with a landmark show at the Whisky A Go-Go on the Sunset Strip (figs. 121, 122), they called the tour their Creepy Crawl, after the term Manson had used for the murderous housebreaking expeditions on which he dispatched his followers. Pettibon generated the images to match, emblazoned with those words, taking the old punk flirtation with the gothic and demonic at grim face value. His Creepy Crawl poster suite, successively promulgated via the flyer as medium, offered a Black Flag story bereft of consolation. There was certainly none on offer for the first-wave Hollywood punks pushed aside by the Hardcore army, though they might have thought Manson an all too appropriate avatar for their rivals.

■

That Pettibon's compelling activity should have anchored itself in a mordant recapitulation of the late 1960s counterculture reinforces once more the underexamined importance of that phenomenon for art, however travestied and bereft of consolation it appears in his rendering. So it probably seemed to the largely white, youthful constituency from which Pettibon took his bearings. But there were at the same moment in Los Angeles a vibrant group of African American artists in their early maturity who looked to one of the most remarkable, unlikely survivors of the 1960s counterculture as offering a template for their own collective undertaking.

Senga Nengudi, one of the principals of the group, had by her mid-thirties built up a considerable portfolio in art and dance between California, Japan, and New York. Recently resettled in Los Angeles, she joined the same Brockman Gallery where David Hammons had shown *Injustice Case* (fig. 53), his defiant celebration of the fortitude of the Black Panther Bobby Seale in 1970. There, her recent "RSVP" series of sculptures, installations fashioned from stretched, stuffed, and weighted nylon tights, had achieved their first, lasting renown. But she had larger, multimedia and multisensory aspirations, inspired in part by a voice that stood for continuity with the communalism and metaphysical flights of the 1960s. As she recalls, "Oh, we couldn't wait for the Sun Ra experience: this whole audience full of people. He might come out of a bag doing 1940s big band music, or progressive jazz, or he might come out of a bag not doing music at all, and just doing a lecture on 'space is the place.'"[27]

Sun Ra (born Herman "Sonny" Blount) was by then in his sixties, though it was always difficult to tell his age under the voluminous robes, awash with glitter, the wigs, and the headdress he sported onstage (fig. 123), as did the members of his large, pulsating ensemble, the Solar Arkestra. Having moved from his native Alabama to Chicago, where he established himself as an accomplished arranger for other jazz artists, Blount underwent a self-proclaimed visionary transformation in the early 1950s: transportation to Saturn in an out-of-body experience with alien beings. From this claimed epiphany came his elaborate, obsessively researched theories, drawing upon a heady mix of occultisms, concerning the extraterrestrial origins and destiny of black African culture via ancient Egypt. By the late 1950s, his growing

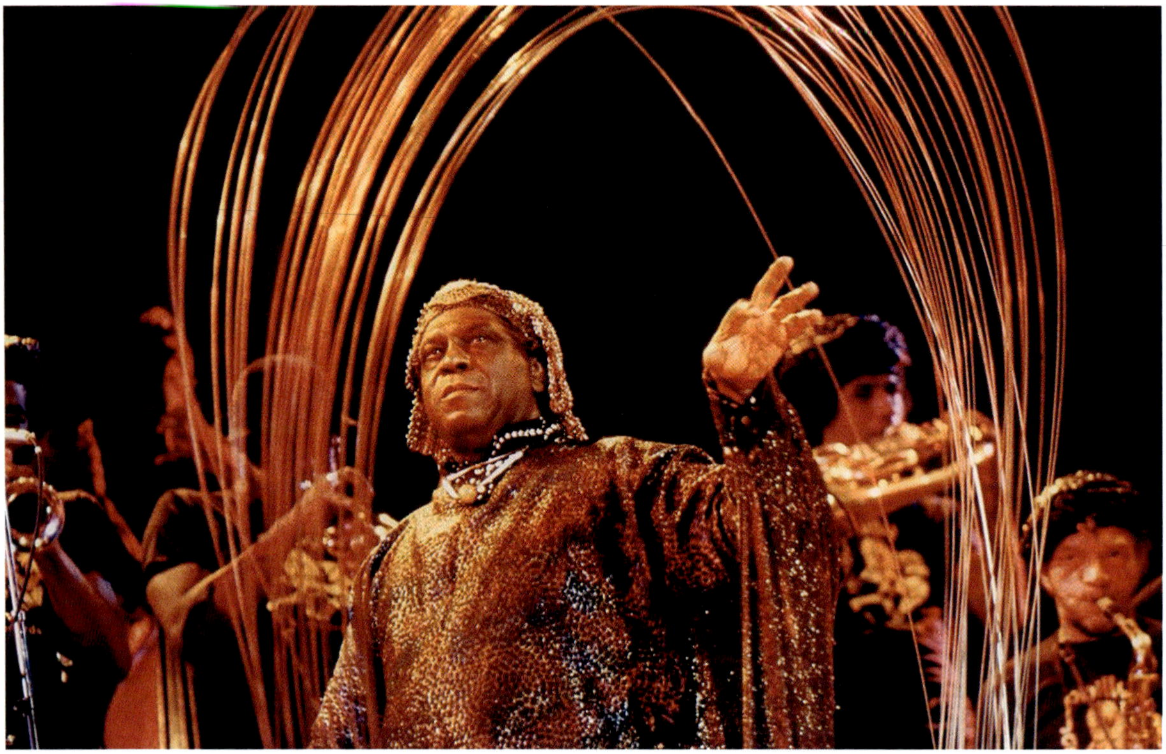

**123** Sun Ra and his Sun Ra Arkestra perform with a steel sculpture on 23 September 1978, at Hill Auditorium in Ann Arbor, Michigan, photograph by Leni Sinclair

band began to dress in the eclectic synthesis of Egyptian and science-fiction costume with which he would be identified for the next three decades, the visual, theatrical embodiment of the latter-day mythos that shaped his band's abrupt transitions from swing to lounge to free jazz to funk to Afro-percussion to unison chant to poetry that so fascinated Nengudi. Out of his deep musical learning, Sun Ra would recapitulate the history of jazz in the twentieth century as the analogue to the expanding self-awareness and attainment of superior consciousness by Black Americans, qualities that transcended the bounded times and places of oppressive history.[28]

As the mystical imaginations fostered by the West Coast counterculture waxed over the course of the 1960s, Sun Ra had already staked out a rich province of that territory in the name of Black experience. And the presumed end of the counterculture did not slow him down in the slightest nor diminish the appetite of his admirers for more of the same. While white rock music descended into posturing stadium spectacle over the course of the 1970s, Sun Ra genuinely kept the faith—as elsewhere incubated by the Ken Kesey Acid Tests and Digger events on the Haight Panhandle—in participatory ritual as the reason for musical performance. Certainly, a remarkable cohort of Black artists, Nengudi being one of them, were predisposed to respond on that basis, to view him as the living exponent of an African-derived centrality of ritual encouraged along more than one vector in the city.

One of these carried an academic provenance. The UCLA specialist in African art history, Arnold Rubin, had been emphasizing since his appointment in 1967 the uses of objects in traditional African cultures as much or more than the formal attributes that had fascinated the Cubists and a generation of modernist-oriented connoisseurs and collectors. His Super 8 films and vivid stories captured the ways in which masks and power objects were presented, manipulated, and worn on ceremonial occasions by the peoples of the arid Benue Valley in northern Nigeria, providing a vivid resource not only for his students but for occasional visitors to his seminar, such as the artist Betye Saar. She regularly credits his 1975 *Artforum* article, "Accumulation: Power and Display in African Sculpture," encountered near the outset of her mature career, as sparking a guiding conviction that collage components could affect viewers of a work in an active manner that surpassed static contemplation.[29] Rubin likewise insisted that ritual abounded in present-day America, ready to be unpacked by eyes attuned to this African attitude toward worked objects as spirit instruments, a view reinforced by two landmark exhibitions curated at UCLA by the visiting Robert Farris Thompson from Yale. To the best of his ability, he enlisted music, dance, and accompanying costume in both exhibitions to lend implied animation to deracinated objects too often drained of life by Euro-American conventions of decorous display.[30]

Into that climate of expectation, Sun Ra would land in Los Angeles like a wave of affirmation. Those artists who were also spending time in New York, as were Nengudi and her friend David Hammons, would already have witnessed his regular Monday night performances at the avant-garde Slug's jazz club on New York's Lower East Side. Over the course of the 1970s, Solar Arkestra extravaganzas were becoming increasingly available on the West Coast—near the start of the decade, Sun Ra even spent a semester in a teaching position at UC Berkeley, offering a course titled "The Black Man in the Cosmos." But it was in Southern California that a cognate response emerged from the visual arts, even though the term "visual" seems too limiting.

With the "total theater" of Sun Ra explicitly in her mind, Nengudi seized on the largely bare, sandy ground heaped beneath the underpasses surmounting Pico Boulevard, south of downtown. Tiny palms and shrubs clung to life amid an arid, artificial terrain that, in her words, "had the sense of Africa," with its own nomadic occupants, present by virtue of "little fire-remnants where they kept themselves warm."[31] Her aim was to consecrate this miniature desert, loomed over by "the very powerful columns," as the setting for a ritual she named *Ceremony for Freeway Fets* ("Fets" a neologism for "fetishes" in the sense of power objects) in simultaneous dimensions of sight, movement, and music (fig. 124). She was helped along in this undertaking by one government program channeled through the Brockman Gallery and

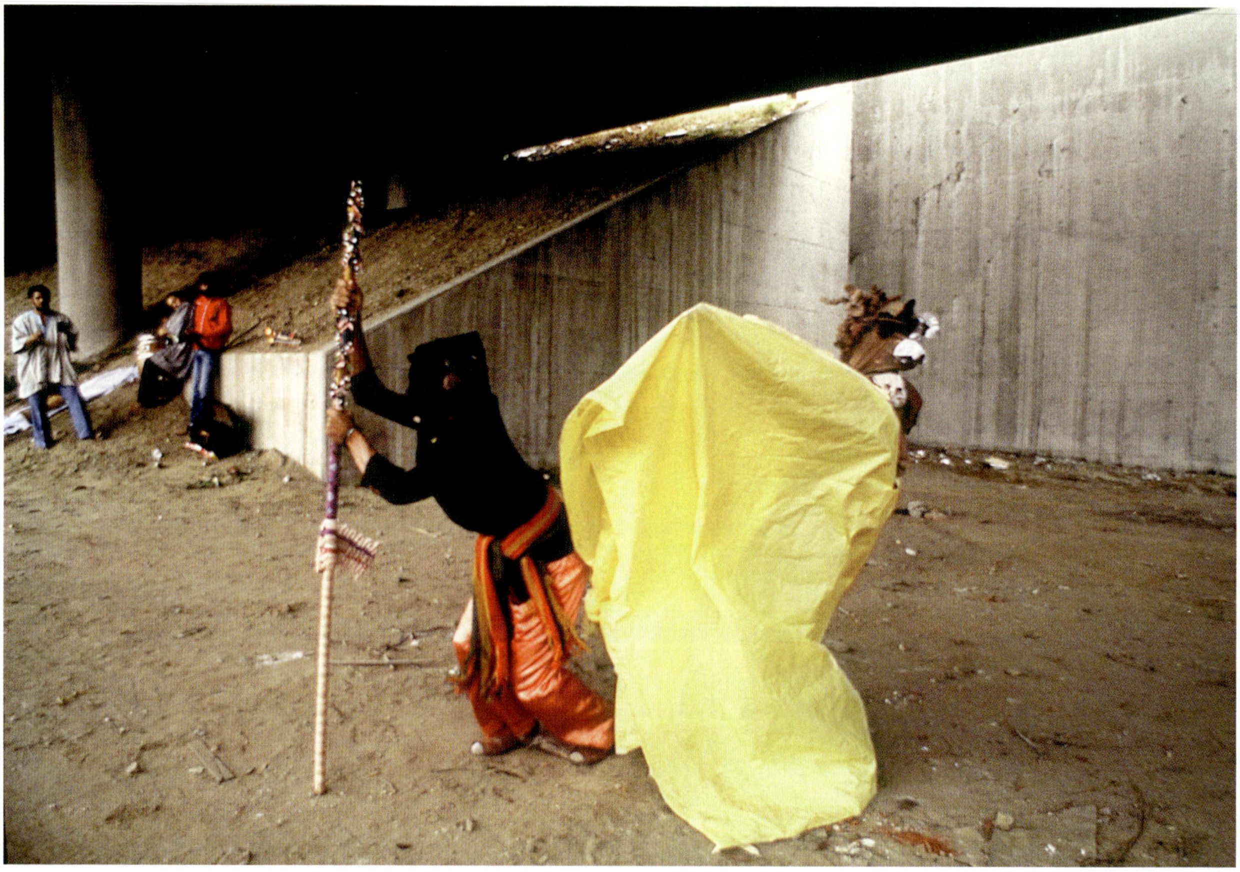

**124** Senga Nengudi, *Ceremony for Freeway Fets* (detail), 1978, C-print, 30 × 45 cm, Sprüth Magers and Thomas Erben Gallery, New York

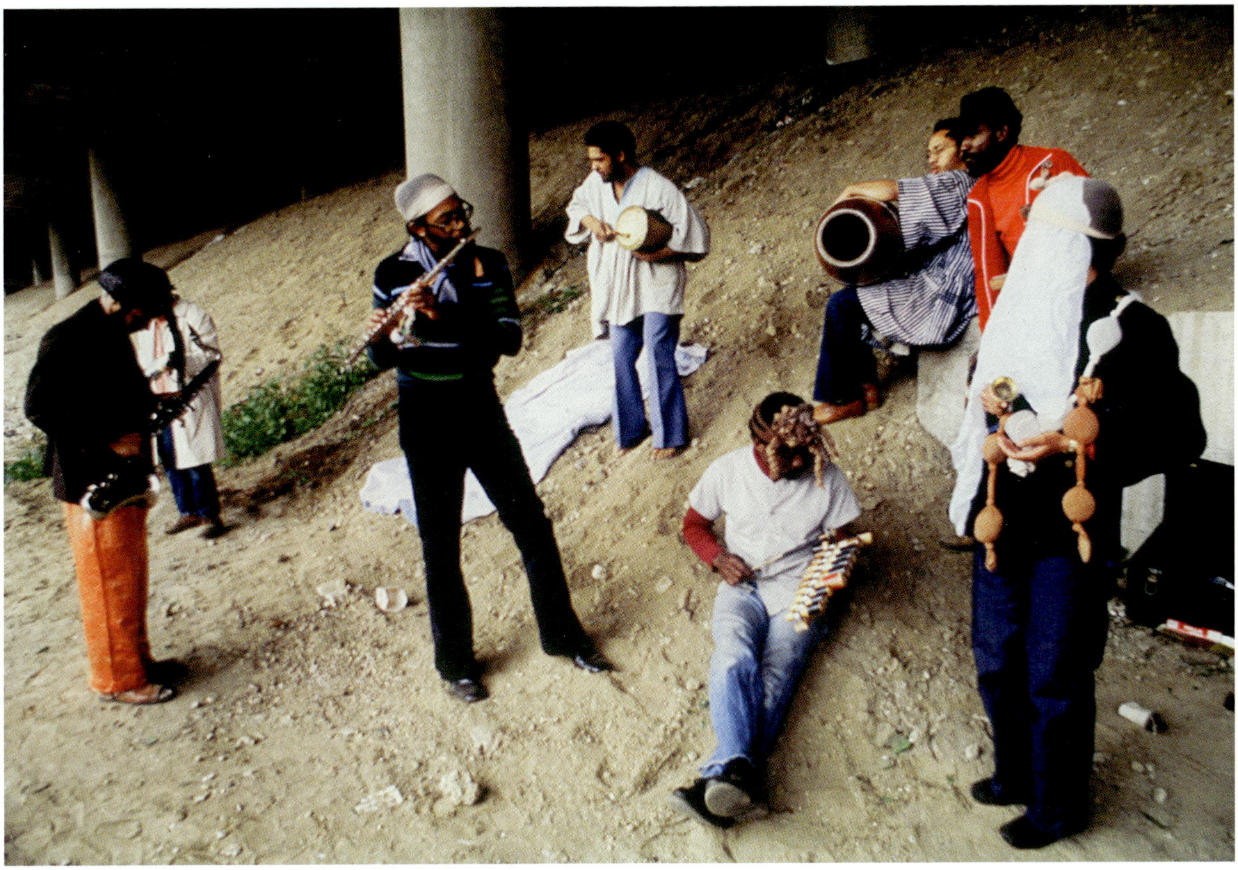

**125** Senga Nengudi, *Ceremony for Freeway Fets* (detail), 1978, C-print, 30 × 45 cm, Sprüth Magers and Thomas Erben Gallery, New York intended to support artists in public projects, and by another set up by the California Department of Transportation (the all-powerful Caltrans) to "beautify" the brutal abutments of the state's freeway system (likewise a backdrop for San Franciscan Bonnie Ora Sherk in the early part of the decade [fig. 70]). Taking advantage of these sources of support, Nengudi conceived an event in the spring of 1978 that would possess all the improvised underground resonances of a North Beach jazz poetry happening back at the counterculture's dawn.

Nengudi possessed the understanding that no straightforward attempt on her part to imitate Sun Ra's lavish panoply would be credible. For his example to cross the boundary from musical performance to art, each of its defining qualities would necessarily have to undergo a reversal. Where the Solar Arkestra seemed nearly perennial, tirelessly persistent, likely to turn up anywhere, Nengudi's counterpart would be momentary, ephemeral, barely touching down in its borrowed landscape—the characteristic means of visual artists being nobly impoverished in keeping with the bare resources possessed by the nocturnal homeless who inhabited the site. The distressed nylon pantyhose she attached to the abutments would attract no more than slight notice from passersby amid the debris that habitually collects in such overlooked pockets of urban space. The masks and headdresses she fashioned for the participants from rolled and stuffed pantyhose would draw the background fabrics, imbued with female significance, into the ensemble's totality. As allies, she recruited from fellow members of the loose collective going by the name of Studio Z—friends and collaborators who came together in a large space maintained by Hammons on Slauson Avenue—with the dancer-artist Maren Hassinger playing an especially salient role by joining the flow of movement with Nengudi under her sweeping yellow tarpaulin.[32] Hammons, back from New York at that moment, brought his own costume and fabric-wrapped staff. He even picked up a saxophone, Nengudi being determined that the musicians be, as she has said, "actually visual artists who knew how to play instruments and everyone there was part of Studio Z" (fig. 125).[33]

Recalling the occasion as "euphoric to harness this collaborative energy," Nengudi would see the work, with no film or video record remaining, recede for many years into almost unremarked history. But its principals and the art historian Kellie Jones have gone a good way toward recovering its affect and significance. It could, indeed, be said that *Ceremony for Freeway Fets* has found its moment, but its occasion of richly chromatic celebration was just as signally important then. Doubtless taking little or no notice of the harshly spartan, unadorned austerity of White Hardcore, Nengudi and Studio Z put down a crucial countervailing marker alongside it.

The next, valedictory chapter will follow a young artist, recently transplanted to Los Angeles at this same moment, as he formed his project expressly between these two poles. For the young Mike Kelley, a perceived, racially marked polarity between the two musicians who have figured most prominently in these pages, Iggy Pop and Sun Ra, provides more than a convenient metaphor: these were the explicit points of reference between which he came to orient his practice, veering closer to one only to be pulled in an opposite direction by the other. And never far from his thoughts was the fate of the counterculture he had only been old enough to experience for a few brief years. Unlike his friend and sometime collaborator Raymond Pettibon, Kelley was not content to leave its memory under the sign of murderous corruption and death. Indeed, he lodged his own protest in 1992 (noted in the Prologue) against the willed forgetting of the counterculture by the "advanced" critics and historians of visual art: "Contemporary American art history is spookily aligned with Reagan/Bush ideology. By excising artworks from the 1960s that mirror the social and political upheavals and countercultural activities of the period, or focusing on works primarily in the formalist tradition, an unspoken alliance is forged with the conservatives: both agree that these unsavory issues are not appropriate for art, and thus for society."[34] That verdict still applies, and one route toward its rectification lies in revisiting Kelley's life and career with exactly that thought in mind.

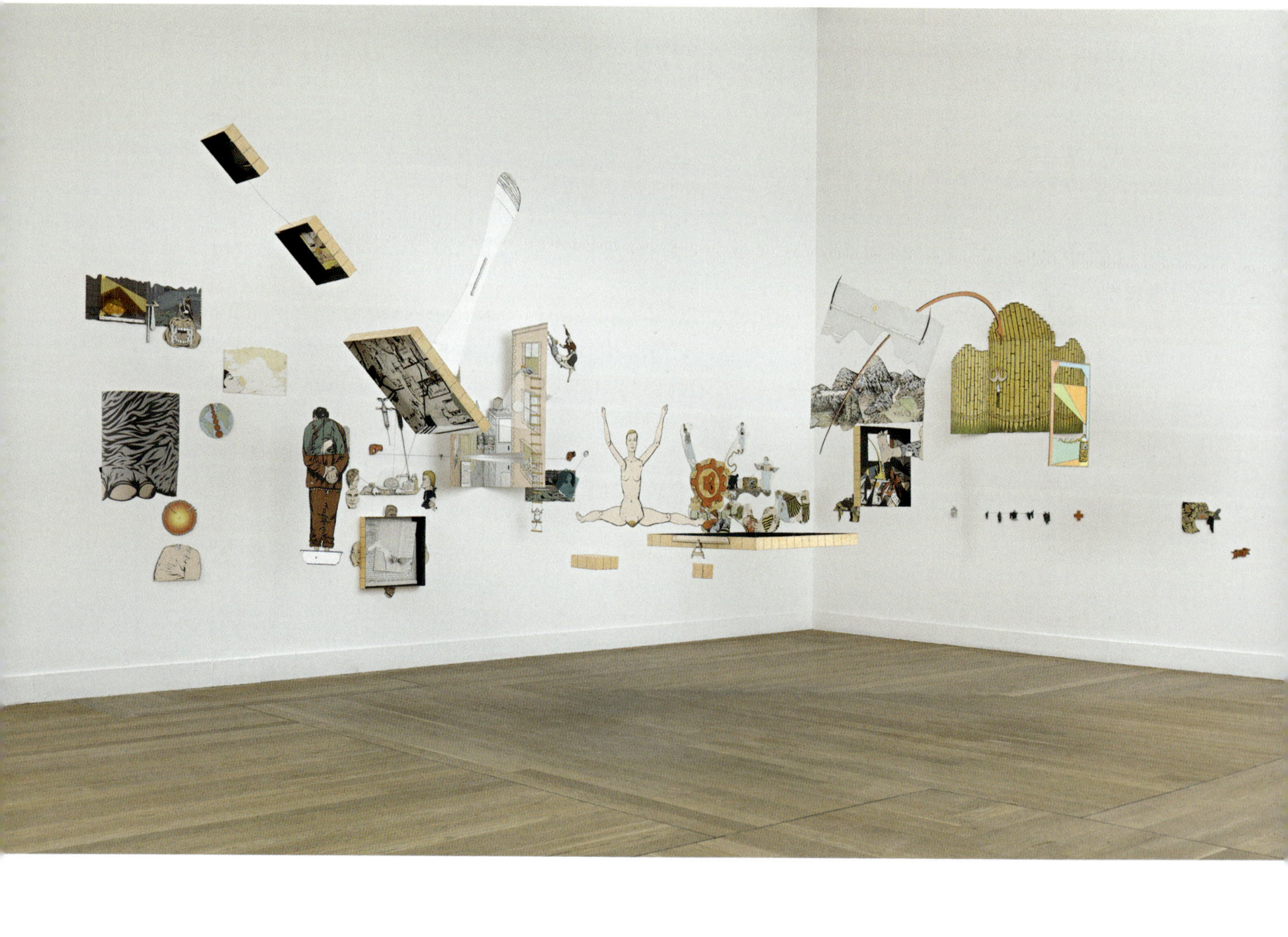

**126** Öyvind Fahlström, *Dr. Schweitzer's Last Mission*, 1965–66, tempera on eight metal boxes, ten cut-out boards, fifty magnetic metal and vinyl cut-outs, 450 × 1020 × 225 cm

TWELVE

# LAST ARTIST OF THE COUNTERCULTURE

"So we beat on, boats against the current, borne back ceaselessly into the past." It seems worth hazarding a literary commonplace to invoke the elegiac concluding sentence of *The Great Gatsby* as a point of entry to the art of Mike Kelley. The line lends appropriate elevation to Kelley's unwillingness ever to let anything go, to his being among the most parsimonious of artists in the way that materials from one project carry over to others until their usefulness might be exhausted—a point that never seems to arrive. An underlying logic and pattern of development persisted over drastic changes in the outward appearances of Kelley's art, from his student works through the physically ambitious, internationally celebrated work of his late career.

His arresting body of writing testifies to the degree to which early memories occupied his thought and made themselves felt in his art. And these are typically unsparing in detailing episodes of failure and embarrassment. One poignant example concerns an invitation he extended, while a student at the University of Michigan School of Art in the mid-1970s, to the Swedish-Brazilian painter and installation pioneer Öyvind Fahlström. A tireless satirist of American Cold War overreach, long resident in New York, Fahlström adapted an eclectic Pop repertoire to sprawling arrangements of silhouetted panels and miscellaneous flotsam (fig. 126). Kelley's tale, as he recounted it in 1995, is one of his own humiliation from beginning to end, as he describes the visit by Fahlström to the Ann Arbor campus, one that Kelley had initiated after encountering the older artist on a trip to New York. He receives minimal support from the School of Art, so must make do from his own meager resources, starting with the rusted-out wreck of a car, with a hole in floor on the passenger side, he is forced to use in meeting Fahlström at the Detroit airport. The rest of the visit, including the sparsely attended artist talk, proceeds in much the same vein of mortifications and mishaps, leavened by one telling bright spot: Fahlström leaves behind in a bar a book of Sylvia Plath's poetry densely annotated with his comments and sketches; when they return hours later, they find the precious volume just where it had been left; "truly a miracle!" Kelley proclaims. But overall, he concludes, "I was ashamed by how things turned out and never spoke to Fahlström again. He died of cancer seven months later."[1]

The vividness and elaboration of the story certainly justifies his appending it to a preceding appreciation of the qualities in Fahlström's work that prompted Kelley's first enthusiasm, as it offers a glimpse into his own convictions at the time of writing in the mid-1990s: "*Opera* was his model," Kelley proposes, "not only because it aspires to synthesis, but because it demonstrates the 'amorality' of art, its readiness to profit from and transform into art anything at all to stimulate and broaden our self-awareness . . . which in turn can or need not be made to serve a political end." He included among Fahström's operatic tendencies his indulgence in science fiction: elaborate "versions of the present illustrated in the terms of a parable." In this vein, Kelley was feeling the renewed force of Fahlström's lesson that the visual artist, like the composer or writer, "should make fewer, bigger, and more complete works."[2] And there is one further addendum to the essay, as Kelley ends the body of the text with a mystery-mongering poem from 1979, titled "The Realm of Myth" by Sun Ra, the visionary jazz musician and futuristically self-fashioned performer introduced at the close of the previous chapter.

Two of its inner stanzas read:

> Everything is of a particular science
> And myth is no exception
> Witness: "Science-fiction"
> . . .
>
> As a science Myth has many dimensions
> And many degrees
> Tomorrow is said to be a dimension of myth
> Or even the very realm of myth itself.[3]

In Kelley's own self-mythologizing, this invocation of Sun Ra (about whom more will emerge below) harks back to the same stage of life conjured up by the Fahlström anecdote:

> I decided to end . . . with a poem by Sun Ra because I have long commingled Falström's and Sun Ra's works in my mind. I discovered them around the same time and see many similarities between them. Both believe in synthesis, in complexity over simplicity, both have a disregard for a signature style; and both proclaim the importance of art as a force for changing consciousness and the world. Both believe that you should not talk down to your audience, yet both use popular modes of address that are radically transformed—perverted, you might say—to get the point across. To borrow a Sun Ra term, they are both "myth scientists" of the highest caliber.[4]

One could take most of this passage and substitute Kelley's first-person singular for the plural third-person pronouns; the result would be as accurate a self-description as he ever wrote, to wit: *I believe in synthesis, in complexity over simplicity . . . I have a disregard for a signature style*

*. . . I believe that you should not talk down to your audience . . . I use popular modes of address that are radically transformed—perverted, you might say—to get the point across.* But the abjection of the story of Fahlström's visit shadows this exaltation, the two extremes held in together in one brief moment of literary self-examination. As will emerge below, the date of this self-lacerating essay, 1995, proved a necessary moment for stocktaking on his part, one that entailed an imaginative transport back to the counterculture as most vividly recalled by the utopian pageantry of Sun Ra's performances and persona. While it may not be immediately obvious that Sun Ra represents such a countercultural touchstone, the Afro-Futurist icon forcibly and abundantly did so in Ann Arbor, Michigan, during the first half of the 1970s. How and why that came to be the case, alongside how and why Kelley came to resurrect that attachment two decades later, will emerge from even a brief account of his early life.

■

The journalist Charlie LeDuff, author of the 2013 *Detroit: An American Autopsy*, comes from Westland, the same suburb of that city as did Kelley. Though situated on the western fringe of the metropolitan area, the name of the town has another source: "Westland is a working class city, and the people there fully embrace their consumer culture," LeDuff relates; "As far as I know, Westland is the only city in the world that named itself after its shopping mall." Roughly a decade younger than the artist, LeDuff recalls his Westland surroundings as dramatizing the full fragility of that consumer-based optimism: "as it is with most things around here, the shopping mall is on the rocks, rundown and made more dismal by the empty storefronts surrounding it and the vacant lot where the Quo Vadis theater once stood."[5] As the larger part of that decay still lay on the horizon, a young Kelley would still have confronted, along with other males of his age, the career prospects of punishing factory or machine-shop work, though Kelley's father had sidestepped the industrial sector, rising from school custodian to janitorial supervisor for the local school district, while his mother worked in the kitchen of a nearby Ford Motor Company commissary. Their dual incomes, along with the male breadwinner's supervisory status, perhaps pointed toward higher aspiration. Even so, the young Kelley's entering the University of Michigan at Ann Arbor in 1972 represents a dramatic leap beyond the normal expectations of Westland. That campus may lie only some thirty miles beyond his family home, but the distance would have seemed far larger when measured in terms of life expectations.

For anyone raised in Michigan, admission to the main campus of the U of M was the functional equivalent to going to the Ivy League—East Coast college recruiters have historically expressed frustration at the difficulty of prying even the most able and affluent candidates away from the flagship university of their home state. Coming from the first generation in his household to seek a post-secondary degree, the more expected step for Kelley, as a bright student from his background, would have been either the more proximate, second-tier Eastern Michigan University or Wayne State in Detroit, with its large working-class and immigrant population. But the status of Ann Arbor appealed to what time would reveal to be Kelley's uncompromising educational ambition, as did its well-staffed and well-equipped School of Art.

That first significant step up the ladder of social and professional advancement, however, left him full of ambivalence, which he dramatized by playing up an identity as a despised outcast from the social hierarchy of the predominantly preppy student body. But he was taking the step, nonetheless, partaking in the apparatus of professional success by following a route designed to lead him away from the vocations and class identity assigned by his early upbringing. His coping strategy—knowingly acting the part of a rustic clown—might have led him no further than an ignominious dead end, had it not been for the fortuitous countercultural flowering in southeastern Michigan during the period just prior to the onset of his college years. It confirms the fractal character of the counterculture that only when coming to grips with an artist whose work came to flourish after 1980 does an overlooked dimension of a 1960s phenomenon come into focus, this being its necessary incorporation of Black liberation on a deep symbolic level—to which Kelley was both the witting and unwitting heir.

Telling this story requires introducing one further main character, that of the local poet and agitator John Sinclair, who personally galvanized what might have been a provincial afterthought without his presence; with it, the Detroit–Ann Arbor axis became the most vital countercultural crucible between the coasts. Sinclair's charisma as a poet stemmed in great part from his embrace of the most adventurous African American jazz as his chief theme and touchstone of profundity: "I came to Detroit in 1964," he later wrote, "as a refugee from white American society attracted to this teeming center of African-American culture. Detroit was the birthplace of the Nation of Islam and the hotbed of bebop, the place where you could hear jazz all night long and cop weed or pills whenever you wanted to."[6] The key date for Sinclair and his whole sensibility came in 1965, just on the cusp of both the wider anti-war and hippie movements, the moment when the John Coltrane Quartet released their album of summation, *A Love Supreme*. Before the travesty of the word in Love Generation ballyhoo, this confessional testament enjoyed an instant embrace by the advanced jazz world as a revelatory watershed, doubt and misfortune overcome on an ascending, Dante-like path to an epiphany of self-transcendence in divine love—albeit through music less beatific than that might imply, as it built toward a raw and urgent entreaty at its peak moments.

Coltrane had been through his own hell, wracked by alcohol and heroin addictions throughout the first decade of his playing career, which ended in 1957 with what he described as an overwhelming experience of inner conversion to higher purpose. Afterward, he abjured intoxicants and dedicated his playing to searching for some yet-veiled form of truth in his music. Second apprenticeships followed with Thelonious Monk and his old partner Miles Davis, as the trumpeter was replacing conventional chord and key changes with slowly shifting modal scales as the improvisor's foundation. From there, Coltrane as a leader seized these and greater liberties, even seeming to abandon his consummate command of his instrument, with overblown declamations and altissimo pleas punctuating extended, trancelike meditations, all with the aim of achieving a new sonics of testifying in the name of inner freedom. By so doing, he self-consciously channeled the Black liberation movements at home and among the emergent independent nations of Africa into the service of a fierce, inward overcoming of inherited American shackles.

The undiminished stature and galvanizing metaphysical force of *A Love Supreme* make its relative lack of prominence in the West Coast counterculture of the 1960s—along with the entire free-jazz movement—a striking occlusion. Small clubs of the Tenderloin and Western Addition in San Francisco had featured the most advanced jazz players since the dawn of bebop in the late 1940s, attracting avid followers among such bohemian intellectuals as the filmmaker Harry Smith. The jazz-loving Bill Graham, the impresario of the Fillmore Auditorium, made efforts to program the groups of the reedmen Charles Lloyd and the late-blooming local John Handy; he would play *A Love Supreme* over the house P.A. as the audience was entering and leaving the hall. *Rolling Stone*'s founder and editor, Jann Wenner, would put Sun Ra on its cover. But the overall whiteness of the hippie milieu, along with its dancing imperative, made their complexities of harmony and rhythm an exceptional sidebar to the various four-to-the-bar permutations of blues-rock.

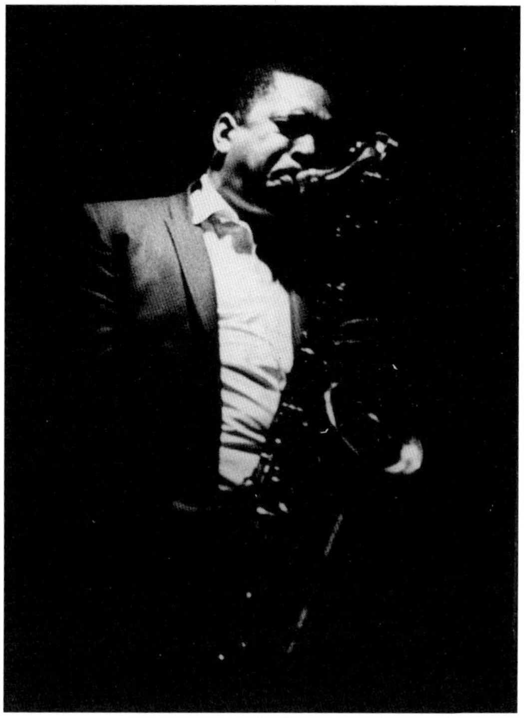

**127** John Coltrane in performance at the Drome Lounge on Dexter Avenue in Detroit in August 1966, photograph by Leni Sinclair

Thanks to Sinclair, this bifurcation proved far less the case in Detroit. In his 1965 chapbook titled *This Is Our Music*, he is credited with being the first to dedicate a poem to Coltrane—a task to which he returned at greater length in the year of the musician's premature death in 1967, alongside paeans to a range of comparable players in the orbit of the late saxophonist.[7] Such homages made eminent sense in a city overflowing with talented Black musicians, among them Coltrane's own drummer Elvin Jones[8] (the pop records issued by Motown owe their rich and inventive instrumental textures to the competitive skills honed by jazz players recruited by the label for studio duty). The photographs of Leni Sinclair, Sinclair's wife, thread through this chapter as only a small sample of her extraordinary visual record of civil rights and anti-war militancy, with accompanying radical music and experimental modes of life that took root and flowered in southeastern Michigan during this period.[9] She caught Coltrane's spot-lit transport when his quartet visited Detroit in 1966 (fig. 127); a companion shot on longer exposure transforms his physical body and horn into an incandescent pattern of fugitive, kinetic traces.[10]

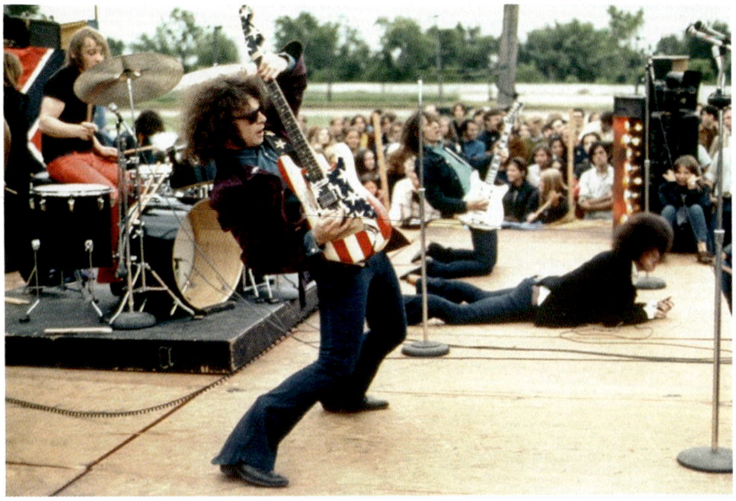

**128** The MC5, Mount Clemens, Michigan, 1969, photograph by Leni Sinclair

Indeed, the Sinclairs were late in coming around to the rock idiom that seemed so natural to the West Coast. When the members of the local group MC5 (MC for Motor City) were angling for the poet's support, they succeeded by working out their own arrangements of compositions by Coltrane, the free-jazz exponent Albert Ayler, or Sun Ra, while combining these musical exertions with a political militancy likewise in keeping with Sinclair's. The outcome proved as overpowering a brand of electric rock as any then going. "Total assault on the culture by any means necessary" had become the Sinclair mantra, and the MC5 defined their music in the same grandiose terms, missing few opportunities to drive the point home on stage—as Leni Sinclair would regularly be there to record (fig. 128)—incessantly regaling their young audiences with the powerful if non-specific exhortation to "Kick out the Jams!"

Under vicious pressure from law-enforcement agencies, the Sinclairs shifted operations to the temporarily more sheltered university town of Ann Arbor. With its central history in the New Left—Students for a Democratic Society and the egalitarian ideals enunciated in its 1962 Port Huron Statement had arisen there, with the first anti-war teach-in following in 1965—Ann Arbor lent a greater political focus to the near-manic level of activity John Sinclair pursued under the Coltranesque rubric Trans-Love Energies.[11] Alongside Black music, he sought in 1968 explicitly to channel the example set by the Black Panthers in politics and community organization. His self-proclaimed White Panther Party was to be "the voice of the lumpen hippie, just like the Black Panther Party was the voice of the lumpen proletariat—which means working class without jobs."[12] And true to that spirit, the MC5 was the only band brave enough actually to set up and play at the 1968 demonstrations outside the Democratic Convention in Chicago.

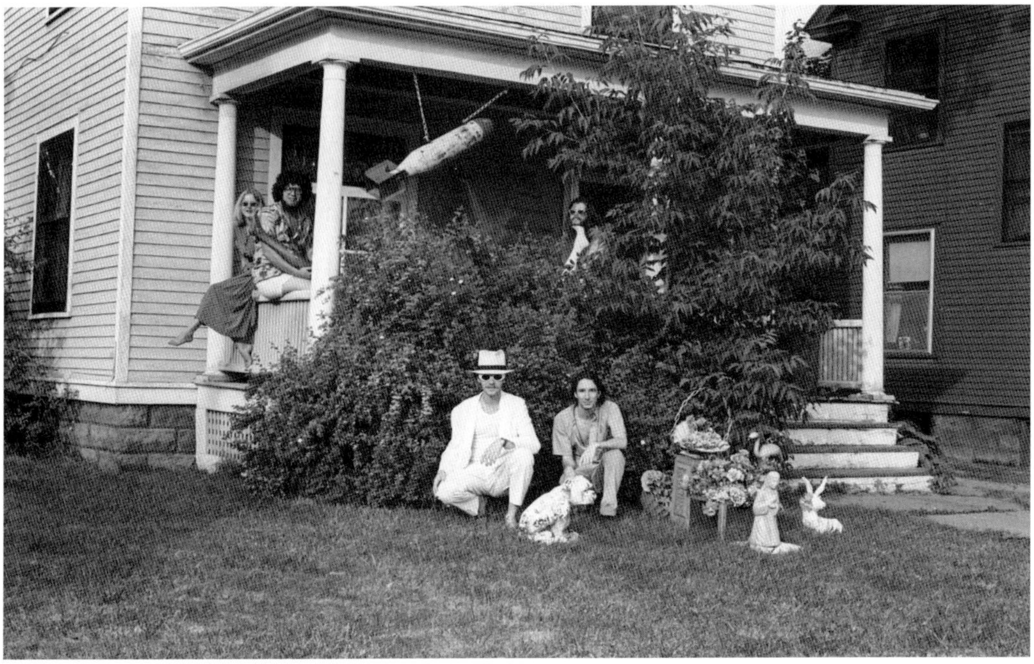

**129** God's Oasis, Mike Kelley's shared Ann Arbor house, from the *Ann Arbor News*, Wednesday, 23 June 1976. Pictured from left: Marju Nemvaltz, Rick Greenvald, and Jim Shaw on the porch; David Owen and Kelley on lawn

Trans-Love Energies undertook management of the MC5 and by 1969 was shepherding the career of no less an act than Sun Ra and the Solar Arkestra. For a time, indeed, the entire ensemble moved in with the Trans-Love commune in a one of the large houses they were renting on Hill Street, Ann Arbor's fraternity row.[13] This conjunction ultimately brought the great Afro-Futurist and his resplendent ensemble into the overawed view of a young Mike Kelley. His friend and collaborator, the artist John Miller, ascribes a formative force to this locally intensified variant of the larger counterculture, stating categorically that Kelley's "practice can be construed as an outgrowth of the carnivalesque youth and countercultures of the 1960s and 70s, exemplified by the Diggers, the Yippies, Sun Ra or John Sinclair's White Panther Party."[14] In light of his apartness from conventional collegiate life, this exceptionally intensified local counterculture, with its more diffused climate of friendly nonconformity and refusal of bourgeois decorum, offered essential support for Kelley's disheveled and alienated public persona (fig. 129). In the intervening years, the town had become a magnet for young vagabonds in hippie garb, a milieu where, by appearance and taste, the young Kelley could readily blend in.

The Psychedelic Stooges, the band formed by the Ann Arbor native Iggy Pop (James Osterberg), held particular appeal by adhering to the most rudimentary level of musical proficiency and thereby releasing an unrelenting, pulsing racket in performance. Free-jazz performances, despite the advanced skills of the players, could sound to the uninitiated ear like chaotic cacophony, a Sinclair-approved effect that validated Michigan rockers like the Stooges in the unleashing of their punishingly industrial noise. The previous chapter crossed Iggy's path at a later period, during his strung-out, mid-1970s sojourn on the Sunset Strip in Los Angeles; but Kelley had caught him in the first blush of local success. Nicknamed for his having once played drums in a band called the Iguanas, Iggy, along with the three backing Stooges, came from the same fringe-middle-class, southeastern Michigan environment as had Kelley, his pale German-immigrant stock the counterpart to Kelley's Irish-immigrant forbears. The young artist's enthusiasm could only have been reinforced by the enduring celebration of Iggy written by the critic Lester Bangs in the fledgling Detroit rock paper *Creem* in 1971, one that resonates with Kelley's cognate self-presentations down the years: "clawing at himself, smashing the mike in his chops, jumping into the crowd to wallow around a forest of legs and ankles and god knows what else while screaming those sickening songs about TV eyes and feeling like dirt and having no fun 'cause you're a fucked up adolescent, horny but neurotic, sitting around bored and lonesome and unable to communicate with yourself or anybody else."[15] Kelley duly joined with Jim Shaw and other artist friends to form their own band, calling themselves Destroy All Monsters after a schlock Japanese horror film. This undertaking surpassed the Stooges along one vector by making no pretense of musicality whatsoever, noise and outrageous performance on absurd "instruments" being its primary purpose (though they later recruited the Stooge guitarist Ron Asheton for some performances).[16]

As observed above, Kelley's written appreciations of other artists regularly function in an allegorical fashion to describe components of his own self-conscious ambitions. Thus, an essay by Kelley of 1991 anticipated his joining of Fahlström and Sun Ra by doing the same with Iggy Pop. He recounts an ordeal of punishing weather and menacing bikers who frequented the venue where Iggy and the Stooges happened to be performing. Feeling anxious as a skinny longhair in hostile territory, he witnessed Iggy wind up the crowd with antics intended to aggravate its antipathies to a breaking point: a theater of provocation with which the young artist had every reason to identify: "He played the audience like fish . . . They would suffer insult after insult, have their faces rubbed over and over again in their own complicity and come running back for more . . . a big biker shouted 'Hey, Poodle Boy,' and hit Iggy with an egg. The next thing I saw was Iggy doing a belly flop into the audience, and then a riot broke out."[17]

Leni Sinclair, well acquainted with Iggy, could portray him as fresh-faced and cheerfully accessible;[18] but on stage (fig. 130) just as demonically possessed and canine-coiffed as he comes across in Kelley's tale, which the artist joins to an extended description of Sun Ra and his ensemble (fig. 131) performing at the regionally renowned Ann Arbor Jazz and Blues

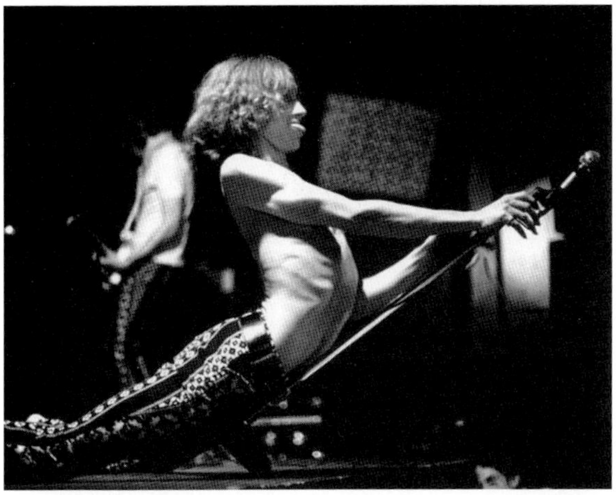

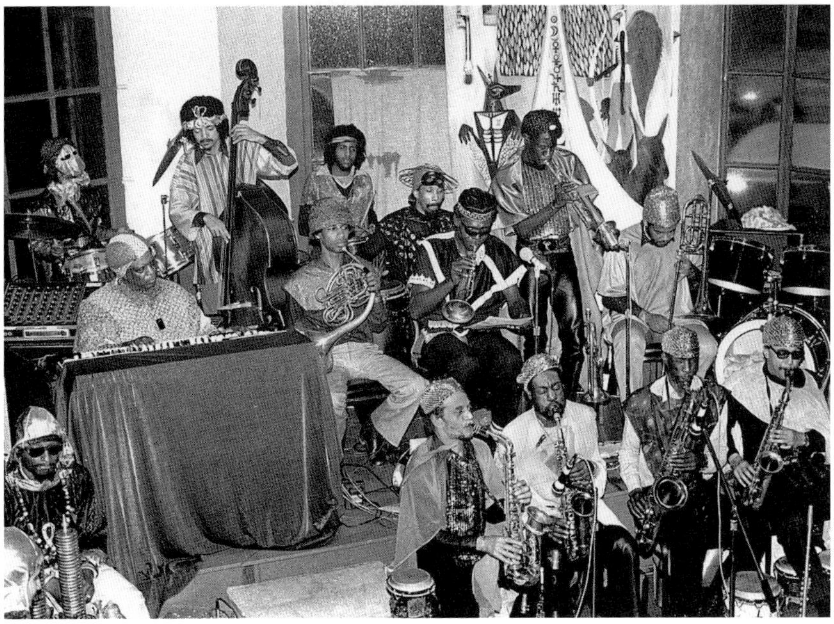

**130 (TOP)** Iggy Pop, c. 1969, photograph by Leni Sinclair

**131** The Sun Ra Arkestra at the Detroit Jazz Center, 31 December 1979 in Detroit, photograph by Leni Sinclair

Festival (very much in the vein of Senga Nengudi's encomium quoted in the previous chapter. By his own account, Kelley attended many concerts in the thriving Detroit–Ann-Arbor musical axis, but these two are virtually the only ones he chose to recount in print: on one side, the lean, bleached-white performance of Iggy's "moronic, contorted dancing," as Kelley put it, against the immobile human backdrop of the other Stooges; on the other, the sprawling, resplendent, multihued, musical and visual cornucopia of Sun Ra's Solar Arkestra. In

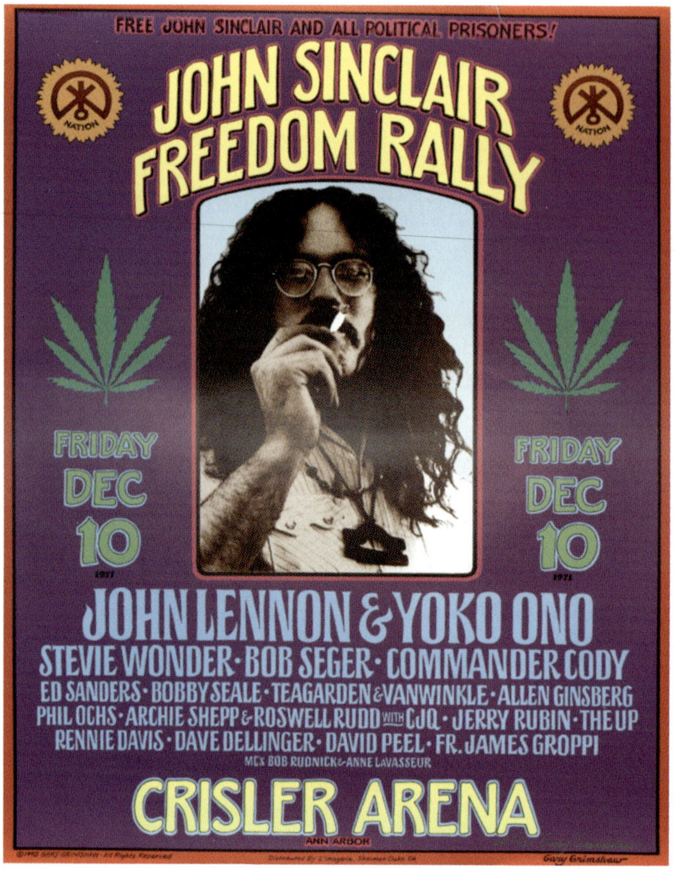


**132** Gary Grimshaw, poster for the John Sinclair benefit concert, Ann Arbor, 1971

tandem, they point up the importance of Ann Arbor as the epicenter of the counterculture for the entire middle of the country and the crucible, in its late stages, for Kelley's discovery of an artist's vocation. But the pathos of that discovery lay in that countercultural arena suffering an eclipse even before he arrived on the scene.

Unfortunately for Sinclair and several of his closest associates, officialdom from the Ann Arbor Police all the way up to J. Edgar Hoover and Richard Nixon took their incendiary White Panther rhetoric as a serious, armed anarchist threat. The core members of Trans-Love Energies were soon in prison on various trumped-up charges, Sinclair famously sentenced in 1969 to ten years in prison for giving three joints to an undercover narc.[19] "Free John!" the campaign for his release, assumed dimensions commensurable with the actual Panthers' "Free Huey!" and "Free Bobby!" campaigns, undertakings touched on in chapter 8 above, with Sinclair's culminating in the famous benefit rally, headlined by John Lennon and Yoko Ono, along with Ann Arbor-born Bob Seger and Motown's Stevie Wonder (no less), with Bobby Seale himself winding up the crowd, which filled the university's Crisler Arena in December 1971 (fig. 132).

For its part, Destroy All Monsters acted out on the level of representation an elegy for those recently passed glories, as did the posters, graphics, and paintings that Kelley and the group produced as a visual penumbra to their performances. "It was connected," he observed in retrospect, "with the death of radical popular music in the late 1960s, with the death of left politics in general, and with the huge economic crash of the 1970s."[20] These became the watchwords for his art making to the end of his life.

■

In his actual studies and production of art, Kelley maintained his uncultivated side with no suspicion of pretense, while at the same time embracing his artistic vocation with fierce application and pride, driven by sheer ability that he could not in good faith deny. The music critic Carl Wilson has written that there is "a talent to having talent and living with it. Talent can seem like an alien invasion of the self, a kind of parasite that requires its host to do things it might not otherwise do."[21] Driving Kelley was the need to serve the talent he possessed, the thing that made him a born artist, someone who could not *not* have been an artist. And in that service, he would leave his social class behind, at least in empirical terms, but would not in the process place himself above his Westland origins. In the face of teaching regimes that grated on his defiant sense of distance from either a cultivated bourgeoisie or a complacent bohemia, he held to his janitor-father's station in life and brandished the signs of the class outsider in nearly all of his art. To that end, the commonplace motifs that Pop art had successfully glamourized needed to be replaced by matter so despised as to thwart upwardly mobile assimilation, from inept adolescent notebook scribblings to the earnest amateurism of Sunday painters to the cultish grotesquerie of the illustrator Basil Wolverton to the Zap Comix stable of cartoonists, who had provided the counterculture with raw satirical exposure to the most unsavory implications of personal liberation. These he combined in a cycle of small paintings in which such disgraced artifacts keep uncomfortable company with abstractly painted passages cribbed from the repertoire of properly abstract painting that he had mastered in his schooling (fig. 133).

It comes as no surprise that he would categorize his demotic visual repertoire under the rubric of "the repressed," which spoke both to its invisibility in the face of the legitimating judgment of the art world and to his own need perpetually to excavate and put on display his most socially disreputable attachments. More profoundly for Kelley, the fate of this cultural refuse paralleled the repression suffered by the liberating energies of the Ann Arbor counterculture, which had put an end to his direct participation in it. The full force of the concept's Freudian implications would subsequently enter into his thinking, but that would follow from the next and equally crucial stage in his educational attainments.

■

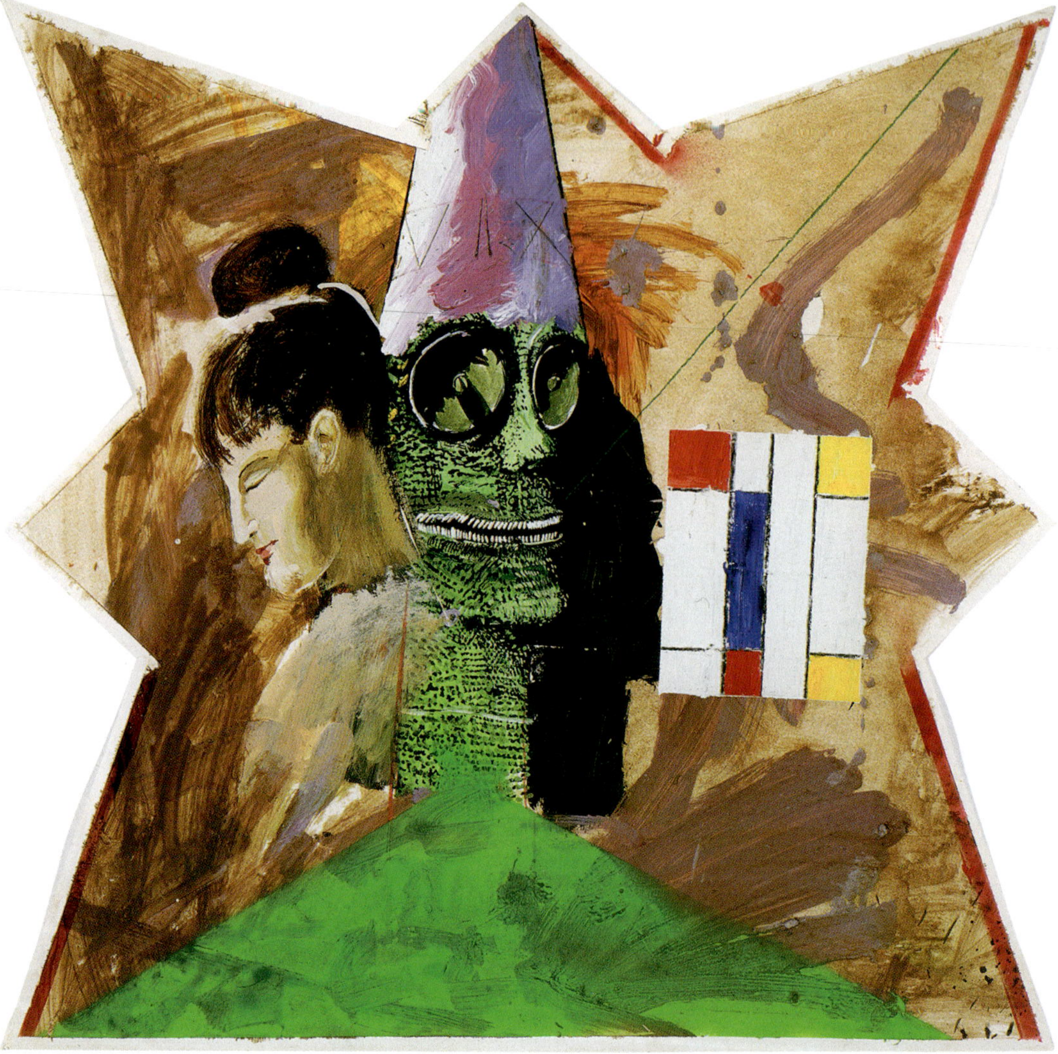

**133** Mike Kelley, *Painting with Hawaiian Mask, Ballerina, and De Stijl Painting*, 1976, mixed media on paper, 61 × 61 cm, private collection

As Kelley's ambitions for his talent rightfully knew no bounds, the best that Michigan had to offer was never going to be enough. Having attained the Midwestern equivalent to the Ivy League, he successfully set his sights on a graduate equivalent of MIT for the fine arts—the distant Valencia campus of California Institute of the Arts. Having disdainfully absorbed the traditional training he never stopped railing against, he advanced himself to an institution innovating a new model of art training, one almost technocratic in its orientation toward cerebral inquiry and research into the fundamental nature of art. While Kelley implicitly embraced that ethos, it was entirely in character that he chose as his work-study assignment to supervise the institute's wood shop, thereby keeping himself as close to basic skills and matter as he could possibly stay. Art-school carpentry would have been close in its range of tools and machinery to those to be found in the garage of any well-equipped hobbyist back in Westland, an implied persona readily imaginable as a school janitor on his day off.

For his master's degree exhibition, Kelley duly applied himself to a series of sculptures that aped the characteristic pastimes of just such an amateur: a series of small sculptures in the shapes of distorted wooden birdhouses. The aviary motif carries overtones of a tranquil natural harmony, which dovetails with themes of shelter, refuge, and home, all condensing around the pastoral poet's idea of untroubled simplicity of life and closeness to nature as antidotes to the anxieties that accompany higher cultivation of manners and intellect. Later configurations of the birdhouse sculptures, however, make their satisfactory occupation doubtful and imply a troubled dimension of perversity in their implied maker. In the pediment of the 1978 *Catholic Birdhouse* (fig. 134) harking back to his early education by nuns, the small upper hole for the righteous bird—labeled *The Hard Road*—bears the penitential marks of tortured efforts at entry. He inscribed the large, unmarked hole below *The Easy Road*. With Kelley's widened circle of fame in his late career, these outwardly modest, folk-like sculptures have begun receiving their share of critical attention, the relative simplicity of their geometric volumes regularly prompting analogies with the high-minded austerity of geometric form in Minimalist sculpture as exemplified in the 1960s by Donald Judd and the early works of Robert Morris.

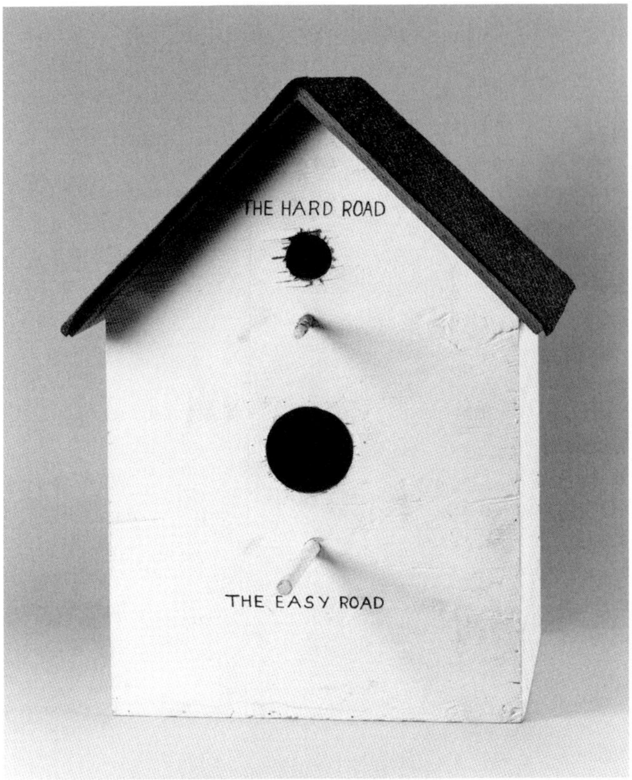


**134** Mike Kelley, *Catholic Birdhouse*, 1978, wood, paint, and composite shingles, 60 × 47 × 47 cm, private collection

One can wonder, however, just how challenged Kelley would have felt by Minimalism, in that its heyday as an aesthetic standard lay more than a decade in the past. Having become in Kelley's eyes an effective caricature of itself, it was Minimalism that needed its dignity restored if it were to serve him as a "legitimizing façade, concealing what is . . . an image of low intent masquerading in heroic garb."[22] Nor did this "historical referencing to reductivist paradigms," as Kelley continued in impeccable, received jargon, begin to exhaust his

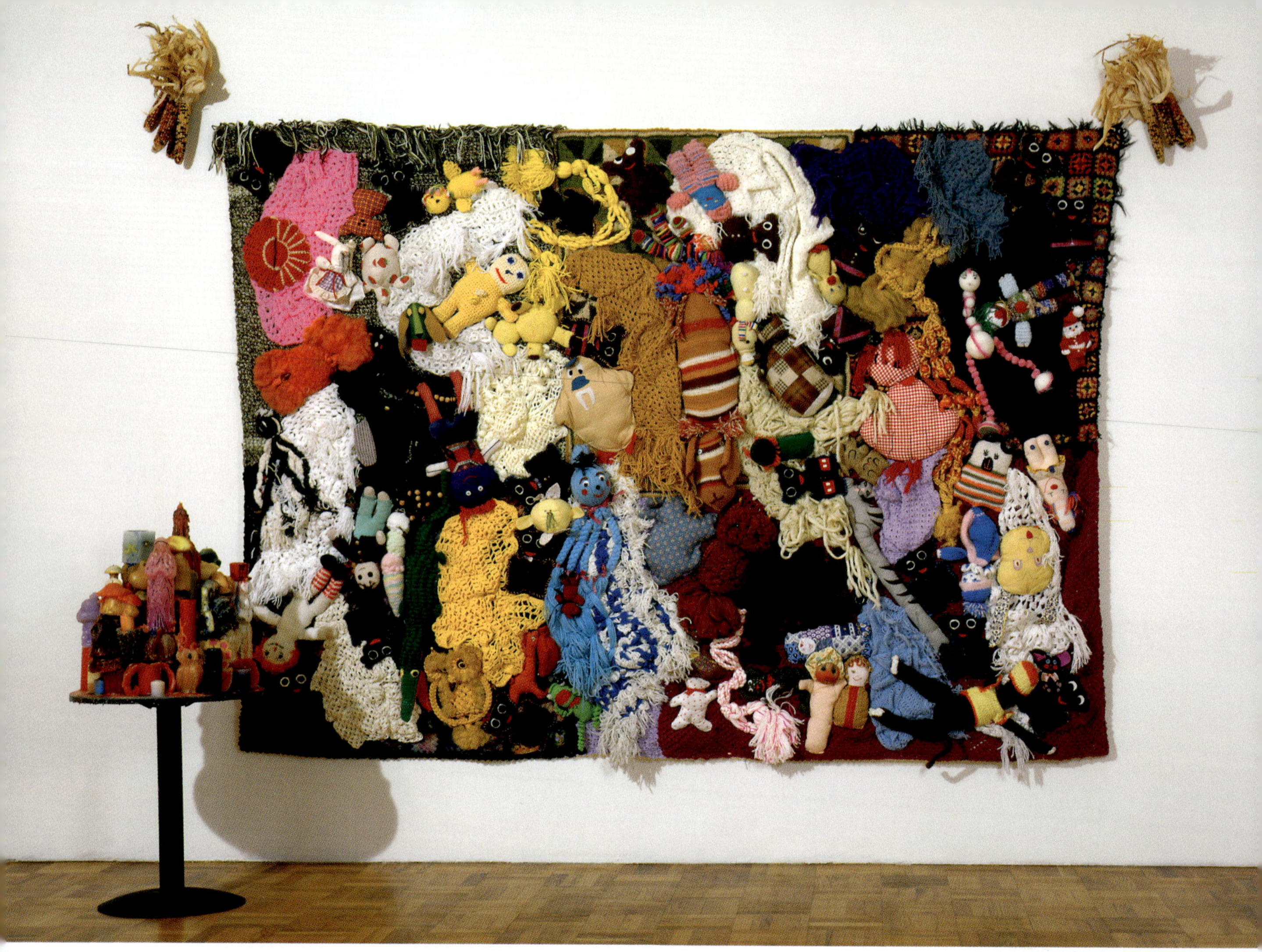

**135** Mike Kelley, *More Love Hours Than Can Ever Be Repaid* and *The Wages of Sin*, 1987, 2 parts: found handmade stuffed animals and afghans on canvas with dried corn; wax candles on wood and metal base 244 × 322.6 × 15 cm and 132 × 58.4 × 58.4 cm, Whitney Museum of American Art, New York

jousting with the lofty concepts at play in the art world.[23] More current at the onset of the 1980s were critical celebrations of art held to expose or demystify the "commodity" status of objects that circulated in the art market and, by extension, the grip that seductive goods for sale maintained on the inner lives of contemporary consumers. But this was never Kelley's attitude, unimpressed as he was by the doyen of this tendency, Hans Haacke, whose work he dismissed as "academic Puritan agitprop."[24] By the later years of that decade, he had set about calling this orthodoxy to account in perhaps his most famous series of works, ones he assembled from knitted children's toys.

In order to gather the material for these pieces, he enlisted friends to help him scour the second-hand outlets of Glendale and Pasadena in search of discarded crocheted dolls and

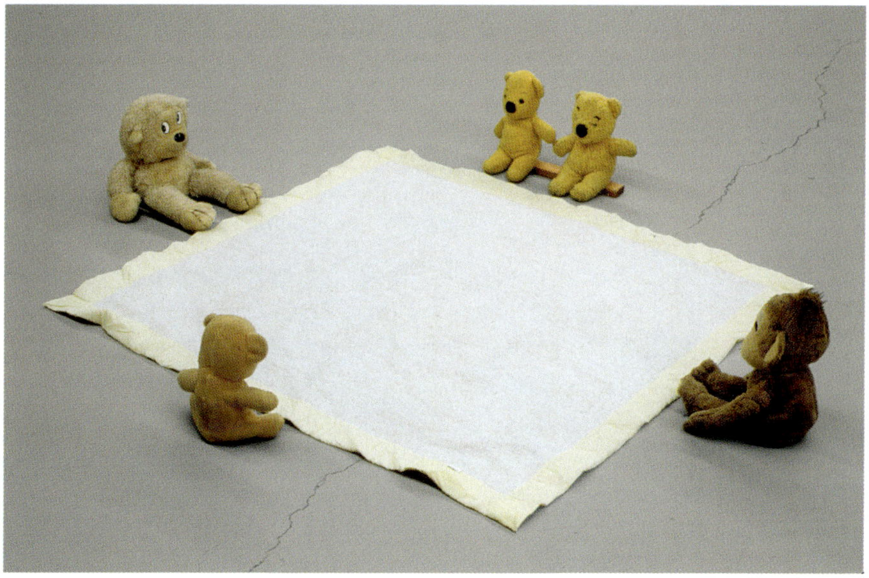

**136** Mike Kelley, *Arena #7 (Bears)*, 1990,
found stuffed animals and blanket,
29.2 × 134.6 × 124.5 cm, private collection

stuffed animals (fig. 135). Many of these objects would have been irreplaceable handmade gifts that time and growing up had rendered into worn and soiled waste objects of next to no market value. These Kelley began assembling into configurations that aped, as had the Birdhouses, high-minded art formats. *More Love Hours Than Can Ever Be Repaid*, mimics a large-scale painting of turbulently dense and abstract forms. Dissatisfied, however, with the way that this approach suppressed the individual outlines of the toys, he began to arrange them, now favoring structured commercial figures that could stand unsupported, into clarified installations around blankets resting on the floor: the Arenas (fig. 136). For all the apparent directness of these arrangements, however, Kelley's move in this direction, he reported, aroused responses of greater intensity than any of his provocations had ever encountered before, an inchoate anxiety that far exceeded the apparent modesty of the provocation. Blotting out the other associations occasioned by these bedraggled child-surrogates, including disgust at their unsanitary appearance, were feelings arising from contemporaneous panics over the sexual abuse of children.

A significant part of this phenomenon, of course, lay in genuine comprehension of widespread crimes, obscured in the past by taboos surrounding the subject and by automatic deference to culpable figures in positions of authority. But boundaries between fact and fantasy were difficult to maintain, as Kelley had no trouble recognizing. The locally explosive trial in Los Angeles of the innocent McMartin family—subjected from 1983 to accusations of abuse at their pre-school, which became increasingly outlandish and improbable as the near-decade-long trial proceeded—impressed him with the scientific gloss given to paranoid witch-hunting. Central to the effort was a new class of expert in "recovered memory syndrome," one who claimed the ability to expose memories of abuse so traumatic that their patients had reacted with involuntary amnesia.[25] Kelley possessed sufficient command of psychoanalytic theory to differentiate the Freudian concept of repression, one in which trauma and fantasy are intermingled, from this new application for the purposes of establishing forensic truth (that having been Freud's original error). The therapist, irrespective of prejudice or self-interest, became the guarantor of veracity through the mouth of the child.

Sensationalist exploitation of such cases in the news and entertainment media was, as Kelley saw it, upending priority given to verifiable observation in favor of what could not be seen. Here was the esoteric psychological concept of repression itself becoming a prime topic for manufactured mass consciousness and spurious notions of reality. But the timing of the soft-toy works, even if initially motivated by the commodity-fetish zeitgeist in the high-art world, threatened him with becoming an abettor of this lumpen abuse panic. What was more, he attested, those who saw or even heard about the Arenas assumed that they were confessional in nature, that he was alluding to his own abuse as a child. Kelley's response was not to contest this insinuation directly, but rather to claim the themes of repression and lost memory for his own purposes, superimposing them onto his master narrative of the repression suffered by the radical impulses liberated during the heyday of the counterculture.

■

As his first vehicle in this quest, Kelley returned to the bleached, quasi-architectural vocabulary of the CalArts Birdhouses. Among their references had been a subtle evocation of the white, corporate-modernist character of the structure that housed the school itself (there was a persistent urban legend among the students that the building had been designed so that, should the school fail, it could be re-purposed as a mental institution). By the late 1980s, the fact that the building featured several basement levels—where the bulk of the instruction and student work took place—had gained a correspondence by analogy to the non-existent basement under the McMartin pre-school, the fictitious setting for the most extreme of the induced memories among the student "witnesses." An effigy of CalArts assumed a culminating position in the 1995 work Kelley titled the *Educational Complex* (fig. 137), an elaborate set of architectural models on a Frank Gehry-like plywood platform, purporting to represent every institution of learning through which he had passed. And the themes that guided the subsequent unfolding of his shortened career revolve around this central project. He stated he had recovered from his own memories the plans for each miniaturized replica, which were then fabricated and assembled in pristine, white-painted foamcore with a team of able student assistants. He left blank any space or feature he could not remember, thus displacing the McMartin drama of repression and recovery from the news cycle to his own life, sublimating the intimacy of a doll (so often used to coax associations out of young patients) to

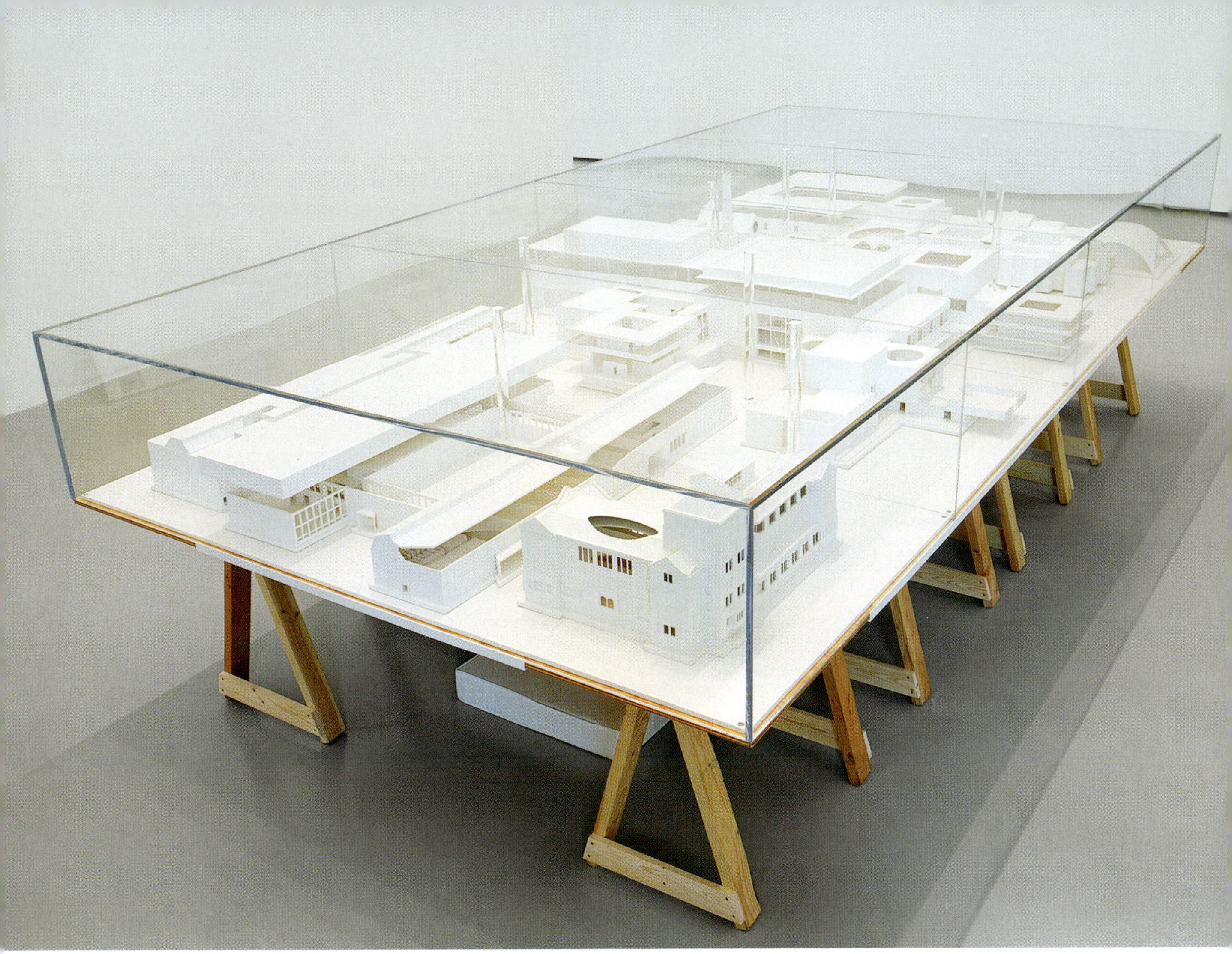

**137** Mike Kelley, *Educational Complex*, 1995, Painted foam core, fiberglass, plywood, wood, plexiglass, and mattress, 46.7 × 488.2 × 244.2 cm, Whitney Museum of American Art, New York

the seemingly impersonal, masculine-coded vocabulary of architecture, but in a way that ineluctably calls to mind the adjective "clinical."

The first and smallest of the structures represents the Kelley family house in Westland. The peculiar oculus in its incongruously large pediment brings the model into close visual alignment with the characteristic round opening of a Birdhouse, revealing a depth in his degree project that few could have perceived in 1978. His parochial and secondary schools are naturally present, as are the art-school buildings (old and new) at the University of Michigan. The quality and prestige of his higher education remained for him evident sources of pride, as he regularly insisted upon his standing as a highly trained professional artist; while the home

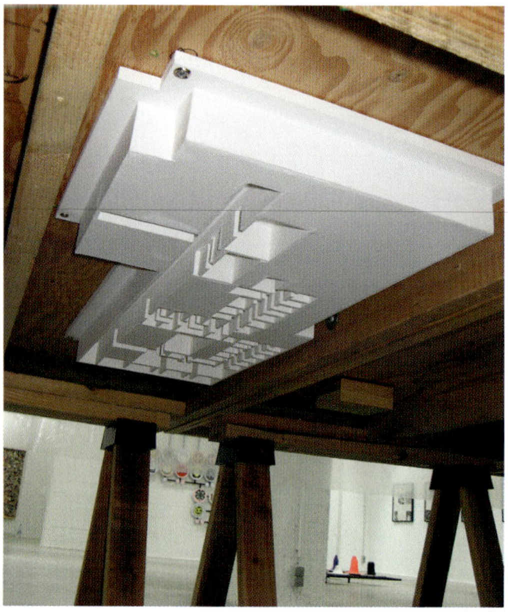

138 View of the CalArts sublevel model located on the underside of the base supporting Mike Kelley's *Educational Complex*, 1995

and Westland schools stand as the sources of the common knowledge and folklore he never subordinated to his higher learning. The model of CalArts mediates between the two registers of learning, its appearance above grade resembling a technological thinktank, its multiple basement levels visible only to those viewers willing to abase themselves by crawling onto a mattress underneath the trestle stand of the platform (fig. 138).

If Kelley had made art that was single-mindedly about his alien, working-class status in the elite stratum of art, the result would have been diverting but one-dimensional. Likewise, any wholehearted embrace of his achieved professional status at the expense of his working-class formation would have been shallow and unseemly. *Educational Complex* diverts the commonplaces about occluded memories toward reconciling this received disjunction within what amounts to an allegorical self-portrait and autobiography. Having accomplished this task, however, did its maker draw the conclusion that this intensely worked, apparently consummating artwork relax too much of the tension between these two poles? Its date of 1995 returns the present account to its beginning, to the forceful re-emergence of Fahlström and Sun Ra into his pre-occupations, both of them masters of expansive abundance, riots of texture, color, and mythic imagery. Such stock-taking entailed his internal pilgrimage back to the time of his own direct participation at the epicenter of the Midwestern counterculture, a mutually dependent convergence between an august institution of higher learning and networks of drugs, protest, and body-shaking music. That memory of carnival presented itself as the necessary, complementary alternative to the whited sepulchers of his latest magnum opus.

■

As Kelley could readily perceive at that juncture, the demands entailed in the making of major art had undergone a change. If not in ways that he applauded, these shifts posed an unavoidable challenge if he were to maintain his visibility and concede no ground to more facile competitors. Half a world away from Los Angeles, the young Damien Hirst was painfully learning how to marshal his own recalcitrant materials of steel, structural glass, formaldehyde, and animal carcasses into a sculptural version of mystifying special effects. Prior to this undertaking, Hirst had been working in the Anthony d'Offay Gallery in London, representatives of Gerhard Richter at the time the German artist was moving toward assembly-line production of his wall-filling abstract canvases, concocted from randomized simulations of expressive paint handling. Jeff Koons had shown the way to hyper-competent outsourcing of fabrication with the "Banality" series of 1988 but had temporarily faltered with "Made in Heaven" during the early 1990s, leaving a door open for the likes of Hirst and Takashi Murakami to take the model further. Post-1995, Kelley confronted this changed landscape, understanding its competitive implications if he was to hold his place at the level of recognition to which his ineluctable talent had propelled him.

The *Educational Complex* taught him what it took to pull off cognate effects of manufactured perfection that depend on expert technical assistance directed at one remove. The invaluable John Miller, an artist and a close friend of Kelley, has pieced together a detailed account of how *Educational Complex* was put together by trial and error with the aid of tireless assistants, a messy process that belies the immaculate impression conveyed by the achieved installation.[26] The rival artists adduced above, however, were surpassing this trial-and-error stage, scaling up to large factory operations, staffed with numerous assistants, and calling, where necessary, on the expertise of expensive engineers and fabricators. If lacking Kelley's ultimate depth, these were all estimable artists who had reached an astute reckoning with the changed character of the art profession. As mega-wealthy collectors like François Pinault and Eli Broad came to dominate the upper end of the market, any artist in their sights had the choice of being a pawn or a peer. To treat with these collectors as an equal required conspicuous wealth and splendid outward display, which are the only attributes genuinely respected by the members of this new plutocratic sphere. Their achievement necessitated making and marketing exceptionally costly works with high visual impact, which in turn could not be manufactured without expensive labor, equipment, and physical spaces. Such terrain of enforced rivalry, however, with its forced proximity to obscene wealth, held patent dangers to the integrity of Kelley's enterprise. Hence his recourse to re-living the truths of his own underground existence in the waning days of the Ann Arbor counterculture, in particular the operatic vividness imprinted on him by Sun Ra's performances.

It took another decade for him to achieve the full realization of that return, a dizzying array of video productions set into sculptural frameworks, to each of which he gave the generic title *Extracurricular Activity Projective Reconstruction*, then grouped together under the collective rubric *Day Is Done* (fig. 139). The blank spaces that stood in *Educational Complex* for repressed memories he now filled with extruded riots of color, sound, and motion at life-sized human scale, overtly channeling the flamboyance of the Solar Arkestra via manic activity, swirling capes, exotic headgear, percussive music, and contrived, multicolored unreality—thus the opposite of the grim "truths" promised by recovered-memory therapies. Remaining in the sphere of institutionalized education, Kelley's "myth science" entailed translating anonymous found photographs from high-school yearbooks, souvenirs of enigmatic folk pageants and theatricals that Kelley had collected and filed under what he called "iconographic" categories: "Religious Performances, Thugs, Dance, Hick and Hillbilly, Halloween and Goth, Satanic, Mimes, and Equestrian Events [the last signifying

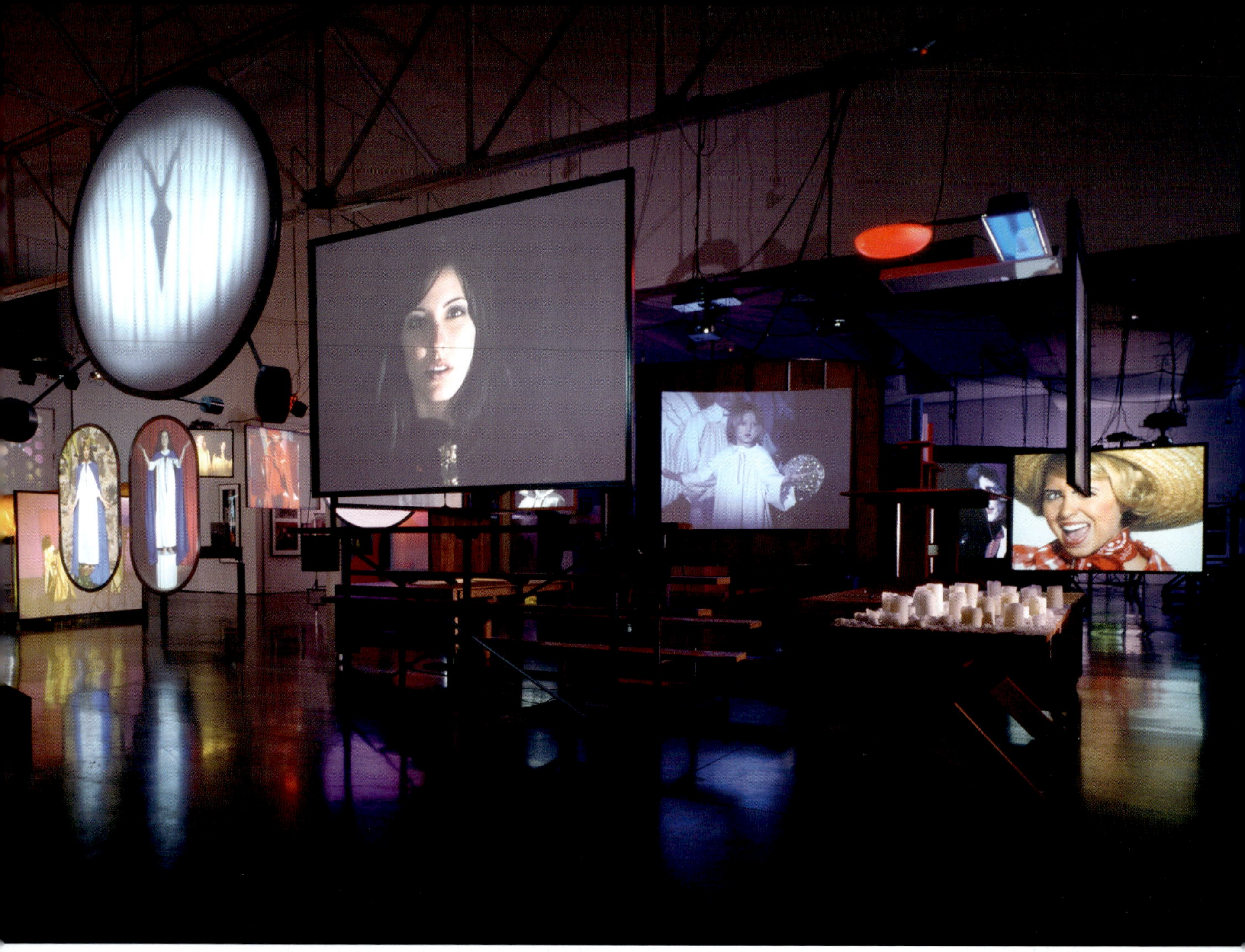

**139** Installation view, *Day Is Done,*
Gagosian Gallery, New York, New York, 2005

horse costumes]."[27] In his interpretation, "They are not standard school events, but carnivalesque events, symbolically at odds with the ordered world of education . . . unlike traditional sports activities, for example, which could be considered propagandistic events designed to inspire in the general population the values of group cooperation and the competitive spirit of capitalism." From the cues encoded in these arcane black-and-white images, he scripted extended performances with singing and speech, aspiring in each one to the highest available production values in the video medium; and in Hollywood these were both unsurpassed and available for hire.

Kelley's physical, imaginative, and capital investments in the production of thirty-two such scenarios—projected in shrine-like enclosures made from the props used in their production—were immense, abundantly fulfilling the dictum, derived from Fahlström, that the ideal artist "should make fewer, bigger, and more complete works." The pathos of the project lay in its being mounted only once as a total production, when all the parts were assembled in 2005 inside the largest of the Gagosian Gallery spaces in New York's Chelsea art district. Kelley called it "a kind of spatialized filmic montage: a feature-length film made up of multiple simultaneous and sequential scenes playing in architectural space." That actual experience of *Day Is Done* was all of that and more, but never to be repeated—as its elements were dispersed to various buyers, it became less and less possible to reassemble them, with only the single-channel video anthology of the individual scenarios remaining. No nonprofit venue stepped forward in time to prolong the life of the piece in its totality, not even in Los Angeles, which remained a deeply felt sore point with Kelley ever after.

■

In his ruminations of 1995, *Day Is Done* seems foretold in his invocation of Fahlström's art, pointing the way toward art more sprawling and splendid in character, approaching grand opera with Wagnerian primal landscapes populated by figures of myth. But the gods of Valhalla were not what he had in mind, as he seized on another consistent feature of the older artist's thematic repertoire: in Fahlström's example, Kelley notes, "Comic books offered a rich pictorial source reflecting contemporary mythologies, values, and belief systems in clear image tropes understandable to the public at large."[28] That might sound a hopefully populist note, but Kelley's way would be to seek out the arcane and inscrutable even in the most familiar of any such comic-art source, the DC Comics character Superman, a universally recognized figure, one who actually possesses what devotees seriously refer to as a "mythos." In his description of the project, Kelly sums up one of its more obscure corners, out of which he generated his last major artistic undertaking: "The popular Superman story recounts the adventures of an alien being sent to earth to survive the complete destruction of his home planet Krypton. . . . As the plot unfolds, it turns out that Kandor, Superman's city of birth (fig. 140), was not destroyed. It ends up in his possession, reduced in size and kept inside a bell jar in his Fortress of Solitude, where it functions as a constant reminder of his past and as a metaphor for his alienated relationship to the planet he now occupies."[29] The inception of the project lay in Kelley's delighted discovery of a dispersed worldwide network of fans specifically dedicated to tracing and savoring all the narrative and visual permutations of Kandor over decades of Superman comic panels. Seeking in 1999 to bring these adepts together via the early internet, he proposed that they then be physically flown to the site of his "Kandor-Con" exhibition in Berlin. The museum's budget, he ruefully had to concede, would not even stretch to building the website, let alone the transport and housing of unknown numbers of enthusiasts. But the psychic investment they would have collectively manifested in the theme moved him to begin translating the vagaries of Kandor renderings on the page into monumental sculpture, starting with the bell jar that holds in the city's alien atmosphere.

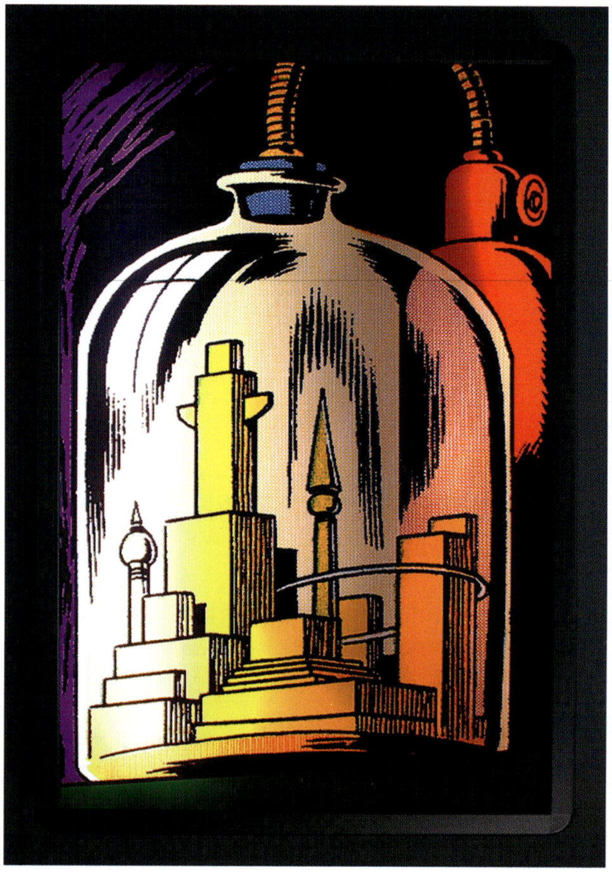

**140** Mike Kelley, *Lenticular 1*, 2007, lenticular panel, lightbox 114.9 × 75.2 × 8.9 cm

Kelley had encased the memory-architecture of *Educational Complex*, like so many rare specimens, beneath a pristine Plexiglas cover, but spent nearly five years perfecting the manufacture of the bell jars for his Kandors. Technical issues intervened, among them the inability of all but one Czech firm to manufacture glass enclosures large enough for his requirements.[30] Disappointing attempts to project video on their surfaces had the fortunate effect of prompting instead his placing inside the jars resin moldings of the fantasy city adapted from the many and various Kandors imagined by the DC comic artists, each lit from below to glow like an extraterrestrial jewel on a heavy molded base styled in a *moderne* homage to the moment of Superman's invention in the 1930s (fig. 141). At the debut during the 2009 Venice Biennale of Pinault's personal museum in the Punta della Dogana, twenty of Kelley's *Kandors* were presented in a large gallery of their own, their iridescent colors the only light in the darkened space.

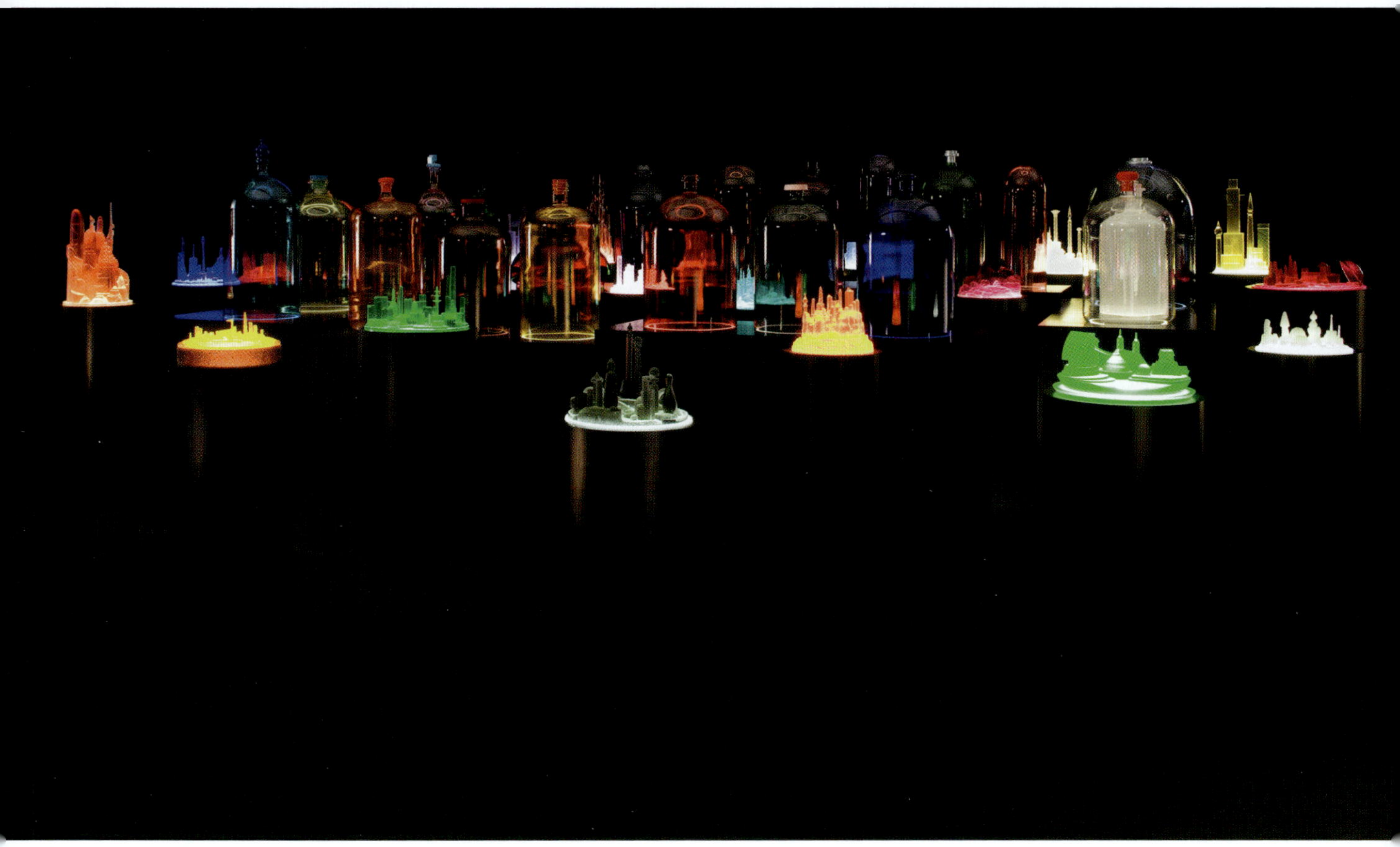

**141** Installation view, *Mike Kelley: Kandors 1999–2011*, Hauser & Wirth, Los Angeles, California, 2017

"Visually opulent" the *Kandors* may be (those were Kelley's words[31]) and catnip for a plutocratic show-off, but theirs is the cold phosphorescence of life rendered inert, of happiness as out of reach as outer space—and no way to get there. Might Kelley have remembered Sun Ra's remarks from 1973 in an interview with John Sinclair (fig. 142), published on the occasion of the Solar Arkestra's appearance at the Ann Arbor Jazz and Blues Festival: "I'm not really talking about freedom . . . because that doesn't help anybody. The only freedom they'll get is over in a cemetery; . . . It's a scientific truth: people are only free when they're dead. And they're always talking about peace, and they'll get that too, when they're dead . . . this planet for thousands of years has been under the law of death and destruction [but] it's moving over into something else which I choose to call MYTH, a MYTH-SCIENCE . . . because I'm interested in happiness for people, which is just a myth, because they're not happy. I would say that the synonym for myth is happiness."[32]

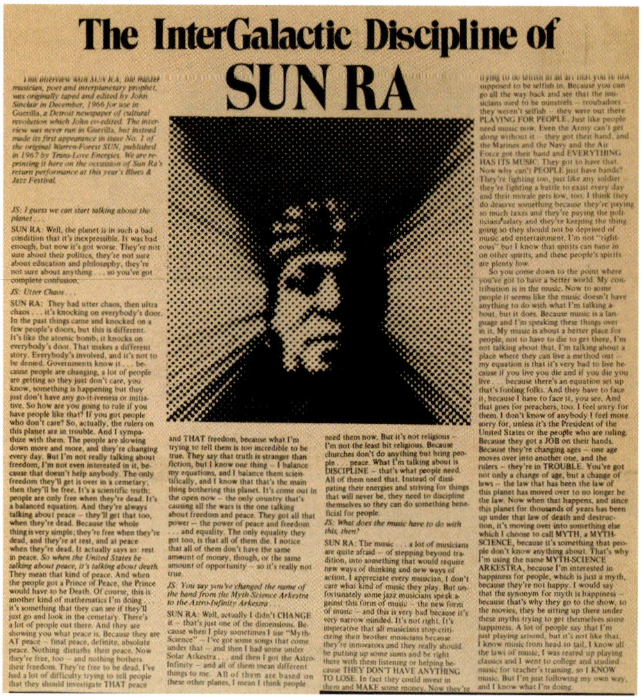

# The InterGalactic Discipline of SUN RA

*This interview with SUN RA, the master musician, poet and interplanetary prophet, was originally taped and edited by John Sinclair in December, 1966 for use in* Guerilla, *a Detroit newspaper of cultural revolution which John co-edited. The interview was never run in* Guerilla, *but instead made its first appearance in issue No. 1 of the original Warren-Forest SUN, published in 1967 by Trans-Love Energies. We are reprinting it here on the occassion of Sun Ra's return performance at this year's Blues & Jazz Festival.*

*JS: I guess we can start talking about the planet . . .*

SUN RA: Well, the planet is in such a bad condition that it's inexpressible. It was bad enough, but now it's got worse. They're not sure about their politics, they're not sure about education and philosophy, they're not sure about anything . . . so you've got complete confusion.

*JS: Utter Chaos . . .*

SUN RA: They had utter chaos, then ultra chaos . . . it's knocking on everybody's door. In the past things came and knocked on a few people's doors, but this is different. It's like the atomic bomb, it knocks on everybody's door. That makes a different story. Everybody's involved, and it's not to be denied. Governments know it . . . because people are changing, a lot of people are getting so they just don't care, you know, something is happening but they just don't have any go-it-iveness or initiative. So how are you going to rule if you have people like that? If you got people who don't care? So, actually, the rulers on this planet are in trouble. And I sympathize with them. The people are slowing down more and more, and they're changing every day. But I'm not really talking about freedom, I'm not even interested in it, because that doesn't help anybody. The only freedom they'll get is over in a cemetary, then they'll be free. It's a scientific truth: people are only free when they're dead. It's a balanced equation. And they're always talking about peace – they'll get that too, when they're dead. Because the whole thing is very simple; they're free when they're dead, and they're at rest, and at peace when they're dead. It actually says so: rest in peace. *So when the United States be talking about peace, it's talking about death.* They mean that kind of peace. And when the people got a Prince of Peace, the Prince would have to be Death. Of course, this is another kind of mathematics I'm doing . . . it's something that they can see if they'll just go and look in the cemetary. There's a lot of people out there. And they are showing you what peace is. Because they are AT peace – final peace, definite, absolute peace. Nothing disturbs their peace. Now they're free, too – and nothing bothers their freedom. They're free to be dead. I've had a lot of difficulty trying to tell people that they should investigate THAT peace and THAT freedom, because what I'm trying to tell them is too incredible to be true. They say that truth is stranger than fiction, but I know one thing – I balance my equations, and I balance them scientifically, and I know that that's the main thing bothering this planet. It's come out in the open now – the only country that's causing all the wars is the one talking about freedom and peace. They got all that power – the power of peace and freedom . . . and equality. The only equality they got too, is that all of them die. I notice that all of them don't have the same amount of money, though, or the same amount of opportunity – so it's really not true.

*JS: You say you've changed the name of the band from the Myth-Science Arkestra to the Astro-Infinity Arkestra . . .*

SUN RA: Well, actually I didn't CHANGE it – that's just one of the dimensions. Because when I play sometimes I use "Myth-Science" – I've got some songs that come under that – and then I had some under Solar Arkestra . . . and then I got the Astro-Infinity – and all of them mean different things to me. All of them are based on these other planes, I mean I think people need them now. But it's not religious – I'm not the least bit religious. Because churches don't do anything but bring people . . . peace. What I'm talking about is DISCIPLINE – that's what people need. All of them need that. Instead of dissipating their energies and striving for things that will never be, they need to discipline themselves so they can do something beneficial for people.

*JS: What does the music have to do with this, then?*

SUN RA: The music . . . a lot of musicians are quite afraid – of stepping beyond tradition, into something that would require new ways of thinking and new ways of action. I appreciate every musician, I don't care what kind of music they play. But unfortunately some jazz musicians speak against this form of music – the new form of music – and this is very bad because it's very narrow minded. It's not right. It's imperative that all musicians stop criticizing their brother musicians because they're innovators and they really should be putting up some sums and be right there with them listening or helping because THEY DON'T HAVE ANYTHING TO LOSE. In fact they could invest in them and MAKE some money. Now they're trying to be selfish in an art that you're not supposed to be selfish in. Because you can go all the way back and see that the musicians used to be minstrels – troubadors – they weren't selfish – they were out there PLAYING FOR PEOPLE. Just like people need music now. Even the Army can't get along without it – they got their band, and the Marines and the Navy and the Air Force got their band and EVERYTHING HAS ITS MUSIC. They got to have that. Now why can't PEOPLE just have bands? They're fighting too, just like any soldier – they're fighting a battle to exist every day and their morale gets low, too. I think they do deserve something because they're paying so much taxes and they're paying the politicians' salary and they're keeping the thing going so they should not be deprived of music and entertainment. I'm not "righteous" but I know that spirits can tune in on other spirits, and these people's spirits are plenty low.

So you come down to the point where you've got to have a better world. My contribution is in the music. Now to some people it seems like the music doesn't have anything to do with what I'm talking about, but it does. Because music is a language and I'm speaking these things over in it. My music is about a better place for people, not to have to die to get there, I'm not talking about that. I'm talking about a place where they can live a method out – my equation is that it's very bad to live because if you live you die and if you die you live . . . because there's an equation set up that's fooling folks. And they have to face it, because I have to face it, you see. And that goes for preachers, too. I feel sorry for them. I don't know of anybody I feel more sorry for, unless it's the President of the United States or the people who are ruling. Because they got a JOB on their hands. Because they're changing ages – one age moves over into another one, and the rulers – they're in TROUBLE. You've got not only a change of age, but a change of laws – the law that has been the law of this planet has moved over to no longer be the law. Now when that happens, and since this planet for thousands of years has been up under that law of death and destruction, it's moving over into something else which I choose to call MYTH, a MYTH-SCIENCE, because it's something that people don't know anything about. That's why I'm using the name MYTH-SCIENCE ARKESTRA, because I'm interested in happiness for people, which is just a myth, because they're not happy. I would say that the synonym for myth is happiness – because that's why they go to the show, to the movies, they be sitting up there under these myths trying to get themselves some happiness. A lot of people say that I'm just playing around, but it's not like that. I know music from head to tail, I know all the laws of music, I was reared up playing classics and I went to college and studied music for teacher's training, so I KNOW music. But I'm just following my own way, and I know what I'm doing.

**142** "The InterGalactic Discipline of Sun Ra," interview with John Sinclair, *Ann Arbor Sun* (5 September 1973), Ann Arbor District Library

As with all of Sun Ra's utterances, the rhetoric is elliptical and the logic circular: myth is happiness because happiness is a myth. But these were exactly the terms with which Kelly chose to end his deeply felt written homage to Öyvind Fahlström in 1995. Occultism and metaphysics are far from the approved protocols of high-minded art discourse. And Kelley was unlikely to have exactly shared Sun Ra's vision of the extraterrestrial origins and destiny of black African culture via ancient Egypt, a latter-day mythos that shaped his band's abrupt transitions between musical and poetic genres that both he and Senga Nengudi found so captivating. Against that deeply meditated mythos of Afro-Futurism, however, all that Kelley may have had to hand in the myth department were some expedient interplanetary contrivances cooked up by the writers and artists of the DC comics company. But the bell jar as a motif called on deeper and more personally resonant memories, *The Bell Jar* having been Sylvia Plath's title for her 1963 autobiographical novel tracking its protagonist's descent into depression.

Thus the glass Kandor envelopes tap the layered recollection of Fahlström's long-ago visit to Ann Arbor, Kelley's memory of his own unworthiness and inadequacy redeemed therein by the miraculously lost-and-found volume of Plath's poetry, dense with the Swedish artist's

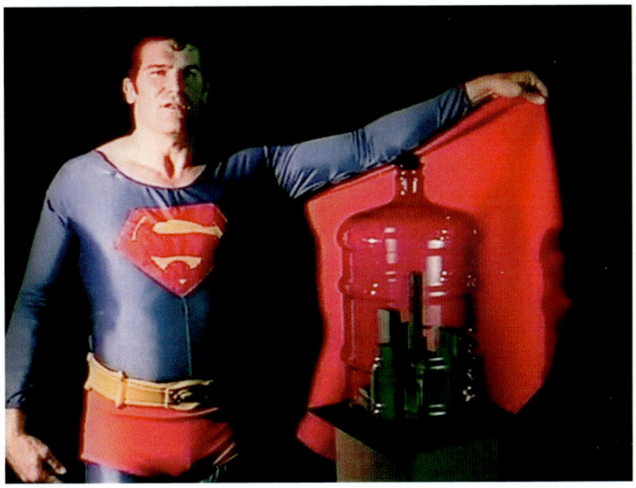

**143** Mike Kelley, still from *Superman Recites Selections from "The Bell Jar" and Other Works by Sylvia Plath*, 1999, video

annotations and marginal drawings. At the first iteration of his Kandor project in 2000, Kelley debuted a video (fig. 143) in which, as he put it, "an actor, who plays the part of Superman, recites those sections of Plath's writings that feature the bell jar."[33] The actor is convincing, and the poignancy of the gender clash affecting, as it drains the sentimentalism that has encrusted the poet's thinly fictionalized memoir of debilitating depression. The general reluctance to address Kelley's own despondency in light of these themes in his art is understandable. The psychological genealogy of Kelley's suicide in 2012, three years after his *Kandors* gleamed in the darkness of Venice, can never be mapped in time nor adequately understood from the outside. But its themes are there to be discerned in his own confessional writing, beginning at least as early as 1995. His return in memory to the mid-1970s, his dwelling on Fahlström's early death at age forty-eight, the talismanic Plath volume, all offer sufficient guidance to their abiding presence in his thoughts. Having acquired something like art-world superpowers, he invested the leading mass-culture superhero with the ineffectuality enacted by his own Ann Arbor persona and by the hapless comic characters of his first CalArts performances. But that kind of actor or character provided a means for achieving conscious control over the built-in antimonies present in the facts of his existence—control that made his art a series of answers to the fundamental moral question: how was this anomalous life to be lived?

It would be both self-evident and intrusively presumptuous to say that he ran out of answers to that fundamental question. It is not for any observer to draw lessons from such a tragedy. But it offers reasons to reflect anew that sustaining art at Kelley's level—so cognitively acute but never detached, so emotionally rich but never ruled by emotion, so painfully self-exposed but defiant of public scrutiny—is never easy, however great the worldly success it might have attained. The requisite intensity and demands on the self, the demands of talent, can be perilous, and the great majority of us never know what that peril can be like.

# NOTES

PROLOGUE | **NEUROPLASTICITY**

1 Facsimile of the catalogue available at http://www.radicalmatters.com/metasound/pdf/Szeemann-Harald_Live-In-Your-Head_When-Attitudes-Become-Form_1969.pdf; for further documentation, see *When Attitudes Become Form: Bern 1969/Venice 2013* (Milan: Fondazione Prada, 2013).

2 See Harald Szeemann, "Zur Austellung," in Szeemann, ed., *Live in Your Head: When Attitudes Become Form, Works—Concepts—Processes—Situations—Information*, exh. cat. (Bern: Kunsthalle Bern, 1969), n.p.; reprinted in English as "About the Exhibition," in Christian Rattemeyer, ed., *Exhibiting the New Art: 'Op Losse Schroeven' and 'When Attitudes Become Form' 1969* (London: Afterall, 2010), 192–93.

3 Marlène Bélos and André Gazut, *Quand les Attitudes deviennent forme*, Geneva, Télévision Suisse Romande, first televised 6 April 1969.

4 Aldous Huxley, in one founding document of the psychedelic movement, *Doors of Perception, and Heaven and Hell* (New York: Harper and Row, 1963), 33, reported that, under the influence of mescaline, "the folds of my gray flannel trousers were charged with is-ness."

5 Theodore Roszak, *The Making of a Counter Culture: Reflections on the Technocratic Society and Its Youthful Opposition, with a New Introduction* (Berkeley and Los Angeles: University of California Press, 1995), xxvi.

6 In the voluminous critical and theoretical literature on this topic, one common point of reference is Michel Foucault, "What is an Author?," trans. D. Bouchard and S. Simon in Bouchard, ed., *Language, Counter-Memory, Practice: Selected Essays and Interviews* (Ithaca, N.Y.: Cornell University Press, 1977), 138: "In short, the subject (and its substitutes) must be stripped of its creative role and analysed as a complex and variable function of discourse."

7 From paper delivered by Dr. Michael C. Agron and discussion by Sidney Cohen, LSD: Clinical And Therapeutic Uses—Napa State Hospital Symposium—November 7, 1961—KPFK—Gordon Skene Sound Collection, https://pastdaily.com/2020/03/28/clinical-and-therapeutic-uses-of-lsd-the-napa-symposium-1961-past-daily-pop-chronicles/.

8 Michael Pollan, *How to Change Your Mind: What the New Science of Psychedelics Teaches Us About Consciousness, Dying, Addiction, Depression, and Transcendence* (New York and London: Penguin, 2018), 214.

9 Andrew Jacobs, "The Psychedelic Revolution Is Coming: Psychiatry May Never Be the Same," *New York Times* (9 May 2021), https://www.nytimes.com/2021/05/09/health/psychedelics-mdma-psilocybin-molly-mental-health.html?searchResultPosition=2.

10 The Menlo Park facility was one site where the CIA, in its persistently ham-handed campaign to enlist LSD as some psychosis-inducing weapon, was sponsoring experiments; see Pollan, *How to Change Your Mind*, 206.

11 Most famously reported, accurately if anecdotally, by Joan Didion in her 1967 article for the conservative, middle-American weekly *Saturday Evening Post*, "Slouching Towards Bethlehem," reprinted in Didion, *We Tell Ourselves Stories in Order to Live: Collected Nonfiction* (New York: Everyman's Library, 2006), 67–97.

12 Mike Kelley, "Death and Transfiguration," in *Foul Perfection: Essays and Criticism*, ed. John C. Welchman (Cambridge, Mass., and London: The MIT Press, 2003), 141–42.

13 Bruce Conner, transcript of a recording made of a lecture given at Carnegie Museum of Art on 10 April 1973 (transcript made November 2015), 7, http://cmoa-records-images.s3.amazonaws.com/download/fv001_002_025_A_transcript.pdf.

14 Daniel Abdal-Hayy Moore, "ON BRUCE CONNER (may he rest in peace) AND ASSORTED KANSAN COHORTS: A Memorial and Memory Lane Meditation" (2008), http://www.vlib.us/beats/bconnermemorial.html.

15 Conner has been fortunate during his life and afterlife in the quality of interpreters most attracted to his work. The present account is deeply indebted to the insightful publications, all cited below, by Anastasia Aukeman, Peter Boswell, Rachel Federman, Rudolf Frieling, Gary Garrels, Johanna Gosse, Kevin Hatch, Laura Hoptman, Bruce Jenkins, Joan Rothfuss, and Rebecca Solnit. But the constraints of shorter forms, individual essays and chapters, or medium-based studies can only sample certain vital connective tissue, consistencies provided, for example, by Conner's commitment to hallucinogen-facilitated psychotherapy, fascination with Black popular music, irrepressible drive to dance, or fierce antagonism toward the American war machine, along with all forms of state violence.

16 From a summary of Michael C. Agron's papers: "Mike Agron found Bruce Conner to be imaginative and inventive—someone he liked a lot and who was quiet, self assured, organized and easy to work with. He was very insightful about what was happening to people and had a keen instinct for publicity. Mike had been introduced to the 'Kansas Group' by a medical colleague, Dr. Sterling Bunnell. Their common interest in creativity, consciousness and art inevitably led to experimentation (sensory perceptions) which was a psychiatric research project at San Francisco Medical School. For Mike Agron the combination of art and psychiatry being part of this group was intoxicating." Agron is quoted in this document testifying to his presence at the Conners' apartment two days before the couple's departure for Mexico in December 1961, the occasion when Bruce Conner altered the worn letters of SLOW (Agron remembers STOP) painted on the street to read LOVE, https://www.eclipticgallery.com.au/gallery3/index.php/Batman-Gallery-Mike-Agron-Collection; see Conner's description of the exploit, transcript of Carnegie Museum of Art lecture, 7.

17 James Meyer, *The Art of Return: The Sixties & Contemporary Culture* (Chicago and London: University of Chicago Press, 2019).

18 See Benjamin H. D. Buchloh, "Conceptual Art 1962–1969: From the Aesthetic of Administration to the Critique of Institutions," *October* (Winter 1990), 105–43.

19 See Philip Leider, "How I Spent My Summer Vacation or, Art and Politics in Nevada, Berkeley, San Francisco and Utah (Read about It in *Artforum*!)," *Artforum* (September 1970), 40–49.

20 See Damon R. Bach, *The American Counterculture: A History of Hippies and Cultural Dissidents* (Lawrence: University Press of Kansas, 2020), 116; Roszak, *Making of a Counter Culture*, xl.

21 Mike Kelley, "Some Aesthetic High Points," in *Kelley, Minor Histories: Statements, Conversations, Proposals*, ed. John Welchman (Cambridge, Mass., and London: MIT Press, 2004), 43.

## ONE | PEYOTE FRONTIER

1 Bruce Conner, interview with Paul Karlstrom, "Oral history interview with Bruce Conner, 1974 August 12," Archives of American Art, Smithsonian Institution, https://www.aaa.si.edu/collections/interviews/oral-history-interview-bruce-conner-12989#transcript.

2 Conner, interview with Paul Cummings, "Oral history interview with Bruce Conner, 1973 April 16," Archives of American Art, Smithsonian Institution, https://www.aaa.si.edu/collections/interviews/oral-history-interview-bruce-conner-12017.

3 Bruce Conner, interview with Paul Karlstrom and Serge Guilbaut, "Oral history interview with Bruce Conner, 1974 March 29," Archives of American Art, Smithsonian Institution, https://www.aaa.si.edu/collections/interviews/oral-history-interview-bruce-conner-13116.

4 See Tara McDowell, *The Householders: Robert Duncan and Jess* (Cambridge, Mass.: MIT Press, 2019).

5 Michael McClure, interview with Anastasia Aukeman, in Aukeman, *Welcome to Painterland: Bruce Conner and the Rat Bastard Protective Association* (Berkeley and Los Angeles: University of California Press, 2016), 13–14.

6 Peter Boswell, personal communication (April 2021).

7 Bruce Conner, interview with Marc Selwyn, "Marilyn and the Spaghetti Theory," *Flash Art*, (January–February 1991), 94.

8 Conner preferred his titles to be rendered in sans-serif type, all in capital letters.

9 The clipping came from a Hearst Corporation Sunday supplement, the *American Weekly*; the Hearst newspaper in San Francisco was the *Examiner*.

10 Rachel Federman, "Fifty Years in Show Business," in Rudolf Frieling and Gary Garrels, eds., *Bruce Conner: It's All True* (Berkeley and Los Angeles: University of California Press, 2016), 32.

11 See Roger Griffith and Megan Randall "The Life, Death, and Resurrection of Bruce Conner's CHILD," in Frieling and Garrels, *It's All True*, 293–98.

12 Conner, interview with Karlstrom and Guilbaut.

13 Thomas Albright, "Meet Bruce Conner, Film-Maker, Rolling Stone (9 March 1968), https://www.rollingstone.com/culture/culture-news/meet-bruce-conner-film-maker-231478/.

14 See Jay Stevens, *Storming the Barricade: LSD and the American Dream* (New York: Grove, 1987), 60–73; also Michael Pollan, *How to Change Your Mind: What the New Science of Psychedelics Teaches Us About Consciousness, Dying, Addiction, Depression, and Transcendence* (New York and London: Penguin, 2018), 144–59.

15 See Michael McClure, *Scratching the Beat Surface: Essays on New Vision from Blake to Kerouac* (Harmondsworth and New York: Penguin, 1994), 5–11; see also Michael Duncan and Kristine McKenna, *Semina Culture: Wallace Berman and His Circle* (New York: DAP/Santa Monica Museum of Art, 2005), passim; also Stephen Fredman, *Contextual Practice: Assemblage and the Erotic in Postwar Poetry and Art* (Stanford, Calif.: Stanford University Press, 2010), 99–124.

16 McClure, *Scratching the Beat Surface*, 5–11.

17 Albright, "Meet Bruce Conner."

18 See Philip Deloria, "Countercultural Indians and the New Age," in Peter Baunstein and Michael William Doyle, eds., *Imagine Nation: The American Counterculture of the 1960s and '70s* (New York and London: Routledge, 2002), 159–88.

19 See William Hjortsberg, *Jubilee Hitchhiker: The Life and Times of Richard Brautigan* (Berkeley: Counterpart, 2012), 189.

20 Bruce Conner, quoted in Rebecca Solnit, *Secret Exhibition: Six California Artists of the Cold War Era* (San Francisco: City Lights, 1990), 62–63.

21 See R. G. Davis, *The San Francisco Mime Troupe: The First Ten Years* (Palo Alto: Ramparts Press, 1975), 9–46; Davis places the studio just south of Market on Brady, "a short street of slum houses tucked around light industry" (p. 18).

22 Conner, interview with Karlstrom.

23 Sidney Felsen, quoted in Duncan and McKenna, *Semina Culture*, 324.

24 Bruce Conner, interview with Paul Cummings, "Oral history interview with Bruce Conner, 1973 April 16," Archives of American Art, Smithsonian Institution, https://www.aaa.si.edu/collections/interviews/oral history interview-bruce-conner-12017.

25 I am grateful to Peter Boswell for that observation.

26 The Menil Collection, Houston, holds a comparatively miniaturized work on the same theme that came from the collection of Walter Hopps.

27 Conner, interview with Karlstrom.

28 Mark Johnston, *Saving God: Religion after Idolatry* (Princeton: Princeton University Press, 2011), 130, 124.

## TWO | MOVIES AND MEXICO

1 Rebay had large ambitions for the role of film in her plans for the new museum, designed by Frank Lloyd Wright, which she envisioned as housing a film laboratory and screening facility. To that end, she offered to support a substantial number of film artists. See John S. Hanhardt, "Rhythm of the In-Between: Abstract Film and the Museum of Non-Objective Painting," in Karole Vail, ed., *The Museum of Non-Objective Painting: Hilla Rebay and the Origins of the Solomon R. Guggenheim Museum* (New York: Guggenheim Museum, 2009), 139–55.

2 See Thomas Crow, *The Long March of Pop: Art, Music, and Design 1930–1995* (New Haven and London: Yale University Press, 2015), 18–32; also Stephen Fredman, *Contextual Practice: Assemblage and the Erotic in Postwar Poetry and Art* (Stanford, Calif.: Stanford University Press, 2010), 76–94.

3 See Carol Bove, "Inkweed Studios," in Rudolf Frieling and Gary Garrels, eds., *Bruce Conner: It's All True*, exh. cat. (Berkeley and Los Angeles: University of California Press, 2016), 22.

4 Bruce Conner, interview with Paul Cummings, "Oral history interview with Bruce Conner, 1973 April 16," Archives of American Art, Smithsonian Institution, https://www.aaa.si.edu/collections/interviews/oral-history-interview-bruce-conner-12017.

5 P. Adams Sitney, *Visionary Film: The American Avant-Garde 1943–2000*, 3rd ed., (Oxford and New York: Oxford University Press, 2002), 246.

6 Conner, interview with Cummings.

7 On this project, see Marci Kwon, *Enchantments: Joseph Cornell and American Modernism* (Princeton: Princeton University Press, 2021), 185–88.

8 Conner, interview with Cummings; see also Tanya Zimbardo, "With Bruce Conner: A 1984 Interview in *REVER-*

SAL," *OTHERZINE* (Fall 2016), http://www.othercinema.com/otherzine/2935-2/.

9 Amelia Does, "Worthwhile Insanity: On Collage Filmmaking and Arthur Lipsett, An Interview with Bruce Conner," *INCITE!* (Winter 2010), http://www.incite-online.net/does2.html.

10 See Peter Boswell, "Theater of Light and Shadow," in Boswell et al., *2000 BC: The Bruce Conner Story, Part II*, exh. cat. (Minneapolis: Walker Art Center, 1999), 69; Matthew Biro ("Bruce Conner: It's all True," *Brooklyn Rail* [October 2016], https://brooklynrail.org/2016/10/artseen/bruce-conner-its-all-true) aptly observes, "A focus on elemental imagery—earth, air, fire, and water—gives A MOVIE a mythological, prescientific resonance, and careful shot selection and rapid-fire editing allow the filmmaker to present the world as protean matter in a continuous state of flux. Paradoxically, A MOVIE seems to acknowledge a postmodern condition in which a flood of simulacra appears to supplant the real, while at the same time suggesting that a still-perceptible conflict of primordial forces exists beneath the play of representations."

11 Bruce Conner, interview with Peter Boswell (1 September 1985), quoted in Gary Garrels, "Soul Stirrer: Visions and Realities of Bruce Conner," in Frieling and Garrels, *It's All True*, 338: Conner goes on, "Or through mystical meditation. Sometimes it happens spontaneously as it happened to me [in a recovered memory] when I was eleven years old."

12 The associate was Lothar Knoth, an East German refugee teaching at the Autonomous University of Mexico City; see Robert Greenfield, *Timothy Leary: A Biography* (Orlando: Harcourt, 2006), 111.

13 Timothy Leary, *High Priest* (New York: College Notes and Texts, 1968), 16.

14 Bruce Conner, interview with V. Vale, in Bruce Conner, *The Afternoon Interviews with V. Vale* (San Francisco: RE/search, 2016), 57–58

15 Ibid., 57; also see Anastasia Aukeman, *Welcome to Painterland: Bruce Conner and the Rat Bastard Protective Association* (Berkeley and Los Angeles: University of California Press, 2016), 223.

16 Jean Conner, interview with Robert Conway, personal communication (April 2021); Conway has also forwarded this remark from a 1973 lecture given by Conner at the Carnegie Museum of Art: "When I was there, Timothy Leary rang my doorbell. I had met him in New York. He said he was in Mexico City and he was going to go around and look at the places where the magic mushrooms grew. He had a map of where they had grown that he had gotten from some department. We started going to those places. All that Mexican footage that was in it, we were in San Pedro Tenancingo looking for mushrooms, not really looking for them to take them. Ostensibly, he said he wanted to talk to them." As if to confuse the issue further, Conner at another point in the talk dates the encounter to 1961, though they had been in Mexico only a few weeks or less during that year; see Bruce Conner, transcript of a recording made of a lecture given at Carnegie Museum of Art on 10 April 1973 (transcript made November 2015), http://cmoa-records-images.s3.amazonaws.com/download/fv001_002_025_A_transcript.pdf.

17 Conner, interview with Vale, 33.

18 See Frieling, "Bruce Conner's Ch-Ch-Changes," in Frieling and Garrels, *It's All True*, 324–25: acting out of ambivalence and approach/avoidance during the 1961 Art of Assemblage exhibition at the Museum of Modern Art in New York (in which Conner was included, having advised the curator William Seitz on his visit to San Francisco), he threw SUPERHUMAN DEVOTION, damaged in transit, over the side of the Staten Island ferry in the company of artist Ray Johnson. Jean Conner offers background on its making (Garrett Caples, "The Rumpus Mini-Interview Project #70: Jean Conner," *The Rumpus* [9 February 2017], https://therumpus.net/2017/02/the-rumpus-mini-interview-project-70-jean-conner/): "SUPER-HUMAN DEVOTION, I think, was two pieces of glass. Everything was stuffed in between the two pieces. He did several works like that and most of them got destroyed because the glass broke; there was no way to put it back together again. They're actually window frames he was using, because he'd get these window frames out of buildings at that time they were tearing down the old Fillmore area, when they were moving out all the black people. He would go out at night and take off with the windows."

19 Yvonne Bond, quoted in Jack Loeffler and Meredith Davidson, *Voices of Counterculture in the Southwest* (Albuquerque: University of New Mexico Press, 2017), 44–46.

20 Walter Hopps, "Bruce Conner," *Bomb*, no. 80 (Summer 2002): 8–11, https://bombmagazine.org/articles/bruce-conner/

21 Bruce Conner, interview with Paul Karlstrom, "Oral history interview with Bruce Conner, 1974 August 12," Archives of American Art, Smithsonian Institution, https://www.aaa.si.edu/collections/interviews/oral-history-interview-bruce-conner-12989#transcript.

22 Boswell, "Theater of Light and Shadow," 44.

23 Jean Conner, quoted in Garrels, "Soul Stirrer," 336.

24 Conner, quoted in Boswell, "Theater of Light and Shadow," 44.

25 Conner, interview with Karlstrom: "When the Art of Assemblage show happened Bill Seitz was here picking up stuff I'd take him down to McAllister Street to second-hand stores. There was a black man who had a second-hand-store. He said he was a Reverend. He had a lot to do with the work I was doing. For example, he'd have a hub cap; on top of that would be a soda glass from an ice cream soda fountain, with a hand mirror in the center, with a marble sitting on top of it, with a doll's head on top, of it, a peacock feather coming out of one eye, and a mirror backover here, and a picture of Martin Luther King. . . . His prices were too high. I bought only a few things from him. He didn't want to sell anything. And he's one of the artists. . . . I don't even know his name. But when I'd take Bill Seitz around town I showed him this place."

26 See Russell Ferguson, *Francis Alÿs: Politics of Rehearsal*, exh. cat. (Los Angeles: Hammer Museum, 2007), 68.

## THREE | BOSTON AND THE LEARY LURE

1 Bruce Conner, interview with Paul Karlstrom, "Oral history interview with Bruce Conner, 1974 August 12," Archives of American Art, Smithsonian Institution, https://www.aaa.si.edu/collections/interviews/oral-history-interview-bruce-conner-12989#transcript.

2 On the Oldenburg Happening, see the illuminating discussion in Antonia Pocock, "The Heartland of Pop: Claes Oldenburg, Jeff Koons, and the Chicago Imagists," PhD dissertation, New York University (2020), 97–101; Michael Kirby provides Oldenburg's script and a detailed description of the work's unfolding in *Happenings: An Illustrated Anthology* (New York: E. P. Dutton, 1965), 234–61; see also Robert Pincus Witten, "The Transformation of Daddy Warbucks: An Interview with Claes Oldenburg [1964]," in Nadja Rottner, ed., *Claes Oldenburg (October Files 13)* (Cambridge, Mass.: MIT Press, 2012), 117–21.

3 Conner, interview with Karlstrom.

4 For a contemporary report on the details of the festival, including Conner's participation, see Lawrence Lindgren, "The Year's FOTA Breaks with Tradition," *Chicago Maroon* (26 April 1963), 1, http://campub.lib.uchicago.edu/view/?docId=mvol-0004-1963-0426#page/1/mode/1up.

5 Bruce Conner, interview with Paul Cummings, "Oral history interview with Bruce Conner, 1973 April 16," Archives of American Art, Smithsonian Institution, https://www.aaa.si.edu/collections/interviews/oral-history-interview-bruce-conner-12017.

6 Sheldon Renan, *An Introduction to American Underground Film* (New York: Dutton, 1967), 138.

7 Daniel Abdal-Hayy Moore, "ON BRUCE CONNER (may he rest in peace) AND ASSORTED KANSAN COHORTS: A Memorial and Memory Lane Meditation" (2008), http://www.vlib.us/beats/bconnermemorial.html.

8 Thomas Albright, "Meet Bruce Conner, Film-Maker, *Rolling Stone* (9 March 1968), https://www.rollingstone.com/culture/culture-news/meet-bruce-conner-film-maker-231478/.

9 On the timing of the move, see Tanya Zimbardo, "With Bruce Conner: A 1984 Interview in *REVERSAL*," *OTHERZINE*, http://www.othercinema.com/otherzine/2935-2/: "when I had an exhibition at the University of Chicago, I was taking down the show, packing it up to take back to Massachusetts, when a couple was just coming in to see my show because a friend of theirs was named Bruce Conner. And after I got back to Massachusetts, I got a news clipping from somebody in Lincoln, Nebraska, about somebody named Bruce Conner. So I decided that there were a lot of me all over the world!"; on the house, see Robert Greenfield, *Timothy Leary: A Biography* (Orlando: Harcourt, 2006), 189.

10 Timothy Leary, *Flashbacks: An Autobiography* (New York: Penguin, 1983), 176; on this period in the IFIF, see Greenfield, *Leary*, 185–206.

11 Charles Giuliano, "Remembering Bruce Conner: A Leading Artist of His Generation" (13 July 2008), https://www.berkshirefinearts.com/07-13-2008_remembering-bruce-conner-1933-2008.htm.

12 David Felton, "The Lyman Family's Holy Siege of America," *Rolling Stone* (23 December 1971), https://www.rollingstone.com/culture/culture-news/the-lyman-familys-holy-siege-of-america-235776/; the most likely article to which Conner is referring appeared in a Mexican journal of anthropological scholarship, but was written and published in English and could have been passed hand to hand: Thomas MacDougall, "Ipomaea Tricolor: A Hallucinogenic Plant of the Zapotecs," *Boletín del Centro de Investigaciones Antropológicas de México*, 6 (March 1960), in which the author, a pioneering plant collector and ethno-botanist in the region, identifies the species of morning-glory vine (badoh) in Indigenous use and, for the first time, describes the grinding of the seeds required for its effective use.

13 See Jay Stevens, *Storming the Barricade: LSD and the American Dream* (New York: Grove, 1987), 199–200.

14 Giuliano, "Remembering Bruce Conner"

15 Ibid.

16 Bruce Conner, interview with V. Vale, in *Bruce Conner, The Afternoon Interviews with V. Vale* (San Francisco: RE/search, 2016), 28–32

17 See Kevin Hatch, *Looking for Bruce Conner* (Cambridge, Mass., and London: MIT Press, 2012), 226.

18 Conner, interview with Karlstrom.

19 See Tony Glover, *Blues Harp* (New York: Oak Publications, 1965), 11.

20 See Thomas Crow, *The Long March of Pop: Art, Music, and Design 1930–1995* (New Haven and London: Yale Univer-sity Press, 2015), 23–34.

21 Jim Kweskin, quoted in Eric Von Schmidt and Jim Rooney eds., *Baby, Let Me Follow You Down: The Illustrated History of the Cambridge Folk Years*, 2nd ed. (Amherst: University of Massachusetts Press, 1979), 176.

22 Ibid., 185.

23 Geoff Muldaur, quoted in ibid., 187.

24 Geoff Muldaur, personal communication (April 2021).

25 See Johanna Gosse, "Pop, Collaboration, Utopia: Bruce Conner's BREAKAWAY in 1960s Los Angeles," *Camera Obscura* (Fall 2015), 14.

26 Giuliano, "Remembering Bruce Conner."

27 Conner, interview with Cummings.

28 Brian O'Doherty, "Conner and His Films: The Artist as Director, Performer and—Occasionally—As Artist," *New York Times* (26 April 1964), section 10, 11.

29 See Anastasia Aukeman, *Welcome to Painterland: Bruce Conner and the Rat Bastard Protective Association* (Berkeley and Los Angeles: University of California Press, 2016), 227, 285 n.33.

30 Bruce Conner, quoted in Rebecca Solnit, *Secret Exhibition: Six California Artists of the Cold War Era* (San Francisco: City Lights, 1990), 74: "Billy Jahrmarkt and Joan opened the gallery. They had shows. But it was hardly ever open. They hardly sold anything. Mainly it was because Bill was an awful lot into drugs and into junk. And it wasn't happening."

31 Paper delivered by Dr. Michael C. Agron and discussion by Sidney Cohen, LSD: Clinical and Therapeutic Uses—Napa State Hospital Symposium—November 7, 1961—KPFK—Gordon Skene Sound Collection; https://pastdaily.com/2020/03/28/clinical-and-therapeutic-uses-of-lsd-the-napa-symposium-1961-past-daily-pop-chronicles/.

32 Yvonne Bond, quoted in Jack Loeffler and Meredith Davidson, *Voices of Counterculture in the Southwest* (Albuquerque: University of New Mexico Press, 2017), 41

33 Conner, interview with Vale, 54–55.

34 Aukeman, *Painterland*, 120.

35 "Correspondence between the Conners and the Agrons from Mexico and other locations," sale item, 2012, Ecliptic Gallery, Melbourne.

36 See Rachel Federman, "Twenty-Four Hour Art: Bruce Conner's Environments," in Rudolf Frieling and Gary Garrels, eds., *Bruce Conner: It's All True*, exh. cat. (Berkeley and Los Angeles: University of California Press, 2016), 307.

37 See Giuliano, "Remembering Bruce Conner."

38 Conner, interview with Karlstrom: "That's Mexican, that Suitcase. I carried that around Mexico. This was my suitcase before I put candles on it. I'd put my clothes in it. I'd go across the border. On the Mexican side the inspectors would say, 'That's really nice.' And the Mexicans would say, 'Oh boy, look at that! Look at that!' It was a lot more colorful; it's faded a lot. Then when I'd get over to the American side nobody saw it at all."

39 *San Francisco Examiner* (12 August 1964), clipping reproduced in Joan Rothfuss, "Escape Artist," in Peter Boswell et al., *2000 BC: The Bruce Conner Story, Part I*, exh. cat. (Minneapolis: Walker Art Center, 1999), 164

40 Conner, interview with Peter Boswell (1985), quoted in Rothfuss, "Escape Artist," 180.

41 Bruce Conner, in "Bruce Conner: A Discussion at the 1968 Flaherty Seminar," *Film Comment* (Winter 1969), 16–25, http://michelle-silva.squarespace.com/news/2017/3/29/03jiw6y9g162amjbtkkaouuurqk4jc.

## FOUR | **PYSCHEDELIC ORACLE**

1 See Anastasia Aukeman, *Welcome to Painterland: Bruce Conner and the Rat Bastard Protective Association* (Berkeley and Los Angeles: University of California Press, 2016), 189–90.

2 See Joan Rothfuss, "Escape Artist," in Peter Boswell et al., *2000 BC: The Bruce Conner Story, Part II*, exh. cat. (Minneapolis: Walker Art Center, 1999), 164; see also Aukeman, *Painterland*, 68–85, on the series of photographs of San Francisco artists, including Conner, taken by Jerry Burchard.

3 Conner, quoted in Rothfuss, "Escape Artist," 164.

4 See the alphabetical biographies in Michael Duncan and Kristine McKenna, *Semina Culture: Wallace Berman and*

*His Circle* (New York: DAP/Santa Monica Museum of Art, 2005), 70–304.

5 Russ Tamblyn, quoted in Duncan and McKenna, *Semina Culture*, 347–48.

6 Wallace Berman, letter to David Meltzer (postmark 29 March 1962), reproduced in ibid., 361.

7 See Johanna Gosse, "Pop, Collaboration, Utopia: Bruce Conner's BREAKAWAY in 1960s Los Angeles," *Camera Obscura* (Fall 2015), 14–15; see entry in "Filmography," in Boswell et al., *2000 BC*, 264.

8 John Russell, quoted in Hariet Vyner, *Groovy Bob: The Life and Times of Robert Fraser* (London: Heni Publishing, 2016), 105.

9 Conner, quoted in Vyner, *Groovy Bob*, 106.

10 Ibid., 105.

11 Geoff Muldaur, personal communication (April 2021).

12 Timothy Leary, Richard Alpert, and Ralph Metzner, *The Psychedelic Experience: A Manual Based on the Tibetan Book of the Dead* (New Hyde Park, N.Y.: University Books, 1966).

13 The incipient Family Dog collective had rented the same venue the previous October, for "A Tribute to Doctor Strange," a costume dance named for the Marvel Comics character, where the Charlatans, Jefferson Airplane, and Great Society (Grace Slick's first band) provided the music. Even Allen Ginsberg made an appearance and led the dancing. See the very useful history by Walter Medeiros, "Mapping San Francisco 1965–1967: Roots and Florescence of the San Francisco Counter Culture," in Christoph Grunenberg and Jonathan Harris eds., *Summer of Love: Psychedelic Art, Social Crisis and Counterculture in the 1960s* (Liverpool: Tate and Liverpool University Press, 2005), 235.

14 Tom Wolfe, *The Electric Kool-Aid Acid Test* (New York: Farrar, Strauss and Giroux, 1968).

15 Charles Perry, *The Haight-Ashbury: A History* (New York: Wenner Books, 2005) 47.

16 Toni Basil, "I'm 28" (composer Graham Gouldman)/ "Breakaway" (composer Ed Cobb), A&M Records, Los Angeles (February 1966).

17 Johanna Gosse, "Pop, Collaboration, Utopia: Bruce Conner's BREAKAWAY in 1960s Los Angeles," *Camera Obscura* (September 2015), 3

18 Ibid., 5

19 See Rothfuss, "Escape Artist," 170.

20 See Barry Miles, *Paul McCartney: Many Years from Now* (New York: Henry Holt, 1997), 233–37.

21 Bruce Conner, quoted in Scott MacDonald, *Canyon Cinema: The Life and Times of an Independent Film Distributor* (Berkeley and Los Angeles: University of California Press, 2008), 122.

22 Conner and McClure produced a second, larger edition in 1970, encased in a presentation box, which is the version most often exhibited and remarked on in the literature, despite forfeiting the winning fragility of the original. For further information, see Steven Fama, *the glade of theoricornithichermetica* (1 February 2010), http://stevenfama.blogspot.com/2010/02/17-reasons-why.html.

23 Quoted in Rachel Federman, "Fifty Years in Show Business," in Rudolf Frieling and Gary Garrels, eds., *Bruce Conner: It's All True*, exh. cat. (Berkeley and Los Angeles: University of California Press, 2016), 122.

24 See Ian MacDonald, *Revolution in the Head: The Beatles' Records and the Sixties* (Chicago: Chicago Review Press, 2007), 192.

25 Ron Thelin, interview with Leonard Wolf, in Wolf, ed., *Voices from the Love Generation* (Boston: Little, Brown, 1969), 227.

26 Allen Cohen, "Notes on the San Francisco Oracle," http://www.rockument.com/blog/haight-ashbury-in-the-sixties/allen-cohen-and-the-s-f-oracle/.

27 Bruce Conner, interview with Paul Karlstrom, "Oral history interview with Bruce Conner, 1974 August 12," Archives of American Art, Smithsonian Institution, https://www.aaa.si.edu/collections/interviews/oral-history-interview-bruce-conner-12989#transcript.

28 Bruce Conner, interview with Bruce Jenkins and Peter Boswell (1 June 1996), quoted in Boswell, "Theater of Light and Shadow," in Boswell et al., *2000 BC*, 70.

29 Bruce Conner, interview with Mary Fuller, "You're Looking for Bruce Conner, the Artist, or What Is This Crap You're Trying to Put over Here?" *Current* (May–July 1976), cited in Joan Rothfuss, "Escape Artist," 167.

### FIVE | LIVING UP TO THEIR REPUTATIONS

1 See Tom Folsom, *Hopper: A Savage American Journey* (New York: ITBooks, 2013), 97; a copy of Ginsberg's *Howl* appears propped up in several interior shots.

2 Bruce Conner, interview with Paul Karlstrom, "Oral history interview with Bruce Conner, 1974 August 12," Archives of American Art, Smithsonian Institution, https://www.aaa.si.edu/collections/interviews/oral-history-interview-bruce-conner-12989#transcript.

3 Johanna Gosse ("Cinema at the Crossroads: Bruce

Conner's Atomic Sublime, 1958–2008," PhD dissertation [Bryn Mawr, 2014], 114) proposes Hopper as Conner's "Jungian shadow—an inverted mirror-image reflecting his darker, less enlightened aspect."

4 Ibid.

5 See R. Gordon Wasson, "The Divine Mushroom of Immortality," in Peter T. Furst, ed., *The Flesh of the Gods: The Ritual Use of Hallucinogens* (Long Grove, Ill.: Waveland Press, 1972), 188–89; Wasson was the ex-banker and amateur mycologist who described his experiences ingesting psilocybin mushrooms in the Mazateca highlands in the mass market *Life Magazine* in 1955, which probably did more to accelerate the movement than any other source of information; see photograph of Hofmann in Joseph Mann, *Turn On and Tune In: Psychedelics, Narcotics, and Euphoriants*, (Cambridge: Royal Society of Chemistry, 2009), 13.

6 William Wilson, "Bruce Conner Paints Tommy the Elephant," *Los Angeles Times* (17 May 1967) part IV, 1, 7

7 Kevin Hatch, *Looking for Bruce Conner* (Cambridge, Mass., and London: MIT Press, 2012), 9.

8 Bruce Conner, interview with William Hjortsberg, in Hjortsberg, *Jubilee Hitchhiker: The Life and Times of Richard Brautigan* (Berkeley; Counterpoint, 2012), 258.

9 See Hjotsberg, *Jubilee Hitchhiker*, 271–332.

10 Bruce Conner, interview with William Hjortsberg, quoted in ibid., 329.

11 Ibid.

12 Joan Rothfuss, "Escape Artist," in Peter Boswell et al., *2000 BC: The Bruce Conner Story, Part II*, exh. cat. (Minneapolis: Walker Art Center, 1999), 168; Luke 11:34–36; 12:2.

13 See Peter Boswell, "Theater of Light and Shadow," in Boswell et al., *2000 BC*, 74.

14 Peter Biskind, *Easy Riders and Raging Bulls: How the Sex-Drugs-and Rock 'n' Roll Generation Saved Hollywood* (New York: Simon and Schuster, 1998), 66.

15 Ibid., 70.

16 For Conner's presence, acknowledged in an unpublished interview, see Gosse, "Cinema at the Crossroads, 114.

17 Quoted in Josh Karp, "Dennis Hopper's Mad Vision: The Making of the Last Movie," *Esquire* (1 October 2018), https://www.esquire.com/entertainment/movies/a23287946/the-last-movie-dennis-hopper/; see also the on-the-spot report by Michael Goodwin, "In Peru with Dennis Hopper Making the Last Movie," *Rolling Stone* 56 (16 April 1970), 26–30.

18 See Folsom, *Hopper*, 163.

19 Johanna Gosse, "Pop, Collaboration, Utopia: Bruce Conner's BREAKAWAY in 1960s Los Angeles," *Camera Obscura* (Fall 2015), 16.

20 Conner, interview with Paul Karlstrom.

21 David Felton, "The Lyman Family's Holy Siege of America," part 1, *Rolling Stone* (23 December 1971), https://www.rollingstone.com/culture/culture-news/the-lyman-familys-holy-siege-of-america-235776/.

## SIX | BEARING WITNESS TO WAR

1 Wally Hedrick, interview with Leslie Goldberg, *di Rosa Artist Interview Series* (16 August 2002), http://www.wallyhedrick.org/pdfs/di_rosa_artist_interview_series.pdf.

2 Wally Hedrick, interview with Paul Karlstrom, Archives of American Art, Smithsonian Institution (1974), https://www.aaa.si.edu/collections/interviews/oral-history-interview-wally-hedrick-12869#transcript: "We weren't really there overtly but we were there. I was starting to hear things on the new broadcasts, 'We're sending 20 advisers.' And I said, 'Uh oh, here we go.' But see, I'd only been out of the Army five years, and somehow I don't think I knew the difference between Korea and Vietnam. To me it was all the same. All I knew was we were there and we were going to get screwed again, you know. So it was sort of in honor of the people being killed, I guess."

3 See, among many sources, Neil Sheehan, *A Bright Shining Lie: John Paul Vann and America in Vietnam* (New York: Vintage, 1989), 351–58.

4 Letters to the *Times*: "Mrs. Nhu Defends Stand," *New York Times* (14 August 1963).

5 Hedrick, interview with Karlstrom.

6 See Peter Selz, *Art of Engagement: Visual Politics in California and Beyond* (Berkeley and Los Angeles: University of California Press, 2006), 40.

7 Irving Petlin, interview with James McElhinney, "Oral history interview with Irving Petlin, 2016, September 13–15," Archives of American Art, Smithsonian Institution, www.aaa.si.edu/collections/interviews/oral-history-interview-irving-petlin-17411#transcript.

8 Ibid.

9 Ibid.

10 Selz, *Art of Engagement*, 155–56.

11 For an excellent overview, see Matthew Israel, *Kill for Peace: American Artists against the Vietnam War* (Austin: University of Texas Press, 2013).

12 See Tom Wells, *The War Within: America's Battle over Vietnam* (New York: Henry Holt, 1996), 23–38.

13 *Los Angeles Free Press* (14 May 1965), 6–7.

14 The informant inside RAND was a Soviet specialist named Roman Kollkowicz, whom Petlin had befriended over their shared objections to the already evident escalation of the American war in Vietnam. Both shared a family background of Holocaust victims. See Israel, *Kill for Peace*, 30–31.

15 Petlin, quoted in John Yau, "Irving Petlin with John Yau," *The Brooklyn Rail* (5 March 2006), static1.squarespace.com/static/59822b3ef14aa166253ed0e8/t/59c5837549fc2b90f037f27b/1506116469405/08_petlin_Brooklyn+Rail_March+2006.pdf.

16 See Francis Frascina, *Art, Politics and Dissent: Aspects of the Art Left in Sixties America* (Manchester and New York: Manchester University Press, 1999), 36. Relying on interviews with Petlin, Frascina describes these police as from the Los Angeles Police Department; given the lawlessness of that force, this is possible, but they would have lacked jurisdiction in the separately incorporated city of Santa Monica.

17 Petlin, quoted in Yau, "Irving Petlin with John Yau."

18 Kurt Von Meier, "Los Angeles Letter," *Art International* (April 1966), 68.

19 These events are reviewed in Frascina, *Art, Politics and Dissent*, 57–87.

20 One county supervisor declared, "Whatever it takes is going to be done. . . . We're not going to surrender that area or any area to beatniks or wild-eyed kids." See Thomas Crow, *The Long March of Pop: Art, Music, and Design 1930–1995* (New Haven and London: Yale University Press, 2015), 255–77.

21 See "Potpourri of Protest," un-sourced press clipping (14 March 1966) in the papers of Charles Britten, box 5:3, special collections, Getty Research Institute, Los Angeles.

22 See Frascina, *Art, Politics and Dissent*, 72.

23 Petlin described the conclusion of the project and the unsuccessful plans to preserve the structure ("Irving Petlin with John Yau"): "When the four months were over and we were trying to figure out what to do, Walter Hopps tried to bring the tower to the Pasadena Art Museum. The museum directors turned it down. Ed Janss, a great collector, was the president of the Center for Constitutional Rights. He wanted a helicopter to airlift it to the center, but his board turned it down. We realized the tower was doomed, and Mark came up with the idea of cutting it up into little pieces and each piece would be like a pillow, because he clipped the piece at two ends and we gave a pillow to each one of the artists who participated, and the artists who sent paintings knew that we were going to use them to continue the struggle against the war. We auctioned them off to raise money for further events in Southern California against the war, and that was the basis for the founding of a new organization—I was leaving, Mark was leaving, and we were starting to work in New York, but that's what happened to the tower."

24 James Turrell, interview with Almine Rech, in Rech, ed., *Rencontres 9/James Turrell* (Editions Almine Rech, Paris, 2005), 24.

25 See David Pagel, "Turn on the Light: You Don't Just See James Turrell's Illuminated Works. You Feel Them," *Los Angeles Times* (21 October 2007).

26 James Turrell, interview with Alison Sara Jacques, in A. S. Jacques and J. Svestka, eds., *James Turrell*, exh. cat. (Madrid: la Caixa, 1992), 57.

27 *Jim Turrell*, Pasadena Art Museum, September–October 1967.

28 Jennifer Licht, letter to Walter Bareiss, 23 September 1969, MoMA archives, quoted in Lise Kjaer, "Awakening the Spiritual: James Turrell and Quaker Practice," PhD dissertation, City University of New York (2008), 139.

29 Douglas Davis, "View from Hill and Main," *Newsweek* (27 October 1969), 111.

30 Hedrick, interview with Karlstrom.

31 Irving Petlin, in "The Artist and Politics: A Symposium," *Artforum* (September 1970), 38. The editor, Phil Leider, who published in the same issue his countercultural manifesto "How I Spent My Summer Vacation" (to be discussed in Chapter 8), had known Petlin during the Artists Protest Committee activities in Los Angeles. Both were by this date living in New York, where Petlin had recently collaborated on the design of the famous anti-war poster "Q. And babies? A. And babies," printed over a photograph taken at the My Lai massacre.

### SEVEN | **FROM WAR ABROAD TO OPPRESION AT HOME**

1 The text was published as "Declaration of Independence from Vietnam," *Ramparts* (May 1967), 32–37; this passage on 33. On the event and responses to it, see Taylor Branch, *At Canaan's Edge: America in the King Years 1965–68* (New York: Simon & Shuster, 2006), 590–97.

2 "Declaration of Independence from Vietnam," 37.

3 See Jason Epstein, "A Special Supplement: The Trial of Bobby Seale," *New York Review of Books* (4 December 1969); for a summary of the case and trial, see Jon Weiner, "Introduction: The Sixties on Trial," in Weiner ed., *Conspiracy in*

*the Streets: The Extraordinary Trial of the Chicago Eight* (New York: The New Press, 2006), 1–43.

4 Kellie Jones, *South of Pico: African American Artists in Los Angeles in the 1960s and 1970s* (Durham N.C.: Duke University Press, 2017), 228.

5 The serious literature on Corita Kent was scanty until relatively recently. See Julie Ault, *Come Alive! The Spirited Art of Sister Corita* (London: Four Corners Books, 2006); Ian Berry and Michael Duncan eds., *Someday is Now: The Art of Corita Kent* (Munich: Prestel, 2014); and Susan Dackerman ed., *Corita Kent and the Language of Pop*, exh. cat. (Cambridge, Mass.: Harvard Art Museums, 2015). My own approach to the subject has been indebted to the deep scholarship of Kristen Gaylord. See Gaylord, 'Catholic Art and Activism in Postwar Los Angeles', in Miguel de Baca and Makeda Best eds., *Conflict, Identity, and Protest in American Art* (Newcastle-Upon-Tyne:Cambridge Scholars Publishing, 2015), 99–120.

6 James Francis McIntyre, Archbishop of Los Angeles, letter of 12 May 1966, reproduced in Anita M. Caspary, *Witness to Integrity: The Crisis of the Immaculate Heart Community of California* (Collegeville, Minn.: Liturgical Press, 2003), 40–41.

7 The poem is included in the Gerald Huckaby collection, *City, Uncity* (New York: Doubleday, 1969), each poem rendered by Kent in her distinctive calligraphy against her high-keyed, full-page designs. For a brief resumé of Huckaby's fascinating life, see the 2017 obituary published by his local newspaper, *the Mendocino Beacon,* http://obituaries.mendocinobeacon.com/obituaries/mendocinobeacon/obituary.aspx?pid=187857440; "Stop the Bombing" was read at his wake.

8 See Branch, *At Canaan's Edge*, 578.

9 Martha Rosler, personal communication (August 2021).

10 Martha Rosler, interview with Melissa Ho (2016), quoted in Ho, ed., *Artists Respond: American Art and the Vietnam War 1965–1975*, exh. cat. (Washington, D.C., and Princeton: Smithsonian Museum of American Art and Princeton University Press, 2019), 93.

11 See the chronology of events compiled by Helene Whitson at *Found SF*, http://www.foundsf.org/index.php?-title=S.F._STATE_STRIKE_1968-69_CHRONOLOGY.

12 Rupert García, interview with Paul Karlstrom, "Oral history interview with Rupert García, September 7, 1995–June 24, 1996," Archives of American Art, Smithsonian Institution.

13 Ibid.

14 On this development, see Thomas Crow, *The Long March of Pop: Art, Music, and Design 1930–1995* (New Haven and London: Yale University Press, 2015), 327–43.

15 García, interview with Karlstrom.

16 See Cary Cordova, *The Heart of the Mission: Latino Art and Politics in San Francisco* (Philadelphia: University of Pennsylvania Press, 2017), 114–15.

17 See Geoff Kaplan, ed., *Power to the People: The Graphic Design of the Radical Press and the Rise of the Counterculture* (Chicago and London: University of Chicago Press, 2013), 104–9.

18 On Douglas's individual career, see Erika Doss, "'Revolutionary Art is a Tool for Liberation': Emory Douglas and Protest Aesthetics at *The Black Panther*," *New Political Science* (June 1999), 245–58; also Jo-Ann Morgan, *The Black Arts Movement and the Black Panther Party in American Visual Culture* (New York and Abingdon: Routledge, 2020), 135–62; for his own testimony about his early life, see the abundant quotations in Elton. C. Fax, *Black Artists of the New Generation* (New York: Dodd Mead, 1977), 256–78.

19 See Joshua Bloom and Waldo E. Martin Jr., *Black Against Empire: The History and Politics of the Black Panther Party* (Berkeley: University of California Press, 2013), 56.

20 See Donald Freed, *Agony in New Haven: The Trial of Bobby Seale, Ericka Huggins, and the Black Panther Party* (New York: Simon Schuster, 1973), 25: "As George Sams traveled around the country, spending large sums of money, certain things began to happen to the Panthers. Each city he visited was thereafter subjected to predawn raids by combinations of city, state, and federal police. But Sams was never caught; he always managed to leave before the raids were made."

21 For a thorough account of the murder, see Mike Davis and Jon Weiner, *Set the Night on Fire: L.A. in the Sixties* (London and New York: Verso, 2020), 430–52.

22 See Bloom and Martin, *Black Against Empire*, 261–62.

23 The Lumpen was also the name of the Panther singing group, which performed during the New Haven rallies and protests.

24 See Harry Gamboa Jr., "In the City of Angels, Chameleons, and Phantoms: Asco, a Case Study of Chicano Art in Urban Tones (or, Asco Was a Four-Member Word)," in Chon Noriega ed., *Urban Exile: Collected writings of Harry Gamboa Jr.* (Minneapolis: University of Minnesota Press, 1998), 77.

25 For a comprehensive, multiauthored overview, see C. Ondine Chavoya and Rita Gonzalez, eds., *ASCO: Elite of the Obscure*, exh. cat. (Los Angeles and Williamstown,

Mass.: Los Angeles County Museum of Art and Williams College Museum, 2011).

26 One motive, they have claimed, was to hold back the supplied colored paints so they could use them in their own paintings. But the effect of the monochrome scheme transcended that expedient motive. Willie Herrón, interview with Jeffrey Rangel, "Oral history interview with Willie Herrón, 2000 February 5–March 17," Archives of American Art, Smithsonian Institution, https://www.aaa.si.edu/collections/interviews/oral-history-interview-willie-herrn-12847.

27 See Harry Gamboa Jr., quoted in "LA Stories: A Roundtable," *Artforum* (October 2011), https://www.artforum.com/print/201108/john-baldessari-thomas-crow-harry-gamboa-jr-liz-larner-andrew-perchuk-ali-subotnick-maurice-tuchman-and-helene-winer-moderated-by-richard-meyer-and-michelle-kuo-29043: "The resulting 35-mm color slide was delivered to various local TV stations and accompanied by the notice that the 'last gang member' had been killed, thereby ending violence in the barrio. The image was televised by at least two TV stations. The project was a response to the incendiary tabloid-style journalism of the two major Los Angeles newspapers, which often listed the names, addresses, workplaces, and gang affiliations of victims or their family members in an effort to maintain high levels of reciprocal gang violence, thus selling more newspapers. The desired effect of *Decoy Gang War Victim* was to generate a pause in the violence in order to rob the newspapers of their daily list of victims."

## EIGHT | TOWARD 1970

1 Mel Bochner, quoted in Amy Newman, *Challenging Art: Artforum 1962–1974* (New York: SoHo Press, 2000), 139.

2 Philip Leider, quoted in Newman, *Challenging Art*, 139.

3 Philip Leider to Michael Fried (March 1966), quoted in ibid., 159.

4 Philip Leider, quoted in Amy Newman, "An Art World Figure Re-emerges, Unrepentant," *New York Times* (3 September 2000).

5 Michael Lydon, "The Rolling Stones—at Play in the Apocalypse," *Ramparts* (March 1970), 28–54.

6 Leider, quoted in Newman, *Challenging Art*, 228.

7 Philip Leider, "How I Spent My Summer Vacation or, Art and Politics in Nevada, Berkeley, San Francisco and Utah (Read about It in Artforum!)," *Artforum* (September 1970), 40–49.

8 Leider, quoted in Newman, *Challenging Art*, 271.

9 Robert Smithson, "The Spiral Jetty," in Jack Flam ed., *Robert Smithson: The Collected Writings* (Berkeley and Los Angeles: University of California Press, 1996), 143.

10 Bruce Glaser, "Questions to Stella and Judd," *Art News*, 65 (September 1966); 58–59; reprinted in Gregory Battcock, ed. *Minimal Art: A Critical Anthology* (New York: Dutton, 1968), 158. On Weber's report, see Timothy Martin, "Enantiomorphic Chambers," in Per Bj. Boym ed., *Robert Smithson Retrospective: Works 1955-1973* (Oslo: Museet for samitidskunst, 1999), 60; though issues of dating may throw this directly causal link to the published interview into doubt, Smithson would have been thoroughly familiar with Stella's line of thought long before. The work had its only exhibition in a 1966 group show at the Finch College Museum of Art in Manhattan, *Art in Process: The Visual Development of a Structure*. Other exhibiting artists included Judd, Sol LeWitt, and Carl Andre.

11 Robert Smithson, "What Really Spoils Michelangelo's Sculpture," in Flam, *Robert Smithson: Collected Writings*, 348.

12 G. Robert Deiro, quoted in William L. Fox, *Michael Heizer: The Once and Future Monuments* (New York: The Monacelli Press, 2019), 84; Fox's oral histories with Deiro, included in the volume, are an invaluable addition to the land art literature.

13 Author interview with Douglas Chrismas, September 2003.

14 Ibid.

15 Smithson, "Spiral Jetty," 146.

16 See Catherine Phillips, in Nancy Holt, ed., *Robert Smithson's Spiral Jetty* (Berkeley and Los Angeles: University of California Press, 2005), 199–200.

17 On the renegade history of Canyon, extending back to the timber camps of the nineteenth century, see John van der Zee, *Canyon: The Story of the Last Rustic Community in Metropolitan America*, 2nd ed., (Kensington, Calif.: Grizzly Peak Press, 2010).

18 Leider, quoted in Newman, *Challenging Art*, 270.

19 On this history, see Scott McDonald, *Canyon Cinema: The Life and Times of an Independent Film Distributor* (Berkeley and Los Angeles: University of California Press, 2008), 1–17.

20 In his account of Heizer's *Double Negative*, Fox (*Michael Heizer*, 99) both acknowledges and qualifies this distinction: "*Double Negative* still strikes most people first as a formal gesture, albeit an impressively large one. But once you descend into one of the trenches, the work becomes

an experience that alters the way you see the world. . . . The surrounding desert is excluded from view, your vision focused on the counterpart of the trench across the way . . . such meta-cognitive maneuvers, when you're simultaneously thinking and watching yourself think, easily become a meditation and a reverence."

21 Bruce Conner, interview with Paul Karlstrom, "Oral history interview with Bruce Conner, 1974 August 12," Archives of American Art, Smithsonian Institution, https://www.aaa.si.edu/collections/interviews/oral-history-interview-bruce-conner-12989#transcript.

22 Bonnie Ora Sherk, interview with Nick Kaye (6 February 2015), http://siteworks.exeter.ac.uk/interviews/bonnieorasherk#portable_parks_i-iii.

23 See ibid. I am indebted also to the unpublished research on Sherk and the San Francisco circle of performance artists by Nicholas Nguyen.

24 For this and subsequent quotations from Terry Fox, see interview with Willoughby Sharp, *Avalanche* 2 (Winter 1971), 70–71.

25 See Susie Cagle, "Richmond versus Chevron: The California City Taking on its Most Powerful Polluter," *Guardian* (9 October 2019), https://www.theguardian.com/environment/2019/oct/09/richmond-chevron-california-city-polluter-fossil-fuel.

26 Fox, interview with Sharp, 70.

## NINE | THE ART OF DISAPPEARANCE

1 See Joan Didion, "Where I Was From," in Didion, *We Tell Ourselves Stories to Live: Collected Nonfiction* (New York: Knopf, 2006), 1019–28; D. J. Waldie, *Holy Land: A Suburban Memoir* (New York: Norton, 2005).

2 John Baldessari, quoted in Coosje Van Bruggen, *John Baldessari*, exh. cat. (Los Angeles and New York: Museum of Contemporary Art and Rizzoli, 1990), 29.

3 Ibid.

4 For an excellent account of the program at UCSD, see Jill Dawsey, ed., *The Uses of Photography: Art, Politics, and the Re-Invention of a Medium*, exh. cat. (San Diego and Berkeley: San Diego Museum of Contemporary Art and University of California Press), 2018.

5 Paul Brach, quoted in Van Bruggen, *Baldessari*, 57.

6 The literature on recent art history has yet to catch up with Baden's importance and impact on younger California artists. For the beginning of a corrective, see Jacob Stewart-Halevy, *Slant Steps: On the Art World's Semi-Periphery* (Berkeley and Los Angeles: University of California Press, 2019), 143–49, which addresses his earlier phase in northern California, including the 1967 work *Irish Position*, the fashioning of which anticipates to some degree his approach to *Augur*.

7 May Beth Jackson, "PC Profs Display Their Own Things," *Claremont Collegian* (9 October 1968), 4. Baden states further, "The qualities that we generally associate with sculpture are a priapic aspect and impenetrability. It may be that we don't have to make sculpture anymore and only to give a set of direct and precise instructions for action."

8 Quoted in Jack Burnham, "On Being Sculpture," *Art-forum* (May 1969), 44.

9 Ibid., 45.

10 Quoted in Robert Horvitz, "Chris Burden," *Artforum* (May 1976), 26

11 Burden had made a previous, cognate piece in the same location that came closer to Baden's concerns. It consisted of a series of semi-circular supports of gradually diminishing dimensions overlain with translucent plastic. For those who entered the passage, the height of the last hoop required getting down close to the earth in order to crawl under and exit the enclosed space. For a full account, see Matthew Teti's invaluable, "From Minimalism to Performance Art: Chris Burden, 1967–1971," PhD dissertation, Columbia University (2018), 105–10.

12 See Grace Kook-Anderson ed., *Best Kept Secret: UC Irvine and the Development of Contemporary Art in Southern California 1964–1971*, exh. cat. (Laguna Beach: Laguna Art Museum, 2011).

13 Quoted by George Melrod, "Interview with Chris Burden," *art ltd.*, http://artltdmag.com/2012/09/interview-chris-burden/. On his preference for Irwin as a mentor, Burden explained, "he would just come to the studio about once every two months and spend whole days at a time. It was really good, because it was on a one-to-one basis. He would come by for a whole week, and sort of do a total head blitz and then leave. You had to sign up for classes, but I just signed up for about three or four with Irwin; that just kind of took care of school." See Chris Burden and Jan Butterfield, "Chris Burden: Through the Night Softly," *Arts Magazine* (March 1975), 68.

14 Quoted in Horvitz, "Chris Burden," 26.

15 For further discussion and details, see Matthew Teti, "Occupying UCI: Chris Burden's *Five Day Locker Piece* as Institutional Critique," *RACAR* (Spring 2018), 39–52.

16 Chris Burden, lecture at the Rhode Island School

of Design (12 November 1974), quoted in Horvitz, "Chris Burden," 28.

17 Glicksman, interview with McGrew, 102.

18 For the author's own discussion along these lines, see Thomas Crow, *Modern Art in the Common Culture* (New Haven and London: Yale University Press, 1996), 136–41.

19 See Barbara Munger, "Michael Asher: An Environmental Project," *Studio International* (October 1970), 162.

20 Hal Glicksman, interview with Rebecca McGrew, in McGrew and Glenn Phillips, eds., *It Happened at Pomona: Art at the Edge of Los Angeles 1969–1973* exh. cat. (Claremont, Calif.: Pomona College Museum of Art, 2011), 103.

21 Note from Michael Asher to Glicksman, 1970, special collections, Getty research Institute, Gift of Hal Glicksman (2009. M.5).

22 Willoughby Sharp, "New Directions in Southern California Sculpture," *Arts* (Summer 1970), 37.

23 James Turrell, interview with Rebeca McGrew, in McGrew and Phillips, *It Happened at Pomona.*

24 Ibid.

25 Hap Tivey, interview with Rebecca McGrew, in McGrew and Phillips, *It Happened at Pomona*, 302.

TEN | **NOIR VORTEX**

1 I am greatly indebted to the deep research by Pedro de Llano into the shape and details of Bas Jan Ader's life, the publication of which will add immeasurably to the wider under-standing of the artist's importance.

2 See Alexander Dumbadze, *Bas Jan Ader: Death Is Elsewhere* (Chicago and London: University of Chicago Press, 2013), 24–25.

3 Quoted in Richard Hertz, ed., *Jack Goldstein and the CalArts Mafia* (Ojai, Calif.: Minneola Press, 2003), 34.

4 Helene Winer, interview with Marie Shurkus, quoted in Shurkus, "Lessons from Post-Minimalism," in Rebecca McGrew and Glenn Phillips, eds., *It Happened at Pomona: Art at the Edge of Los Angeles 1969–1973*, exh. cat. (Claremont, Calif.: Pomona College Museum of Art, 2011), 75.

5 Quoted in Hertz, *Jack Goldstein*, 3, 55.

6 Ibid., 62. Hertz's savvy compilation of oral histories has been indispensable to the present study.

7 Ibid., 157

8 Quoted in ibid., 25–6, 55

9 Quoted in ibid., 65. The artist Michael Brewster testifies that the signal came from EKG sensors rather than the heartbeat monitor, which had failed to function, and Goldstein was extricated from the burial soon after the start of his performance; see Marie Shurkus, "Jack Goldstein's Sculpture: Image before Its Consequences," in McGrew and Philips, *It Happened at Pomona*, 194.

10 Quoted in Yves Aupetitallot, *Jack Goldstein: 03.02–28.04.2002* (Grenoble: Magasin-Centre National d'Art Contemporain, 2002), 154.

11 Quoted in ibid., 93.

12 Quoted in Roger Ebert, "Chris Burden: The 'Body Artist'," *Chicago Sun-Times* (8 April 1975).

13 Mark Johnston, *Surviving Death* (Princeton and Oxford: Princeton University Press, 2011), 45.

14 Quoted in Peter Schjeldahl, "The Art World: Chris Burden's Art of Extremity," *New Yorker* (14 May 2007), 152.

15 See Jennie Klein, "Feeding the Body: The Art of Barbara T. Smith," *PAJ* (January 1999), 30–31; for an essential overview of Smith's art and career, see Rebecca McGrew et al., *The 21st Century Odyssey Part II: the Performances of Barbara T. Smith* (Claremont, Calif.: Pomona College Museum of Art, 2005).

16 E .H. Gombrich, *Art and Illusion: A Study in the Psychology of Pictorial Representation* (Princeton and Oxford: Princeton University Press, 1960).

17 Vija Celmins, interview with Robert Gober, in Lane Relyea et al., *Vija Celmins* (London: Phaidon, 2004), 25.

18 Ibid., 16.

19 Ibid. 25.

20 My thanks to Claire Rifelj for her attention to this work.

21 Quoted in Richard Armstrong, ed., *Alexis Smith*, exh. cat. (New York: Whitney Museum of American Art, 1992), 15

22 Allen Ruppersberg, interview with Frédéric Paul, in Paul, ed., *Allen Ruppersberg: Books, Inc.*, exh. cat. (Limousin: FRAC, 1999), 38.

23 Robert Towne, "It's Only LA, Jake: . . . ," *Los Angeles Times* (29 May 1994), https://www.latimes.com/archives/la-xpm-1994-05-29-bk-63320-story.html.

24 Ruppersberg, interview with Paul, 38.

25 Ibid., 36.

26 See Marie Shurkus, "Lessons from Post-Minimalism," in McGrew and Philips, *It Happened at Pomona*, 90.

27 For a parallel discussion, see Allen McCollum, "Allen Ruppersburg: What One Loves about Life Are the Things That Fade," in Paul, *Allen Ruppersberg*, 11.

28 For an insightful account of the piece in its multiple iterations, see Alexander Dumbadze, *Bas Jan Ader: Death*

*Is Elsewhere* (Chicago and London: University of Chicago Press, 2013), 93–101.

29 Walter Benjamin, "Little History of Photography," in Benjamin, *The Work of Art in the Age of Its Technological Reproducibility*, ed. Michael W. Jennings et al (Cambridge, Mass.: Harvard University Press, 2008), 274.

30 Raymond, Chandler, "The Simple Art of Murder" (1944), in Chandler, *The Simple art of Murder* (New York: Vintage, 1988), 18.

31 See Marion van Wijk, *In Search of the Miraculous: Bas Jan Ader, Discovery File 143/76* (Amsterdam: Dalstar Veenman, n.d.) 207.

### ELEVEN | SECRET CEREMONIES

1 For the interview, see "Gronk: No Movie Maker," reprinted in Harry Gamboa Jr., "In the City of Angels, Chameleons, and Phantoms: Asco, a Case Study of Chicano Art in Urban Tones (or, Asco Was a Four-Member Word)," in Chon Noriega, ed., *Urban Exile: Collected Writings of Harry Gamboa Jr.* (Minneapolis: University of Minnesota Press, 1998), 44–50.

2 Peter Plagens, quoted in Max Benavidez, *Gronk* (Los Angeles: UCLA Chicano Studies Center Press, 2007), 39.

3 Willie Herrón, interview with Jeffrey Rangel, "Oral history interview with Willie Herrón, 2000 February 5–March 17," Archives of American Art, Smithsonian Institution, https://www.aaa.si.edu/collections/interviews/oral-history-interview-willie-herrn-12847.

4 Genesis P. Orridge quoted in Marc Spitz and Brendan Mullen, eds., *We Got the Neutron Bomb: The Untold Story of L.A. Punk* (New York: Three Rivers, 2001), 20.

5 See Paul Trynka, *Iggy: Open Up and Bleed* (New York: Broadway Books, 2007), 183–85.

6 Chuck E. Starr, quoted in Spitz and Mullen, *Neutron Bomb*, 26.

7 Diane Gamboa, sister of Harry, emerged at this moment of punk as an important photographer.

8 See Bryan Ray Turcotte and Christopher T. Miller, *Fucked Up and Photocopied: Instant Art of the Punk Rock Movement* (Corte Madera: Gingko Press, 1999), 66–69.

9 Marty Goldberg (Hal Negro), quoted in Spitz and Mullen, *We Got the Neutron Bomb*, 72.

10 Alice Bag, quoted in ibid., 75.

11 See Jenny Lens, *Punk Pioneers: When Punk Was Fun* (New York: Universe, 2008); her formidable counterpart was Melanie Nissen, staff photographer of *Slash* magazine, on whose work, see now, Nissen, *Hard + Fast* (Los Angeles: Blank Industries, 2022).

12 Lens, *Punk Pioneers*, 22.

13 Ibid.

14 Jon Savage, "The Screamers—122 Hours of Fear," *Guardian Music Blog* (27 July 2010), https://www.theguardian.com/music/musicblog/2010/jul/27/screamers-122-hours-fear.

15 Bruce Conner, *The Afternoon Interviews with V. Vale* (San Francisco: RE/search, 2016), 104.

16 Richard Alden Peterson, "Special Report: A Photographer Remembers Artist Bruce Conner, Part 1," *American Photography's Pro Photo Daily* (16 January 2017).

17 Ibid.; Peterson also describes Conner's embrace of another venue, where he seems not to have taken photographs, which revived more of the sensory adventures of the previous decade. Another Punk promoter had secured the rented hall of San Francisco's Deaf Club in the Mission District, where the non-hearing members had been gathering since the 1930s. Peterson reports that blotter acid "was included with your admission ticket at some shows at another Punk club where Bruce danced ecstatically. At The Deaf Club, where Bruce held a personal party in the early Punk days, the deaf members stood at the back of the room holding balloons to feel the pulsing music. Bruce told me he thought the Deaf Club was a place of heightened physic energy." ai-ap.com/publications/article/20262/special-report-a-photographer-remembers-artist-br.html.

18 Bruce Conner, quoted in Greil Marcus, "Bruce Conner at the Mabuhay Gardens, San Francisco, 1978," *Aperture* 183 (Summer 2006), 65.

19 Conner, quoted in ibid.

20 Conner, quoted in *Afternoon Interviews*, 76.

21 His immersion in the scene fostered seeds of collaboration with the Dead Kennedys in particular, the one San Francisco punk band to gain national recognition and begin touring widely. As Stephanie Katsias has brought to light, Conner traded some art with a friend in exchange for recording studio time in 1978, briefly and unsuccessfully stepping in as their fledgling album producer. When the lead singer Jello Biafra ran for mayor of San Francisco in the following year, he reprised in a similarly serio-comic mode Conner's own city electoral campaign of a decade or so before; Katsias, "'Combat Photography': Bruce Conner, *Search & Destroy*, and the Politics of the San Francisco Punk Scene" (master's thesis, Institute of Fine Arts, New York University, 2021) draws on Michael Stewart Foley, *Fresh*

*Fruit for Rotting Vegetables* (New York and London: Bloomsbury Academic, 2015), 56; the present account is indebted to her original insights into Conner's optic on the Mabuhay Gardens performers.

22 See Stevie Chick, *Spray Paint the Walls: The Story of Black Flag* (London: Omnibus, 2009), 171–74.

23 Craig Lee and Shreader, in Peter Belisto and Bob Davis, *Hardcore California: A History of Punk and New Wave* (Berkeley: The Last Gasp of San Francisco, 1983), 54.

24 Kristine McKenna, "How to Build a New World Then Tear It Down," in John Doe and Tom DeSavia eds., *Under the Big Black Sun: A Personal History of LA Punk* (Philadelphia: Da Capo, 2016), 240–41; McKenna, as cited above, became an important historian and documentarian of the early Los Angeles underground, particularly the circle around Wallace Berman.

25 On family and early life, see Chick, *Spray Paint*, 15–26.

26 See ibid., 62.

27 Senga Nengudi, in Elana Mann and Vera Brunner-Sung, "My Tribe: An Interview with Senga Nengudi," https://www.elanamann.com/writing/my-tribe-interview-senga-nengudi.

28 For this period in the career of Sun Ra, see the definitive biography by John Szwed, *Space Is the Place: The Lives and Times of Sun Ra* (New York: Da Capo, 1998), 244–75.

29 Arnold Rubin, "Accumulation: Power and Display in African Sculpture," *Artforum* (May 1975), 35–47; see "Influences: Betye Saar," *Frieze* (October 2016), https://www.frieze.com/article/influences-betye-saar.

30 These were *African Art in Motion* in 1974 and *African Gods and Kings: Yoruba Art at UCLA* in 1976. Both Rubin and Thompson, in their vision of art participating in common rituals at every perceived level of culture, were taking up the then-eclipsed legacy of Aby Warburg. Rubin put his ideas into action by undertaking a deep investigation into the year-round apparatus responsible for the Tournament of Roses parade in Pasadena every New Year's Day, involving his students and becoming deeply invested in the designers and builders of the floats. What later surfaced in academia as "visual culture" could be said to have started with them.

31 Senga Nengudi, quoted in "Studio Z's Constellation" (Chicago: Museum of Contemporary Art), https://mcachicago.org/Publications/Websites/West-By-Midwest/Stories/Studio-Zs-Constellation; Nick Stillman, "Senga Nengudi's *Ceremony for Freeway Fets* and Other Los Angeles Collaborations," *East of Borneo* (7 December 2011), https://eastofborneo.org/articles/senga-nengudis-ceremony-for-freeway-fets-and-other-los-angeles-collaborations/.

32 For a thorough unpacking of the themes and details of the performance (absent Sun Ra), see Kellie Jones, *South of Pico: African American Artists in Los Angeles in the 1960s and 1970s* (Durham, N.C.: Duke University Press, 2017), 194–207.

33 Nengudi, quoted in "Studio Z's Constellation."

34 Mike Kelley, "Death and Transfiguration," in *Foul Perfection: Essays and Criticism*, ed. John C. Welchman (Cambridge, Mass., and London: The MIT Press, 2003), 141–42.

## TWELVE | LAST ARTIST OF THE COUNTERCULTURE

1 Mike Kelley, "Myth Science (on Öyvind Fahlström)," in *Foul Perfection: Essays and Criticism*, ed. John C. Welchman, 173–74.

2 Ibid., 164.

3 Ibid., 172.

4 Ibid., 172.

5 Charlie LeDuff, *Detroit: An American Autopsy* (New York: Penguin, 2013), 87.

6 John Sinclair, "I Just Want to Testify" (1979), in Sinclair, *It's All Good: A John Sinclair Reader* (London: Headpress, 2009), 42.

7 See Scott Saul, *Freedom Is, Freedom Ain't: Jazz and the Making of the Sixties* (Cambridge, Mass.: Harvard University Press, 2003), 294–97.

8 See Reggie Carter and John Sinclair, "Elvin Jones on Detroit Jazz in the '50s," *Ann Arbor Sun* (25 March 1976), 9, 14.

9 For a full record, see the remarkable recent volume, which Kelley encouraged before his death: Leni Sinclair, *Motor City Underground: Photographs 1963–1978*, ed., Cary Loren and Lorraine Wild, exh. cat. (Detroit: Museum of Contemporary Art, 2021).

10 See ibid., 53.

11 For an excellent overview, see Jeff A. Hale, "The White Panthers' 'Total Assault on the Culture,'" in Peter Baunstein and Michael William Doyle, eds., *Imagine Nation: The American Counterculture of the 1960s and '70s* (New York and London: Routledge, 2002), 125–56.

12 Sinclair, quoted in Saul, *Freedom Is, Freedom Ain't* , 296.

13 See John Szwed, *Space Is the Place: The Lives and Times of Sun Ra* (New York: Da Capo, 1998), 244–75; the MC5 prided themselves on playing 'heavier' than any of the famous bands for which they regularly opened at the Grande

Ballroom in Detroit. For the sound and performance of the MC5, refer to the live concert album, *Kick out the Jams*, released on Elektra records in January 1969; though poorly recorded, it provides an invaluable document.

14 John Miller, *Mike Kelley: Educational Complex* (Cambridge, Mass., and London: The MIT Press and Afterall Books, 2015), 10.

15 Lester Bangs, 'Of Pop & Pies & Fun: A Program of Mass Liberation in the Form of Stooges Review, Or, Who's the Fool?' parts 1 and 2, *Creem* (November, December 1971).

16 See Mike Kelley and Dan Nadel, *The Return of the Repressed: Destroy All Monsters 1973–1977* (New York and Los Angeles: Picture Box/Prism, 2011).

17 Mike Kelley, "Some Aesthetic High Points," in Kelley, *Minor Histories: Statements, Conversations, Proposals*, ed. John Welchman (Cambridge, Mass., and London: MIT Press, 2004), 42–43.

18 See Sinclair, *Motor City Underground*, 263.

19 See Hale, "The White Panthers' 'Total Assault on the Culture,'" 144.

20 Mike Kelley, interview with Eva Meyer-Hermann, in Meyer-Hermann and Lisa Gabrielle Mark, eds., *Mike Kelley*, exh. cat. (Amsterdam: Stedelijk Museum and Prestel, 2014), 377.

21 Carl Wilson, "A new book revisits Alex Chilton's lifelong struggle with his own talent," *Bookforum* (February–March 2014), https://www.bookforum.com/print/2005/a-new-book-revisits-alex-chilton-s-lifelong-struggle-with-his-own-talent-12773.

22 Kelley, "Foul Perfection: Thoughts on Caricature" (1989), in *Foul Perfection*, 21.

23 Ibid.

24 Mike Kelley, "Death and Transfiguration," in *Foul Perfection*, 145.

25 John Miller, *Mike Kelley: Educational Complex* (Cambridge, Mass., and London: The MIT Press and Afterall Books, 2015), 40–46, provides an acute summary. For a recent, dispassionate summary of the relevant events, see Richard Beck, *We Believe the Children: A Moral Panic in the 1980s* (New York: Public Affairs, 2015).

26 See the fascinating, detailed account of the fabrication process and the personnel involved that Miller provides, ibid., 15–23.

27 Kelley, "*Day Is Done: Extracurricular Activity Projective Reconstructions #2–32*," in Anne Potégnie ed., *Mike Kelley: Educational Complex Onwards 1995–2008* (Brussels: Wiels Contemporary Art Centre, 2008), 166.

28 Kelley, "Myth Science," 162–64.

29 Mike Kelley, "Kandors," in *Mike Kelley: Kandors*, exh. cat. (Berlin: Jablonka Gallery and Hirmer, 2007), 53.

30 Ibid., 55–57.

31 Ibid., 56.

32 John Sinclair, "It Knocks on Everybody's Door: Detroit Sun Interview with Sun Ra" (1966), in Sinclair ed., *Sun Ra: Interviews & Essays* (www.worldheadpress.com, 2012).

33 Kelley, "Kandors," 54–55.

# ACKNOWLEDGMENTS

Making a book on art is as much a matter of gathering images as it is about prose exposition and argument. My deepest gratitude goes to the artists and the stewards of artists' legacies who have made the former task feasible and rewarding. Firstly, Robert Conway and Michelle Silva, representing Jean Conner and the Conner Family Trust, have been wonderfully responsive and resourceful in helping this book come into being. Mary Clare Stevens, executive director of the Mike Kelley Foundation for the Arts, joined by Amy Via, likewise embraced the spirit of the project. Yayoi Shionoiri, executive director of the Chris Burden Estate, could not have been more helpful in facilitating the visual representation of this old friend, whose loss is irreparable, just as are the absences of Mike Kelley and Michael Asher. Karen Dunbar, executive director of the Michael Asher Foundation, assured the faithful accounting of his legacy. Rebecca McGrew, chief curator of the Benton Museum of Art at Pomona College, has provided generous advice and assistance over many years. Anna Meliksetian and Michael Briggs, representing the Estate of Bas Jan Ader, graciously responded to my requests. Claire de Dobay Rifelj, at the Los Angeles Sprüth Magers Gallery, graciously went out of her way to make crucial connections, while Tracey Schuster adroitly navigated the byways of the special collections at the Getty Research Institute on my behalf. As befits the geographical focus of the book, Bay Area colleagues—Sue Grinois at the Fine Arts Museums of San Francisco and David Senior at SFMOMA—creatively responded to all my requests.

Among the artists who graciously cooperated in the book's production, Allen Ruppersberg opened his archives with the utmost generosity, while Mowry Baden did the same with his personal image collection, having shared memories and wisdom over a decade. I thank Nancy Rubins for her warm conversation and Hiro Kosaka for the encouraging words. Both Jenny Lens and Martha Rosler imparted invaluable first-hand knowledge along with the crucial reproductions of their work. Hal Glicksman seems always to have some gem to reveal from his storied career. Blues master Geoff Muldaur, musical companion to the Conners from early days, tapped his priceless store of recollections for my benefit. Looking back, the work of Christopher Williams brought Bas Jan Ader out from the shadow cast by his early death. And I owe a debt to Dennis Parks for taking me around to the Ader bungalow all those years ago and for much inspiration besides. Nancy Barton, Ann Goldstein, and John Miller illuminated from their first-hand experience Mike Kelley's life and commitments.

All have joined with the wonderfully able and stimulating interlocutors whose thoughts and knowledge have materially sustained the project. Robert Slifkin, in his remarkable range and quality of mind, has been the stimulating, warm-spirited colleague everyone wants to have. I am greatly in Pedro De Llano's debt for his friendship and generously shared, ground-breaking research and insight into the art of Bas Jan Ader. Alexander Dumbadze's expertise encompasses Ader, Ruppersberg, Jack Goldstein, and much else about their formative place and time. Marci Kwon generously gave the manuscript a critical reading at an early stage, and Antonia Pocock provided vital Chicago intelligence. Exchanges with Peter Boswell smoothed my path into the complex world of Bruce Conner, while Matthew Teti has done the thorough, in-depth investigation that Chris Burden's life and work deserve.

Participating in the landmark Smithsonian exhibition and catalogue organized by Melissa Ho, *Artists Respond*, immensely enriched the chapters on the anti-war and Third World liberation movements; exchanges with Rupert García and Harry Gamboa Jr. at the museum were both enlightening and hugely pleasurable. The sections on Los Angeles in the 1970s would be the poorer had not Paul Schimmel invited me to synthesize an account for his LAMOCA exhibition *Under the Big Black Sun*. In seminars over fourteen years, the extraordinary enterprise and ideas of the graduate students at the Institute of Fine Arts, NYU, have immeasurably contributed to these inquiries. And a kind invitation from Sid Sachs to speak at the University of the Arts about dispersed, local avant-garde scenes helped spark my setting out to write.

I have indeed been fortunate to have been able to work again with Michelle Komie, art and architecture publisher at Princeton University Press, along with Terri O'Prey, Steven Sears, Kenneth Guay, and Annie Miller in all the details of book production, and what's more to have had the remarkable guidance and design provided by my very first editor and art-publishing legend, Gillian Malpass. Catherine Phillips has received my heartfelt thanks many times on pages such as these. I offer them again here with special gratitude for her deep expertise on southern Mexico, its flora, and its indigenous botanical lore, matters of vivid interest to Bruce Conner and countless adherents to the countercultural life.

# INDEX

# ILLUSTRATION AND COPYRIGHT CREDITS

References are to figure numbers

© Conner Family Trust, San Francisco / Artists Rights Society (ARS), New York: front and back jacket, 3, 4, 5, 6, 8, 11, 12, 13. 14, 16, 17, 18, 19, 20, 21, 22, 24, 25, 26, 27, 28, 29, 31, 32, 33, 34, 35, 36, 37, 39, 40, 41, 43, 44, 45, 46, 117, 118, 119

Alamy Stock Photo: 6, 101

AKG Images: 8

Image licensed by Art Resource, New York: 10, 53, 66

© Artists Rights Society (ARS), New York: 54, 55, 56, 62, 63

Digital image © The Museum of Modern Art / licensed by SCALA / Art Resource, New York. Courtesy Martha Rosler © Mitchell Innes & Nash: 57

Photograph by Seymour Rosen, Smithsonian American Art Museum, licensed by Art Resource, New York: 64

Image courtesy Cinewest Archive, UC San Diego Library: 65

Photograph by Josh Brasted (24 January 2021), Getty Images: 68

Photograph by Eric Broder Van Dyke, Alamy Stock Photo: 67

Image courtesy Artforum: 69

Photograph courtesy the archives of the San Francisco Museum of Modern Art: 70, 71, 72

© Estate of Terry Fox, Cologne: 71, 72

© John Baldessari 1966–68, courtesy Estate of John Baldessari © 2022; courtesy Sprüth Magers: 74

© John Baldessari 1968, photograph by Phillip T. Jones, courtesy Estate of John Baldessari © 2022: 75

© John Baldessari 1970, courtesy Estate of John Baldessari © 2022; courtesy Sprüth Magers: 76

Courtesy the artist: 77, 78

© Chris Burden / licensed by The Chris Burden Estate and Artists Rights Society (ARS), New York: 79, 80

Licensed by The Chris Burden Estate and Artists Rights Society (ARS), New York: 81, 82, 83, 95, 96

Photograph by Frank J. Thomas, courtesy the Frank J. Thomas Archive and the Benton Museum of Art at Pomona College © Michael Asher Foundation: 84, 85

Photograph by Kenneth M. Bernstein, courtesy of Pomona College Museum; Michael Asher installation © Michael Asher Foundation: 73

Photograph by Lewis Baltz, Pomona College Museum of Art: 86

Photograph by Peter Kirby, Pomona College Museum of Art: 87

Richard Barnes Collection, Special Collections and Libraries, Claremont Colleges Library: 88

© Estate of Bas Jan Ader / Mary Sue Ader Andersen, 2016 and Artists Rights Society (ARS), New York, courtesy Meliksetian | Briggs, Los Angeles: 89, 90

Photograph by Robert Wedemeyer, courtesy the artist: 92

© Vija Celmins, courtesy Matthew Marks Gallery: 97

Courtesy the artist and Garth Greenan Gallery, New York: 98, 99

Courtesy the artist: 100, 103, 104

Photograph by Gary Krueger, courtesy the artist: 102, 105

© Estate of Bas Jan Ader / Mary Sue Ader Andersen, 2016 / The Artist Rights Society (ARS) New York: 106, 107, 108, 109, 110

© 1976, Harry Gamboa, Jr.: 112

Michael Ochs Archives/Getty Images: 113, 127, 128, 130, 131

© 1976-Now Jenny Lens, MFA: 111, 114, 115, 116

© Raymond Pettibon, courtesy the artist and David Zwirner: 121, 122

Getty Images: 123

© Senga Nengudi, courtesy the artist, Sprüth Magers and Thomas Erben Gallery, New York, photograph by Quaku/Roderick Young: 124, 125

Courtesy the Öyvind Fahlström Foundation and Archives: 126

Photograph by Larry E. Wright. Image courtesy the Ann Arbor District Library: 129

© Mike Kelley Foundation for the Arts. All Rights Reserved Licensed by VAGA, New York, NY ARS: 133, 134, 135, 136, 137, 138, 139, 140, 141, 143

Courtesy the Mike Kelley Foundation for the Arts and Hauser & Wirth, photo: Fredrik Nilsen: 141, 143